# Economic and Political Integration
# in Europe:
# Internal Dynamics and Global Context

# Economic and Political Integration in Europe:
# Internal Dynamics and Global Context

*Edited by*

## Simon Bulmer and Andrew Scott

Blackwell Publishers

ISBN 0-631-19039-2


First published 1994


Blackwell Publishers
108 Cowley Road, Oxford OX4 1JF, UK
and
238 Main Street, Cambridge, MA 02142, USA

*British Library Cataloguing-in-Publication Data*
A catalogue record for this book is available
from the British Library

*Library of Congress*
Cataloging in Publication Data applied for




Printed in Great Britain on acid free paper by
Whitstable Litho, Kent

# CONTENTS

# About the Editors and Contributors

**Simon Bulmer** is Reader in the Department of Government, University of Manchester. He is Joint Editor of the *Journal of Common Market Studies*.

**Andrew Scott** is Jean Monnet Senior Lecturer in the Economics of the European Community in the Europa Institute, University of Edinburgh. He is Joint Editor of the *Journal of Common Market Studies*.

**Zenon Bańkowski** is Reader in Jurisprudence in the Faculty of Law, University of Edinburgh.

**Anne-Marie Slaughter Burley** is Assistant Professor of Law, University of Chicago Law School.

**Andrew Hughes Hallett** is Professor of Economics, University of Strathclyde and Visiting Professor in the Department of Economics, Princeton University.

**Christopher Hill** is Montague Burton Professor of International Relations, London School of Economics.

**Alexis Jacquemin** is Adviser to the Commission of the European Communities and Professor of Economics, Université Catholique de Louvain, Belgium.

**Brigid Laffan** is Jean Monnet Professor of European Politics, University College, Dublin.

**Deepak Lal** is James S. Coleman Professor of International Development Studies, University of California, Los Angeles and Professor of Political Economy, University College London.

**Leon Lindberg** is Professor of Political Science at the University of Wisconsin - Madison.

**David Mayes** is a Senior Researcher, National Institute for Economic and Social Research and is Director of the Single Market Initiative of the Economic and Social Research Council, London.

**Andrew Moravcsik** is Assistant Professor of Government, Department of Government, Harvard University.

**Peter Robson** is Professor of Economics, St Andrew's University.

**Michael Smith** is Professor of International Studies, Coventry University.

**Niels Thygesen** is Professor of Economics, University of Copenhagen and Associate Senior Research Fellow, Centre for European Policy Studies, Brussels.

**Helen Wallace** is Professor of European Studies and Director of the Sussex European Institute, University of Sussex.

**William Wallace** is Walter F. Hallstein Fellow at St Antony's College, Oxford.

**Joseph Weiler** is Professor of Law, Harvard Law School, Harvard University and Director of the Academy of European Law, European University Institute, Florence.

**Jacek Saryusz-Wolski** is Under-Secretary of State, Council of Ministers, Republic of Poland.

**Stephen Woolcock** is Senior Research Fellow, Royal Institute of International Affairs, London.

**David Wright** works for the Commission of the European Communities, Brussels.

# Preface

In November 1992 a conference was held in Edinburgh, Scotland, to mark the 30th anniversary of the *Journal of Common Market Studies*. Founded in 1962 by Uwe Kitzinger, the *Journal of Common Market Studies* has, over the intervening 30 years and under a number of eminent editors, established its place as a leading journal of research into the economics and politics of international integration in general, and European economic and political integration in particular. For the idea of convening a conference to mark the 30th anniversary of the *Journal of Common Market Studies* we are, of course, indebted to Loukas Tsoukalis. It was the conference that he – then Editor of the journal – convened in 1982 to celebrate the 20th anniversary of the journal that provided the inspiration for convening the Edinburgh conference. We sincerely hope that the present collection of the papers, delivered in the University of Edinburgh in November 1992, will be as influential in setting the research agenda for European Community studies in the 1990s as the 1982 volume (Tsoukalis, 1983) proved to be for the 1980s.

The timing of the Edinburgh conference could not have been better. It was held immediately before the European Council meeting which marked the conclusion of the UK presidency of the Council of Ministers. That summit was also held in Edinburgh. Thus the conference took place against the backdrop of a city awash with a seemingly endless series of European activities. We are grateful to Jacek Saryusz-Wolski, Minister with responsibility for European matters in the Government of the Republic of Poland, who presented the keynote address which opened the conference. We were also pleased that the

Right Honourable Tristan Garel-Jones, MP, Minister of State at the Foreign and Commonwealth Office (European Minister), was able to accept an invitation to address conference delegates. His presentation provided valuable insights into the workings of the presidency. Finally, delegates were also able to attend a lecture given by the Right Honourable John Smith, MP, Leader of the Labour Party, who was one of the many eminent speakers who participated in the inaugural Lothian European Lectures series (Prince, 1993).

As the title of the volume implies, our objective in convening the conference was a combination of retrospective and prospective analyses of the development of European integration within a global context. Contributors to the conference were asked to complement their commentary concerning the ongoing develop-ment of the European Community as an economic, political and legal system with judgements about the challenges and issues that will confront the Commu-nity as it moves towards the twenty-first century. We also wanted to ensure that the conference proceedings reflected the place of the evolving European Community within the global system, and did not focus solely on domestic matters. In convening this conference, we were guided by the view that the *Journal of Common Market Studies* exists not only to present the results of leading researchers, but also to be a force in identifying the intellectual problems, and contributing to the theoretical debates, that will continue to preoccupy scholars as integration proceeds.

As usual in undertakings of this nature, thanks are due to a large number of individuals and organizations without whose support the conference could not have taken place. In particular, we would take this opportunity of expressing our deep gratitude to the Ford Foundation for providing the necessary financial support for the conference, and to Séamus Ó'Cléireacáin of that organization for his help. Both the Scottish Office and the Economic and Social Research Council (Single Market Initiative) contributed to the costs of the conference, and we are grateful to David Brew and David Mayes respectively of these institutions for their support. We are indebted to the Europa Institute of the University of Edinburgh for hosting the conference. The University of Edin-burgh proved to be a first-class venue, and the ambience and considerable hospitality afforded by the Old College was greatly enjoyed and appreciated by all the delegates. Our thanks go to the staff of the Old College who contributed so much to the success of the conference. We are also grateful to Eva Evans of the University Association for Contemporary European Studies (UACES) and Margaret Ainslie of the Europa Institute for providing essential support at key moments. Wolfram Kaiser deserves particular thanks for providing secretariat support before, during, and after the conference with courtesy and efficiency extending well beyond the call of duty. It almost goes without saying that we are extremely grateful to those who contributed directly to the conference proceedings, and whose papers are reproduced in this volume. We thank them for sharing their expert analyses with us, and we thank the discussants for their commentary and the individuals who chaired the various sessions. The Round Table which concluded the conference provided an opportunity for three eminent scholars to present their thoughts on the future research agenda for the economic, political, and legal areas of European Community studies. Finally, a special vote of thanks must be accorded to the Chairman of the Conference organizing committee, Professor Willie Paterson, Director of the Europa Institute at the University of Edinburgh. His unflagging support and contagious enthusiasm were essential ingredients for the success of the venture, and his contributions to all aspects of the conference proceedings demonstrated his prodigious energy and intellect.

Most of the papers presented in this volume were previously published in the September and December 1993 issues of the *Journal of Common Market Studies*. Included in this volume are the discussants' comments to these papers, and the contributions made at the Round Table that did not appear in the journal.

## References

Prince, G. (ed.) (1993) *A Window on Europe: The Lothian Lectures 1992* (Edinburgh: Canongate Press).

Tsoukalis, L. (ed.) (1983) *The European Community: Past, Present and Future* (Oxford: Blackwell).

# Introduction:
# Economic and Political Integration
# a Decade On

SIMON BULMER
and
ANDREW SCOTT

The period between the 20th and the 30th anniversaries of the *Journal of Common Market Studies* has witnessed a number of momentous events which together have redefined the political and economic map of Europe. Today we can, justifiably, speak of a 'new' Europe in which the post-war distinction between 'west' and 'east' Europe has lost much of its relevance. The European Community (EC) is at the heart of this new Europe: indeed, given the importance of the Community's economy and its evolving political role in the global arena, it is appropriate to describe the EC as the heart of the new Europe. The issues that confront the European Community today reflect, in large measure, significant changes that have occurred since the early 1980s. Then, the European Community was languishing in the political and economic doldrums, riven by internal disputes which threatened to undermine the consensual nature of the intergovernmental bargaining process which lies at the centre of Community decision-making, and without which the entire edifice would be weakened, possibly fatally. Rather than laying plans for the next stage in the construction of the community of Europe, the EC heads of state and government were preoccupied with crisis-management: the dispute over the UK contributions to the budget and reform of the CAP being two of areas of acute internal conflict. Practical matters and political expediency were the currency of deliberations in successive European Councils, while only in the corridors of the politically

© Basil Blackwell Ltd 1994, 108 Cowley Road, Oxford OX4 1JF, UK and 238 Main Street, Cambridge, MA 02142, USA

emasculated European Parliament was any serious consideration being given to the future of the European construction.

The process of integrating the economies of the EC Member States had come to a virtual standstill by the early 1980s. The immediate challenge confronting the Community was to prevent the progress that had been made during the previous two decades in establishing a 'common market' from being undermined by what was, in essence, a revival of protectionism. National governments were preoccupied with tackling deep-seated economic problems, often in different and sometimes in divergent ways. This period is remembered as the era of 'Euro-sclerosis', when Western Europe's industrial economies were plagued by ever-rising unemployment, low rates of economic growth, stagnating international trade, falling investment and an apparent erosion in the competitiveness of their multinational corporations. Macroeconomic policy co-ordination within the EC still had far to develop as monetary and fiscal policies within some Member States remained incompatible with stability in international currency markets. The European Monetary System (EMS) was, at the time, an unstable arrangement with an uncertain future. The preoccupation with domestic economic problems not only created an environment in which the further development of 'common' EC policies was difficult to achieve, there were in any event fundamental differences in philosophy between Member States both on what public policy could achieve, and what role the Community's institutions should play in delivering such policy. In short, during the early 1980s the process of European integration appeared to have encountered the classical 'limits to positive integration'.

By the second half of the 1980s, however, economic conditions throughout the EC had improved considerably. Economic growth had been restored to an acceptable level, though unemployment still was comparatively high in many Member States as macroeconomic policies remained firmly targeted at restraining inflationary pressures. The Exchange Rate Mechanism (ERM) of the EMS had settled down and become a framework for macroeconomic policy convergence. The ERM entered, from 1987, a period of more or less uninterrupted stability of nominal exchange rates (some would say 'excess' stability) which lasted until September 1992. This stability not only indicated a convergence between the macroeconomic policies of Member States, but also an increasing (though not complete) convergence in their underlying economic performance. Unsurprisingly, the pace of international economic integration towards ultimate objectives tends to quicken, and to encounter less resistance, when it takes place against a backdrop of buoyant economic performance. As the history of the European Community clearly demonstrates, the converse also holds.

The decision in 1985 to implement a package of measures aimed at completing the Community's Internal Market is now widely regarded as a key moment in the revival of the momentum for further economic and political integration within the EC. Ostensibly aimed at assisting the recovery of the Community's flagging economy, the Internal Market programme – the elimination of all remaining barriers to the free movement of goods, services, capital and labour between EC Member States by 31 December, 1992 – had effects which extended well beyond the strictly economic arena. The Internal Market programme was presented formally as a White Paper from the Commission to the European Council Summit at Milan in June 1985. The White Paper listed some 300 measures, subsequently reduced to 279. When enacted and in conjunction with observance of the principle of 'mutual recognition', rendering inoperable the remaining (in practice the overwhelming share of) intra-EC obstacles to the integration of product and factor markets, this would complete the process of establishing the common market that had been initiated in 1958. Considered solely as an economic event, completion of the Internal Market held out the prospect of significant gains accruing to Member States' economies. Eliminating intra-Community barriers to the 'four freedoms' would benefit consumers by allowing them access to lower cost supplies from partner Member States (the classical gains from trade creation). At the same time, the corporate sector would be able to exploit the cost savings in production associated with servicing an enlarged market (the gains from economies of scale), thereby enhancing their competitiveness in markets globally. With only a few exceptions, all the legislation needed to create a Single Market throughout the EC was in place by 31 December 1992.

As Moravcsik (1991) recounts, the presentation of the Internal Market programme in 1985 represented a culmination – rather than the beginning – of a period of intense intergovernmental negotiations concerning the future direction of European integration. Although the Single Market programme was the core element in what became the 're-launching' of integration, it was not only the Community's economic configuration that was being addressed. In the run-up to the Milan Summit, discussions on political integration were also underway. Reform to the Community's institutional structure and to the cumbersome decision-making procedures in the Council of Ministers figured on this agenda, both being considered necessary for implementing the measures needed to complete the internal EC market. Meanwhile Altiero Spinelli had initiated a wide-ranging debate concerning the future constitutional and institutional structure of the Community in the European Parliament. The results of Parliament's deliberations were contained in the influential 'Draft Treaty Establishing the European Union' agreed upon in 1984 by a majority of MEPs. The explicitly 'federalist' provisions for political union detailed in the Draft Treaty went well beyond anything likely to be acceptable to Member States. But the Treaty did provide a rallying point around which those Member States advocating closer political union could gather. Institutional reform and enhanced political integration, in addition to the Internal Market project, were now fixed on the Community's agenda.

The Fontainebleau Summit in June 1984 acknowledged the need for a comprehensive review of the Community's procedures and structures. Consequently, an Ad Hoc Committee for Institutional Affairs (the Dooge Committee) was formed to consider reform of the Community's economic, political, and institutional configuration. The Dooge Committee Report endorsed the Single Market objective, and supported the greater use of qualified majority voting in the Council of Minister's decision-making and an extension of Community competences to include foreign policy. In response to the Commission's White Paper and the Dooge Committee report, the Milan Summit in June 1985 initiated an Intergovernmental Conference (IGC) from which the Single European Act (SEA) emerged. The SEA was signed by EC Foreign Ministers in February 1986, although a delay in its ratification meant that it did not enter into force until July 1987.

Intended at the outset to be a device for ensuring the successful implementation of the Internal Market programme, the SEA ultimately proved to be instrumental in reviving the dynamic of EC political as well as economic integration. The SEA was significant in five respects. First, it provided the legal basis for completion of the Internal Market according to a fixed timetable: that is, by 31 December 1992. Second, the SEA enhanced both the treaty provisions for qualified majority voting as well as, by providing new momentum to integration, its actual practice. Third, the SEA included an explicit commitment to furthering 'economic and social cohesion' within the Community and mandated the Commission to bring forward proposals for reforming existing regional and social policies with a view to achieving this. Fourth, the SEA established a framework for further elaboration of concerted action in the area of foreign policy. Finally, the SEA introduced a new co-operation procedure that enhanced, albeit modestly, the powers of the European Parliament.

Although the principal purpose of the SEA was to extend the process of negative integration by proscribing national measures which restricted market access, it also heralded a new era of policy co-ordination and, subsequently, positive integration in the EC. Developments in two policy areas illustrate the extent to which implementation of the provisions of the SEA directly resulted in a significant 'deepening' of economic integration.

An express provision of the SEA was that Community regional and social (structural) policies should be reformed in pursuance of the objective of 'strengthening economic and social cohesion' (SEA, Art. 23). The Internal Market project seemed to promise much for the industrially advanced Member

States but rather less for the poorer countries characterized by economic backwardness – Greece, Spain, Portugal and Ireland. The decision to prioritize 'cohesion' was, therefore, an explicit recognition that the economic gains from the Single Market should be 'shared' throughout the EC. This has led some experts to depict Article 23 as little more than a 'side payment' to these poorer Member States in return for which these countries would endorse the SEA (Moravcsik, 1991; Marks, 1992). Be this as it may, the reforms to the Community's structural policies initiated by Art. 23 of the SEA were substantively significant in two respects. First, the reforms resulted in the redistributive function of the Community budget being strengthened; under the Delors I package of 1988 it was agreed that the funds assigned to structural programmes should be doubled (in real terms) over the period to end-1992. This increase in expenditure on measures promoting (economic and social) 'cohesion' was financed by the introduction of a fourth source of Community revenue linked to the GNP of each Member State. Second, the 1988 reforms to the structural funds introduced new criteria of eligibility for Community assistance. Henceforth, assistance would be concentrated in areas of greatest need (defined by reference to five new objectives of structural policy), and the Commission would have enhanced powers of supervision in the national distribution of monies allocated under Community programmes. Moreover, the reform of the structural funds made explicit provision for a closer involvement of sub-national authorities, as well as the 'social partners' in the formulation and implementation of Community structural policies. Consequently, the reform of the structural funds effected a modest reconfiguration in the policy-making process within the EC; a reconfiguration that was at the expense of the position of national governments by enhancing the supranational element in Community structural policies and by requiring the participation of sub-national authorities in the Community's structural policy process. Closer involvement of sub-national authorities in the Community's policy process has been taken one stage further by the provision in the Maastricht Treaty on European Union for the establishment of the (advisory) Committee of the Regions.

However, it has been in propelling the EC towards monetary union that the impact of the Single Market and the SEA has been most profound. By the late 1980s a consensus was emerging that realizing the objective of a truly unified EC market required the Community to move beyond the stage of the classical 'common market' and become a fully-fledged 'Economic and Monetary Union'. Although there were already signs of growing political support for monetary union, chiefly as a way of diluting the Bundesbank's dominance in the Community's monetary arrangements, a report by a group of experts chaired by Tommaso Padoa-Schioppa (Padoa-Schioppa, 1987) demonstrated that unless further convergence of monetary policies within the EC took place, completion of the Single Market would jeopardize the prevailing (EMS) exchange rate arrangements thereby undermining the notion of a Single Market.

In June 1988, the Hanover meeting of the European Council set up a committee to 'study and propose stages' leading towards Economic and Monetary Union (EMU) under the Chairmanship of Commission President Jacques Delors. The Delors Committee Report (Delors Committee, 1989), presented in April 1989, provided a blueprint for the transition, through three stages, to a single currency. Each stage involved a combination of ever-closer convergence of Member States' monetary policies accompanied by institutional reforms that progressively would shift responsibility for monetary policy away from Member States to a transnational para-public agency in the form of an EC Central Bank. The Madrid Summit in June 1989 produced agreement to begin the staged transition to monetary union on 1 July 1990. Stage 1 would involve, *inter alia*, the liberalization of intra-EC capital movements, the inclusion of all EC currencies in the ERM of the EMS, and formal economic and monetary policy co-ordination between Member States. At the Strasbourg Summit in December 1989 it was mooted that an IGC should be convened during 1991 to prepare 'an amendment of the Treaty with a view to the final stages of economic and monetary union'. That Conference produced detailed proposals for a fundamental treaty revision to provide for eventual monetary union, later incorporated in the Treaty on European Union agreed upon at the Maastricht Summit in December 1991, and formally signed by the foreign and finance ministers on 7 February 1992.

There is, therefore, a direct lineage beginning with the Single European Act of 1987 and culminating five years later with the signing of the Maastricht Treaty on European Union. Significantly, this lineage appears, at first sight, to conform rather well to certain aspects of the neo-functionalist account of 'spillover' to which is assigned the dynamic role in the process of international integration. Undoubtedly moves towards monetary union owed much to the realization that measures of 'negative' economic integration alone were insufficient to establish a genuinely common market. Co-ordination between and, arguably, complete convergence of, monetary policies would also be required. However, appearances must not be confused with causality, and the question concerning the underlying dynamics of the evolution of monetary co-operation within the EC is a matter upon which further light is cast in an important article by Andrew Moravcsik in this volume.

The dynamic underpinning the revival of integration within the Community from the mid-1980s was, in the main, economic rather than political in its orientation. The SEA notwithstanding, rather less was being achieved in the arena of political union. Advocates of closer political union in Europe focused on two main themes: an extension of Community competences beyond strictly economic matters (where there had been a gradual extension of EC competence during the 1980s), and reform of the Community institutions to address the emerging 'democratic deficit'. On the first issue little progress had been made. The inclusion of foreign policy co-operation within the Community framework as provided for in the SEA amounted to a formal recognition of prevailing inter-governmental practice. However, the momentous events of the late 1980s which saw the end of the Cold War and the prospective unification of Germany confronted the Community with, among other things, the inadequacy of its prevailing modalities of foreign policy co-operation. It was these events, more than any other factor, which led to the decision to convene an IGC on political union.

Second, the institutional reforms introduced by the SEA had not attended to the democratic deficit. Two aspects of this deficit were identified. The first related to the Community's decision-making procedures which were portrayed as secretive and lacking in accountability. Secondly, federalists argued that the weakness of legislative powers on the part of the European Parliament meant that common policies lacked democratic legitimacy. Moreover, as the pace of economic integration intensified, it was becoming clear that closer co-operation between Member States over a range of civil matters, hitherto excluded from formal Community scrutiny, would be necessary. This raised new concerns that common policies over highly sensitive issues would be decided upon through prevailing intergovernmental procedures rather than within a reformed supra-national framework.

Against this background agreement was reached at a special Dublin Summit in April 1990, to convene an Intergovernmental Conference on political union to address the twin issues of Community competences and institutional reform. This IGC ran alongside the IGC on monetary union. Proponents of political union sought an extension of Community competences within the framework of the existing treaties. Instead, what emerged was the so-called 'temple' model, according to which there would be three distinct 'pillars' which collectively would constitute the European Union.[1] The central pillar was the Community pillar – that is the European Community *per se* with its competences and institutional structure as defined in the Treaties (now amended to include economic and monetary union). To this would be added two new 'pillars': on Common Foreign and Security Policy (CFSP) and Justice and Home Affairs respectively. Institutional reform was accommodated by further revision to the Community Treaties to extend the legislative powers of the European Parlia-

---

[1]Initially there were to be four pillars, the fourth being a pillar derived from the Social Charter. However, on the basis of the British government's opposition, this was relegated to a protocol to the Treaty.

ment. Specifically, the co-operation procedure established by the SEA was extended to cover a greater number of issues, while the European Parliament was granted a new, negative assent procedure. Finally, the Parliament will be able to request the Commission to make a legislative proposal, though it will not enjoy an independent legislative capacity.

Although the new Treaty provides for joint action on matters falling under the two new pillars,[2] decisions will be taken intergovernmentally by the foreign or home affairs ministers of the 12 Member States. Further, policy will be decided upon only with the unanimous consent of all Member States; each Member State will, therefore, have a right of veto. On the other hand, measures implementing joint decisions in the area of CFSP can be taken by qualified majority vote if the Council unanimously so decides, while measures implementing conventions unanimously agreed upon under the Justice and Home Affairs pillar can be taken by a two-thirds majority. There is a limited role for the Community institutions under the provisions applying to the new pillars. To ensure consistency between decisions pertaining to CFSP and external economic policy – the latter falling within the exclusive competence of the Community – the Commission will be involved in Council deliberations on CFSP, though it will not be able to vote. The European Parliament will only be consulted about policies under both pillars. Significantly, while there is provision for the jurisdiction of the European Court of Justice to extend to issues falling within the Justice and Home Affairs pillar – if agreed to by Member States – there is no similar provision pertaining to CFSP.

The Treaty on European Union is regarded by some as providing the framework within which the goal of political and economic unification in Europe will, progressively, be realized. Whether the Treaty on European Union will constitute such a framework, and as Helen Wallace suggests in Chapter 3 of this volume it is far from self-evident that it will do so, nonetheless the Treaty does extend the formal boundaries of common EC competences to include monetary union, while the two new pillars of the Union constitute an extension of the terrain of inter-state co-operation. In so doing – as both Art. B and Art. C of the Treaty explicitly acknowledge – the Treaty of European Union represents an opportunity to extend the *acquis communautaire*. It is, however, paradoxical that the extension of joint action, particularly to the CFSP and Justice and Home Affairs pillars, represents a strengthening of the kind of intergovernmental arrangements which exacerbate the democratic deficit.

[2] CFSP is taken to mean that a common EC foreign and security policy will evolve, including defence. The Justice and Home Affairs pillar includes joint activity in the areas of asylum policy, controls on the Community's external borders, immigration policy and policy regarding nationals of third countries, combatting drug addiction and fraud, criminal and civil judicial co-operation, and co-operation between national police and customs authorities.

It is not only the consequences that have flowed from the 'relaunching' and subsequent 'deepening' of European economic and political integration that have to be addressed by the Community and Member State agencies at the moment. There are equally profound questions pertaining to a 'wider' Europe that have to be answered. In the medium term, the Community is set to undergo a fourth round of enlargement as the Scandinavian countries, along with Austria, begin negotiations that will almost certainly culminate in EC membership sometime in the second half of the decade. Over the longer term the Community will have to respond to membership applications from beyond its eastern borders. The collapse of the Berlin Wall in 1989 heralded a period of momentous political change throughout eastern and central Europe as the old communist regimes were swept away to be replaced by new, democratic structures. The ever-quickening pace of the reform process in central and eastern Europe has laid before the West in general and the European Community in particular a series of challenges to which their response will (continue to) illuminate the integrity of their commitment to defending and advancing the cause of political and social justice in these fledgling democracies. As is clear from the article which opens this volume, already there are doubts in the minds of some of the new leaders of the eastern and central European countries whether the European Community's response thus far has been adequate.

Although the European Community certainly has moved far from the conditions which pertained during the early years of the 1980s, it is evident today that some of the problems that plagued Member States then have returned a decade later. In particular, the economies of the EC Member States today are beset by recessionary forces that are giving rise to high levels of unemployment and low rates of economic growth. Further, the cracks that appeared in the ERM in September 1992 as both sterling and the lira were forced out of the regime, and which saw the end of a period of over five years during which no re-alignments to central rates were made, did indeed become fundamental 'fault lines' by July 1993 when intense speculation against some currencies resulted in the decision to abandon the narrow band of fluctuation in favour of a uniform 15 per cent band either side of central rate parity. The hope was that freeing EC countries from their exchange rate obligations would enable them to implement a fiscal and monetary package appropriate to tackling domestic economic problems. Certainly, the fiscal problems that confront a number of Member States (Belgium, Italy, Spain) are becoming ever more serious as the recession deepens. Cyclical budget deficits are adding further to the volume of outstanding (structural) debt and this, in turn, is putting upward pressure on interest rates, thereby postponing yet further the economic recovery. Prevailing economic conditions undoubtedly pose a major challenge to the realization of monetary union according to the timetable set out in the Maastricht Treaty. It seems unlikely that many countries will satisfy the so-called convergence criteria by 1997, or even by 1 January 1999. If indeed monetary union is to be postponed until a greater degree of convergence between the main economies has been achieved, then it would appear to be essential that the benefits deriving from monetary policy co-operation and co-ordination are not victims of the current instability.

Finally, the global environment has changed significantly over the past decade. In 1986 a new round of multilateral trade negotiations was initiated under the aegis of the GATT – a trade Round widely regarded as the most ambitious in the history of the GATT. The Uruguay Round has thrown up problems and disputes which have, to date, delayed agreement being reached on the breadth of the trade policy reforms to be implemented. However, the European Community has, from the outset, declared its commitment to securing a successful conclusion to the Uruguay Round, and continues to work towards this objective. In particular, the EC introduced extensive, and internally contested, reforms to its much criticized Common Agricultural Policy in an effort to advance the chances of achieving a successful conclusion to the Round. Undoubtedly the sheer range of complex and interrelated matters being addressed within the Uruguay Round has contributed – and continues to contribute – to the delay in agreement being reached. However, it has not only been with respect to the many functional matters of trade policy reform under review that the GATT presently is subject to pressure. At the same time, some analysts have questioned the viability of the GATT as an arrangement for resolving trade disputes in a global community which increasingly is becoming characterized by regional trading blocs. The emergence of large trading blocs – generally referred to as 'global regionalism' though the phrase is rarely defined – is one that has attracted considerable academic interest as it has variously been viewed as an alternative structure for resolving conflicts in international trade and thus to be encouraged, or as a harbinger of a new era in which regional will replace national protectionism and as such posing a profound threat to the international economy. What is certain is that the EC now constitutes the largest unified market in the world, and as such has considerable responsibility for maintaining intact the fabric of international commercial diplomacy. Certainly there are signs of a revival of protectionist instincts within the EC and elsewhere at the present time, as is to be expected during bouts of global recession. However, as the EC has demonstrated in the past, regional integration need not occur at the expense of multilateral trade diplomacy: nor need it be accompanied by the spectre of protectionism.

## The Scope of the Book

This volume brings together a number of articles which address major themes currently confronting scholars of European integration. In Chapter 1, Jacek Saryusz-Wolski, Minister for European Affairs in the Republic of Poland, considers the response of the EC to the seismic changes that have occurred in the economic and political configuration of central and eastern Europe. It is evident that he considers that the Community needs to go further in its response. This chapter builds on a theme which Saryusz-Wolski refers to as the 'costs of half-Europe'; that is, the losses to both the countries of central and eastern Europe and to the European Community if the former are not able, within a reasonable timescale, to become full members of the EC. Within this overall framework, two specific themes are developed. The first concerns the need for the countries of central and eastern Europe to have clearly defined criteria before the EC would contemplate their membership. These criteria should, it is argued, be determined jointly and should reflect the positions from which the countries are developing. It might well be counterproductive for the Community to insist on criteria being met which simply are outside of what is possible for these countries over the medium term.  Saryusz-Wolski's second theme addresses the Community's response to the serious economic problems which these countries are experiencing in the meantime. How committed is the Community to the economic development of the countries on its eastern borders? He questions whether the market access provisions and the financial help offered by the EC under the Association agreements are sufficient to achieve the desired improvement in economic conditions. And what are the consequences – for both the EC and for central and eastern Europe – if the assistance is not enough to achieve economic development?

In Chapter 2, Andrew Moravcsik examines the core theoretical propositions surrounding the process of international integration. Moravcsik's thesis is that the policies and institutional provisions of the EC are best regarded as the outcome of negotiations between independent but interdependent and rational governments, each of which is motivated by self-interest and whose primary objective is to remain in office. Moravcsik labels this approach 'liberal inter-governmentalism' and presents it as an alternative to the neo-functionalist theories that remain the bedrock of academic analyses of the European Community. We are presented with a Community in which inter-state bargaining positions reflect preferences formed at the national level which are, in turn, the outcome of struggles between interest groups operating within the nation-state. In this approach it is the existence of international interdependence that provides the motivation for inter-state bargaining (of which the European Community represents a sophisticated model) as interdependence otherwise may constrain or compromise national governments from realizing national objectives. Inter-dependence itself arises as a consequence of national policies which have been implemented in order to meet the expectations of dominant national interest groups.

Moravcsik details two models in his article. The first model examines the manner in which national preferences are fashioned and, by extension, the complex bargaining process which ultimately leads a government to adopt particular policies. Unlike the neo-functional model, which accords consider-able autonomy to supranational actors, liberal intergovernmentalism sees national actors as being constrained in their policy options by the need to meet the expectations of their domestic constituents. The second model details a process of intergovernmental bargaining in which specific policy outcomes reflect the underlying distribution of bargaining power between the participants and – in the context of a zero-sum game – the extent to which the 'losers' from any policy choice can be compensated by the 'winners'. Throughout his article, Moravcsik illuminates the theoretical core of his approach by detailed commen-tary drawn from the EC's experience of policy co-ordination in the context of ever-closer economic integration. Moravcsik's chapter provides a comprehen-sive and intellectually challenging account of the evolution of economic policy co-ordination within the EC. His analytical construct constitutes an important contribution to the theoretical debate surrounding the ongoing process of European integration. It is particularly valuable in locating the study of integra-tion within the international political economy literature and away from the *sui generis* tendencies which characterize much of neo-functionalism.

In Chapter 3 Helen Wallace focuses on the evolution of the EC as a system of governance and considers the underlying challenges to which the Community will need to respond over the medium term. Whilst recognizing the political importance of the debate that surrounded the ratification of the Treaty on European Union, Helen Wallace illuminates four deep-seated problems which go beyond the immediate matter of Treaty ratification. The first concerns the 'economic sustainability' of the Community – that is, the extent to which the Community has the economic strength to manage the complex economic, social and demographic forces that are acting upon it and to resist resurgence of protectionist tendencies within particular Member States. A second problem revolves around policy-making at the Community level; what is referred to as the problem of 'political sustainability' within the Community. Specifically, Community policy increasingly is confronting a crisis of legitimacy as the influence exerted by narrow sectoral interests and political elites rises at the expense of the wishes of a broader constituency. Indeed, it is difficult for the wishes of the broader constituency to be represented within the EC policy-making process. Third, the forces that propelled the post-war integration of western Europe are no longer as powerful as once they were. With the end of the Cold War and the unification of Germany much of the Community's original *raison d' être* has gone and has not been replaced. Finally, Helen Wallace asks whether there is within the Community a collective objective which is held with sufficient conviction to provide the impetus necessary for further 'deepening' of economic and political integration.

Europe's international role is examined by Christopher Hill in Chapter 4. Hill's central thesis is that a gap has developed between the international role that Europe is expected to play and that which it is capable of playing. In conceptualizing the EC's role in world affairs, Hill builds upon the twin notions of 'actorness' and 'presence'. Actorness refers to the extent to which the EC may be considered to be a genuine actor in the international political arena, while presence is gauged by the extent to which EC actions have a discernible impact on international affairs. Although the EC is accepted as an international actor with presence, the divided nature of responsibilities in the field of foreign policy between the Member States and the EC institutions restricts the extent to which the Community can exercise these twin functions. Hill identifies a number of international roles that the Community might play in a world where all the usual post-1945 assumptions concerning the configuration of international affairs are no longer relevant. But if the EC is to develop an enhanced presence in global affairs by developing a common foreign policy, three problems will have to be tackled: its ability to reach agreement, the lack of resources, and the availability of instruments at its disposal. In short, the Community must be able to take decisions and to stick to them. That presently it does not and cannot represents the source of what Hill refers to as the capability–expectations gap, a gap which he considers to be dangerous as it encourages initiatives and raises expectations which the Community is unable subsequently to discharge. Whilst acknowledging that this gap might be closed over time, Hill proposes that a proper appreciation of the complexities of the Community's foreign policy might prevent such a gap opening in the first place. In other words, there is a need to conceptualize the Community's role in international affairs in a manner that recognizes the inherent difficulties associated with formulating and implementing a common foreign policy position within the Community system. In the Community system Member States wear different hats in the various international fora which address foreign policy issues. In this situation it is difficult to achieve consistency and sustainability of foreign policy between Member States. It may be the case that a common foreign policy will need to await a significant movement towards an explicitly federal European Union.

In Chapter 5 Joseph Weiler presents a retrospective assessment and prospective analysis of the evolving role of the European Court of Justice (ECJ) within the process of European integration. The chapter is structured around two sections. The first section presents a retrospective of the contribution of the ECJ to the dynamic of EC integration, and examines the origins of the considerable influence which the ECJ has been permitted to exercise in this regard. Consequently, Weiler is interested here in exploring the acceptance, and the process of legitimization, of ECJ decisions within Member States – much of the explanation for which requires argument drawn from the sphere of political science – rather than in the doctrinal basis of these decisions, which is a matter of legalistic or constitutional interpretation. Why has the ECJ been so successful in restricting the 'sovereignty' of Member States? Weiler identifies three 'sets of interlocutors' each of which has, implicitly, empowered the ECJ by facilitating the incorporation of Court rulings in the domestic context – the national judiciaries in Member States, Member State governments themselves, and academia. Weiler presents a persuasive rationale that accounts for collaboration on the part of each interlocutor in accepting and enforcing ECJ rulings, including those which patently restricted the sovereignty of the nation-state. This rationale revolves around mutual empowerment (judiciary to judiciary), respect and reasoned self-interest (Member State to ECJ) and myopia (academia to ECJ).

In the second section of his essay, Weiler considers the future role of the ECJ. His thesis is that the provisions of both the Single European Act and the Treaty on European Union jointly will necessitate the ECJ adjudicating on issues and disputes which, by their nature, will expose the ECJ to considerable public scrutiny and, inevitably, will invite greater criticism. In particular, the restrictions which the Treaty on European Union implies on the activities of the Community in certain policy areas, along with the emphasis placed upon 'subsidiarity', will require the ECJ to rule over disputes concerning competence. Consequently, the ECJ may become enmeshed in disputes which, hitherto, it has been able to avoid and this will intensify the general scrutiny that is applied to ECJ rulings.

The next three chapters address the question of regional economic integration (REI) from a variety of perspectives. In Chapter 6 Peter Robson considers the relevance of recent developments in the theory of REI for the developing countries. While contemporary REI theory increasingly reinforces the conventional wisdom that REI raises welfare in the participating countries, Robson notes that studies into the effects of REI between developing countries have, on the other hand, tended to reject this proposition. Robson accepts that for a number of reasons REI between developing countries has not, in the past, been particularly successful, due partly to their failure to ensure that the gains from integration were evenly distributed between participating countries and partly to structural conditions of the economies. However, this should not be used as evidence that REI between developing countries can never be successful.

Robson argues that changes in the structural context of developing countries has removed a major obstacle to their successful integration, where this is taken to mean the ability of these countries to exploit the classical gains from trade creation. Robson's argument and conclusions represent an important contribution to the debate concerning the appropriate strategy for developing countries. Specifically, he takes issue with the prevailing wisdom, represented mainly by the World Bank, that REI is not a strategy that developing countries should favour.

In Chapter 7 Deepak Lal presents a critical assessment of the consequences for the global economy resulting from the emergence of regional trading blocs in general, and the EC and the North American Free Trade Area (NAFTA) in particular. Whilst accepting that both the EC and the NAFTA are trade creating – thus welfare enhancing – Lal nonetheless warns that these arrangements may well weaken the role of the GATT and in so doing jeopardize an arrangement which has been central to post-1945 global economic prosperity. Lal argues that the attention that is being given to regional economic integration is at the expense of the multilateral system at the very moment when that system is in greatest need of support. The essential problem with regional trading blocs is that they are discriminatory and, argues Lal, discrimination is likely to beggar discrimination to the detriment of free trade. Lal also is highly critical of much of what goes under the heading of 'new' trade theory which forms the intellectual basis for strategic industrial policies implemented within these trading blocs, policies which involve some element of protection.

A different perspective on regional trading arrangements is given by Stephen Woolcock in Chapter 8. Rather than regarding regional blocs necessarily as counter to the interests of the GATT, Woolcock considers the extent to which such arrangements might be complementary to the GATT in the sense that they are better able to address the 'challenges of increased interdependence'. Specifically, Woolcock considers the evidence supporting the contention that the trading rules which underpin the EC and which determine its external trading relations are consistent with the multilateral trading system. Based on a comparative assessment of trade policy in three sensitive areas – technical barriers to trade, public procurement and services and investment – Woolcock concludes that EC policy does conform with existing multilateral rules, and that the principles and approaches adopted by the EC are similar to those which inform GATT policy. Of course, the progress recorded by the EC in eliminating commercial restrictions in these three areas has been considerably greater than that recorded through the aegis of the GATT. In large measure this can be attributed to the adjudicative approach to dispute settlement that is a key element in the EC's prevailing *acquis communautaire*. One implication is that if the GATT is to progress in tackling trade disputes it will need to acquire a stronger adjudicative role.

In Chapter 9 Alexis Jacquemin and David Wright consider the corporate challenges and priorities that will inform Europe's business decisions post-1992. Already, they argue, there is evidence of greater intra-industry specialization within the EC, and in part this has been a response – and one that economic theory would predict – to the completion of the Internal Market. Elsewhere, completion of the EC market has prompted foreign direct investment and has induced corporate restructuring through increased merger and takeover activities. But what of the future? In the second section of their paper, Jacquemin and Wright report the findings from a study, conducted by the Forward Studies Unit of the Commission, which sought to establish the major factors that together would 'shape' the economic environment within which EC companies will operate in the future, and the priorities which EC business identify for the post-1992 period. The priorities for business that emerge from the study focus, unsurprisingly, on practical matters such as improvements in communications and infrastructure systems, greater flexibility of the labour market, and enhanced competitiveness of EC technology. It appears that business wishes to see a consolidation of the Internal Market rather than the development of any new initiatives.

The increasingly complex issue of Europe's monetary arrangements is addressed by Niels Thygesen in Chapter 10. Written prior to the decision to reform the ERM and widen the fluctuation bands to their present 15 per cent either side of parity, here Thygesen assesses the likely consequences for the goal of monetary union should the ERM be reformed. As one of the reform proposals he considers is to relax the intervention limits for ERM currencies, his analysis has considerable relevance in the present context. A particular concern is that such a strategy will jeopardize the significant contribution that the ERM has made to the disinflation that characterized all ERM countries during the 1980s, and which persuaded policy-makers that the time was right for proceeding to full monetary union. Moreover, Thygesen argues that the re-entry of those currencies that have exited the ERM (i.e. sterling and the lira) will not be assisted by such a strategy. Throughout his paper, Thygesen warns of the consequences that might arise from exchange rate policy and EC institutional developments becoming marooned somewhere between the prevailing ERM arrangements – which may not guarantee stability in currency markets – and a definite move to monetary union. There is, as Thygesen makes clear, a trade-off between the policy autonomy afforded to a national government by widening the margin of fluctuation, and the credibility of the central rate (and by implication the transition to monetary union) associated with a narrowing of the fluctuation margin. In this light it would appear that the decision to increase the ERM band will have set the entire monetary union timetable back.

The final chapter in this volume presents the conclusions from a Round Table event at which three leading authorities from the disciplines of economics, political science and EC law gave their thoughts concerning the future research agenda for scholars in the area of EC studies.

## References

Delors Committee (1989) *Report on Economic and Monetary Union in the European Community* (Brussels: Committee for the Study of Economic and Monetary Union).

Marks, G. (1992) 'Structural Policy in the European Community'. In Sbragia, A., *Euro-politics: Institutions and Policymaking in the 'New' European Community* (Washington: Brookings Institution).

Moravcsik, A. (1991) 'Negotiating the Single European Act'. In Keohane, R. and Hoffmann, S., *The New European Community: Decisionmaking and Institutional Change* (Boulder, Col.: Westview).

Padoa-Schioppa, T. (1987) *Efficiency, Stability and Equity: A Strategy for the Evolution of the Economic System of the European Community* (Oxford: Oxford University Press).

# 1.
# The Reintegration of the 'Old Continent': Avoiding the Costs of 'Half Europe'

JACEK SARYUSZ-WOLSKI

The whole European continent faces major challenges arising from its reintegration in the aftermath of the end of the Cold War. I will make some remarks about this challenge, as seen from the perspective of Poland and the Visegrad countries. These remarks may seem somewhat blunt, but it is important that our perspective is understood. Is the European Community now looking east? Is reintegration now inevitable? Or, more pessimistically, do we now face an economically divided continent? And what would be the potential costs of a 'half-Europe'?

## I. The Challenge

The question which one could put since the dramatic changes took place in central and eastern Europe in 1989, is whether the western response or west European response to this development has been appropriate, as related to the magnitude of the challenge. Certainly there have been important policy developments but, perhaps, it was not a happy coincidence that it was at approximately the same time that the three Association Agreements were initialled (in November 1991) that the Maastricht Treaty was being negotiated (December

1991). The Association Agreements with Poland, Czechoslovakia and Hungary were somehow overshadowed by the magnitude of the Maastricht Treaty, with which there have been so many problems relating to ratification.

What should be said is that both the Maastricht Treaty and the Association Agreements can be situated in the same logic of history. From our point of view this signing of the Association Agreements is an institutional means to integration in the world order. That is to say, from the point of view of European integration, it is a move away from the path of *west* European integration, along which you have been proceeding for the past decades, to a truly *pan*-European integration. The problem which we are facing in both western and eastern Europe is whether we will be able finally to overcome this division of Europe or whether we will have another, this time economic, 'Yalta'. We are trying – I mean mainly the Visegrad countries but to some extent it concerns also other southern neighbours in central Europe – to catch up with historical developments in western Europe. This, of course, is the historical process which started with the Treaties of Paris and Rome and is a course of events which we have been looking at with jealousy but from which we have been separated by the artificial division of Europe. So, from our point of view, the Association process is very much in the same logic of history, leading to full integration. However, to the extent that integrating the east will be guided by the same dynamics as guided the west, problems may ensue.

However much we invoke Jean Monnet's saying that 'Europe is inevitable', some words of caution are still necessary. Historically, Europe has been both united but also divided and fragmented. And today there are still some elements of these three possibilities. A few years ago it was very fashionable to talk about the end of history. What we are witnessing today is very much the opposite, namely a return to history; at least that is how things appear from a central/eastern European perspective. It was much simpler when we were looking at the situation in 1989. Today the situation appears to be immeasurably more complex than it did during that glorious autumn of 1989.

The west is committed in principle to assist in our development and transformation, but in terms of substance there is still no real take-off of this effort. The negotiated Association Agreements, whilst welcome, are not a sufficient response to the problems which we are facing. The new governments of central/eastern Europe are facing formidable challenges and confronting many difficulties. A democratically elected western government would hesitate to try to tackle a single one of these difficulties if it hoped to be re-elected! This tends to be neglected in the west. Indeed, it is important for both sides of Europe not to be surprised by political instability in these circumstances or be overtaken by the events, as has already happened in the case of the former Yugoslavia.

Probably in the immediate future Europe's new architecture is likely to be baroque rather than classical: to consist of interlocking systems. We hope this Europe will not be divided by a new economic Iron Curtain, with poverty somewhere east of the old Curtain. The question is how both 'sides' of Europe can proceed towards a more structured, classical new architecture without ante-rooms and without ante-chambers.

European integration is very often confronted with a dilemma of widening versus deepening. However, from our standpoint this is a false dilemma because it is hard to imagine that deepening of the European construction can be successful without responding to the challenge of central/eastern Europe: the challenge on the eastern borders of the Community. So one might take the opposite view that widening and deepening go together and that widening could to some extent play the role of catalyst in the processes of deepening in the European Community. From our standpoint the delays in the two processes are unfavourable developments. We should not forget that the time factor is especially important in central/eastern Europe and that we could lose the battles in our domestic arenas. In the central/eastern European countries we are not interested in premature accession to the European Community; we think that this should only happen when the time is right. The question is how to define the right time, and I will return to that later.

## II. The Potential Costs

At the same time, besides the time factor, one should also consider something which – to paraphrase the EC's study on the Single Market – might be called 'the cost of half-Europe'. Arguably, there is such a thing as the cost of half-Europe. I think the cost will be significant for both sides and these costs should be identified. The reintegration of central/eastern Europe, whatever politicians do or do not do, is already under way. Since 1989 there has been a significant change in the direction of trade. In fact, in terms of importance of trade flows, the European Community has replaced COMECON for the Visegrad countries and probably for other central/eastern European countries as well. This is something which should be reflected somehow in the sphere of institutions and institutional linkages.

The present institutional arrangements are proudly called Europe Agreements or Association Agreements. They consist of three main elements. The first is a political signal that EC membership might be a possibility at the end of the reform process, but this is a very unclear signal. The second element is something which might be called selective access to the markets with the stress on selective as, in fact, there has been very little success in accessing the EC market. The third element of the Europe Agreements consists of the financial commitments or financial co-operation, a very weak aspect. Certainly, the whole notion of a political dialogue is welcome, and could be improved and exploited. However, it cannot substitute for deficiencies in the other three elements.

If one agrees that the Europe Agreements are not sufficiently far-reaching, then one must acknowledge that there is a danger that they will be an instrument to keep the central/eastern European countries in something like cold storage. And, as we all know, fruit does not ripen in refrigerators. It is quite clear from our perspective, given the bare economic facts, that we cannot wait until our level of economic development reaches the average level of EC economic development. The problem is to define criteria which will indicate when we are 'ready' for membership.

Already the process which is under way has effects on western Europe and the European Community. First, my fear is that the peace dividend – arising from the removal of the threat from the east – is probably being consumed by the countries of the west rather than being used to facilitate economic assistance to the central/eastern European countries. Second, in the longer-term perspective there is unquestionably the possibility of a positive macroeconomic effect on the western European side. And that effect also concerns central/eastern Europe, for the degree to which it can help the transformation process depends on the degree of liberalization of east–west economic relations. From our point of view – and this is based on very sound economic simulations – the smaller the access to markets that we get, the slower will be the pace of reform and the slower will be the pace of economic transformation.

During negotiations with the EC, we based our positions on a very simplified model of two scenarios: a restricted one and a liberal one. In the event we were offered the restricted one, with consequentially inferior effects on growth, on employment, on inflation and all the macroeconomic indicators. The question is, whether this can be improved.

Our plea is that the EC response to the needs posed by the central/eastern European challenge should be stronger. And the number of our expectations is not that great but qualitatively they are significant. First, there is the question of EC membership as a distant but precisely described objective which we think that both sides should treat as a common goal. For the time being, the Preambles of the Association Agreements state that it is our aspiration but not the goal of the EC. Second, there should be some kind of a calendar – a time-frame indicating what should happen and when. And this is very important from the point of view of the psychological behaviour of our societies. Third, there should be a convergence plan, and this should involve provisions for improved market access and improved financial co-operation.

When we review developments, we see a very clear picture of what is a divergence between political declarations, on the one hand, and political 'openings' and economic 'offerings' made to central/eastern Europe, on the other hand. What has appeared quite clear – and I think this was a revelation for both sides but more so for the Community – was that these 'openings' and 'offerings' leading to the reintegration of central/eastern Europe would necessitate economic adjustment on both sides; that is, including the Community. For that purpose there is a need to have a much stronger European Community *Ostpolitik*. But that also necessitates political will, which for the time being is missing. And it requires a different concept of what we are going to do in the coming decades in Europe. Going back to the forefathers of European construction – Monnet, Schuman, Adenauer – I would say that we should reflect again whether we want Europe as a *'projet politique'* or we want Europe as a *'Europe des marchands'*. And if we give a clear answer to this question, we can then proceed to talk about trade, investment and other more concrete issues.

It is quite clear that in the medium and long term, the improvement of the conditions for the reintegration of central eastern European countries will have a politically stabilizing effect. This is not an insignificant matter, I think, for our western partners. What we are looking for is a fair chance for our economies, not a charity-type action, something which might be called an enlightened self-interest that is in the longer-term self-interest of Western Europe. Unfortunately, what has been happening over the last long months of negotiation has revealed that there is a conflict between the short- and long-term reasoning and interests. In principle, we agreed on the long-term interest, in both an economic and political sense. However, when we came down to the short-term perspective there was a clear divergence between vested sectoral Community interests on the one hand, and the pursuit by eastern producers of market access on the other. This was, then, an internal Community conflict. The under-articulation of the interests of consumers in the EC and the over-articulation of some of the sectoral interests of pressure groups – these deficiencies in the EC's decision-making mechanism – bring about a situation where the Community is not able to assure the fulfilment of its long-term political interest because of the over-articulation of short-term vested sectoral interests.

This is quite clearly a fault of the political process – possibly in time we will be in the same situation – but perhaps we should reflect on how to negotiate in order not to endanger the longer-term interest. What would be needed would be a cost–benefit analysis in this wider sense, one which would include all elements – political, economic and matters relating to security – and assess these in a long-term perspective.

I have already referred to the adjustment which has to happen on both sides. We need solid, dynamic and open partners in the European Community. What we have discovered paradoxically is that adjustment is more difficult for the EC than for us. Although for us the EC represents nearly 55–60 per cent of our global trade, for the Community we only represent some 2–3 per cent.

Looking in a cool way at the situation, we have to say that there are barriers on both sides. We should work together first to identify them, and then to build up a plan to overcome them. The barriers on the eastern side are clear. It is very often said, and it is a view shared by some EC member countries, that we are not yet ready for EC membership; that we should be ready; and that we should wait until we are ready. That is a very vague notion of 'readiness'. We know very clearly that we need to achieve the economic stability that is essential to the structural change of our economies; we have to approximate our laws; we have to adjust to the *acquis communautaire*; and our economies have to be sound. However, if we look today at the macroeconomic criteria for Economic and Monetary Union as described in the Maastricht Treaty, some of our countries fulfil them to a higher extent than do some of the EC Member States. What we are proposing is that the criteria are based more on the health rather than the wealth of our economies. The main economic indicators that we proposed are set out in the Visegrad Memorandum presented to the Community in October 1992, and are along similar lines to the convergence philosophy set out in the Maastricht Treaty. These criteria are macroeconomic liberalization and control of inflation; microeconomic liberalization; continued external liberalization of relations with convertibility of currencies; and further structural change with continued privatization. Some of our countries have already fulfilled some of the criteria, but we need continued encouragement and further assistance.

The barriers on the EC side are equally real. They are the following. First, there is the problem of adjustment in sensitive sectors – agriculture, textiles, steel and coal – which has to be faced; the Community has considerable experience in adjusting internally. Second, there is the fear of migration; this is very much exaggerated. It should not threaten western Europe if there is prosperity and sustainable growth in central/eastern Europe. And then there is the question of budgetary cost. This is difficult to quantify precisely but is not overwhelmingly great. The fourth barrier on the EC side is the internal decision-making process. This is quite clearly linked to the issue – already referred to – of deepening. The EC's decision-making has to be effective; we are not at all interested in paralysing the Community.

If we accept reverse reasoning, we could ask what is the cost of non-enlargement, for there is such a cost and it would be paid on both sides. The experience of Yugoslavia is instructive. The first cost of non-enlargement would be losing the peace dividend which we have been hoping for. Second, there would be no positive demonstration effects to all the territories from the Polish eastern border to Vladivostok, with all the negative and threatening consequences of their withdrawal from the path of democratization and marketization. Third, it would be against the flow of history: it would put Europe back into the position of a quarrelling club. Fourth, it would compromise the political elites who initiated the changes in Prague, Warsaw and Budapest; also with significant consequences. Fifth, it would lead to some kind of a peripheralization of eastern/central Europe – the creation of a grey zone – again with costs to be paid for. And last there would be an economic cost which could be calculated as a loss of economic opportunities because, besides the short-term perspective, these economies are complementary to those in the west. A bigger, reunited Europe can enjoy faster economic growth, greater prosperity and stability. Thus the main conclusion from this statement that there are barriers on both sides, on the EC side and on the central/eastern European side, is that the pace of our march towards the Community should be dictated by *our* ability to adjust, and not by the EC's ability to adjust.

### III. The Way Ahead

I do not know whether the reintegration of central/eastern Europe should be looked upon from a moral, historical, economic, political or some other perspective, but it is our deep conviction that the pace and the timing should be dictated by our ability to adjust. We, for sure, will not reverse our commitment to the reform process in central/eastern Europe, even if the response is so hesitant. We will continue in our attempts to stabilize and modernize our economies as far as we are able. There are already very positive signs. Poland is the first country to move out of recession, and recovery is occurring as production increases. This confirms that the so-called shock therapy, which was so much criticized in the west, was the correct response. We are moving towards the approximation of legislation and the gradual adoption of the *acquis communautaire*. We have begun to re-establish, and will be further re-establishing, the natural productive structure of our economies. But the pace at which this occurs will be dictated by the extent to which we have unfettered access to EC markets. We will seek to prevent frustration in public opinion about being prevented from this 'return to Europe'. And on all fronts we will be continuing the regulatory reforms.

These various processes have to be accompanied by the proper reaction on the Community's side in terms of further liberalization of access to the markets, based on the principle of preferential treatment; by a progressive increase in financial co-operation, financial transfers and private direct investment. These last two points are very closely connected because no one would invest at present in Poland or Hungary without being able to sell back to their home market. Market access is vital; otherwise a vicious circle might ensue. All of the elements of economic assistance are interlinked and could be operationalized within a convergence plan which would define membership conditions, criteria and a timetable. It is quite clear from my point of view that is possible to set criteria that would be so high that it would be the twenty-second century before they were met. We think that treatment of central/eastern Europe should not be very different from the treatment of the southern flank: the Iberian enlargement of the EC. What is needed is a reasonable time-frame for membership with appropriate transitional arrangements.

Already there is scope to go beyond the Europe Agreements; to abolish more identified barriers and to apply what we call a dynamic and evolutionary interpretation of Association. In the absence of a dynamic perspective – for which the political will is needed – it is not possible to have far-reaching economic solutions. We are told that by saying or fixing some kind of timetable or criteria, we will raise hopes which, if unfulfilled, will result in frustration, and conditions may deteriorate; this is the view of some politicians in the west. We think that the reverse is the case. A clear perspective will motivate and dynamize our reforms, and set a good example to others. This also implies that central/eastern European countries should not be treated en bloc. Treatment should be proportional to economic achievements and discipline, together with the safe-guard of human rights and democratic principles.

The common elements in the expectations, hopes, positions, and plans of the Visegrad states is the clear perspective of EC membership to which I have referred. It is very important to understand that the Visegrad countries accept the changing nature of the European Community. We fully appreciate that we would be joining in, let us say, the year 2000, a different Community. We know that. For that reason we have to march more quickly. But to march more quickly we need better treatment.

The Visegrad countries want to realize as soon as possible all the potential which is in the Europe Agreements. But we also want to go beyond them, for they were negotiated at a very specific moment and already the circumstances for us have changed. We are asking for an acceleration of the reintegration process and an improvement in the offers and concessions included in the Europe Agreements.

The accelerated development of a regular and extended political dialogue is already becoming a political fact. We are keen to participate in this 'European political space' but neither it nor any other form of political co-operation could be regarded as an alternative to enlargement. By no means could such a development displace or delay full membership. We know that in the political thinking in western Europe there is a temptation to offer us a substitute. On the Visegrad side we are not interested in such substitutes.

We are also interested in closer and stronger links with the Western European Union as this evolves. We are interested in bringing our societies together. Our societies have been victimized by the tragic course of world history, and the artificial divide of Europe should be eliminated as quickly as possible and we should recover losses. It is not only the economy which counts, for stability and security are built upon more than purely economic well-being.

We expect assistance from the EC in terms of approximating our laws and standards and developing our infrastructure to facilitate a further opening of markets and trade. We also expect that the Twelve will change the mechanism of assistance, moving towards investment and away from the predominance hitherto of technical assistance by which some of the countries are suffocated, at least in some sectors. We also expect an increase in resources and some kind of a doctrine of treatment, or philosophy behind the assistance – treating the assistance as an instrument of reintegrating our countries.

Assistance should not be purely a developmental tool as under the Lomé Convention or under traditional linkages between big European states and their former colonies. Instead, it should be an instrument of reintegration, and the question of what instruments to use should be a subordinate matter to the overriding objective of the reintegration of the central/eastern European countries. We would also expect a broad interpretation of the financial co-operation provisions of the Europe Agreements. To our disappointment we have discovered that there is a dichotomy between the thinking and political action on the part of the Community countries. The EC Member States behave quite differently when they sit in the IMF in Washington from the way they behave when they sit in the EC bodies in Brussels. These different, if not schizophrenic, attitudes have very important implications for us. The recipes which we are offered by the Bretton Woods institutions are, as you know, very tough. At the same time we are trading with western Europe: 60 per cent of our trade is equivalent to the average inter-Community trade of other Member States. And we are often being advised to go towards softer economic policies: soft in terms of respecting social criteria, social tensions, political necessities, and so on. But, as you probably know, this is not the philosophy of the Bretton Woods institutions, so the position in that respect is inconsistent, and if you look into the financial chapter of the Europe Agreement, you will see that everything is conditional. The Community will not do a single thing without asking the Bretton Woods institutions. We think that the time has come to have a consistent approach to our countries.

We expect accession by the end of the century. Some people say that we are completely unrealistic. We – the Visegrad countries – share the same main targets of the economic policy which I mentioned, and which we propose to be the evaluation criteria. And we propose a start to formal negotiations. Beyond that, and bearing in mind the proposed intergovernmental conference in 1996, we are trying to keep pace with events in the EC. We also think that further action will be needed to ensure the gradual elimination of the economics disparities to which I referred at the beginning.

These then are the tasks ahead. How far the two sides of the formerly divided continent succeed in avoiding the 'costs of half-Europe' remains for future analysis.

# 2.
# Preferences and Power in the European Community: A Liberal Intergovernmentalist Approach

ANDREW MORAVCSIK*

## I. Introduction

The European Community (EC) is the most successful example of institution-alized international policy co-ordination in the modern world, yet there is little agreement about the proper explanation for its evolution. From the signing of the Treaty of Rome to the making of Maastricht, the EC has developed through a series of celebrated intergovernmental bargains, each of which set the agenda for an intervening period of consolidation. The most fundamental task facing a theoretical account of European integration is to explain these bargains. Today many would revive neo-functionalism's emphasis on *sui generis* characteristics of EC institutions, in particular the importance of unintended consequences of previous decisions and the capacity of supranational officials to provide leadership.

This article joins the debate by reasserting the self-critique, advanced almost two decades ago by Ernst Haas and other leading neo-functionalists, who

* The first version of this article can be found in Chapter 1 of Moravcsik (1992a). A subsequent version was delivered at the conference of the European Community Studies Association (Washington, May 1993). I am grateful to Simon Bulmer, Anne-Marie Burley, James Caporaso, Renaud Dehousse, Robert Keohane, Leon Lindberg, Giandomenico Majone, and Gideon Rose for detailed comments on earlier drafts, to Helen and William Wallace for their generous support, and to the New York University School of Law for logistical assistance.

suggested that European integration can only be explained with reference to *general* theories of international relations. The basic claim of this article is that the EC can be analysed as a successful intergovernmental regime designed to manage economic interdependence through negotiated policy co-ordination. Refinements and extensions of existing theories of foreign economic policy, intergovernmental negotiation, and international regimes provide a plausible and generalizable explanation of its evolution. Such theories rest on the assumption that state behaviour reflects the rational actions of governments constrained at home by domestic societal pressures and abroad by their strategic environment. An understanding of the preferences and power of its Member States is a logical starting point for analysis. Although the EC is a unique institution, it does not require a *sui generis* theory.

The article is divided into five sections. The first reviews the legacy and limitations of neo-functionalist theories of regional integration, and introduces an alternative approach, liberal intergovernmentalism, drawing on contemporary theories of international political economy. The second and third present the components of liberal intergovernmentalism: a liberal theory of how economic interdependence influences national interests, and an intergovernmentalist theory of international negotiation. The fourth suggests how international institutions augment, rather than restrict, the ability of governments to achieve domestic goals. Applications and extensions of theories of regimes and 'two-level games' predict the circumstances under which governments delegate and pool sovereignty. A brief conclusion summarizes the results.

## II. From Pre-Theory to Theory

*The Limitations of Neo-Functionalism*

The theoretical core of scholarship on the EC is over a quarter of a century old. Neo-functionalism, developed and refined between 1955 and 1975 by Haas, Philippe Schmitter, Leon Lindberg, Stuart Scheingold, Donald Puchala, Joseph Nye and 'many others, remains the most comprehensive and sophisticated attempt to provide a general theory of European integration and a touchstone for subsequent scholarship (Haas, 1958; Lindberg, 1963; Lindberg and Scheingold, 1970; Nye, 1968; cf. Taylor, 1983; Pentland, 1973). Since 1975, despite many insightful case studies of specific issue-areas, overviews of EC history, and criticisms of neo-functionalism, no comparable theoretical synthesis has appeared (Wallace *et al.*, 1983; George, 1985, 1992; Bulmer, 1986).

The neo-functionalists' central prediction was that European economic integration would be self-sustaining. The theoretical basis for this prediction was the concept of 'spillover', whereby initial steps toward integration trigger endogenous economic and political dynamics leading to further co-operation. Underlying spillover is a form of 'economic determinism' based on the 'end of ideology' and the advent of a world in which 'the technocrat has become the *eminence grise* of all government ... national and regional'. Economic planning at the regional level is an inevitable response to the complexity of modern economies. It is 'merely the adaptation ... of forms of social and economic organization which evolved historically at the national level'(Haas, 1964a, p. 62; Haas and Schmitter, 1964, p. 707; cf. Lindberg and Scheingold, 1970). Yet the same complexity is likely, over the longer term, to trap governments in a web of unintended consequences spun by their own previous commitments. Neo-functionalists identify two sorts of spillover, each of which deepens and widens integration by working through interest group pressure, public opinion, elite socialization or other domestic actors and processes (George, 1985).

The first, *functional spillover*, occurs when incomplete integration under-mines the effectiveness of existing policies, both in areas that are already integrated and in related sectors of the economy, thereby creating pressure for deepening and widening policy co-ordination. Functional spillover is econom-ic: it reflects the tightly interlinked nature of modern economies, in which government intervention in one sector engenders economic distortions else-where. Any 'halfway house' between sovereignty and integration is therefore unstable; without continuously strengthened policy co-ordination, the EC would fail to cope with 'complexly linked and highly controversial issues on the European agenda' and thus lose its legitimacy (Haas, in Caporaso and Keeler, 1993, p. 20).

The second, *political spillover*, occurs when the existence of supranational organizations sets in motion a self-reinforcing process of institution-building. The regulation of a modern integrated international economy requires techno-cratic oversight by supranational authorities. In the case of the EC, these are officials, judges and parliamentarians in Brussels, Luxembourg and Strasbourg. These authorities inevitably gain a certain measure of autonomous initiative. Neo-functionalists stress in particular the political role of the Commission, 'the archetype of an activist bureaucracy'. 'Administrators' in the Commission 'engineer integration' by 'seizing upon crises' to engage in 'creative personal action', articulating goals, recruiting and organizing officials, proposing new policies, or brokering bargains (George, 1993; Pentland, 1973, p. 117; Lindberg and Scheingold, 1970, pp. 82–95).

Despite the richness of its insights, neo-functionalism is today widely regarded as having offered an unsatisfactory account of European integration (Hoffmann, 1966; Hansen, 1969; Taylor, 1983; Haas, 1975; Keohane and Nye, 1975; Webb, 1983; Keohane and Hoffmann, 1991; Cornett and Caporaso, 1992). The most widely-cited reason is empirical: neo-functionalism appears to mispredict both the trajectory and the process of EC evolution. Insofar as neo-functionalism advances a clear prediction about the trajectory of EC over time, it was that the technocratic imperative would lead to a 'gradual', 'automatic', and 'incremental' progression toward deeper integration and greater supranational influence (Haas, 1964a, p. 70; 1967, p. 327; 1976, p. 176) . Instead, however, the process of Community-building has proceeded in fits and starts through a series of intergovernmental bargains. Nor has the process by which integration takes place supported the neo-functionalist view. Integration has only intermittently spilled over into related sectors and policies and, at least until recently, the autonomous influence of supranational officials has increased slowly and unevenly, if at all.

While empirical critiques of neo-functionalism are not without merit, they should not be overstated. To be sure, the empirical evidence does not seem to confirm the stress placed by neo-functionalism on political spillover and the autonomy of supranational officials. But other premises, particularly the focus on economic interests, may still be viable. It remains plausible, for example, to argue that integration is a distinctive policy response of modern welfare states to rising economic interdependence.

A more incisive criticism of neo-functionalism is theoretical, namely that it failed to generate an enduring research programme because it lacked a theoretical core clearly enough specified to provide a sound basis for precise empirical testing and improvement. Only the early variants of neo-functionalism predicted a steady development toward federalism. Faced with the failure of European integration to advance steadily, and variation in integration across issues, time-periods or countries ('spillback', 'spill-around', 'encapsulation'), however, neo-functionalism provided no clear direction for revision.[1]

As a result, further development in neo-functionalist theory seemed to converge toward an increasingly complex and indeterminate ideal-typical description of the single case of the EC. Increasing numbers of epicyclical modifications and alternative causal mechanisms were introduced, until the predictions became so indeterminate as to preclude precise testing. Descriptions of alternative causal mechanisms proliferated, some diametrically opposed to the theory's initial focus on technocratic management and economic planning. The uneven development of the EC in the 1960s, for example, was interpreted as a result of the influence of 'dramatic political actors', of which de Gaulle was the archetype – an account theoretically unrelated to Haas's earlier predictions and, moreover, empirically unsatisfying, since the malaise outlasted de Gaulle's

---

[1] Haas (1976) p. 183. In Lindberg and Scheingold, there are five alternative models, only one of which is spillover; Nye expanded this to seven process mechanisms or 'actor strategies', only two (1 and 3) of which related to spillover. cf. Pentland (1973) p. 119; Lindberg and Scheingold (1970) pp. 134–9; Schmitter (1971) pp. 232–64. For an overview, see Nye (1971) pp. 64–75.

presidency. By the end of the 1960s, almost any process of decision-making among democratic states was consistent with the theory (Lindberg and Scheingold, 1971).

Underlying neo-functionalism's failure to develop predictions about variations in the evolution of the EC was its lack of grounding in underlying general theories of domestic and international political economy. In international political economy, as in other social phenomena, it is widely accepted that prediction and explanation, particularly over time, require theories that elaborate how self-interested actors form coalitions and alliances, domestically and internationally, and how conflicts among them are resolved. Such theories must be derived independently of the matter being studied, in the sense that they require a set of restrictive microfoundations – assumptions specifying the nature of the fundamental social actors, their preferences, and the constraints they face.[2] In this regard, neo-functionalism is both oddly apolitical and lacking in any aspiration to generality, in that it advances long-term predictions about the future of the EC without underlying, more specific theories that identify the decisive determinants of politicians' choices among competing alternatives. While stressing the domestic politics of economic policy co-ordination, neo-functionalism lacks an equivalent to modern theories of trade policy, which explain government choices on the basis of models of pressure from predictable distributional coalitions. Neo-functionalism, as Lindberg and Scheingold put it, describes domestic processes, but 'says little about *basic causes*' of variation in national demands for integration (Lindberg and Scheingold, 1970, p. 284, emphasis in original). Neo-functionalist analyses of international bargaining point to the existence of dynamics such as log-rolling, compromise, and upgrading the common interest through linkage and supranational mediation, but offer no explanation – except the variable skill of supranational leaders – of how governments choose among them.

Neo-functionalism's *ad hoc* approach eventually detached it from rich currents in general theories of international political economy over the past two decades (cf. Keohane and Nye, 1975). With the exception of a few studies of (largely unsuccessful) attempts at regional integration among developing countries, the EC came to be treated as a *sui generis* phenomenon, thereby impeding efforts at theoretical generalization.[3] This was based in large part on the *a priori* expectation that Europe would develop in a federal direction, which led neo-functionalists to stress the uniqueness of its institutional structure, rather than analogies to other forms of interstate co-operation. The possibility of explaining integration in terms of theories of interdependence, regimes or other generaliz-

---

[2] For a general defence of this approach, see Coleman (1990).

[3] An empirical exception is Haas (1966) pp. 93–130. Haas examines other international regimes, but his theoretical explanation is inductive, rather than grounded in micro-analysis of processes.

able phenomena was thereby lost, while the potential for useful comparison and theoretical development remained limited (Pentland, 1973, pp. 189–94). For this reason, neo-functionalism remains today an inductively derived ideal-type, rather than a general theory – in the words of its creator, a 'pre-theory' of regional integration (Haas, 1976).

## The Legacy of Neo-Functionalism

The success of the EC in recent years has fuelled efforts among scholars to resurrect neo-functionalist models, in particular those that stress the unintended consequences for Member States of leadership exercised by supranational actors, including Commission officials and European parliamentarians ( Ross, 1992; Peterson and Bomberg, 1993; Sandholtz, 1992; Pederson, 1992). This body of work repeats many neo-functionalist themes, if sometimes by other names. Yet current efforts to resurrect neo-functionalism rarely address the *conclusions that neo-functionalists themselves drew* about the weaknesses of their approach, nor do they consider the implications for current theory-building of theoretical developments in international relations theory over the intervening two decades. The functionalist legacy, combined with contemporary theories of international political economy, suggests at least three important conclusions.

First, by 1975 leading neo-functionalists were nearly unanimous in arguing that 'regional integration theory', which had sought to explain the progress of the EC along the *sui generis* path toward a future federalist endpoint, should be supplemented, perhaps supplanted, by a *general* theory of national policy responses to international interdependence. Rather than focusing on the future aspirations that make the EC unique, neo-functionalists argued that the emphasis should be on generalizable aspects of the current activities of the EC. Recognizing the central importance of economic management among those activities, Haas came to believe that 'the study of regional integration should be both included in and subordinated to the study of changing patterns of interdependence' (Haas, 1975).

In the language of modern theories of international political economy, this implies that the EC should be treated as an international regime designed to promote policy co-ordination. As Hoffmann, Haas's erstwhile critic, asserted in 1982, 'the best way of analyzing the EEC is … as an international regime' (Hoffmann, 1982, p. 33). International regimes promulgate 'principles, norms, rules, and decision-making procedures around which actor expectations converge' in given issue-areas, through which 'the actions of separate individuals or organizations – which are not in pre-existing harmony – [are] brought into conformity with one another through a process of negotiation … often referred to as policy co-ordination' (Krasner, 1983, p. 1; Keohane, 1984, p. 51). Regime theory provides a plausible starting point for analysis – a set of common conceptual and theoretical tools that can help structure comparisons with other international organizations, as well as internal comparisons among different cases of EC policy-making. At the same time, however, contemporary regime analysis requires refinement to take account of the unique institutional aspects of policy co-ordination within the EC, as evidenced by the depth of its purported goals, the richness of the networks it sustains, and, above all, the solidity of its supranational legal identity (Keohane and Hoffmann, 1991).

Second, the neo-functionalist legacy suggests that explanations of integration require stronger underlying theories of variation in substantive, as well as institutional, outcomes. The neo-functionalists were concerned overridingly with tracing progress toward a terminal condition called *political community* – the evolution of a unique, potentially federal political structure in Europe that would prevent war and guarantee 'peaceful change' (Haas, 1966, p. 94; Lindberg and Scheingold, 1970, p. 99). Accordingly, they limited their definition of integration almost exclusively to institutional characteristics of the EC – the scope and institutional form of common decision-making. This discouraged attention to distributional conflicts in the EC over issues such as the level of external tariffs, agricultural prices, or regulatory harmonization, which require attention to the substantive measures of policy co-ordination. An instructive example is the creation of the CAP in the 1960s. While the neo-functionalists emphasize the Commission's success in creating a policy *formally* under the control of the EC, they overlook the fact that it was a defeat for the Commission's original *substantive* proposal, which foresaw a prudently limited, self-financing, relatively low-price regime.[4]

A broader definition of European integration might consider four dimensions of policy co-ordination: (1) the *geographical scope* of the regime; (2) the *range* of issues in which policies are co-ordinated; (3) the *institutions* of joint decision-making, implementation and enforcement; (4) the *direction and magnitude of substantive domestic policy adjustment*. These four elements may be thought of as different dimensions of the same underlying variable, namely policy co-ordination. While the first three are similar to those employed by neo-functionalists, the fourth – the direction and magnitude of substantive policy adjustment – is based on the view that policy co-ordination is most significant where it imposes greater adjustment on domestic policy. Since the costs and benefits of the necessary adjustments generally vary across countries, the measure also helps in the analysis of distributional conflict.

---

[4] Lindberg's otherwise insightful analysis in *Political Dynamics* largely overlooks this distinction. See also Von der Groeben (1982).

Third, by the 1970s, many neo-functionalists had concluded that unicausal theories are unable to account for EC policy-making. More than one theory is required (Puchala, 1972; Pentland, 1973, pp. 189–94; Cornett and Caporaso, 1992). Modern theories of international political economy suggest a number of empirical, theoretical and philosophical reasons, discussed in more detail in the next section, to treat the need for multicausal explanation as a *general* principle. Empirically robust explanations of international policy co-ordination are likely to incorporate, at a minimum, theories of both national preference formation and intergovernmental negotiation, each grounded in explicit assumptions about actor preferences, constraints and choices (Moravcsik, 1992b). The vagueness of neo-functionalist predictions suggest, moreover, that only such theories can explain, rather than simply describe, the evolution of the EC. Only by meeting these criteria, most neo-functionalists felt, could scholars move from 'pre-theory' to theory.

## Liberal Intergovernmentalism and the Rationality Assumption

Rather than resurrecting neo-functionalism, the approach introduced here takes seriously the self-criticisms of neo-functionalists examined above. They point toward a conception of the EC more closely in line with contemporary theories of international political economy. Such theories suggest that the EC is best seen as an international regime for policy co-ordination, the substantive and institutional development of which may be explained through the sequential analysis of national preference formation and intergovernmental strategic interaction.

This section proposes a framework within which to construct such an explanation, termed 'liberal intergovernmentalism'. Liberal intergovernmentalism builds on an earlier approach, 'intergovernmental institutionalism', by refining its theory of interstate bargaining and institutional compliance, and by adding an explicit theory of national preference formation grounded in liberal theories of international interdependence (Moravcsik, 1991). Various specific points seek to refine and extend the existing literature, but the result is broadly consistent with current theories of international political economy, in particular endogenous tariff theory, negotiation analysis, and functional explanations of international regimes.

At the core of liberal intergovernmentalism are three essential elements: the assumption of rational state behaviour, a liberal theory of national preference formation, and an intergovernmentalist analysis of interstate negotiation. The assumption of rational state behaviour provides a general framework of analysis, within which the costs and benefits of economic interdependence are the primary determinants of national preferences, while the relative intensity of national preferences, the existence of alternative coalitions, and the opportunity for issue linkages provide the basis for an intergovernmental analysis of the resolution of distributional conflicts among governments. Regime theory is employed as a starting point for an analysis of conditions under which governments will delegate powers to international institutions.

Much contemporary international relations theory is based on the assumption of state rationality. State action at any particular moment is assumed to be minimally rational, in that it is purposively directed toward the achievement of a set of consistently ordered goals or objectives.[5] Governments evaluate alternative courses of action on the basis of a utility function. The approach taken here departs decisively, however, from those theories in international relations, most notably realist and neo-realist approaches, which treat states as 'billiard balls' or 'black boxes' with fixed preferences for wealth, security or power. Instead, governments are assumed to act purposively in the international arena, but on the basis of goals that are defined domestically. Following liberal theories of international relations, which focus on state–society relations, the foreign policy goals of national governments are viewed as varying in response to shifting pressure from domestic social groups, whose preferences are aggregated through political institutions. National interests are, therefore, neither invariant nor unimportant, but emerge through domestic political conflict as societal groups compete for political influence, national and transnational coalitions form, and new policy alternatives are recognized by governments. An understanding of domestic politics is a precondition for, not a supplement to, the analysis of the strategic interaction among states (Moravcsik, 1991, 1992b).

The model of rational state behaviour on the basis of domestically-constrained preferences implies that international conflict and co-operation can be modelled as a process that takes place in two successive stages: governments first define a set of interests, then bargain among themselves in an effort to realize those interests. Metaphorically, these two stages shape demand and supply functions for international co-operation. A domestic preference formation process identifies the potential benefits of policy co-ordination perceived by national governments (demand), while a process of interstate strategic interaction defines the possible political responses of the EC political system to pressures from those governments (supply). The interaction of demand and supply, of preference and strategic opportunities, shapes the foreign policy behaviour of states.[6]

---

[5] Such goals are best seen not as defined across alternative policies or strategies (e.g. a free trade regime, fixed exchange rates), but across alternative future states of the world (e.g. higher levels of economic transactions, exchange rate stability). Rational choices among policies and strategies must generally take into account the expected reactions of other states and the resulting strategic interactions among them, while preference across future states of the world do not. The latter are 'pre-strategic' preferences. On this distinction more generally, see Elster (1986).

[6] To avoid confusion, it is important to remember that nested within the domestic definition of the demand function is also a national process of societal demands for and governmental supply of policies. The domestic use of the metaphor of demand and supply is drawn from Shepsle's analyses of legislative politics (Shepsle, 1992).

Figure 1: The Liberal Intergovernmentalist Framework of Analysis

| Liberal Theories | Intergovernmentalist Theories |
|---|---|
| (International demand for outcomes) | (International supply of outcomes) |
| Underlying societal factors: pressure from domestic societal actors as represented in political institutions | Underlying political factors: intensity of national preferences; alternative coalitions; available issue linkages |

NATIONAL     configuration     INTERSTATE ──▶ OUTCOMES
PREFERENCE ──▶ of state     NEGOTIATION
FORMATION     preferences

This conception of rationality suggests that parsimonious explanations of international conflict or co-operation can be constructed by employing two types of theory sequentially: a theory of national preference formation *and* a theory of interstate strategic interaction. Unicausal explanations of European integration, which seek to isolate either demand or supply, are at best incomplete and at worst misleading. 'Demand-side reductionism' – the narrow attention to variation in domestic preferences while ignoring the strategic context in which states interact – or 'supply-side reductionism' – exclusive emphasis on interstate bargaining or international institutions without considering the underlying distribution and variation in preferences – risk omitting essential variables and encouraging misleading inferences about those that remain. Explaining the emergence in 1978–9 of the European Monetary System, for example, requires that we understand both the convergence of macroeconomic policy preferences, which led European governments to favour monetary co-ordination, *and* the determinants of the outcomes of the tough interstate bargaining that took place over the precise terms under which it would take place.

Thus liberal intergovernmentalism integrates within a single framework two types of general international relations theory often seen as contradictory: a liberal theory of national preference formation and an intergovernmentalist analysis of interstate bargaining and institutional creation.[7] In the sections that follow, these sequential components are developed in more detail.

[7] Sections IV and V of this article deal respectively with two different aspects of interstate strategic interaction: distributional bargaining and the delegation or pooling of decision-making in international

## III. Liberalism, National Preference Formation and the Demand for Integration

*Liberalism and State–Society Relations*

The theory of national preference formation set out in this section is liberal in inspiration. Liberal theories of international relations focus on the effect of state–society relations in shaping national preferences. They assume that private individuals and voluntary associations with autonomous interests, interacting in civil society, are the most fundamental actors in politics. State priorities and policies are determined by politicians at the head of the national government, who 'are embedded in domestic and transnational civil society, which decisively constrains their identities and purposes.'[8] The most fundamental influences on foreign policy are, therefore, the identity of important societal groups, the nature of their interests, and their relative influence on domestic policy. Groups that stand to gain and lose a great deal *per capita* tend to be the most influential. The identity, interests, and influence of groups vary across time, place and, especially, issue-area, according to the net expected costs and benefits of potential foreign policies. The factors that determine the identity, interests and influence of domestic groups are themselves both domestic and transnational. In this sense, 'second image reversed' theories, which assume that international constraints create patterns of societal interests that influence governments via the 'transmission belt' of domestic politics, are characteristically liberal.[9] But so are theories that stress purely domestic state–society relations, due to the nature of domestic political and socio-economic institutions.

Groups articulate preferences; governments aggregate them. For liberals, the relationship between society and the government is assumed to be one of principal– agent; societal principals delegate power to (or otherwise constrain) governmental agents. The primary interest of governments is to maintain themselves in office; in democratic societies, this requires the support of a coalition of domestic voters, parties, interest groups and bureaucracies, whose views are transmitted, directly or indirectly, through domestic institutions and practices of political representation. Through this process emerges the set of national interests or goals that states bring to international negotiations.

---

regimes. Regime theory is treated as a theory of strategic interaction, in the sense that the institutional measures for compliance shape the range of potential bargains. The latter might also be thought of not as an element of strategic interaction, but as a separate 'compliance' stage of policy co-ordination. For a model of this kind, see Moravcsik (1989).

[8] Moravcsik (1992b) from which the argument in this section is drawn.

[9] See Gourevitch (1978). To the extent that international factors, such as economic interdependence or external threats to national security influence preference formation, they must pass through the domestic polity.

This is not to say that all foreign policy proposals begin with direct pressure from pluralist groups, only that state leaders must construct governing coalitions out of influential groups with specific interests. Sometimes the influence of societal groups is indirect. In economic affairs, for example, some firms and groups, particularly those with fixed investments and assets, may seek to influence governments directly, exercising the option of 'voice'; others, particularly those with more mobile investments and assets, may find it less expensive to shift investments to alternative activities or jurisdictions, exercising the option of 'exit' (Hirschman, 1970; Magee *et al.*, 1989, pp. 13, 93, 102; Bates and Lien, 1985; Lindblom, 1977). In the liberal view, even the latter constraint ultimately rests on the desire of politicians to avoid imposing costs on – and thereby alienating – those social groups whose support maintains them in office.

Yet the interests of societal groups are not always sharply defined. Where societal pressure is ambiguous or divided, governments acquire a range of discretion. While domestic societal groups impose a basic constraint on governments, the nature and tightness of this constraint varies with the strength and unity of pressures from social groups. At times the principal–agent relationship between social pressures and state policies is tight; at times, 'agency slack' in the relationship permits rational governments to exercise greater discretion.[10]

The liberal focus on domestic interests and state–society relations is consistent with a number of plausible motivations for governments to support (or oppose) European integration. These include federalist (or nationalist) beliefs, national security concerns and economic interests. The *federalist* motivation views European integration as a cosmopolitan ideal, justified by a sense of a common European identity and purpose. (Ideological opponents of integration may be motivated by an equally ideological commitment to a conception of the nation that places value on the preservation of sovereignty.) The liberal *national security* motivation is premised on the view of economic interdependence and common institutions as means of reinforcing peaceful accommodation among democratic states with an historical legacy of conflict, assuring a common front against the anti-democratic Soviet Union, or guaranteeing political support for specific, democratically legitimate national projects, such as German unification.[11] The *economic interdependence* motivation views the EC as a means of co-ordinating policy to manage flows of goods, services, factors of production,

---

[10] Here I do not mean to imply that all cases in which governments do not serve the interests of particularistic groups should be thought of as 'autonomous' action, but simply that the greater the 'slack' in the relationship between particularistic opponents of co-operation, the greater the possibility of pursuing a policy targeted at a larger domestic constituency or, in some cases, at realizing the preference of these in office.

[11] It is unhelpful to associate all national security arguments with realism. Liberalism and realism both place a high value on national security, but view threats as emanating from different sources. Realists highlight objective power and uncertainty, liberals the societal sources of aggressive intentions. Hence their differing predictions about the distribution of conflict and co-operation (Moravcsik, 1992b).

and economic externalities more effectively than unilateral policies. Elsewhere these alternative specifications of liberal theory are tested against one another (Moravcsik, 1992a); here the focus is on motivations that stem from economic interdependence and the ways in which they constrain governmental preferences in international negotiations.

## Interdependence, Externalities and Co-operation

At the core of liberal theories of economic interdependence lies the claim that increasing transborder flows of goods, services, factors, or pollutants create 'international policy externalities' among nations, which in turn create incentives for policy co-ordination. International policy externalities arise where the policies of one government create costs and benefits for politically significant social groups outside its national jurisdiction. Where the achievement of domestic governmental goals depends on the policies of its foreign counterparts, national policies are interdependent and policy externalities can arise (Cooper, 1986, pp. 292–3).

National governments have an incentive to co-operate where policy co-ordination increases their control over domestic policy outcomes, permitting them to achieve goals that would not otherwise be possible. This situation arises most often where co-ordination eliminates *negative* international policy externalities. (A second motivation for co-operation whereby governments employ international institutions as part of a 'two-level game' strategy to increase the initiative of the government, is discussed in the final section of this article.) Negative policy externalities occur where the policies of one nation imposes costs on the domestic nationals of another, thereby undermining the goals of the second government's policies. Examples include protectionist barriers against flows of foreign goods and capital, competitive devaluation, and lax domestic environmental pollution standards. Each of these policies may impose costs on foreign nationals, thereby undermining the policy goals of foreign governments. (The opposite, positive policy externalities, occur when domestic policies confer benefits on foreign groups, thereby strengthening national policies. Unilateral openness, an overvalued currency, high domestic welfare standards, and strong regulations on industrial air pollution are typical examples.) Where externalities are negative, the possibility of ameliorating them through policy co-ordination generates an incentive for co-operation; where externalities are positive or insignificant, however, or where unilateral policies can be cost-effectively adjusted to counteract the effects of such a foreign government's policies, little incentive for co-operation exists.

In the modern international political economy, policy co-ordination has two major purposes, each of which aims at removing a negative policy externality. The first is the accommodation of economic interdependence through *recipro-*

*cal market liberalization.* Restrictions on imports and exports are not simply of interest to domestic societal groups, but to their counterparts abroad as well. The liberalization of the movement of goods, services and factors of production may promote modernization and a more efficient allocation of domestic resources, favouring producers in internationally competitive sectors and owners of internationally scarce factors of production. Restrictions on imports of goods and factors impose policy externalities on potential foreign exporters, investors and immigrants.

The second major purpose of economic policy co-ordination is *policy harmonization* in order to assure the continued provision of public goods for which the state is domestically responsible, such as socio-economic equality, macroeconomic stability and regulatory protection. National welfare provision, monetary policy, labour market controls, product regulation and many other domestic policies rely for their effectiveness on the separation of markets for goods, services, factors and pollutants. Where economic interdependence links jurisdictions, divergent national policies may undermine each other's effectiveness. Co-ordinated (or common) policies may therefore result in greater *de facto* control over domestic policy outcomes than unilateral efforts (Cooper, 1972).

Contrary to the beliefs often attributed to them, liberals do not argue that co-operation to achieve trade liberalization and the common provision of public goods is inevitably supported by all governments. The vulnerability of governments to negative externalities may vary greatly: some are able to sustain effective policies autonomously, others remain vulnerable to negative externalities from policies abroad. While the latter have an incentive to support international policy co-ordination, those that produce negative externalities or benefit from the positive externalities of others have an incentive to free ride on the domestic policies of their neighbours, rather than co-operate (Keohane and Nye, 1989, 12ff). Only where the policies of two or more governments create negative policy externalities for one another, and unilateral adjustment strategies are ineffective, inadequate or expensive, does economic interdependence create an unambiguous incentive to co-ordinate policy.[12]

## The Distributional Consequences of Policy Co-ordination

Even where agreements are mutually beneficial, governments often have different preferences concerning the distribution of the benefits, leading to conflict over the precise terms of co-operation.[13] The costs and benefits of

---

[12] This diverges from the common analysis of regimes as providing public goods. The institutional infrastructure of regimes itself may be thought of as a public good, as can some common goals of regimes. For the most part, however, the benefits of the EC are excludable and, to an extent, rival goods; co-operation stems from interdependence – the effects of national policies on the opportunities for foreigners.

[13] This is overlooked by Grieco (1988), but captured by Keohane and Nye (1989), and Krasner (1991).

policy co-ordination are often unevenly distributed among and within nations, rendering nearly inevitable a measure of international and domestic conflict between winners and losers. To the extent that it takes domestic and international distributional conflict into account, liberal interdependence theory does not, as some have suggested, assume the existence of a harmony of interests or a simple correlation between potential transactions and co-operation. Nations and domestic groups that are disadvantaged by policy co-ordination are likely to oppose it. Only where governments can collectively overcome such opposition is co-operation possible. The distribution of expected net societal costs provides a means of predicting the nature of political conflict and co-operation in the EC, both internationally and domestically.[14]

Domestically, governments participating in international negotiations are both empowered and constrained by important societal groups, which calculate their interests in terms of the expected gains and losses from specific policies (Milner, 1988; Gourevitch, 1986; Frieden,1991a; Odell, 1982). Powerful groups disadvantaged by co-operation will seek to obstruct government policy, even where such policies generate net gains for society as a whole. To understand and predict the likelihood of international co-operation in any given instance, therefore, requires a more precise specification of domestic societal interests in particular issue-areas and the ways in which those interests constrain governments.

Societal pressure on national governments reflects not only the expected magnitude of gains and losses, but also the uncertainty and risk involved. The magnitude, certainty and risk of domestic distributional effects of policy co-ordination determine not only the goals of respective governments, but the extent to which governments can afford to be flexible in negotiation. At one extreme, where the net costs and benefits of alternative policies are certain, significant and risky, individual citizens and firms have a strong incentive to mobilize politically. In such circumstances, unidirectional pressure from cohesive groups of producers or organized private interests imposes a strict constraint on government policy. The prospects for international agreement will depend almost entirely on the configuration of societal preferences; in negotiations, governments have little flexibility in making concessions, proposing linkages, managing adjustment or otherwise settling on the 'lowest common denominator'. International agreement requires that the interests of dominant domestic groups in different countries converge; where they diverge, co-ordination is precluded. Such conditions are approximated in EC negotiations over agricultural prices, and EC bargaining positions are dictated by pressures from interest groups.

---

[14] The existence of such a predictive theory distinguishes liberalism from the neo-functionalist tradition of Haas and others (Haas, 1964).

At the other extreme, where the net costs and benefits of alternative policies are diffuse, ambiguous or insignificant, and the risk is low, the societal constraints on governments are looser (cf. Buchanan and Tullock, 1962, pp. 78–9). Under such circumstances, leading politicians enjoy a wider range of *de facto* choice in negotiating strategies and positions. More than one policy is likely to be consistent with the basic desire of politicians to remain in government. The slack in the principal–agent relationship between society and the state permits governments to assume more political risk by taking a more 'enlightened' or longer-term view, balancing winners and losers to construct broader coalitions, accepting short-term losses for long-term gains, or pursuing more ideologically controversial goals.

## Policy Areas and National Preferences in the EC

Different policy areas engender characteristic distributions of costs and benefits for societal groups, from which follow variations in patterns of domestic political mobilization, opportunities for governments to circumvent domestic opposition, and motivations for international co-operation.[15] EC policy areas can be divided into three categories on the basis of policy objectives: the liberalization of the exchange of private goods and services, the provision of socio-economic collective goods, and the provision of non-economic collective goods.

*Commercial policy, market access and producer interests.* At the core of the EC is its Internal Market. The most basic EC policies – including internal market policy, agricultural policy, competition policy, industrial policy, and research and development policy – are designed to liberalize or eliminate distortions in markets for private goods and services. Modern theories of commercial policy begin by assuming that individual and group support for liberalization and protection reflects, to a first approximation, the net expected costs and benefits of the policy change (Magee *et al.*, 1989; Hillman, 1989). Social groups with an intense interest in a given policy are more likely to mobilize than those with a weak interest, since higher *per capita* gains support the costs of locating, organizing, monitoring and representing concentrated groups. This tends to create a systematic political bias in favour of producers *vis-à-vis* those with more diffuse interests, such as tax-payers and individual consumers, or those with no direct access to the political process, such as foreign producers (Olson, 1965; Hillman, 1989). Following endogenous tariff theory, the approach employed here assumes that societal groups mobilized around commercial policy issues are composed almost exclusively of domestic producers, whether drawn from labour or capital, who organize by sector on the basis of calculations

---

[15] A more detailed model would take variations in domestic institutions into account.

of net expected costs and benefits resulting from the introduction of new policies.[16]

Among producers, the net expected costs and benefits of liberalization reflect the following factors. First, *the extent to which individual producers profit from commercial liberalization depends most fundamentally on their competitive position in domestic and international markets*.[17] Protectionist policies not only redistribute domestic wealth from consumers to sheltered producers, but also create negative policy externalities for exporters excluded from potential markets. Accordingly, exporters and multinational investors tend to support freer trade, which increases their profits; import-competing producers tend to oppose free trade, which undermines their profitability. Where adjustment is relatively costless or compensation between winners and losers can be arranged, distributional effects need not create opposition to free trade. Where adjustment and compensation are costly, however, a domestic prisoner's dilemma among domestic veto groups – each of which seeks to be exempted from disadvantageous policy changes, leading to a suboptimal outcome for society as a whole – translates into an international prisoner's dilemma, in which each government seeks to shelter its weakest sectors from international market pressure. Policy co-ordination helps overcome these dilemmas by balancing the gains and losses of free trade within and across countries, thereby creating viable domestic coalitions in favour of liberalization.[18]

Import-competing sectors and firms with low levels and profits and growth are particularly likely to press for protection. Sectors and firms that are sheltered or undiversified, that face chronic surplus capacity, cyclical downturn or long-term decline, or have large irreversible investments are more likely to press for protection; expanding, profitable, diversified industries are less likely to do so. For declining sectors with immobile investments, market adjustment by shifting future adjustment is more costly, benefits are more visible, while the possibility exists that rents will be competed away by the entry of new firms. The losers from liberalization, because they are more easily identifiable, tend to be over-represented, while the potential winners remain under-represented.

---

[16] Under conditions of high domestic factor mobility, one would expect coalitions to form between capital and labour; according to the Stolper–Samuelson theory, protection will be sought by factors of production that are relatively scarce – capital in labour-abundant countries, and labour in capital-abundant countries. In the long term, this may be valid (see Rogowski, 1989). In the short and medium term, however, many factors are unable to move between industrial sectors, due in part to high fixed investments in human and physical capital. Hence a specific-factors (Ricardo–Viner) approach is more appropriate, in which owners of capital (or land) and labour work together to form sectoral coalitions (Magee *et al.*, 1989).

[17] This is the cornerstone of most modern empirical studies of commercial policy. For empirical support, see Lavergne (1983).

[18] Since protectionist policies can easily be implemented unilaterally, the incentive for international co-operation in these areas typically stems from opportunities to co-ordinate the liberalization of market access.

Second, *cross-cutting or balanced patterns of interests internalize the costs and benefits of trade liberalization* to the same sets of firms and sectors, creating a cross-cutting set of interests that undermines opposition to liberalization. Most importantly, intra-industry trade and investment patterns reduce the net effects on the positions of individual producers and sectors.[19] Even producers facing substantial import-competition have an incentive to support free trade if loss of domestic market share is offset by exports, control over foreign producers, or receipts from foreign investments. The risk of a large loss is reduced as well. Producers of finished goods also form concentrated interest groups in favour of free trade in raw materials and intermediate inputs.

Third, *where the effects of policy changes are uncertain, organized opposition to government initiatives is diluted.* Uncertainty about the effects of co-operation arises where policies are stated vaguely, left to future negotiation, mediated by complex market processes, or applied in an unpredictable way across a population. Uncertain policies engender less opposition than those that are immediate, precise and targeted. Policies often become more controversial as specific provisions are negotiated and the real effects become evident – as occurred in implementing EC agricultural, transport and competition policy in the 1950s and 1960s.

In many cases, pressure from private economic interests is enough to convince governments to liberalize. Where the net expected costs and benefits to firms and sectors are significant, unambiguous and predictable for important segments of domestic producers, pressures from producer interests will impose a relatively tight constraint on state policy. Most agricultural sectors, as well as industries with chronic surplus capacity, are characterized by inter-industry trade patterns, uniform and calculable interests, and high fixed, irreversible investments and assets. Net commodity exporting countries demanded liberalization; net commodity importing countries resisted it. In the CAP, interstate bargains have been possible only on the basis of lowest common denominator log-rolling agreements in individual sectors, with the costs passed on to consumers and foreign producers. Direct pressure from producer interests in the EC has created and maintained a system of high agricultural prices and managed trade, regardless of the preferences of politicians.

In other cases, the decision to liberalize reflects not just pressure from narrow interests, but a broader calculation on the part of the government. When net expected costs are insignificant, ambiguous, balanced or uncertain, governments enjoy a greater autonomy from particularistic domestic groups that oppose co-operation, which they can employ to create support for broader societal goals. This they can do by negotiating international compromises and issue linkages, which creates viable coalitions by balancing winners against

[19] Milner (1988) stresses intra-industry trade.

losers. By subsidizing the costs of adjustment, or by balancing losses of domestic market share with gains in foreign markets, they can also mute opposition to liberalization. Both agricultural trade liberalization in Germany and industrial trade liberalization in France were accompanied by large domestic subsidies to uncompetitive producers expressly designed to finance adjustment. The more governments are able to act independently of groups disadvantaged by a policy, thereby trading off gains and losses over a larger constituency, the more we should observe the compromises and 'upgrading the common interest' predicted by neo-functionalists. Whereas neo-functionalism stresses the autonomy of supranational officials, liberal intergovernmentalism stresses the autonomy of national leaders.

Governments independent of pressure from particular opponents of liberalization are able to pursue broader national industrial strategies. Such strategies, like narrower policies, may be designed in the long term to promote re-election through economic growth and socio-economic public goods provision. Neo-classical trade theory argues that even unilateral liberalization is wealth-maximizing, because it promotes the efficient allocation of resources and reinforces competition, domestically and internationally, thereby expanding consumption possibilities through specialization, which more fully exploits economies of scale and underlying international cost differentials. It is not simply pressure from domestic exporters that generates pressure for free trade, but also the desire of governments to employ international agreements to force adjustment on domestic producers in the interest of overall economic growth and efficiency – a 'two-level game' to which we shall return in the final section of this article. Inefficiency can become politically intolerable for numerous reasons. Often the desire to adopt such a policy is a response to broad underlying shifts in competitive position or manifest policy failure, signalled by a crisis of low investment and growth, unsustainable external disequilibria, or intolerable fiscal expenditures. In 1950 and 1958, for example, the perceived failure of French industrial strategies based on protection led to a push for pan-European liberalization (Institut Charles de Gaulle, 1992). In 1978 and 1985, a generalized sense of macroeconomic policy failure contributed to the acceptance of, respectively, the EMS and the Single European Act.

*Socio-economic public goods provision.* EC policies are not limited to the co-ordination of explicit market liberalization policies, but include also the co-ordination of domestic policies designed to redress market failures or provide public goods, such as those that assure macroeconomic stability, social security, environmental protection, public health and safety standards, and an acceptable distribution of income. Rising economic interdependence often exacerbates the tension between unco-ordinated national policies, the effectiveness of which often requires that either national markets be separated or national policies be harmonized (Cooper, 1972). Transborder inflows of air and water pollution can undermine the effectiveness of national environmental policies; capital out-flows can undermine the credibility of domestic monetary policy; 'social dumping' can undermine the competitiveness of industry and the viability of social compromises.

As with commercial policy, an incentive for international policy co-ordina-tion exists when the configuration of domestic policies produces negative policy externalities – domestic problems that cannot be resolved through domestic regulation, because of interference from policies pursued by foreign governments – for more than one country. Negotiated policy co-ordination typically involves some surrender of domestic policy autonomy in exchange for a similar surrender on the part of other countries. Where domestic policy instruments remain effective, governments will continue to maintain them; but where governments have exhausted all cost-effective domestic means of achiev-ing domestic policy targets, they have an incentive to turn to international co-ordination. Accordingly, policy co-ordination will typically be sought particu-larly by smaller governments, with little control over their domestic markets and high economic interdependence, and by those, generally with high levels of domestic public goods provision, whose policies are particularly vulnerable to disruption.

Many socio-economic public goods policies have important implications for international commerce. The effects of unco-ordinated policies – exchange rate shifts, disparate production and product standards, or divergent social welfare policies – may distort or obstruct international commerce. Therefore, in contrast to pure commercial liberalization, the international co-ordination of such policies raises a 'two-dimensional' issue, in that governments must strike a balance between two independently valued policy targets: flows of economic transactions and levels of public goods provision. To the extent that govern-ments are concerned about trade liberalization, the incentives for international and domestic co-operation and conflict will resemble those in issues of pure commercial policy. However, where governments are primarily concerned with the provision of domestic public goods, the level of conflict and co-operation among governments depends on the extent to which national policy goals are compatible. When governments have divergent macroeconomic, environmen-tal and social goals, then co-ordination is likely to be costly and difficult. International conflict emerges over the division of the burden of adjustment. The more divergent national policies are to begin with, the greater the costs of co-operation. Nonetheless, where these costs are outweighed by the interest in reducing negative policy externalities, international policy co-ordination can help governments reach an optimal balance between increased market access and the maintenance of regulatory standards.[20]

Due to the 'two-dimensional' nature of the public goods issues, the range of mobilized interests is typically broader than in commercial policy. Whereas in pure commercial policy, the 'public interest' is pursued almost entirely by national governments, backed by broad coalitions of interested parties, the public interest is represented in public goods concerns by pressure from public interest groups and mass publics. Where existing domestic policy reflects widespread popular support, domestic regulations are likely to be resistant to the changes required to achieve international harmonization. Alongside producer interests, non-producers may either influence policy directly, as when environmental interest groups mobilize opposition, or punish or reward the government for the results of policy, as when voters respond to recent macroeconomic performance.

As in commercial policy, the level of constraint on governments varies, depending on the intensity and calculability of private interests. Policies involving the direct regulation of goods and production processes tend to engender strong mobilization of producer groups, while the co-ordination of policies to provide macroeconomic public goods, including pollution, inflation, unemployment and the aggregate distribution of income, generates a more diffuse pattern of societal interests. Most producers have more ambiguous and variable interests in public goods provision – e.g. the value of the currency, the level of domestic inflation, or the aggregate level of pollution – than in issues of pure commercial policy. Where strong commercial or public interests are unified in their demands for policy co-ordination, governments will act accordingly. Often, however, the results of negative externalities and policy failure are more diffuse, leading to a more general economic or regulatory crisis. In the latter case, governments may act without direct pressure from interested parties.

Macroeconomic policy provides an illustrative example. While groups do organize around the trade-related costs and benefits of monetary management (Frieden, 1991b), these incentives are often offset by other concerns. While currency depreciation increases the competitiveness of domestically-produced tradeable goods, it also raises the costs of imported intermediate inputs and raw materials, as well as increasing the risk of longer-term inflation. Domestic monetary policy is influenced by the autonomy of domestic monetary institutions and the identity of the party in power, among other things. Recent steps toward European monetary integration, for example, reflect a set of national commitments to macroeconomic discipline imposed by the unsustainability of domestic policies in the face of increased international capital mobility. Only

[20] This is not to imply that the two are always in conflict. See the examples drawn from EC regulatory harmonization cited below.

once domestic policies had converged substantially did more intensive international co-operation become conceivable. When they diverged, the system once again came under pressure.

*Political co-operation, EC institutions, and general income transfers.* Some EC policies cannot be interpreted as direct responses to policy externalities imposed by economic interdependence. Some, such as a common foreign and security policy, aim to provide non-socio-economic collective goods; others, such as general European Community institutions and transnational (regional and structural) income transfers, exist either for their own sake or to facilitate other policies. Liberal theory suggests that fundamental constraints on national preferences will reflect the costs and benefits to societal actors; where these are weak, uncertain or diffuse, governments will be able to pursue broader or more idiosyncratic goals.

The costs and benefits created by *political co-operation* for private groups are diffuse and uncertain. Private producers take little interest in political co-operation, leaving domestic influence over the policy almost exclusively to partisan elites, with a secondary, intermittent constraint imposed by mass publics. The reasoning used to justify policies tends to be symbolic and ideological, rather than calculated and concrete. The inherent incalculability of gains and losses in these policy areas accounts for a troubling neo-functionalist anomaly, namely the manifest importance of ideologically motivated heads of state ('dramatic-political' actors) in matters of foreign policy and institutional reform. The difficulty of mobilizing interest groups under conditions of general uncertainty about specific winners and losers permits the positions of governments, particularly larger ones, on questions of European institutions and common foreign policy, to reflect the ideologies and personal commitments of leading executive and parliamentary politicians, as well as interest-based conceptions of the national interest. This may help explain the ability and willingness of nationalists like Charles de Gaulle and Margaret Thatcher to adopt an uncompromising position toward the dilution of national sovereignty, as well as support by various European leaders for direct elections to the European Parliament, the creation of the European Council, and the quiet development of European Political Co-operation – each an issue in which the costs and benefits to organized interest groups is near impossible to calculate.

Similarly, the politics of decisions about *EC institutions* vary widely, depending on the nature of the decision-making process to be institutionalized. Where the consequences of institutional decisions are calculable and concrete, national positions will be instrumental, reflecting the expected influence of institutional reforms on the realization of substantive interests. This is, for example, generally the case with decisions about majority voting on specific

Figure 2: Economic Interdependence and National Preferences

| | **PREDICTIONS** | |
| | *Sources of*<br>*Societal Interests* | *Determinants of*<br>*State Action* |
| --- | --- | --- |
| **ISSUE AREA**<br>**Commercial**<br>**Liberalization**<br>(e.g. tariffs and quotas,<br>agricultural price<br>policy) | Overt pressure, mostly from<br>producers, whose net<br>expected gains and losses<br>reflect competitive position in<br>international markets, levels<br>of intra-industry trade, and<br>the certainty of policy<br>outcomes | Where producer interests strong,<br>unified and certain, governments<br>will conform to them; otherwise,<br>they are more likely to risk<br>liberalization when faced with<br>overt and intractable policy<br>failure, signalled by low<br>investment and growth,<br>unsustainable external<br>disequilibria, and/or intolerable<br>fiscal compensation |
| **Socio-economics**<br>**Public Goods**<br>**Provision**<br>(e.g. monetary,<br>environmental,<br>social and regulatory<br>policies) | Two-dimensional pressure:<br>from producers, based on the<br>criteria above, and from the<br>public in favour of public goods<br>provision | When societal interests strong<br>and unified, governments<br>conform; when not, they<br>co-ordinate actions to combat<br>policy failure, judged on either<br>of the two dimensions |
| **Political, Institutional**<br>**or Redistributional**<br>**Policies**<br>(e.g. EPC, Euro-<br>parliamentary affairs,<br>structural funding) | Pressure from narrow groups<br>only where the implications are<br>calculable, otherwise only a<br>loose public or elite opinion<br>constraint | Except where implications are<br>calculable, governments and<br>parliamentary elites enjoy<br>relatively broad autonomy to<br>pursue symbolic goals or side<br>payments |

economic policies. Moreover, some delegations of power are viewed as necessary for the effective functioning of the EC. These institutions – to which we shall return in Section IV below – include common representation in international negotiation, the Commission's power of proposal under qualified majority voting, and enforcement of EC rules by the European Court of Justice and the Commission.

The more general and less predictable the implications of decisions on the relative power of institutions, the larger the space for leading politicians and partisan elites to act on the basis of ideological predilections. National interests would lead one to expect large, self-sufficient and uncompetitive countries, as well as those that hold outlier preferences on questions of public goods provision, to be relatively unwilling to accept stronger supranational institutions, such as majority voting or a European Parliament. British and French policy provides some support for this view, but Italy's consistent federalism remains an exception. Similarly, smaller countries might be expected to support strong supranational power. The Benelux countries have indeed done so, yet Danish, Greek and Irish support has been less consistent. National parliamentary elites appear to play an important role in countries like Italy, Germany and the Netherlands, which support federalist institutions.

   *Regional and structural policies* – since they are neither significant enough to provide major benefits to the donors, nor widely enough distributed to represent a policy of common interest – are most plausibly interpreted as side payments extended in exchange for other policies.

*Conclusion*

This section has employed and extended contemporary theories of international political economy to predict the national preferences of EC Member States across three types of issues: commercial policy, socio-economic public goods provision, and other institutional, political or structural policies. In each case, the magnitude, distribution and certainty of net expected costs and benefits to private groups were employed to predict policy preferences of governments, as well as their range of relative autonomy *vis-à-vis* those domestic groups that oppose co-operation (summarized in Figure 2). This defines the demand for international co-operation; in the next section, we turn to the capacity of the international system to supply co-operation.

### IV. Intergovernmentalism, Interstate Bargaining, and the Supply of Integration

Intergovernmentalist theory seeks to analyse the EC as the result of strategies pursued by rational governments acting on the basis of their preferences and power. The major agenda-setting decisions in the history of the EC, in which common policies are created or reformed, are negotiated intergovernmentally, but can they be consistently explained in terms of a theory of interstate bargaining? Like many international negotiations, EC decisions of this kind can thus be thought of as a game of co-ordination with distributional consequences – in other words, a bargaining game over the terms of co-operation (Sebenius, 1991; Krasner, 1991;   Garrett, 1992). The configuration of domestically determined national preferences defines a 'bargaining space' of potentially viable agreements, each of which generates gains for one or more participants. Governments, if they are to pursue a common policy, must collectively select one. The choice between different agreements often has important distributional consequences; governments are therefore rarely indifferent among them. Negotiation is the process of collective choice through which conflicting interests are reconciled.

Bargaining games raise two analytical problems. Lax and Sebenius (1986) refers to these as problems of 'creating' and 'claiming' value. They might be thought of also as co-ordination and bargaining aspects of strategic interaction. The first problem concerns the efficiency of negotiations. Negotiations create value by facilitating mutually beneficial exchanges, but excessive costs of identifying, negotiating and enforcing bargains may obstruct co-operation. Strategic behaviour may lead governments to withhold information about mutually beneficial bargains, negotiation may require costly threats, enforcement may be expensive or impossible. International institutions can help to ameliorate some of these problems by proposing potential agreements, providing rules for decision-making, and the adjudication of disputes. The second problem concerns the distributional implications of interstate bargaining. The choice of a specific outcome from among many possible ones determines the distribution of expected costs and benefits among national governments. Governments bargain hard for advantage. In order to explain bargaining outcomes, it is necessary to understand the factors that account for the relative power.

Creating and claiming value often occur simultaneously, but they can be divided for analytical purposes. In the following section, the focus is on the distributional implications. Strategic interaction is assumed to be efficient, the choice of agreements is restricted to those along the Pareto-frontier, and the analysis focuses on the international distribution of gains and losses. In the following section, in which the role of supranational institutions in assuring efficient bargaining outcomes is addressed, these assumptions are then relaxed.

*Bargaining Power and the Intensity of Preferences*

Negotiation analysis has identified numerous factors that may influence the distributional outcomes of international bargaining, among them the nature of the alternative policies and coalitions, the level and symmetry of information, the extent of communication, the sequence of moves, the institutional setting, the potential for strategic misrepresentation of interests, the possibility of making credible commitments, the importance of reputation, the cost-effectiveness of threats and side-payments, and the relative preferences, risk-acceptance, expectations, impatience, and skill of the negotiating parties (Raiffa, 1982; Harsanyi, 1977). In the abstract, any of these factors might be important predictors of bargaining outcomes.

To generate precise and accurate predictions about a set of comparable cases, such as major EC decisions, detailed assumptions must be made about the situation in which the parties are bargaining. In justifying the selection of assumptions, formal theory, while useful, cannot substitute for detailed empirical knowledge of the context in which bargaining takes place. Given the range of possible theoretical solutions to the bargaining problem and the difficulty of rigorous hypothesis-testing by the case study method, the use of congenial, convenient or conventional assumptions and concepts without contextual justification poses a high risk of generating irrelevant or illusory results. Assumptions lacking explicit empirical justification should therefore be viewed with scepticism.[21]

The following three assumptions about interstate bargaining offer a plausible starting point for analysis of EC decision-making. First, intergovernmental co-operation in the EC is voluntary, in the sense that neither military coercion nor economic sanctions are threatened or deployed to force agreement. Democratic governments are risk-averse and tend to avoid the high costs of conflict. Not only do they decline to ally or wage war against one another, but also the tactical use of economic sanctions (as opposed to the threat of exclusion that might occur through the self-interested pursuit of national interests), while occasionally employed in trade disputes among liberal capitalist states, tends to be relatively rare among the highly interdependent nations of the EC (cf. Martin, 1992). Thus, fundamental decisions in the EC can be viewed as taking place in a non-coercive unanimity voting system. Second, the environment in which EC governments bargain is relatively information-rich. National negotiators are able to communicate at low cost and possess information about the preferences and opportunities facing their foreign counterparts, as well as the technical implications of policies that are of the greatest interest to them (Moravcsik, 1993). Third, the transaction costs of intergovernmental bargaining are low. Negotiations within the EC take place over a protracted period of time, during which member governments can extend numerous offers and counter-offers at relatively little cost. Side-payments and linkages can be made. Governments

---

[21] The specification of applied bargaining models *generally* requires information beyond the basic assumptions of all such models. Harsanyi, in his general theory of classical bargaining games, notes that 'a satisfactory definition of a given game will often require a specification of *additional parameters* to those which by traditional game theory would be included in the definition of the game ... if such parameters are left unspecified, any given game can have a wide *variety* of alternative outcomes' (emphasis in the original). Harsanyi (1977), p. 6; Binmore and Dasgupta (1987), ch. 1. For similar sentiments among international relations theorists, see Axelrod and Keohane (1986); Jervis (1988); Fearon (1991).

can credibly commit themselves to substantive policies through explicit institutional arrangements. Technically, it is possible to design efficient institutions to monitor and enforce any agreement at any desired level. (The assumption of low transaction costs is relaxed in a later section of this article.)

The assumption of a non-coercive, information-rich, deliberative, institutionalized setting may not be perfectly realized at all times during the history of the EC, but it is a reasonable first approximation of the context in which European governments typically negotiate. One implication of these assumptions is that bargaining outcomes should be efficient, in the sense that conflicts are generally resolved Pareto-optimally. Opportunities for useful bargains are exploited. Moreover, these assumptions reduce the importance of various factors that influence bargaining outcomes elsewhere, such as first mover advantages, strategic sequencing, strategic misrepresentation, the use of costly coercive threats, and the role of unilateral precommitments. EC negotiations can be viewed as a co-operative game in which the level of co-operation reflects patterns in the preferences of national governments.

Yet even in this relatively benign environment, relative power matters. Bargaining leverage stems most fundamentally from asymmetries in the relative intensity of national preferences, which reflect, according to the analysis in the previous section, the relative costs and benefits of agreements to remove negative externalities. In negotiating policy co-ordination, the terms will favour those governments able to remove negative externalities by opening markets to which others intensely desire access, modifying policies others intensely desire to change, or distributing resources others intensely desire to share. The more intensely governments desire agreement, the more concessions and the greater effort they will expend to achieve it. The greater the potential gains for a government from co-operation, as compared to its best alternative policy, the less risk of non-agreement it is willing to assume and, therefore, the weaker its bargaining power over the specific terms of agreement.

Theories of bargaining and negotiation suggest three likely determinants of interstate bargaining power under such circumstances: (1) unilateral policy alternatives ('threats of non-agreement'); (2) alternative coalitions ('threats of exclusion'); and (3) the potential for compromise and linkage.

*Unilateral alternatives and threats of non-agreement.* A necessary condition for negotiated agreement among rational governments is that each perceive the benefits of co-operation as preferable to the benefits of the best alternative available to it. Where there exists a policy more desirable than co-operation, a rational government will forgo agreement. *The simple, but credible threat of non-agreement – to reject co-operation in favour of a superior alternative – provides rational governments with their most fundamental form of bargaining power*. The more attractive a government's policy alternatives – often termed 'outside options', 'reservation values', 'concession limits', or 'best alternatives to negotiated agreement (BATNAs)' – the less intense its preference for agreement and the greater its bargaining leverage.[22] Governments with attractive alternatives will not tolerate inconvenient agreements, while governments with unattractive alternatives gain from co-operation even if they have to compromise.[23] Leaving aside for the moment alternative coalitions, linkages and side-payments, the 'threat of non-agreement' guarantees that the outcomes of rational bargaining must fall within a set of agreements, termed the 'feasible set', ranging from an outcome in which all the joint gains accrue to one country to those in which they accrue to another, that is, a set is bounded by the best policy alternatives available to governments. Only agreements within this set are viable.[24]

The most basic type of alternative is simply the unilateral policy that a government is able to pursue without an agreement, that is, under the institutional *status quo*. When bargaining on the basis of unilateral alternatives, governments have only one threat, that of non-co-operation. In negotiations over trade liberalization, for example, the bargaining power of unilateral alternatives stems from asymmetrical interdependence: governments that are less dependent on internal trade than their negotiating partners, and therefore stand to gain less from agreement, enjoy greater bargaining leverage. Thus, even if democratic governments rarely apply tactical or punitive sanctions, *implicit* sanctions – the credible threat to retain protection as the best alternative to agreement – remain a fundamental source of bargaining power.[25] In negotiations over public goods policies, governments with greater domestic policy autonomy enjoy leverage over those whose policies are ineffective or vulnerable to external disruption. In both these bargaining situations, governments of large, prosperous, relatively self-sufficient countries tend to wield the most influence, because they gain relatively little from agreement, compared to their smaller, poorer, more open neighbours. The former can therefore afford to be more discriminating about the terms they will accept.

One implication of bargaining on the basis of the intensity of preferences is that the need to compromise with the least forthcoming government imposes the

[22] Raiffa (1982) pp. 252–5; Zartman (1991), pp. 69ff; Keeney and Raiffa (1991); Dixit and Nalebuff,(1991), pp. 290–2. Keohane and Nye (1988) refer to this as 'vulnerability'; Hirschman develops the same concept. I employed the phrase 'opportunity cost of non-agreement and exclusion' in Moravcsik (1992a) ch. 1. Garrett (1992) has applied this idea to the EC.
[23] The importance of opportunity costs in this context was pointed out by Haas (1993, p. 186).
[24] Sebenius (1991), pp. 332–4. Where a welfare-reducing agreement is reached, it is unlikely to be ratified or implemented. Putnam (1988).
[25] Hirschman (1945), p. 16, notes that 'the power to interrupt commercial or financial relations with any country ... is the root cause of the influence or power position which a country acquires'. See also Keohane and Nye (1977).

binding constraint on the possibilities for greater co-operation, driving EC agreements toward the *lowest common denominator*. Let us assume, for example, that European governments are selecting by unanimity vote among a set of possible agreements, arrayed in order of increasing divergence from the *status quo*. If each government favours agreements closest to its preferred point and is willing to accept only those agreements that it prefers to the *status quo*, it is the government with a preferred point closest to the *status quo* whose veto ultimately limits the extent of reform. A 'lowest common denominator' outcome does *not* mean that final agreements perfectly reflect the preferences of the least forthcoming government – since it is generally in its interest to compromise somewhat rather than veto an agreement – but only that the range of possible agreements is decisively constrained by its preferences.

The evolution of the EC illustrates the importance, but also some important limitations, of unilateral alternatives as determinants of interstate bargaining outcomes. In negotiations over the terms of European monetary integration since the late 1970s, Germany's alternative to negotiated agreement – *de facto* monetary autonomy – has been more attractive than the alternative of its neighbours, which is increasing dependence on the Bundesbank. As a result, the German government has been able to demand that monetary integration take place through convergence to Germany's low-inflation standard, without which Germany would have had little incentive to depart from the institutional *status quo*. Similarly, Britain has traditionally been viewed as indispensable to the credibility of European Political Co-operation. Its interests have been accommodated by those whose unilateral foreign policy options are limited, including Germany, Italy and many smaller states.

Another example of this dynamic is the negotiation over agricultural prices in the 1960s. The German government's control over its lucrative, protected agricultural market, to which French producers desired access, afforded it considerable bargaining power *vis-à-vis* France. The German government employed this leverage to force common EC prices to high German levels, without which its participation would have probably been blocked domestically. French farmers gained the most from the agreement in absolute terms and, in part as a result, the final agreement was closest to the demands of German farmers. This was aided by the fact that while the French government preferred somewhat lower prices (and a correspondingly larger share of the German market), higher prices were not unwelcome to French farmers. By contrast, German markets for *industrial* goods, although lucrative, were already open and threats to close them were not credible. Germany gained little bargaining power from agreeing to keep its markets open, demonstrating that governments can activate the potential bargaining power of their markets best where the threat to restrict market access constitutes a viable unilateral alternative, rather than a tactical expedient.

Agreement at the lowest common denominator does not, however, inevitably mean adoption of the lowest possible common standard. In numerous cases, less environmentally conscious governments in Britain, Spain and elsewhere have accepted environmental product standards far higher than those prevailing domestically. Relatively high environmental and public health standards, such as high air pollution and recycling standards, do not disconfirm the prediction of lowest common denominator agreements. Some of these decisions reflect the dynamics of qualified majority voting, yet even under unanimity, these apparent anomalies are quite consistent with the model of bargaining on the basis of preference intensity, *if preferences are specified properly*. In the EC context, regulatory issues are often 'two-dimensional', linking commercial and public welfare concerns. High national standards operate as permissible non-tariff barriers under Article 36 of the Treaty of Rome. Often the regulation of environmental product standards creates unexpected alliances, as illustrated by the cases of auto emissions standards, recycling laws for bottles and packaging, and standards for toxic chemicals (Vogel, 1992; Majone, 1992; Levy, 1991). Such regulations are thus more acceptable to business in Germany, Denmark and the Netherlands than they otherwise might be. Better yet, however, from the perspective of business in these high standard countries, much of which is multinational, would be an integrated market with high *EC* environmental standards. Producers in low standard countries would gain as well, since access to markets with high standards, cut off by unilateral barriers, would thereby be assured. Far from sparking a race to the bottom, the creation of a single market under 'lowest common denominator' bargaining often creates incentives for the EC to harmonize at a high level.[26]

*Alternative coalitions and the threat of exclusion.* Where the only alternatives to agreement are unilateral policies, EC negotiations over major reforms can be thought of as taking place within a unanimity voting system in which agreement requires that the minimal demands of each country be satisfied. Sometimes, however, the best alternative to agreement is not unilateral action, but the formation of an alternative coalition from which certain states are excluded. Where alternative coalitions are possible, a government must calculate the value of an agreement by comparing it not to unilateral policy options, but to its gains from alternative coalitions it could join or from 'going it alone ... as [it] faces various coalitions' (Raiffa, 1982, p. 253). *The existence of opportunities to form attractive alternative coalitions (or deepen existing ones), while excluding*

---

[26] The European Parliament's role was also important in this case. See Aizenman (1993).

*other parties, strengthens the bargaining power of potential coalition members* vis-à-vis *those threatened with exclusion.* In the EC context, such bargaining power may result either from the threat to co-operate with non-EC countries or, more common today, from the possibility of forming or deepening alternative institutions within Europe, while leaving some members behind – a 'two-track' or 'multi-speed' Europe (Moravcsik, 1991). Such coalitional dynamics tend to favour large states, whose participation is necessary for viable coalitions, and governments with preferences close to the median of the EC, since they are potential members of more viable coalitions.

By creating negative policy externalities, the formation of an alternative coalition creates an incentive for recalcitrant governments to compromise. Due to the much greater market power involved, the threat of exclusion from a coalition is a more powerful incentive to co-operation than a single state's threat of non-agreement. To a much greater extent than unco-ordinated policies, alternative coalitions – for example an exclusive free trade arrangement – can create negative policy externalities for those left outside it. By diverting investment, credit, trade, political influence, or market confidence, exclusion from an alternative coalition may impose significant costs, even in the absence of military and economic coercion (Binmore and Dasgupta, 1987, p. 9). Under these conditions, a government may seek to avoid exclusion by agreeing to terms of co-operation that leave it *worse off in absolute terms than the* status quo ante – although, of course, the agreement is Pareto-improving in the sense that the government is better off as compared to its position if the failure to reach agreement had led to the formation of an alternative coalition.

A number of major events in the history of the EC can be interpreted as responses to the threat of exclusion from an alternative coalition. The initial British response to the formation of the Common Market in the 1950s and 1960s is an illustrative example. The British government initially sought to undermine European integration by proposing an alternative free trade area. When this failed, the British sought to dilute the Common Market by negotiating a free trade deal directly with it, and subsequently formed a parallel organization, the European Free Trade Association (EFTA). Only when each of these strategies had failed did Britain finally apply for membership of the EC – only to find that the adjustment of other countries to the Common Market had shifted relative bargaining power even further against it. This is a case in which Britain, while it would have gained from membership, would nevertheless have preferred the *status quo ante.*

History repeated itself in the negotiations over the Single European Act, when the French and German governments publicly threatened to move ahead without Britain if the British government failed to accept formal treaty revisions to mandate majority voting – a threat clearly understood as such at high levels in the British government. Britain, it was thought at the time, would be doubly disadvantaged by exclusion, not only renouncing the material advantages of reform, but also losing its voice in decisions about their precise form. Since reform was in the interest of all other Member States, even if Britain were excluded, the threat was credible (Moravcsik, 1991).

Yet alternative coalitions do not always create negative externalities for excluded states and, therefore, pressure for geographical spillover. Where a policy of exclusion has *positive* externalities, a contrary dynamic occurs. Where free trade is assured, for example, governments with low social standards often have a clear incentive to free ride, rather than to compromise on common harmonized standards. This helps explain why the threat of exclusion was powerless to block the British government's striking last-minute 'opt-out' of social policy at Maastricht. Exclusion from the social policy provisions of the Maastricht Treaty, insofar as it had any effect at all, promised to make British firms *more* competitive on a European market from which they cannot be excluded. The adoption of high EC social protection standards is thus likely to be possible only through linkage or side payments, which play such an important role in cementing co-operation with the Mediterranean countries.

The distinction between positive and negative externalities provides a means of predicting which policies are 'inherently expansive' – thus resolving an ambiguity in neo-functionalist theory. Where policy externalities are negative, non-members have an incentive to join the organization, which will lead them to compromise on common standards. Where policy externalities are positive, non-members have an incentive to free ride, rather than compromise, and agreements above the lowest common denominator are possible only through linkages and side payments, to which we now turn.[27] This not only helps to explain the dynamics of geographical expansion in the EC, but also the dynamics of current bargaining over regulatory issues.

*Compromise, side-payments and linkage at the margin.* Unilateral and coalitional policy alternatives define a range of viable agreements which all participants prefer to the *status quo*. Within that range, the precise point at which negotiators will compromise is more difficult to predict, particularly when more than two states are involved. In general, bargaining power will depend on the intensity of preference at the margin. Where uncertainty exists about the breakdown of negotiations or time pressure, concessions tend to come dispro-

---

[27] While the existence of alternative coalitions has been presented here as a source of power in broad negotiations over the future scope of the EC, it is relevant also to qualified majority voting on more specific issues. In bargaining among themselves over the precise terms of a directive or regulation, national governments weigh the costs of compromise, which results in a winning coalition of which they are a member and an outcome closer to their preferred point, against the risks of intransigence, which may result in exclusion from the winning coalition and an outcome more uncongenial to them.

portionately from governments for which the failure to reach agreement would be least attractive – that is, from those governments which stand to lose the most if agreement is not reached. Where such uncertainty does not exist, the terms of the final agreement will reflect the relative intensity of preferences at the margin, which defines the shape of the feasible set: governments that place a greater value on  concession at the margin will gain more from negotiations.[28]

More importantly for our purposes here, governments often have differential preference intensities across issues, with marginal gains in some issue-areas being more important to them than to other governments. Under these circumstances, it may be to the advantage of both parties to exchange concessions in issue-areas about which their preferences are relatively weak for concessions in other areas about which they care more. Even where a set of agreements, taken individually, would each be rejected by at least one national government, they may generate net advantages for all if adopted as a 'package deal'. Such linkages can increase the welfare of both parties, thereby helping to overcome one of the major disadvantages of bargaining on the basis of unilateral and coalitional alternatives, namely that governments tend to have the least bargaining power on precisely those issues which are relatively most important to them. Issue linkages are most advantageous where two countries have highly asymmetrical interests in various issues, which permit each to make concessions valuable to the other at relatively low cost.

The major limitation on linkage strategies is domestic opposition. Linkages have important domestic distributional consequences. They tie together into 'package deals' issues in which domestic groups benefit with those in which domestic groups lose. Package deals tend to create winners and losers in *all* countries that are party to them. Where domestic gains and losses produced by linkage are only imperfectly fungible through compensation across issues, linkage becomes a complex and politically risky strategy. Since losers tend to generate more political pressure than winners, for a domestic trade-off to be tolerable, adjustment costs to important domestic groups must be moderate, or substantial compensation must be paid.

The importance of domestic costs and benefits suggests a number of predictions about linkage. First, linkages are most likely in areas where the preferences of domestic groups are not intense. Minor issues are more likely to be sacrificed to a linkage. Wherever possible, therefore, financial or symbolic side-payments between states, rather than linkages between substantive issues are employed. The Maastricht agreement was typical, in that issues implicitly

---

[28] This is the Nash bargaining solution, whereby a marginal redistribution in either direction between two actors with concave utility functions would lead to an equal percentage change in their utility. This is also the equilibrium of an offer-counteroffer game in which both sides are assumed to be equal in all respects other than their preferences. See Binmore and Dasgupta (1987).

linked to monetary policy included highly fungible resources, such as increases in structural funds, or symbolic issues, such as deletion of 'federalist' language and increased powers to the European Parliament. Second, package deals are most likely in the final stage of bargaining – that is, at the margin to balance gains and losses among issues in which all parties are close to being net beneficiaries – rather than among issues in which nations are large net winners and losers. Third, linkages are most likely between closely related issues – within, rather than between, sectors. Where the costs and benefits are internalized to sectors or firms, there is more possibility for producers to adjust, diversify, or to balance gains and losses, just as in the case of intra-industry trade. Sectoral organizations may neutralize opposition by aggregating sectoral support and opposition into a single position. Linkages between disparate sectors are most likely to occur where the possibilities for intra-issue compromise or linkage between related issues have been exhausted. Fourth, if linkages do impose real losses on domestic sectors, they are more likely to be effective when accompanied by domestic side-payments from governments to disadvantaged private groups. In the 1960s and 1970s, industrial subsidies in France and agricultural subsidies in Germany were explicitly designed to ease adjustment to liberalization.

Linkage is thus a politically costly, second-best strategy for integration. Linkages that attempt too much – such as the linkage between the Common Agricultural Policy and strong supranational institutions in the 1960s – are often unstable and are circumvented at a later stage. The limitations on linkage are illustrated by the purported linkage on which the EC is said to be founded, namely that between German access to French industrial markets and French access to German agricultural markets. While such a linkage existed on the margin, it was less central than is often asserted. Industrialists and farmers in both countries gained. French industry's objections to the Common Market were in fact relatively minor; by 1959, before tariff reductions had begun in earnest, they were already among the strongest supporters of acceleration. Opposition to a common agricultural policy came primarily from economic liberals in the German government, who opposed high prices, and farmers, who feared low prices. The final agreement left farmers in every country, including Germany, with higher average support prices than they had enjoyed previously. Those elements of the CAP price structure that most disadvantaged certain farmers were offset by domestic compensation and adjustment assistance. In the 1970s, any residual loss to German farmers was more than offset by the compensation for currency movements and the subsequent 'renationalization' of the CAP, leaving only division of the much smaller budgetary expenditures as an outstanding issue. In contrast to neo-functionalism, which viewed linkage as the core of the EC, it is seen here as a strategy best pursued on the margin and of lesser importance than intra-sectoral trade-offs. Linkages that impose large losses on important domestic groups are unstable.

So far this analysis has focused primarily on the sources of national preferences and the distributional outcomes of intergovernmental negotiations over commercial liberalization, domestic public goods provision, and general political and institutional questions. We turn now from an analysis of the distributional outcomes of intergovernmental bargaining to an analysis of its efficiency. Modern regime theory views international institutions as deliberate instruments to improve the efficiency of bargaining between states.

## V. Supranational Institutions and the Efficiency of Decision-Making

Strong supranational institutions are often seen as the antithesis of intergovern-mentalism. Wrongly so. The decision to join all but the most minimalist of regimes involves some sacrifice of national autonomy, which increases the political risk to each Member State, in exchange for certain advantages. In the intergovernmentalist view, the unique institutional structure of the EC is acceptable to national governments only insofar as it strengthens, rather than weakens, their control over domestic affairs, permitting them to attain goals otherwise unachievable.

EC institutions strengthen the power of governments in two ways. First, they increase the efficiency of interstate bargaining. The existence of a common negotiating forum, decision-making procedures, and monitoring of compliance reduce the costs of identifying, making and keeping agreements, thereby making possible a greater range of co-operative arrangements. This explanation relies on the functional theory of regimes, which focuses on the role of regimes in reducing transaction costs (Keohane, 1984). However, in order to explain the unique level of institutionalization found in the EC, this body of theory must be extended to include the delegation and pooling of sovereignty. Second, EC institutions strengthen the autonomy of national political leaders *vis-à-vis* particularistic social groups within their domestic polity. By augmenting the legitimacy and credibility of common policies, and by strengthening domestic agenda-setting power, the EC structures a 'two-level game' that enhances the autonomy and initiative of national political leaders – often, as noted above, a prerequisite for successful market liberalization. With a few important excep-tions, EC institutions appear to be explicable as the result of conscious calculations by Member States to strike a balance between greater efficiency and domestic influence, on the one hand, and acceptable levels of political risk, on the other.

## Supranational Institutions and Functional Regime Theory

Much of the institutional structure of the EC can be readily explained by the functional theory of regimes, which argues that where transaction costs – the costs of identifying issues, negotiating bargains, codifying agreements, and monitoring and enforcing compliance – are significant, international institutions may promote greater co-operation by providing information and reducing uncertainty. In the conventional regime-theoretical view, EC institutions serve as a passive structure, providing a contractual environment conducive to efficient intergovernmental bargaining. As compared to *ad hoc* negotiation, they increase the efficiency of bargaining, facilitating agreements that would not otherwise be reached (Buchanan and Tullock, 1962; Keohane, 1984; Levy *et al.*, 1992).

The functional regime theory view of international institutions as passive, transaction-cost reducing sets of rules readily explains the role of EC institutions as a framework for negotiating major decisions, from the Treaty of Rome to Maastricht. The *acquis communautaire* of the EC functions to stabilize a constantly evolving set of rules and expectations, which can only be altered by unanimous consent. Institutions promote international co-operation by providing a negotiating forum with bureaucratic institutions that disseminate information and policy ideas; a locus for representatives of business, political parties, national bureaucracies, and interest groups to discuss issues of common concern; joint decision-making procedures; a common set of underlying legal and political norms; and institutions for monitoring and defining national compliance. Greater information and predictability reduce the cost of bargaining and the risk of unilateral non-compliance. Like the GATT, the G-7 and other international regimes, EC institutions provide fora in which to craft linkages and side-payments that render policy co-ordination more viable domestically. Package deals linking regional funds and British entry or structural funds and the Single European Act were surely easier to reach within a common international institution. Yet the large political risk inherent in open-ended decisions about the future scope of EC activities means that Member States remain hesitant to delegate authority to supranational or majoritarian institutions. [29] The essence of the EC as a body for reaching major decisions remains its transaction-cost reducing function, as explicated by contemporary regime theory.

When we turn from major constitutional decision-making to the process of 'everyday' legislation, administration and enforcement, however, the EC seems to be a far more unusual international institution – more than a passive set of

---

[29] This is akin to the problem of designing constitutional protection of minority rights (Buchanan and Tullock, 1962, pp. 129–30).

rules codifying previous decisions. The EC differs from nearly all other international regimes in at least two salient ways: by *pooling* national sovereignty through qualified majority voting rules and by *delegating* sovereign powers to semi-autonomous central institutions. These two forms of transferring national sovereignty are closely related. Qualified majority voting, for example, not only makes the formal decision-making of any single government more dependent on the votes of its foreign counterparts, but also more dependent on agenda-setting by the Commission.

In order to understand the conditions under which Member States will forgo *ad hoc* decision-making under the unanimity rule in favour of a common agreement to pool or delegate sovereignty, contemporary regime theory must be extended. An insightful starting point, suggested by Garrett and Weingast in their analysis of the European Court of Justice, is to view delegation as a response to the problem of incomplete contracting. Predicting the circumstances under which future contingencies will occur is often difficult and costly, sometimes impossible (Garrett and Weingast, 1991). Where member governments have shared goals, but are unable or unwilling to foresee all future contingencies involved in the realization of common goals, they may have an incentive to establish common decision-making procedures or to empower neutral agents to propose, mediate, implement, interpret and enforce agreements.

The metaphor of incomplete contracting *per se*, while a useful starting assumption, fails to explain variation in either the level or the form of delegation (or pooling) of sovereignty. Delegation is, after all, only one of a number of possible responses to future uncertainty. Many unpredictable EC decisions – including the annual determination of CAP prices and the definition of new issues under Art. 235 – are neither delegated nor pooled; others – the determination of international negotiating positions and administered protection against third countries – are pooled, but not delegated. Elsewhere in the international system, delegation is even rarer, despite many cases of incomplete contracting. Even within the EC, governments often refuse to assume the political risk of delegation, preferring instead imperfect enforcement and inefficient decision-making, to the surrender of sovereignty. Incomplete contracting appears to be neither a necessary, nor a sufficient, condition for delegation.

What, then, distinguishes cases of delegation or pooling from cases of *ad hoc* unanimity voting? Following public choice analyses of domestic constitutional choice, intergovernmentalist theory views the decision to adopt qualified majority voting or delegation to common institutions as the result of a cost–benefit analysis of the stream of future substantive decisions expected to follow from alternative institutional designs. For individual Member States carrying out such a cost–benefit calculation, the decision to delegate or pool sovereignty signals the willingness of national governments to accept an increased political risk of being outvoted or overruled on any individual issue in exchange for more efficient collective decision-making on the average.[30] Movement beyond unanimous voting and *ad hoc* negotiation for a class of decisions can thus be thought of as a means of deliberately encouraging implicit linkages across various related issues within an iterated game among governments. By facilitating linkages, delegation or pooling is likely to produce more decisions at a lower cost in time and energy than the laborious negotiation of *ad hoc* package deals. Compared to unanimity voting, delegation and pooling of sovereignty are more efficient, but less controlled forms of collective decision-making. Of the two, delegation involves greater political risk and more efficient decision-making, while pooling through qualified majority voting involves less risk, but correspondingly less efficiency.

Examining this trade-off more precisely, the following three conditions should encourage national governments to support a movement from unanimity to delegated or pooled decision-making: (1) *The potential gains from co-operation.* Where time pressure, previous failures to reach agreement, the desire to implement a prior decision, or a shift in national preferences requires more rapid decision-making, delegation or pooling is more likely. *Ceteris paribus,* the less attractive the *status quo* and the greater the expected gains from increased co-operation, the greater the corresponding incentive to pool or delegate. Levels of economic transactions and, in particular, intra-industry trade, which are higher among the EC countries than among any comparable set of industrialized countries, are likely to lead eventually to pressure for greater delegation and pooling of sovereignty. Where large numbers of similar decisions are involved, the efficiency gains are correspondingly greater (cf. Keohane, 1983).

(2) *The level of uncertainty regarding the details of specific delegated or pooled decisions.* Lack of precise knowledge about the form, details and outcome of future decisions not only precludes more explicit contracts, as noted above, but also helps defuse potential opposition from those who would be disadvantaged by the implicit linkages. Where agreements can be foreseen, some governments and domestic groups would have more reason to prefer direct bargaining under unanimity, as occurred in setting the initial levels of the Common External Tariff and agricultural prices, in order to block policies disadvantageous to them.

---

[30] This analysis assumes that the transaction costs of institutional creation and reform are relatively low, but the transaction costs of individual decision-making are high. The limitations to more 'optimal' international institutions stem not from transaction costs of creating them, but from the interests of governments in reducing domestic political risk. This leads them to promote a set of decision-making rules consistent with a specific trade-off between efficiency and risk.

(3) *The level of political risk for individual governments or interest groups with intense preferences*. Political risk can be understood as the probability of a large downside loss to a government or interest group. Risk-averse governments will assent to procedures where the scope and magnitude of expected and potential losses are minimized, given the goals of co-operation. Governments have an incentive to delegate authority only when there is little probability that the cumulative distributional effects of delegated or pooled decisions will be biased in an unforeseen way against the interests of any national government or major domestic group.[31] The form of third-party representation, agenda-setting and enforcement should involve the minimal transfer of sovereignty needed to achieve desired outcomes. One way to limit the scope of delegation and pooling, often employed in the EC, is to nest specific decisions inside a set of larger decisions already reached by unanimity, thereby both diversifying and limiting political risk.

Each of the three most important instances in which the Treaty of Rome delegates Member State authority to supranational officials – external representation, agenda-setting and enforcement – appears to fulfil these conditions.

*External representation*: Since the EC is a customs union with a common external tariff, negotiations with third countries require a single agent to represent common positions. In order for national governments to trust the agent, it must be perceived as neutral. While this requires that an agent be delegated, only limited independent decision-making for short periods of time is required to carry out designated tasks. Close monitoring and oversight by national governments is to be expected. In the common commercial policy of the EC, for example, the Commission represents the Community, but tight control is maintained by the Article 113 Committee. Only where time pressure in the midst of negotiations forces a rapid decision and national governments are deadlocked can supranational officials advance independent initiatives. These are still subject to *ex post* approval, but may transfer some marginal power to the Commission. In European Political Co-operation, where fewer decisions are taken and a common external position is viewed as less imperative, the EC is generally represented by the foreign ministers of its Member States.

*Agenda-setting*: Where a wide consensus exists on a broad substantive agenda, it can often be realized more efficiently by granting a measure of agenda-setting power to a supranational institution, in this case the Commission. As a reliable source of independent proposals, the Commission assures that technical information necessary for decision is available. More importantly, as a neutral arbiter, it provides an authoritative means of reducing the number of proposals to be considered. Majorities may exist for a number of alternative

---

[31] Some institutions may be biased in a predictable manner, for which a rational government would demand compensation in negotiations.

proposals on a single issue, with governments unable to reduce them to a compromise through their vetoes. This is particularly important where governments have sought to increase the efficiency of bargaining by employing qualified majority voting (QMV). In such circumstances, agenda-setting power can be decisive in deciding which proposal prevails. In the EC, delegating the power of proposal to the Commission provides a means of setting the agenda, thereby avoiding time-consuming or inconclusive 'cycling' between difficult proposals or an arbitrary means of proposal selection.[32] Most states are likely to consider a supranational body to be more neutral than even a randomly chosen national government. Delegating the preparation of proposals to the Commission thereby reduces the risk to national governments that decisions will be delayed by an inconclusive struggle among competing proposals or that the final decision will be grossly unfair – a matter of particular importance to small countries, which often lack the administrative means to prepare or assess proposals.

Yet the ability to select among viable proposals grants the Commission considerable formal agenda-setting power, at least in theory. The power is particularly decisive when the *status quo* is unattractive, creating general support for joint action, yet there is considerable disagreement between national governments over what should replace it. Often a number of proposals might gain majority support, among which the Commission's choice is decisive. The most controversial cases of implementing the White Paper agenda, including a number in telecommunications, environmental and social policy, stand as examples. (For a similar analysis of parliamentary power, see Tsebelis, 1992.)

*Enforcement*: The possibilities for co-operation are enhanced when neutral procedures exist to monitor, interpret and enforce compliance. Neutral enforcement permit governments to extend credible commitments, thus helping to overcome the almost inevitable interstate prisoner's dilemma of enforcement, whereby individual governments seek to evade inconvenient responsibilities, thereby undermining the integrity of the entire system. By taking the definition of compliance outside of the hands of national governments, a supranational legal system strengthens the credibility of national commitments to the institution. The cost of such delegation, which goes beyond the monitoring functions of classical international regimes, is increased political risk. Functions of this type in the EC include competition policy, administered by the Commission, and the interpretation and application of EC law, carried out by the European Court of Justice (Garrett and Weingast, 1991).

---

[32] Under unanimity voting, this is less of a problem: each government can compel compromise by vetoing any proposal that does not accommodate its views, leading to a compromise among proposals. Hence the sequence in which proposals are voted upon is less essential.

In each of these three cases, there is a substantive commitment to the achievement of broad goals, while the political risk is small, insofar as each delegated decision is relatively insignificant. Perhaps most important, the scope of delegation is explicitly limited by national governments. The scope of representation in third-party negotiations is constrained by close oversight, the scope of legislative agenda-setting power by the Council's previous delegation of power and ultimate decision, and the scope of enforcement by existing EC law, as well as the willingness of national governments and their courts to comply with ECJ and Commission decisions.

Of the three types of delegation, only the enforcement power of the ECJ appears to have resulted in a grant of independent initiative to supranational bodies beyond that which is minimally necessary to perform its functions – and beyond that which appears to have been foreseen by governments. The ECJ has constitutionalized the Treaty of Rome, built alliances with domestic courts and interest groups, pre-empted national law in important areas, and opened new avenues for Commission initiative, as in cases like *ERTA* in common commercial policy, and *Cassis de Dijon* in technical harmonization.

The expansion of judicial power in the EC presents an anomaly for the functional explanation of delegation as a deliberate means by national governments of increasing the efficiency of collective decision-making. While supranational delegation undoubtedly creates benefits for governments, the decisions of the Court clearly transcend what was initially foreseen and desired by most national governments (Burley and Mattli, 1993). The 'constitutionalization' of the Treaty of Rome was unexpected. It is implausible, moreover, to argue that the current system is the one to which all national governments would currently consent, as recent explicit limitations on the Court in the Maastricht Treaty demonstrate. Nor is the current institutional form of the Court functionally necessary. Supranational dispute resolution need not take the form, almost unique among international organizations, of a semi-autonomous legal system. Such a system is not *a priori* more appropriate for settling disputes between rival interpretations and applications of a statute than a dispute resolution panel, as exists in the GATT, or the Council of Ministers acting under qualified majority, as exists in EFTA. The Member States might simply have reserved the right to pass legislation to clarify ambiguities. Neither incomplete contracting nor functional analysis can account for the precise form or historical evolution of the ECJ.

The unique role the ECJ has come to play may reflect instead, as Burley and Mattli argue, a number of factors idiosyncratic to the EC. First, the technical complexity of EC law made it difficult to foresee the consequences of early Court decisions, giving those who favoured a strong ECJ some leeway in drafting the treaty (Pescatore, 1981). Second, the referral of cases by domestic courts, and their subsequent enforceability in the same forum, renders ECJ judgments difficult to ignore. Finally, and most importantly, unanimous consent of Member States would now be required to curb its power. Over the years, the Court has pursued a sophisticated strategy, remaining just within a negative consensus that protects it. Any attempt to alter the current arrangements might be challenged by European federalists, by those who favour strong enforcement, and by smaller countries, which would be less well served by a system in which qualified majority voting was employed to adjudicate disputes (Burley and Mattli, 1993).

While the creation of common rules and procedures in functional regime theory alters only the information and expectations of national governments, the EC goes further, pooling decision-making through arrangements for qualified majority voting and delegating authority over representation, formal agenda-setting and enforcement to semi-autonomous institutions. Yet the delegation and pooling of authority in the EC, like the construction of common norms and principles in other regimes, can be explained by extending the central insight of functional regime theory, namely that institutions are means of reducing the transaction costs of identifying, negotiating and enforcing intergovernmental agreements under uncertainty. National governments strike a balance between increased decision-making efficiency and the political risk of uncontrolled issue linkage. The greater the potential gains, the greater the uncertainty about specific decisions, and the lower the political risk, the more likely governments are to delegate power in these ways.

Viewed in light of this trade-off, independent actions by the Commission or outcomes that contravene the interests of a single Member State, taken in isolation, do not constitute decisive evidence against the intergovernmentalist view that the EC is grounded fundamentally in the preferences and power of Member States. Only where the actions of supranational leaders *systematically* bias outcomes away from the long-term self-interest of Member States can we speak of serious challenge to an intergovernmentalist view. While some cases of supranational autonomy, such as certain actions of the European Court of Justice, may pose such a challenge, most fit comfortably within it.

## Supranational Institutions and 'Two-Level Games'

Traditional regime theory focuses primarily on the role of regimes in reducing the transaction costs of collective decision-making for national governments. Yet EC institutions perform a second function as well, namely to shift the balance of domestic initiative and influence. On balance, this shift has strengthened the policy autonomy of national governments at the expense of particular groups (for a dissenting view, see Marks, 1991).[33] Particularly where domestic interests are weak or divided, EC institutions have been deliberately designed to assist national governments in overcoming domestic opposition. Where institutions did not initially serve this purpose in the Treaty of Rome, new institutions were created in order to strengthen this function – the strengthening of the Council bureaucracy in the 1960s, the genesis of the European Council in the 1970s, and the reservation of powers over political co-operation to the Member States being prime examples.

National governments employ EC institutions as part of a 'two-level' strategy with the aim of permitting them to overcome domestic opposition more successfully (cf. Putnam, 1988). The EC fulfils this function in two ways: by according governmental policy initiatives greater domestic political legitimacy and by granting them greater domestic agenda-setting power. Let us briefly consider each. The mantle of the European Community adds legitimacy and credibility to Member State initiatives. Domestic coalitions can be mobilized more easily in favour of policy co-ordination. This adds weight in domestic debates to both major reforms and everyday decisions emanating from the EC. Second, the institutional structure of the EC strengthens the initiative and influence of national governments by insulating the policy process and generating domestic agenda-setting power for national politicians. National governments are able to take initiatives and reach bargains in Council negotiations with relatively little constraint. The EC provides information to governments that is not generally available. Intergovernmental discussions take place in secrecy; national votes are not publicized. Domestically, parliaments and publics generally have little legal opportunity to ratify EC agreements and decisions; where they do, there is rarely an opportunity to amend or revise them. National leaders undermine potential opposition by reaching bargains in Brussels first and presenting domestic groups with an 'up or down' choice – just as 'fast track' procedures are employed to speed trade agreements through the US Senate (Destler, 1986). Greater domestic agenda-setting power in the hands of national political leaders increases the ability of governments to reach agreements by strengthening the ability of governments to gain domestic ratification for compromises or tactical issue linkages. Whereas governments might be pressured for exemptions, oversight over implementation is placed instead in the hands of the more credible European and national court systems. Ironically, the EC's 'democratic deficit' may be a fundamental source of its success.

From the very beginning, much EC decision-making has been difficult to explain except as a two-level game. The reflexive support of both committed

---

[33] Marks argues, on the basis of an analysis of the structural and regional funds, that the EC is catalysing a process of diffusion, whereby the 'decisional powers' of the state are being shifted both to subnational and supranational authorities.

European federalists and those who favour the general economic goals of the EC greatly assisted the early development of specific EC policies. In the initial negotiation of the Treaty of Rome, the liberalization of French industrial trade offers a striking example. In the 1950s Germany, the hub of the European trading system, was engaging in *unilateral* tariff reductions. French exports to Germany were increasing rapidly with little evidence of any protectionist reaction across the Rhine (Milward, 1992). The major incentive for France to accept the EC was not to solve an international prisoner's dilemma by assuring access to the German market, as much modern trade theory would have it. Instead, as French leaders made clear at the time and de Gaulle was to reiterate even more forcefully, it was to employ the legitimacy of the EC to force French firms to modernize – a goal that French governments had been promoting for almost a decade without success (Institut Charles de Gaulle, 1986).

Today we are witnessing an analogous phenomenon, as the credibility of efforts to achieve macroeconomic convergence in countries like Italy and Spain is bolstered by the impression, deliberately exploited by member governments, that the imposition of anti-inflationary discipline is necessary for full involvement in Europe. To be sure, there is little evidence that member governments actually pursue macroeconomic stabilization for 'federalist' reasons, nor that European rhetoric actually reduces the economic cost of macroeconomic stabilization, nor that other EC policies are critically dependent on the achievement of monetary integration. It is plausible to argue, however, that the legitimacy of the EC may reduce the domestic *political* costs of imposing economic discipline. It follows that appeals to Europe should be less efficacious in countries, like the UK, where popular support for the EC is weaker, and more efficacious in countries, like Italy, where the EC enjoys legitimacy. Even among those countries more hostile to current EC policy, supranational institutions may play an important role as scapegoat for unpopular policies or undemocratic processes supported by member governments at the European level.

The proposed independent Eurofed offers a more recent example of the advantages of insulating agenda-setting policy implementation from domestic pressures – to an extent that has been widely criticized – in order to achieve goals that would otherwise be unachievable. Domestic control over exchange rate policy (as well as the legitimacy of European integration), has permitted German Chancellor Helmut Kohl to pursue a policy of monetary integration without the strong backing of either business or the Bundesbank, although the limits imposed by domestic consensus have subsequently become clear. In addition, the proposed European Central Bank will be doubly insulated from domestic pressures in a way designed to make the common European policy credible on domestic and international markets. The Maastricht referendum in France is an exception that proves the importance of secrecy and agenda-setting power, in that it demonstrates the potential consequences when governments lose firm control of domestic agendas or take needless risks in ratification.

## VI. Conclusion: Beyond Liberal Intergovernmentalism

The liberal intergovernmentalist view seeks to account for major decisions in the history of the EC by positing a two-stage approach. In the first stage, national preferences are primarily determined by the constraints and opportunities imposed by economic interdependence. In the second stage, the outcomes of intergovernmental negotiations are determined by the relative bargaining power of governments and the functional incentives for institutionalization created by high transaction costs and the desire to control domestic agendas. This approach is grounded in fundamental concepts of international political economy, negotiation analysis, and regime theory.

The net economic interests of producers and popular preferences for public goods provide a solid foundation for explaining agricultural policy and industrial trade liberalization, as well as socio-economic public goods provision, within the EC. These preferences tell us the goals of states, their alternatives, and – through the level of societal constraint on governments – the extent to which governments are willing to compromise. The distributional outcomes of intergovernmental negotiations are shaped by the unilateral and coalitional alternatives to agreement, as well as the opportunities for compromise and linkage.

Like other international regimes, EC institutions increase the efficiency of bargaining by providing a set of passive, transaction-cost reducing rules. But EC institutions cannot be explained entirely on the basis of existing regime theory. Instead, at least two other functions of international institutions need to be taken into account. First, EC institutions delegate and pool sovereignty, taking key decisions about linkage out of the hands of national governments. The delegation and pooling of authority in the EC can be explained by extending existing functional regime theory, which focuses on the reduction of transaction costs. Governments delegate authority and provide for qualified majority voting in order to increase the efficiency of bargaining at the expense of slightly increased political risk for domestic groups. While existing regime theory focuses on the risk of defection, the major concern of EC states tends to be the risk that the consequences of the agreement, even if all comply, will turn out to be less advantageous for key domestic groups than expected. Thus governments weigh the potential gains from co-operation against the domestic political risk. Second, EC institutions structure a 'two-level game', which increases the initiative and influence of national governments by providing legitimacy and domestic agenda-setting power for their initiatives. To explain this function, regime theory must be supplemented by theories of domestic politics and two-level games.

By bringing together theories of preferences, bargaining and regimes, liberal intergovernmentalism provides plausible accounts for many aspects of the major decisions in the history of the EC in a way that is sharply distinct from neo-functionalism. Where neo-functionalism emphasizes domestic technocratic consensus, liberal intergovernmentalism looks to domestic coalitional struggles. Where neo-functionalism emphasizes opportunities to upgrade the common interest, liberal intergovernmentalism stresses the role of relative power. Where neo-functionalism emphasizes the active role of supranational officials in shaping bargaining outcomes, liberal intergovernmentalism stresses instead passive institutions and the autonomy of national leaders. Ironically, the EC's 'democratic deficit' may be a fundamental source of its success.

Moreover, liberal intergovernmentalism provides explanations for some nagging anomalies inherited from neo-functionalism. Variation in the tightness of domestic societal constraints is employed to explain the disruptive role of dramatic-political actors and the distinction between those issues where linkage or compromise is possible and those in which log-rolling or lowest common denominator solution prevails. The distinction between positive and negative externalities helps explain which issues generate common solutions and spark geographical spillover, and which do not. The introduction of a 'two-level game' analysis explains why France sought industrial trade liberalization with Germany in the 1950s, despite the unilateral openness of the German economy at the time.

Critics may challenge the approach proposed here in three ways. First, they may dispute the basic framework, arguing that state behaviour is not purposive and instrumental, that preference formation does not precede the formulation of strategies, or that national preference and intergovernmental bargaining are so completely manipulated by supranational officials as to be meaningless categories. Second, they may challenge the liberal understanding of state preferences employed here, which draws on contemporary theories of economic interdependence to explain national preferences. Alternative conceptions of economic interest are certainly possible, as are (liberal and non-liberal) explanations based on ideology or geopolitics. Third, they may question the Intergovernmental theory of bargaining, with its stress on bargaining power rooted in unilateral alternatives, competing coalitions, the possibilities for linkage, and the controlled delegation of power to supranational institutions under conditions specified by functional theories of regimes and 'two-level' games views of domestic polities. Such debate is to be welcomed.

Yet few would go so far as to deny the importance of preferences and power altogether. Indeed, a strong liberal intergovernmentalist theory is widely seen as a precondition for the development of more complex theories of integration, such as neo-functionalism. Without explicit theories of state interests, interstate bargaining, and international regimes, it is impossible to determine when consequences are truly unintended, the common interest is truly being upgraded, or supranational officials are truly acting autonomously. This vindicates Haas's judgement that debate between *general* theories of domestic and international politics is necessary. Such a debate is surely preferable to a clash between 'intergovernmentalist' and 'supranationalist' ideal-types, without any specification of the conditions under which each might be expected to apply.

It is certainly true that liberal intergovernmentalism accords supranational institutions and officials less weight and prominence than neo-functionalism once did. Committed integrationists typically read such conclusions as a disparagement of the unique achievement and future potential of the EC. Yet the real achievement and hope of the Community may lie not in the transcendence of traditional state preferences and power, but in the underlying domestic and international forces that have shaped national preferences and power in the direction of greater co-operation. Liberal intergovernmentalism assimilates the EC to models of politics potentially applicable to all states, thereby specifying the conditions under which a similar process of integration may occur elsewhere.

## References

Aizenman, N. (1993) 'The European Parliament's Quest for Legislative Power: Conditions for Success'. Harvard University, undergraduate thesis.

Axelrod, R. and Keohane, R. (1986) 'Achieving Cooperation under Anarchy'. In Oye, K. A. (ed.), *Co-operation under Anarchy* (Princeton: Princeton University Press), pp. 226–54.

Bates, R. and Lien, H.D. (1985) 'A Note on Taxation, Development and Representative Government'. *Politics and Society,* Vol. 14, pp. 53–70.

Binmore, K. and Dasgupta, P. (1987) *The Economics of Bargaining* (Oxford: Blackwell).

Buchanan, J.M. and Tullock, G. (1962) *The Calculus of Consent: Logical Foundations of Constitutional Democracy* (Ann Arbor: University of Michigan Press).

Bulmer, S. (1986) *The Domestic Structure of European Community Policy-Making* (New York: Garland).

Burley, A.-M. and Mattli, W. (1993) 'Europe before the Court: A Political Theory of Legal Integration'. *International Organization,* Vol. 47, pp. 41–77.

Caporaso, J. and Keeler, J. (1983) *The European Community and Regional Integration Theory.* University of Washington, mimeo.

Coleman, J.S. (1990) *Foundations of Social Theory* (Cambridge, Mass.: Harvard University Press).

Cooper, R. N. (1972) 'Economic Interdependence and Foreign Policy in the Seventies'. *World Politics*, Vol. 24, January, pp. 159–81.

Cooper, R.N. (1986) 'Interdependence and Co-ordination of Policies'. In *Economic Policy in an Interdependence World: Essays in World Economics* (Cambridge, Mass.: MIT Press).

Cornett, L. and Caporaso, J.A. (1992) "And it Still Moves!'. State Interests and Social Forces in the European Community'. In Rosenau, J.N. and Czempiel, E.-O. (eds.), *Governance without Government: Order and Change in World Politics* (Cambridge: Cambridge University Press), pp. 219–49.

Destler, I.M. (1986) *American Trade Politics: Systems Under Stress* (New York: Institute for International Economics).

Dixit, A. and Nalebuff, B. (1991) *Thinking Strategically: The Competitive Edge in Business, Politics and Everyday Life* (New York: Norton).

Elster, J. (1986) 'Introduction'. In Elster, J. (ed.), *Rational Choice* (Cambridge: Cambridge University Press), pp. 1–33.

Fearon, J.D. (1991) 'Counterfactuals and Hypothesis Testing in Political Science'. *World Politics*, Vol. 43, pp. 169–95.

Frieden, J.A. (1991a) *Debt, Development and Democracy: Modern Political Economy and Latin America* (Princeton,N.J.: Princeton University Press).

Frieden, J.A. (1991b) 'Invested Interests: The Politics of National Economic Policies in a World of Global Finance'. *International Organization*, Vol. 45, pp. 425–52.

Garrett, G. (1992) 'Power Politics and European Integration'. Stanford, Cal.: Unpublished ms.

Garrett, G. and Weingast, B. (1991) 'Interests and Institutions: Constructing the EC's Internal Market'. Paper presented at the American Political Science Association Meeting, September.

George, S. (1985) *Politics and Policy in the European Community* (Oxford: Clarendon Press).

George, S. (1992) *Britain and the European Community: The Politics of Semi-Detachment* (Oxford: Clarendon Press).

George, S. (1993) 'Supranational Actors and Domestic Politics: Integration Theory Reconsidered in the Light of the Single European Act and Maastricht'. Sheffield, mimeo.

Gourevitch, P. (1978) 'The Second Image Reversed'. *International Organization*, Vol. 32, Autumn, pp. 881–912.

Gourevitch, P. (1986) *Politics in Hard Times: Comparative Responses to International Economic Crises* (Ithaca: Cornell University Press).

Grieco, J.M. (1988) 'Anarchy and the Limits of Cooperation: A Realist Critique of the Newest Liberal Institutionalism'. *International Organization*, Vol. 42, pp. 485–508.

Haas, E.B. (1958) *The Uniting of Europe: Political, Social and Economic Forces, 1950–1957* (Stanford, Cal.: Stanford University Press).

Haas, E.B. (1964a) 'Technocracy, Pluralism and the New Europe'. In Graubard, S.R. (ed.), *A New Europe?* (Boston: Houghton Mifflin), pp. 62–88.

Haas, E.B. (1964b) *Beyond the Nation State: Functionalism and International Organization* (Stanford: Stanford University Press).

Haas, E.B. (1966) 'International Integration: The European and the Universal Process'. In *International Political Communities: An Anthology* (New York: Doubleday), pp. 93–130.

Haas, E.B. (1967) '"The Uniting of Europe" and "The Uniting of Latin America"'. *Journal of Common Market Studies*, Vol. 5, pp. 315–44.

Haas, E.B. (1975) *The Obsolescence of Regional Integration Theory* (Berkeley, Cal.: Center for International Studies).

Haas, E.B. (1976) 'Turbulent Fields and the Theory of Regional Integration'. *International Organization*, Vol. 30, Spring, pp. 173–212.

Haas, E.B. and Schmitter, P.C. (1964) 'Economics and Differential Patterns of Political Integration: Projections about Unity in Latin America'. *International Organization*, Vol. 18, Autumn, pp. 705–37.

Hansen, R. (1969) 'Regional Integration: Reflections on a Decade of Theoretical Efforts'. *World Politics*, Vol. 21, pp. 242–71.

Harsanyi, J. (1977) *Rational Behaviour and Bargaining Equilibrium in Games and Social Situations* (Cambridge: Cambridge University Press).

Hillman, A.L. (1989) *The Political Economy of Protection* (New York: Harwood).

Hirschman, A.O. (1945) *National Power and the Structure of Foreign Trade* (Berkeley, Cal.: University of California Press).

Hirschman, A.O. (1970) *Exit, Voice and Loyalty: Responses to Decline in Firms, Organizations and States* (Cambridge, Mass.: Harvard University Press).

Hoffmann, S. (1966) 'Obstinate or Obsolete? The Fate of the Nation State and the Case of Western Europe'. *Daedalus*, No. 95, Summer, pp. 892–908.

Hoffmann, S. (1982) 'Reflections on the Nation-State in Western Europe Today'. *Journal of Common Market Studies*, Vol. 21, pp. 21–37.

Institut Charles de Gaulle (1986) *1958, La Faillite ou le miracle, Le Plan de Gaulle-Rueff* (Paris: Economica).

Institut Charles de Gaulle (1992) *De Gaulle en son siècle: moderniser la France* (Actes des Journées internationales tenues à l'Unesco, Paris, 19–24 November 1990, Vol. 3, Paris: Documentation Française).

Jervis, R. (1988) 'Realism, Game Theory and Cooperation'. *World Politics*, No. 40.

Keeney, R.L. and Raiffa, H. (1991) 'Structuring and Analysing Values for Multiple-issue Negotiations'. In Peyton Young, H. (ed.), *Negotiating Analysis* (Ann Arbor: University of Michigan Press), pp. 131–51.

Keohane, R.O. (1983) 'The Demand for International Regimes'. In Krasner, S.D. (ed.), *International Regimes* (Ithaca: Cornell University Press), pp. 325–55.

Keohane, R.O. (1984) *After Hegemony: Cooperation and Discord in the World Political Economy* (Princeton: Princeton University Press).

Keohane, R.O. and Hoffmann, S. (1991) 'Institutional Change in Europe in the 1980s'. In Keohane, R.O. and Hoffmann, S. (eds.), *The New European Community: Decision-Making and Institutional Change* (Boulder, Col.: Westview), pp. 1–40.

Keohane, R. and Nye, J.S. (1975) 'International Independence and Integration'. In
  Greenstein, F. and Polsby, N. (eds.), *Handbook of Political Science* (Andover,
  Mass.: Addison-Wesley), pp. 363–414.
Keohane, R. and Nye, J.S. (1977) *Power and Interdependence: World Politics in
  Transition* (Boston: Little, Brown).
Krasner, S.D. (1983) 'Structural Causes and Regime Consequences: Regimes as
  Intervening Variables'. In Krasner, S.D. (ed.), *International Regimes* (Ithaca:
  Cornell University Press), pp. 1–22.
Krasner, S.D. (1991) 'Global Communications and National Power: Life on the Pareto
  Frontier'. *World Politics*, Vol. 43, pp. 336–66.
Kremenyuk, V. (ed.) (1991) *International Negotiations, Analysis, Approaches, Issues*
  (San Francisco: Jossey-Bass).
Lavergne, R. (1983) *The Political Economy of US Tariffs: An Empirical Analysis* (New
  York: Academic Press).
Lax, D.A. and Sebenius, J.K. (1986) *The Manager as Negotiator: Bargaining for Co-
  operation and Competitive Gain* (New York: Free Press).
Levy, M. (1991) 'The Greening of the United Kingdom: An Assessment of Competing
  Explanations'. Paper presented at the 1991 APSA Convention, Cambridge, Mass.,
  mimeo.
Levy, M.A., Keohane, R.O. and Haas, P.M. (1992) 'Conclusions; Improving the
  Effectiveness of International Environmental Institutions'. Cambridge, Mass.,
  mimeo.
Lindberg, L.N. (1963) *The Political Dynamics of European Economic Integration*
  (Stanford, Cal.: Stanford University Press).
Lindberg, L.N. and Scheingold, S.A. (1970) *Europe's Would-Be Polity: Patterns of
  Change in the European Community* (Englewood Cliffs, N. J.: Prentice-Hall).
Lindberg, L.N. and Scheingold, S.A. (eds.) (1971) *Regional Integration: Theory and
  Research* (Cambridge, Mass.: Harvard University Press).
Lindblom, C.E. (1977) *Politics and Markets: The World's Political-Economic Systems*
  (New York: Basic Books).
Loriaux, M. (1991) *France after Hegemony: International Change and Financial
  Reform* (Ithaca: Cornell University Press).
Magee, S.P., Brock, W.A. and Young, L. (1989) *Black Hole Tariffs and Endogenous
  Political Theory: Political Economy in General Equilibrium* (Cambridge: Cam-
  bridge University Press).
Majone, G. (1992) 'Cross-National Sources of Regulatory Policy-making in Europe
  and the United States'. *Metroeconomica*, Vol.11, pp. 79–106.
Marks, G. (1991) 'Structural Policy, European Integration and the State'. Chapel Hill,
  N.C., University of North Carolina, mimeo.
Martin, L.L. (1992) *Coercive Cooperation: Explaining Multilateral Economic Sanc-
  tions* (Princeton, N.J.: Princeton University Press).
Milner, H.V. (1988) *Resisting Protectionism: Global Industry and the Politics of
  International Trade* (Princeton, N.J.: Princeton University Press).

Milward, A.S. (1992) *The European Rescue of the Nation-State* (Berkeley, Cal.: University of California Press).

Moravcsik, A. (1989) 'Disciplining Trade Finance: The OECD Export Credit Arrangement'. *International Organization*, Vol. 43, pp. 173–205.

Moravcsik, A. (1991) 'Negotiating the Single European Act: National Interests and Conventional Statecraft in the European Community'. *International Organization*, Vol. 45, Winter, pp. 19–56.

Moravcsik, A. (1992a) *National Preference Formation and Interstate Bargaining in the European Community, 1955–86* (Cambridge, Mass.: Harvard University Press).

Moravcsik, A. (1992b) Liberalism and International Relations Theory. Harvard University, CFIA Working Paper No. 92–6.

Moravcsik, A. (1993) 'Armaments among Allies: Franco-German Weapons Cooperation, 1975–1985'. In Evans, P.B., Jacobson, H.K. and Putnam, R.D. (eds.), *Double-Edged Diplomacy: International Bargaining and Domestic Politics* (Berkeley, Cal.: University of California Press).

Nye, J.S. (ed.) (1968) *International Regionalism* (Boston: Little, Brown).

Nye, J. (1971) *Peace in Parts: Integration and Conflict in Regional Organization* (Boston: Little, Brown).

Odell, J.S. (1982) *U.S. International Monetary Policy* (Princeton, N.J.: Princeton University Press).

Olson, M. (1965) *The Logic of Collective Action: Public Goods and the Theory of Groups* (Cambridge, Mass.: Harvard University Press).

Pederson, T. (1992) 'Political Change in the European Community: The Single European Act as a Case of System Transformation'. In Kelstrup, M. (ed.), *European Integration and Denmark's Participation* (Copenhagen: Copenhagen Political Studies Press), pp. 184–209.

Pentland, C. (1973) *International Theory and European Integration* (New York: Free Press).

Pescatore, P. (1981) 'Les travaux du "Groupe juridique" dans la négotiation des Traités de Rome'. *Studia Diplomatica*, Vol. 34, pp. 159–78.

Peterson, J. and Bomberg, E. (1993) 'Decision-making in the European Union: A Policy Networks Approach', York, mimeo.

Puchala, D. (1972) 'Of Blind Men, Elephants and International Integration'. *Journal of Common Market Studies*, Vol. 10, pp. 267–85.

Putnam R.D. (1988) 'Diplomacy and Domestic Politics'. *International Organization*, Vol. 42, pp. 427–61.

Raiffa, H. (1982) *The Art and Science of Negotiation* (Cambridge, Mass.: Harvard University Press).

Rogowski, R. (1989) *Commerce and Coalitions: How Trade Affects Domestic Political Alignments* (Princeton, N.J.: Princeton University Press).

Ross, G. (1992) 'European Community Politics and the New Europe'. Cambridge, Mass., mimeo.

Sandholtz, W. (1992) *High-Tech Europe: The Politics of International Co-operation* (Berkeley, Cal: University of California Press).

Schmitter, P. (1971) A Revised Theory of Regional Integration'. In Lindberg and Scheingold (eds.), pp. 232–64.

Sebenius, J.K. (1991) 'Negotiation Analysis'. In Kremenyuk, V. (ed.), pp. 203–15.

Shepsle, K. (1992) 'Congress is a "They", Not an "It": Legislative Intent as Oxymoron'. *International Review of Law and Economics*, Vol. 12, pp. 239–56.

Taylor, P. (1983) *The Limits of European Integration* (London: Croom Helm).

Tsebelis, G. (1992) 'The Power of the European Parliament as a Conditional Agenda Setter'. Paper presented at the Annual Meeting of the American Political Science Association, September.

Vogel, D. (1992) 'Environmental Protection and the Creation of a Single European Market'. Berkeley, Cal., mimeo.

Von der Groben, H. (1982) *Aufbaujahre der europäischen Gemeinschaft: Das Ringen um den Gemeinsamen Markt und die politische Union (1958–1966)* (Baden-Baden: Nomos).

Wallace, H., Wallace, W. and Webb, C. (1983) *Policy-making in the European Community* (2nd edn) (Chichester: Wiley).

Webb, C. (1983) 'Theoretical Perspectives and Problems'. In Wallace *et al.* (1983), pp. 1–42.

Zartman, W.I. (1991) 'The Structure of Negotiation'. In Kremenyuk, V. (ed.), pp. 65–77.

# Comment on Moravcsik

LEON N. LINDBERG

This is a very rich, dense and elegantly reasoned article which deserves much closer reading and a much more reasoned comment than I am able to give it. To those of you who are familiar with Moravcsik's past work (1991a, b), this piece develops further, fills in and fleshes out the category of liberal intergovernmentalism which remains somewhat obscure in those two previous works. This article is also richly informed by detailed empirical analysis and knowledge of EC politics and policies.

The development of the article is based on a careful and quite fair critique of neo-functionalism, as well as a critique of realism and liberal institutionalist approaches to the EC. As Moravcsik said at the end, his goal is to set up situations in which theories can be sufficiently specified to be tested against plausible alternatives. He challenges those who want a neo-functionalist emphasis to specify adequately, and he is quite right that that body of theorizing has not done that. He is also quite right, I think, in the emphasis he puts on the cost of the neglect of the EC by mainstream international relations theories.

I particularly liked this article from my current perspective as a retired neo-functionalist. I have only recently returned to study the EC after doing other things for 20 years and in doing so I have been looking for points of re-entry that would be different from the place I left it two decades ago. When I think back to where neo-functionalists were in 1970 – for instance the books Stuart

Scheingold and I wrote on Europe's 'would-be polity' and the theory volume
(Lindberg and Scheingold, 1970, 1971) – we were launched on an internal
debate. We were incorporating elements of intergovernmentalism; we were
rejecting the automaticity of integration in the early theories; we were talking
about the symbiosis of supranationalism and intergovernmentalism. We had
abandoned the idea of linear progression and indeed I had projected an extended
period of stasis: a plateau or equilibrium.

In fact, the results of that theoretical discourse which we had started in 1970
were probably indeterminate in that the theories were underspecified. However,
we did not have at that time the theories that Moravcsik has been able to draw
on. I think we took the debate as far as we could, but it was in no sense closed.
Now Moravcsik stresses that the discourse in a sense was broken off, that
integration theorizing became detached from the main body of political economy, co-operation theory and international theory, and I agree that was a pity.

I found on returning to this literature – I am looking at what appeared
between 1970 and 1990 – that surprisingly the neo-functionalism that was
portrayed was a kind of caricature, a kind of straw man. It was not the theory we
thought we were working on when we laid down our pens and turned it over to
our students. It was not reflecting the directions in which we thought we were
moving and I think, thanks to Moravcsik's work and that of others, that
discourse is now rejoined. Thus a trajectory is re-established and I think this
article is especially important because it opens up the possibilities of continuing
the discourse about integration theory. In particular, it also opens up the
possibility of joining a discourse between political scientists and economists
and lawyers: something which remains a great problem in integration studies.
I think Moravcsik develops his argument in a language which is very amenable
to this kind of discourse.

Now let me comment a little as an institutionalist instead of as a
neo-functionalist. What I have been working on is an attempt to join a discourse
between institutionalists' and rationalists' theories of political economy, in
particular in some work on the historical development of the American economy (Campbell et al., 1991). By institutionalism I mean what Peter Hall means
by institutionalism (Hall, 1986), or Steven Krasner (1988), namely the discourse between institutionalists' and rationalists' analyses.

I think there is a clear route that leads from neo-functionalism to an interest
in institutionalism or 'new institutionalism'. Thinking about Moravcsik's piece
from that perspective, I would not surprisingly give more weight to supranational institutions than Moravcsik. And I think he might do too, within the logic of
his own approach. I am not sure it is necessary to maintain a distinction between
liberal institutionalism and liberal intergovernmentalism but that may be
necessary for career construction! I think what is involved is a difference in

taste: my taste is for slightly more comprehensive theories and I think Moravc-sik's taste is for more sharply focused or, as he would put it, less ambitious ones.

But let me take two examples from the paper that I think will suffice. First, in Moravcsik's discussion of 'interdependence and national preference forma-tion' there is an excellent discussion of the circumstances under which state political elites or leaders can gain *relative* autonomy from social pressures (producer groups and electorates) in the course of EC bargaining. This analysis draws very nicely on the political economy literature on the autonomy of the state and state–society relations. He specifies these things which he has talked about – intra-sectoral splits which permit political leaders to play off sectoral interests against one another, uncertainty about costs and benefits that permits leaders to delay politicization, diffusion of interests permitting costs to be shifted to unorganized groups, and issue linkages which permit politicians to mobilize opposing constituencies. He might have said something about the manipulation of rates of time preference, which is another way in which political leaders can get autonomy. Rates of time preference refers to the discount rates that actors use in cost–benefit calculations. As Cohen points out, 'any value attached to the future is in the eye of the beholder' and can 'in principle be revised' (Cohen, 1989).

Of course, exactly the same analysis can be applied to an understanding of the relative autonomy of the Commission in this process of national interest formation! This is, of course, what neo-functionalists were trying to do or what I think I was certainly trying to do. Institutionalists talk about the role of institutions in determining interests, in influencing the process of interest perception or the formation of interest when it comes to the analysis of national economic policy-making. This is true in Peter Hall's work to take a solid, empirical case (Hall, 1986). Similarly, I think the Commission has some ability to play the same game; in a sense you can talk about the relative autonomy of the Commission. The Commission obviously depends upon the governments' positions. However, I am not so sure that governments' interest perceptions are so autonomous of the Commission, which is playing with some of those same factors.

A second example, which is similar, relates to bargaining and intensity of national preferences and opportunity cost of non-agreement and lowest com-mon denominator outcomes. I think this issue of lowest common denominator outcomes is really important: whether you can talk about splitting the difference and upgrading common interests at all within Moravcsik's framework, I am not sure. Again I think his approach assumes that governments can find an agreement. All of these approaches of a rationalist kind tend to reason back-wards: the outcome is obvious once you understand the underlying distribution of preferences, or of preference orderings.

I really do not think that is the case. I think that governments perhaps do not really know what their preferences are. Even if they do, it is not clear that they can find an area of agreement. We know that positions are not stable. We know that in certain cases a proposal, a well-chosen proposal from the Commission, can change the whole nature of bargains and bring in new issues. In that sense I think in a system like the EC, in which intergovernmentalism is as much a process of integration as is supranational behaviour – because I think that was an argument that neo-functionalists were clearly making, at least in 1970 – everyone is locked into a system in which the costs of failure are fairly high. And it is not so clear that you can find those package deals. I do not think governments know how to put them together. I do not think governments know how to discern exactly the point at which the others will agree. I think that is a function which could easily be theorized in Moravcsik's framework or in a similar one.

Let me make one final point. The kind of analysis that Moravcsik's article presents, which is a form of rationalist analysis, can be very powerful especially when it is combined with institutional analysis, and especially when it is based on a deep knowledge of the issue areas. I think of the work of Fritz Scharpf, for example his classical article on the decision trap (Scharpf, 1988). Other work that Scharpf has done is powerful, not because he has a rational actor point of departure, but because he is well informed on his subject and has a solid institutional basis from which to operate. The danger of rationalist forms of analysis, particularly done by Americans, is that it is very easy to do this without ever setting foot in Europe or without ever learning anything about the EC and the details of the issue areas.

This is not at all a problem with Moravcsik's work because his analysis is steeped in an empirical understanding of what is going on. I think Europeans find themselves in this position of knowing a great deal about what is going on but not really having a strong set of theoretical tools to make sense of it, so I hope we can have a nice transatlantic discourse in this kind of area. I think the potential of this is greater and I have always been devoted to a kind of Weberian approach to theory building in which you move back and forth between theory and detailed empirical analysis.

I think Moravcsik does that. I think neo-functionalists wanted to do that. And I obviously think that is the way forward.

# References

Campbell, J.L., Lindberg, L. N. and Hollingsworth, J.R. (eds.) (1991) *Governance of the American Economy* (Cambridge: Cambridge University Press).

Cohen, B. J. (1989) 'European Financial Integration and National Banking Interests'. In Guerrieri, P. and Padoan, P. (eds.) *The Political Economy of European Integration* (New York: Harvester Wheatsheaf).

Hall, P. A. (1986) *Governing the Economy: the Politics of State Intervention in Britain and France* (Cambridge: Polity Press).

Krasner, S. (1988) 'Sovereignty: An Institutional Perspective', *Comparative Political Studies*, Vol. 21, pp. 66–94.

Lindberg, L. N. and Scheingold, S. A. (1970) *Europe's Would-Be Polity: Patterns of Change in the European Community* (Englewood Cliffs, N.J.: Prentice-Hall).

Lindberg, L. N. and Scheingold, S. A. (eds.) (1971), *Regional Integration: Theory and Research* (Cambridge, Mass: Harvard University Press).

Moravcsik, A. (1991a) 'Negotiating the Single European Act: National Interests and Conventional Statecraft in the Euroepan Community', *International Organization*, Vol. 45, No. 1, pp. 651–88.

Moravcsik, A. (1991b) 'Negotiating the Single European Act'. In Keohane, R. and Hoffmann, S. (eds.) *The New European Community: Decisionmaking and Institutional Change* (Boulder, Col.: Westview), pp. 41–84.

Scharpf, F. (1988) 'The Joint-Decision Trap: Lessons From German Federalism and European Integration', *Public Administration*, Vol. 66, pp. 229–78.

# 3.
# European Governance in Turbulent Times

HELEN WALLACE

## I. Introduction

European governance in general has come under fire in the 1990s, not just the governance of the European Community (EC). The old polities of western Europe are brittle, while the new polities of central and eastern Europe are under test. The issues for both analysts and practitioners are whether the problems of western Europe are cyclical or structural, and to what extent the EC is itself a source of the recent malaise as distinct from the underlying alteration in the context in which the EC is situated. The signs that are visible are of a 'renationalization' of politics in western Europe, alongside a 'denationalization' of the real economy under pressures of global markets, in which so many economic actors have become politically rootless.

It has to be recalled that the origins of the EC lay precisely in an attempt to build hopes of better governance for (western) Europe through the integration project. This was the clear aspiration of the protagonists and swiftly identified by the early integration theorists as crucial to the process. Two features of the integration experiment were identified in this regard: the opportunity that integration might provide for innovation and 'progress'; and the value of appeals to the shadow of a better future. Both were identified as necessary for the participants to be willing to sustain burdens as well as to extract gains. Both required that the participants be prepared to invest in institution and regime-

© Basil Blackwell Ltd 1994, 108 Cowley Road, Oxford OX4 1JF, UK and 238 Main Street, Cambridge, MA 02142, USA

building, as well as in devising packages of susbstantive measures. These features of the EC process are common ground to a wide range of analysts, from those who have seen integration as a means to bypass the nation-state to those who have interpreted the EC experiment as a vehicle for restoring the resilience of the nation-state.

To put these last points in slightly different terms, the integration experiment was focused on efforts to project 'cosmopolitanism' as preferable to 'parochialism' – the early language was about antidotes to nationalism, or at least counterproductive forms of nationalism – and to persuade participants to be extrovert and not introvert. For these purposes the encapsulation of sustainable collaboration within a robust framework of institutions was viewed as crucial. Those would require repeated investments in institution-building, until a new form of polity emerged. The statists, on the contrary, expected such investments to be limited and to leave the 'hard core' of the nation-state intact.

Whichever model of analysis is preferred, the empirical evidence of recent times has been characterized as much by disinvestment in institutions as about new investment. Or at least the terms of Maastricht, the Treaty on European Union and the debates over its ratification, can be interpreted as easily as marking efforts to set a ceiling on, even roll back, the forces of supranationalism as they can be seen as crossing a new threshold on the route towards a European transnational polity. The reasons for the cogency of such an interpretation lie not simply in the EC-level debate, but also in the changes that have taken place within individual European countries. As Milward (1992) has argued, the origins of the EC belong to a period of remarkable extensions in state power within Western Europe, as governments extended their grasp over economic and social arenas. In contrast, the trends of the 1980s and early 1990s have been towards the 'privatization of public space'. The UK, with over a decade of fierce privatization and reduced welfare provision behind it, may be an extreme case, but the reduction of public functions and of the citizen's dependence on the state has become a common theme of political debates and public policy in many west European countries.

## II. Competing Perspectives on Reform

The history of the EC has been of continuous jostling between integrationist and intergovernmentalist pressures. The constitutional documents, institutional structures and discussions of policy competences have persistently reflected this competition of perspectives. The texts of both the Single European Act (SEA) and of the Treaty on European Union (TEU) reflect this antithesis. Yet the SEA tilted towards the more integrationist, while the TEU tilted towards the more intergovernmentalist, each in two senses as regards, first, key concepts and, second, crucial procedures. The SEA focused its treaty amendments on two 'communitarian' themes, namely the unification of the Single Market and the establishment of the principle of cohesion. Crucial procedures established in both areas confirmed new mechanisms for sustaining these policy goals, mechanisms that gave all the EC institutions opportunities for greater impact *vis-à-vis* the institutions of the Member States.

In contrast, the TEU made more explicit the language of states' rights, through the extended references to subsidiarity, and of intergovernmentalism, as the integrity of the Community method was weakened by the many ambiguities in the TEU text as to when and whether a shift might be made from an intergovernmental mode to a communitarian mode. The presence of 'passerelle' clauses to permit such a shift retained options for further supranational integration, but attached conditions and thresholds that would have to be agreed for the various 'passerelles' to be used. Moreover the 'opt-in'/'opt-out' vocabulary that came to be associated with the TEU and its subsequent 'clarification' at the European Council in Edinburgh in December 1992 at the very least reflected these ambiguities in the texts.

In the Intergovernmental Conferences (IGCs), in 1985 and 1991, the participants wittingly set aside explicit debate on the fundamental antithesis between integration and intergovernmentalism, preferring to pursue their objectives in the debates about incremental additions to the Treaties, rather than a recasting of the basic framework. There was, after all, another option on each occasion, namely to draft a 'constitution' for the EC, as some in the European Parliament argued on each occasion, with varying degrees of support from the Benelux and Italian governments. Instead, however, the 1985 IGC (promoted partly by the results of the sifting process conducted by the Dooge Committee) did not deal with the issues of, for example, the residual right to veto under the Luxembourg Compromise, or the role of the Commission.

Similarly the 1991 IGC on political union deliberately sought to leave 'the balance between the institutions' undisturbed (to echo the comments of many of those involved), while grafting on additional pillars and, in practice, rather modest alterations to the EC proper. This is not to prejudge the eventual impact of the TEU changes to the powers of the European Parliament, which some believe to be of serious potential significance. However, the TEU text in particular neither enhanced the powers of the Commission nor provided ratchets for its reform. Nor did it address at all the issue of whether the Council's methods of functioning should be revised beyond the extensions of qualified majority voting. And the essence of the inherited 'balance' between the Council and the Commission was left as it was. In any case the severe division between the integrationists and the vehemently determined intergovernmentalists from the UK (and, as we subsequently discovered, from Denmark) made it very difficult for a discussion about improving the governance of the EC itself to be pursued – *vide* the fate of the more radical Dutch text on the 'Black Monday' in September 1991, when not even the Belgians and Luxemburgers were ready to support their Dutch colleagues. Ironically it was not until after the negative Danish referendum result of June 1992 that EC governments came to admit that malfunctions in the Council and the Commission needed to be addressed, a task which they approached sideways on at the Edinburgh European Council in the non-treaty form of muddled exhortation.

The language of the 1991 IGC was of political union, but without systematic discussion of the EC 'polity'. The term 'political' was hijacked by the debate on foreign and security policy as the essence of the political, a curious distortion of language long embedded in EC vocabulary. Meanwhile, in the debate in the parallel IGC on economic and monetary union, core political and governance issues were addressed, but subsumed within the detailed texts on the degree of independence of the proposed European Central Bank and the processes for handling convergence criteria. In this respect critics of Maastricht have been right to point out that a key issue of political authority was being swept along under cover of an expert debate on strategies for achieving a single currency.

### III. The Apparent Problem

The apparent problem for the EC in 1992–3 was the ratification of the Treaty of Maastricht, a document negotiated in a room without windows, into which public opinion had subsequently bulldozed its unwelcome and critical presence. The irony was that in the closing months of 1992, the EC and its Member States should have been in festive mood, celebrating the achievement of a real and important goal and poised to exploit the competitive advantage of a unified market. Indeed, the EC members were scheduled to be joined in this same enterprise on 1 January 1993 by seven EFTA countries sharing the same European Economic Area (EEA). The persistent controversy in Denmark and the UK over Maastricht left European Union seriously at risk, whether *tout court* or for all 12 Member States remained to be seen, as some spoke of a fast-track Union for the really committed. Yet the ripples of criticism of Maastricht in other EC countries, notably France and Germany, suggested a more widespread problem and found the defenders of the TEU advocating its approval less as virtuous in itself and more as the least worst option available. The Swiss referendum of December 1992, rejecting the EEA, put the parallel treaty also at risk. Indeed in early 1993 it was still unclear when this would be ratified in several EC countries.

Meanwhile politicians and policy-makers struggled to get the old show back on the road – work was still needed to make a functioning reality of the Single

Market and its external trade regime awaited renewal in the GATT – and to hang on to some kind of future agenda. The British and Danes between them, familiar harbingers of dissent about integration, kept the rest of the Community waiting. The Commission, visibly beleaguered and with a curtailed two-year term of office, grappled with palliatives, but was ill-placed to provide active leadership. The pressures of the electoral cycles and domestic preoccupations of several, even most, EC member governments were additional distractions.

Some attached great expectations to the refinement of the concept of subsidiarity as perhaps offering a golden key to unlock the problem. During 1992 it became something of a cure-all in British political discourse and the conclusions of the Edinburgh European Council, under a troubled British presidency, added some textual footage to the subsidiarity discussion. An alternative solution was canvassed in the mutterings about a 'two-tier' Community, but it did not produce a conceptual reformulation, perhaps because it was mainly cover for the potential marginalization of the dissident British and Danes. The fashionable talk was about openness and transparency, notions that some believed might provide antidotes to the 'neo-Gaullist' vocabulary of national independence, national interest and national identify. Yet the opacity of the EC stemmed more from the reluctance to confront the results of disjointed incrementalism in the overall institutional framework than from particular procedural deficiencies.

Outside the deliberative chambers in which the politicians continued their arcane discourse on these issues, the west European economy was strained by recession, one set to last some time before a recovery would be sustainable. Much was left dependent on the recovery of the UK and German economies. Distributional issues hung in the discussion of the budget and cohesion, but also echoed wider concerns about who would emerge as the winners and losers from the Single Market. The immediate issues were resolved with the agreement at Edinburgh on the Delors-II package, but there was no agreement on an economic recovery package. To the extent that any solutions to this were on the table, they were old solutions, not new ones – some combination of growth incentives and investment in public works and infrastructure.

The debate about both the politics and the economics of the integration project had a very familiar ring. Yes, there was a problem and the economic climate was rough, but this was a bad point in the cycle. Given time and patience to reach a more favourable point in the cycle, there was a chance of regaining familiar ground. Intergovernmentalists and integrationists alike, neo-liberals and adherents of European *Ordnungspolitik* alike, all hoped that what would follow from the period of malaise would be their own prior view vindicated and resilient. No new prescription was on the table, rather a clutch of familiar and competing remedies.

## IV. The Real Problem

The real problem may well lie elsewhere and go beyond the issue of ratifying the TEU. It perhaps consists of four different elements: economic sustainability, political sustainability, the shadows of the past and the shadows of the future. Each of these touches issues *within* EC countries, as well as issues *between* EC countries, and all are touched by circumstances elsewhere in Europe and in the wider international environment.

First, then, the economic sustainability of the west European economy in its old guise is at issue, given the evidence of structural change. A combination of different production patterns, demographic shifts, globalization of financial markets and severe international competition was throwing into question the capability of west European economics, individually and collectively, to regenerate and adapt. The project to establish the Single Market was designed precisely to address some of the consequences, with, for some, EMU as the next logical step. Yet the Single Market was still dependent on the emergence of a governance system capable of implementing its new rules and of ensuring that recession did not produce a new version of non-tariff barrier protectionism or, more crudely, non-compliance with the rules. On this it should be noted both that the recent Sutherland Report only touched the surface of the governance issue, and that the subsidiarity debate was producing pressures for a 'nationalization' of the implementation process (Sutherland Report, 1992). On this last there is an important distinction to be drawn between a sensible decentralization of enforcement mechanisms and the fragmentation of executive responsibilities. Much of the burden will be left, not for the first time in the EC's history, on the judicial system of the EC.

As for EMU, the EC confronted in 1992–3 both major obstacles to the EMU project itself and challenges to the viability of the European Monetary System. But other issues have hardly been addressed. The 'social dimension', a source of strident controversy, would need to be pursued in very different terms to deal with the fall-out from neo-liberal policies or to tackle the 'post-Fordism' type of analysis. Meanwhile the consequences of demographic shifts risked being encapsulated in a hysterical debate about immigration and asylum that, quite apart from its political repercussions, was likely to miss the point about changing patterns of labour and mobility and the inverted age pyramid of western Europe. Here again the question of how far the EC can be a source of innovative debate is crucial, particularly if the redefinition of the post-war welfare state is the real question on the table. Some people in the European Commission have been thinking about precisely these issues. What remains to be seen is whether they will have the opportunity to develop debate and proposals in this field.

Second, the political sustainability of several west European polities was in crucial respects open to question, and all were subject to challenges to the post-war patterns. To summarize a subject that deserves much more extended treatment: the gap between governors and governed is visible in most west European countries. Declining membership of, confidence in, and loyalty to political parties are structural shifts, as the mismatch between socio-economic profile and political channels of representation have grown. The reduced resonance for left-of-centre parties is also evident, complicated by the lost credibility of socialist ideologies since the collapse of communism. New social and political movements are jostling for political space, both the more benign, e.g. ecological, and the more malign, extreme right and racist. In some 'nation-states' there is declining attachment to the established political territory and state structures, as regional movements assert themselves.

Meanwhile – labels for the causes vary – corporatism or sectorization or complexity and overload – or perhaps simply a political vacuum – permit vested and special interests often to exercise a very tight grip on particular areas of politics and policy. This phenomenon is not new to western Europe, where regulatory capture, clientelism and powerful veto groups have in varying degrees been recognized as relevant features of the political process. However, the weakening of other channels for aggregating interests and securing political arbitrage makes individual polities more prone to such influences. Moreover the EC, with its particularly weak forms of broader political accountability and its peculiarly obscure processes of decision-making, perhaps lends itself to the effective intrusion of special interest into the policy process. The results may be more or less benign. Some see scope for the legitimation of EC policies directly through the groups that are most directly engaged and affected. Others identify the disproportionate influence of particular groups on EC policies as inimical to the pursuit of wider public interests. Either way there is an important issue of core politics that deserves more extended assessment, particularly in relation to the development of mechanisms to regulate the Single Market.

Some of these debates are the result of recession, but many have longer histories and political roots. The EC system is built in the image of the old consensus about political representation, political process and the definition of public goods, some of which might be better provided, so the argument went, by EC-level policies. Yet the EC system was also handicapped from the outset by being only a partial polity, without an independent legitimacy or direct political authority. Part of the political vacuum which this left at the EC level was seen by both practitioners and theorists as an advantage, precisely because it left space for a combination of benevolent technocrats and interest-propelled economic groups to build transnational coalitions in support of European policies and to undermine the scope for national policies. Yet the persistence of the political vacuum has been aggravated by the drive to establish a single market and competitive European firms on the back of an alliance with business, including a very close alliance with particular firms. There is a political distortion which follows from the very privileged access of these special interests to the EC policy process and a lack of balance between public interest and private interests. It is no coincidence that the Commission is currently being driven to establish a code for lobbying. It is significant that some 20 per cent of Commission staff are 'irregulars', far removed from the Weberian model, many of these irregulars being drawn from the private sector and with some functions of policy implementation now farmed out to the large army of consultants clustered round Brussels.

These questions also take on a different complexion as the definition of the boundary between the public sphere and the private sphere – the other side of the subsidiarity coin – alters and is contested. The post-Second World War consensus on what constitutes a public good has been disturbed, as is evident in the areas of education, health and such like, as well as the more economic areas of activity. In the early years of the EC, the reach of the individual west European state was sufficiently extensive to produce rather long lists of agreed or potentially agreeable public goods. Thus policy-makers at the EC level rarely had to make a case for public policy as such and could rather concentrate their attentions on which variant of policy might be advocated at the EC level and efforts to justify the EC as the appropriate level at which to set policy. By the 1990s it had become much less clear what could be widely agreed as a public good at all, thus making it much harder to run the argument for additional policy roles and functions at the EC level. The single market process for a time appeared neatly to avoid the issue by shifting to the vocabulary of deregulation. But the implied abnegation of intrusive public power distracted attention from the corollary task of investing in institutional capabilities to execute regulatory responsibilities. Nor was this an issue which claimed attention in the negotiations over the TEU.

Third, the shadows of the past no longer provide the driving force for integration that they once did. Indeed the shadow of the past as regards Germany was supposed to be one of the drivers of the plan for European Political Union, but turned out to be too insubstantial. Fears about a strengthened German neighbour have played a part in both Danish and French public debates and electoral preference, but not so as to make intensified integration seem the necessary remedy. The very mundaneness of the 'normalization' of the unified Germany made such fears seem a little unreal, concerned though many may be about a Germany overstretched politically and economically by the burden of its eastern Länder. This burden also deprives German leaders of some of the old incentives to invest in west European integration.

Nor has the Soviet shadow of the past been replaced by any comparable shadow of external aggression within Europe or towards Europe. However many potential threats to European security may now be identified, there is no consensus of analysis over either particular threats or their intensity to propel political cohesion or a common defence identity. The debate is left to cerebral and arcane debate amongst the expert ranks with little resonance in the wider political arena. While there is much room for debate about how far the old dynamics of European integration depended on 'external federators', it is not contested that external factors were important or that the overhang of both the Second World War and the Cold War contributed greatly to west European solidarity and provided over-arching arguments against the temptations of parochialism.

Then there is the shadow of the future. Much of the bedrock of the original European integration came from the attachment to it of aspirations about a future that could be made better than the past. The EC was seen as a provider of innovation and renewal, both economically and politically. It provided opportunities to exploit a new political arena that would counteract narrow and over-competitive national interests, to deliver needed policies of economic stabilization and prosperity and to offer the prospects of political and economic modernization.

Some of the shadow of the future that might be identified as a successor provider of aspirations for Community solidarity no doubt would have to address the socio-economic agenda. The debate about immigration might emerge as a favoured candidate, given the inclination of several EC governments to pass the buck to the Community. Yet it has to be asked whether a Community built on such foundations would be wise, if the resulting policy proved to be essentially xenophobic and religiously or racially discriminatory. The Maastricht debate sought to set up the Common Foreign and Security Policy as a desirable shadow for the future and for an investment in solidarity. So far it has not generated the resonance and support that would be required to leverage an investment in building further integration.

The question which hangs in the air is whether a stabilized, secure and reasonably prosperous Europe is what would have to be defined as the key goal in order to attract the continuing solidarity and sense of political purpose which would be needed, either to reassert the place for the EC in Europe or to move to the next phase of confrontation between integrationists and intergovernmentalists. So far most of the orthodox integrationists have preferred to stress a deepening of integration among the Twelve, while the British, the most explicit intergovernmentalists, have argued the case for the wider Europe on grounds that have been perceived as subversive.

But this debate may be shifting, in that there are some signs that the Germans have concluded that deepening and enlargement have to be corollaries and that there are at least some in Paris who have moved towards the same conclusions. On this argument the enlargement debate now about the EFTA states and the partnership debate about Central and Eastern Europe will be crucial barometers of where the static and dynamic forces of integration may be found. After all it will be in the light of these that the next IGC will be convened.

Attached to this debate is another very important issue of how west European public opinion will line up on the issue of Community goals that relate to the incorporation of those other Europeans into the family, especially since this cannot be achieved without sacrifice. Bosnia was perhaps a more important challenge for European governance than most west European political leaders seemed to appreciate. The stabilization of the rest of Central and Eastern Europe may be an equally important test – as Saryusz-Wolski has argued in Chapter 1, an economic Yalta may be a scenario that needs to be addressed much more explicitly to assess the 'cost of half-Europe'

## V. The EC – A Lop-sided Political Regime

To summarize on the weaknesses of the EC that have become evident: technocracy and an elite-driven process seem no longer an adequate basis for EC governance. The gap between governed and governors within and between countries is serious and created havoc in the debate about Maastricht to which technical and legalistic devices seem an inappropriate response. The EC is too convenient a scapegoat. Regulatory capture is endemic and stifles certain kinds of policy development. The privatization of public space and the dissensus about European public goods make it much harder for the EC to retain effective footholds.

The shadows of a troubled future are visible: parochialism versus cosmopolitanism; enlargement and Eastern Europe versus the self-interests embedded in current Community policies; the question marks about the need for German resilience; the competition between immediate material interests and historic reconstruction. For a form of sustainable European governance to emerge that would address this agenda would indeed be demanding. It would require more than marginal adjustment within the existing Member States of the EC, countries that are also faced with domestic challenges of governance.

## References

Millward, A.S. (1992) *The European Rescue of the National-State* (London: Routledge).
Sutherland Report (Report to the EEC Commission by the High Level Group on the Operation of Single Market) (1992) *The Internal Market After 1992: Meeting the Challenge* (Brussels: CEC).

# Comment on Wallace

BRIGID LAFFAN

There are many unresolved analytical and conceptual questions about the nature of the EC polity, the driving forces of integration and the dynamics of the integration process. The emphasis in the Wallace article on European governance and the Community as a governance structure is to be welcomed. The Community's part-formed political system represents governance without government. A focus on governance enables us to analyse the nature of the EC polity and should lead us to examine the EC in terms of comparative public policy and comparative politics. This is a useful corrective on the approach that views the Community as simply one of many forms of intergovernmental policy co-operation in the world. The Wallace article brings sharply into focus the great challenges facing European governance in these turbulent times. My comments will focus on two themes that surface in the article, namely, the Community's capacity and legitimacy deficits, and on two issues that are not treated, nationalism and regionalism.

## Better Governance

The article rightly draws our attention at the outset to the importance of a shared objective to the integration project. Integration was about better governance. The resurgence of formal integration in the EC from the mid-1980s onwards was equally dependent on what Keohane and Hoffmann term the 'preference convergence' model which allowed for agreement on a deregulatory project. Without common goals the integration project will falter. A single currency and the aspiration towards a common foreign and security policy were to provide the political cement for integration in the 1990s. The Maastricht ratification debate, the crisis in the Balkans and turbulence in the financial markets undermined the credibility of these goals.

The Wallace article is organized around an analysis of the cyclical or structural nature of the governance challenges facing Europe. The central conclusion is that these challenges are indeed structural. What the article fails to do is to distinguish carefully enough between challenges facing the integration project and the underlying political, social and economic realities. Many of the issues raised relate to fundamental issues of economy and society in Europe. European integration went hand-in-hand with the enhancement of the state's role in economic governance and as orchestrator of a new class compromise and social consensus (Milward, 1992, pp. 20–45). The breakdown of the post-war golden age has placed a severe strain on the 'European polity' and its model of social provision.

Deregulation and the growing internationalization of the world economy have reduced the ability of the state to play a role in the governance of the economy. Traditional instruments on macroeconomic management are no longer as effective as they once were. Rising unemployment is placing considerable strain on the West European welfare state and the capacity of the state to maintain its present levels of social provision. This is bound up with issues of competitiveness, labour costs and labour mobility. The deregulatory ethos of the 1980s brought the public/private line sharply into focus, making it doubly difficult to reach agreement on what constitutes a European public good when there is conflict about the public/private line in many European states. A balanced assessment of the driving forces of integration and governance in Europe requires a renewed focus on the role of the contemporary European state and its relationship to civil society (Laffan and O'Donnell, 1993). The Wallace article hints at many issues that require more careful assessment.

## The Community's Double Deficit

The Community's part-formed polity suffers from a political vacuum, highlighted in the Wallace article. From the outset, it lacked an independent source of direct political authority and legitimacy. While this strategy of integration by stealth was an advantage for many decades, as it allowed technocrats and economic interest groups to build coalitions in support of EC policies, it has run its course. The Community is now facing increased politicization, or what Nye has identified as the problem of premature politicization which occurs when supportive attitudes among the mass public are not intense enough to deal with the incursion of integration on national sovereignty and the identitive functions of the state (Nye, 1971, p.89). The costs to the Community of integration by stealth are now being borne not only in terms of democracy, but also in terms of political authority and effectiveness. The EC suffers the double burden of a capacity deficit and a legitimacy deficit.

The Community's bargaining and negotiation system has proved to be reasonably robust and is more efficient with the extension of qualified majority voting. Yet it is ill suited to the governance challenges facing the Community and the wider Europe. The EC's weakness of political capacity has been amply demonstrated during the crisis of confidence that has beset the integration project since the signing of the Maastricht Treaty in early 1992. The Community has been niggardly in its response to the countries of central and eastern Europe for market access, reactive in response to the break-up of Yugoslavia and ineffectual in response to the currency crisis. The latter highlighted the gaps in the Ecofin system when the Council and its committees were unable to respond to the crisis other than agreeing to a review of the ERM. Communication channels between finance ministries and central banks were clearly inadequate in the run-up to Black Wednesday.

There is also a management deficit in relation to the 1992 project. Markets do not operate in a vacuum, but need regulation and management. The Internal Market is dependent on the emergence of a governance system based on horizontal links across Member States that will ensure fraud is controlled, that health and safety standards are met, and that the system of public management has adequate information to ensure that there is compliance with the rules (Metcalfe, 1992). This requires investment in institutions and reform of the Commission to take account of its management function. The Delors presidency has concentrated on strategic goal-setting with an organization that has not much altered its way of doing things over 30 years.

The Community had added competences, enlarged its membership and responded to a changing external environment without a root and branch overhaul of its institutional system. The prospect of several more rounds of enlargement may well force the Community to deal with some of the basic institutional issues. Yet there is little evidence that the EFTA enlargement will occasion a rethinking of the basic intellectual framework. This will simply postpone the debate for a later date and will make the debate more difficult because of the increased number of states involved.

The Maastricht ratification crisis and the Danish 'No' brought the Community face to face with democratic politics and the Europe of the electorates. The referendum debates in Denmark, France and Ireland showed that there was public unease about the direction of integration and the complex nature of its multi-levelled system. Discussion of the democratic deficit in the Community is frequently reduced to a debate on the powers of the European Parliament. The legitimacy crisis has deeper roots. Regulation and regulatory politics form the core of market integration. The fragmented nature of the Community's policy process and the weakness of political accountability allow for regulatory capture. The darker side of regulatory politics has been exacerbated by the drive to create the internal market. The Commission and the European Parliament are only now in the process of developing a code to regulate lobbying. Community institutions have shallow roots. The West European state, notwithstanding different traditions and historical experiences, is the primary focus of allegiance and loyalty. It provides the framework for democratic politics. According to Habermas:

> That the nation states constitute a problem along the thorny path to a European Union is, however, less due to their insurmountable claims to sovereignty than to another fact: democratic processes have hitherto only functioned within national borders. So far, the political public sphere is fragmented into national units. (Habermas, 1991)

This assertion draws our attention to the state as a normative order and has considerable bearing on the tension between integration and democracy.

## Nationalism and Regionalism

A focus on the state as a frame for democratic politics leads us to the identitive functions of states. Does the continuing existence of European nations, and of states which are the expression of the national identities determine the form which European integration takes, and define the limits of the process? Scholarly analysis of integration and governance in Western Europe has paid far too little attention to the national element in Europe and its implications for European integration.

Issues of territoriality and regionalism must also be revisited in any analysis of governance in Europe. The role of regional authorities and agencies in economic management has increased as national governments run out of macroeconomic instruments. Local regions seek to enhance their competitiveness by deploying regional policy instruments. In many parts of Europe, the enhanced role of regional government in economic policy has gone hand-in-hand with the emergence of regional political movements. There has been a considerable deconcentration and devolution of political power in many West European states. Does this, however, mean that the state is being eroded from below, or does the state continue to set the boundaries? The balance between the competences of the EC, national governments and regional authorities will remain central to European integration in the 1990s.

## Conclusions

The governance challenges facing Europe are of more than academic relevance; they go to the heart of democratic politics, security and economic well-being. How these issues are confronted in the 1990s will have a bearing on the relationship between states and markets, between states and the integration project and between economics and politics.

## References

Habermas, J. (1991) 'Citizenship and National Identity: Some Reflections on the Future of Europe'. Paper given to a Symposium on 'Identity and Diversity in a Democratic Europe: Theoretical Approaches and Institutional Practices', Brussels.

Keohane, R.O. and Hoffmann, S. (1991) *The New European Community* (Boulder, Col.: Westview).

Laffan, B. and O'Donnell, R. (1993) 'Economy, Society and Politics in the European Community: A Framework for Analysis'. Paper presented to the ECSA Third Biennial International Conference, Washington, 27–29 May.

Metcalfe, L. (1992) 'After 1992: Can the Commission Manage Europe?'. *Australian Journal of Public Administration*, Vol. 51, No. 1, pp.117–30.

Nye, J.S. (1971) *Peace in Parts: Integration and Conflict in Regional Organizations* (Boston: Little, Brown).

# 4.
# The Capability–Expectations Gap, or Conceptualizing Europe's International Role

CHRISTOPHER HILL

## I. Introduction

In 1982 Bull and Kahler surveyed different aspects of the European Community's role in the world for the twentieth anniversary of the *Journal of Common Market Studies*.[1] Even if not died in the wool realists, they both evinced considerable scepticism about the external achievements claimed for the Community during the 1970s, based as they had been on a 'civilian' diplomacy but not on military force. Bull, with typical directness but also foresight, argued that the Europeans would need to develop a military capability through the Western European Union if they were ever to be taken seriously on the great issues of international relations. Even then, this would only be a form of 'concert' or alliance. Supranationalism would not work in foreign policy. Kahler, for his part, had little time for the grandiloquent claims made for the Lomé Conventions concluded by the Community with the group of African, Caribbean and Pacific countries (the ACPs) as a model for a new North–South future. In his view the Community's development policy was rather a fading remnant of colonialism largely engineered by France for its own national purposes.

In writing this article, I have benefited from the comments of many colleagues, but in particular from those of David Allen, Renaud Dehousse, Philipp Borinski and Michael Smith.
[1] Wolfgang Hager also wrote a piece on the external dimension, but this dealt with the specific question of protectionism.

Looked at from the perspective of 1993, Bull and Kahler seem coolly prescient. Recent dramas over the Gulf, the Uruguay Round and Yugoslavia seem to show that the Community is not an effective international actor, in terms both of its capacity to produce collective decisions and its impact on events. The realist view that the state is the basis of power and interest in the international system, and that the uneven distribution of military strength is a still a formidable factor in determining outcomes, has correspondingly damaged the Community's image as a powerful and progressive force in the reshaping of the international system. This article goes a certain way towards reinforcing such a view (in that it cautions against expecting too much of the European Community as an international actor), but it does not do so in terms of a debate between realism and idealism, between the idea of the Community as a loose amalgam of independent nation-states and the concept of a civilian power whose example might transform international relations. The aim here, in working to a brief of conceptualizing Europe's international role, is to look at the functions which the Community (EC) might be fulfilling in the international system, but also at the perceptions which are held of its role by third parties. The central argument is that the Community's capabilities have been talked up, to the point where a significant *capability–expectations gap* exists, and that this is already presenting the EC with difficult choices and experiences that are the more painful for not being fully comprehended. The article ends by trying to sketch a more realistic picture of what the Community does in the world than that presented either by its more enthusiastic supporters or by the *demandeurs* beyond its borders.

## II. Starting Points

Since it is often necessary to go back a little in order to advance further, I want here to clear some of the methodological ground necessary for such a discussion. In the first instance, it is important to stress that although the intention is to show how we might think accurately about Europe's international capability – that is, to 'conceptualize' it – this does not mean that the more ambitious undertaking of providing a theory which might explain and predict Europe's behaviour is being undertaken. The attentive reader will uncover even more theoretical assumptions in the analysis than those which are explicitly spelled out, but the whole enterprise is essentially pre-theoretical in the sense that it fashions certain general ideas and arguments which might be useful in the construction of a wider theory, without attempting the systematic linking together characteristic of theory proper.

In any case, it is possible to argue that the experience of 'European foreign policy' over the last 20 years or so has been so unique that the search for one theory to explain its evolution is doomed to fail and that we must fall back on history. This is not to say, of course, that various different kinds of social science theories, depending on the level of analysis chosen, are not highly relevant to an understanding of the phenomenon in question. One might, for example, use theories of bureaucratic behaviour to look at the Commission and national foreign ministries, and theories of dependency to look at European relations with the Third World. Neither would focus sharply or parsimoniously enough on the central issue of what European foreign policy is and how its evolution may be understood,[2] but each would contribute one layer of insight into a complicated and multifaceted problem.

Perhaps the problem is essentially normative, and simpler than we imagine. One observer's response to a question about Europe's international role was to say that Europe's task was to compete with Japan and the United States.[3] There would be no shortage of people keen to join issue with this interpretation, and a primarily political discussion would ensue. But one of the starting points here is that too much of the discussion thus far has been normative, and that it has obscured the analysis of what actually has been happening. Rather more conceptual unpicking is required than has so far been the order of the day.

A further starting point is that to try to identify a distinctive 'role' for Europe in the world is something of a mare's nest, not least because this too requires a normative debate, but this time masquerading under the spurious objectivity of an analytical taxonomy. The idea of a role as the basis for any foreign policy has severe limitations (Hill, 1979). It assumes that an actor can and should find for itself something approximating to a part played on a stage, namely a distinctive, high-profile and coherent identity. But if all were to seek this in international relations, then nationalism inexorably would follow, whereas, when the most powerful do so they are likely to be deluded into looking for 'a place in the sun', 'the leadership of the free world' and other apparent panaceas, instead of concentrating on the more tedious work of crafting the endless necessary compromises between national interests and the long-run requirements of a working international system.

So, 'conceptualizing Europe's international role' is taken here to involve using concepts to understand Europe's various activities in the world; it does not mean outlining a single 'role' which Europe does or might follow. But this in turn brings us to the last definitional problem – what is 'Europe'? This dilemma bedevils all who think about the theory and practice of modern international relations, particularly in the post-1989 period. Several recent works have reflected helpfully on the multiple identities of contemporary Europe – the EC

---

[2] In the interests of brevity this discussion does not distinguish between positivist theories and 'verstehen' approaches, set against each other in Hollis and Smith (1991), even if it leans towards the latter.
[3] Susan Strange, in a seminar at the European University Institute, Fiesole, November 1992.

as Europe or as a nucleus of Europe, Europe as a wider security community, Europe as a grouping of developed capitalist economies (OECD Europe), Europe as an exclusive cultural entity (Neumann and Welsh, 1991) and so on. The criteria can be geographical, political, institutional, economic, moral or any combination of the five (Wallace, 1990; Barbé and Grasa, 1992). The focus here will be on the record in world affairs over the last 25 years of the EC and its Member States – a difficult enough task given the unique combination the concept represents of a semi-supranational entity working alongside sovereign states. If we try to take wider geo-political areas which are still in a state of flux, such as CSCE-Europe, or even the more limited idea of Europe from Brest to the Caspian, it becomes impossible to say anything durable or precise, not least because the whole question of who is going to be in and who outside the EC is highly uncertain.

   The focus of the discussion in this article is therefore on the pattern of activity of the Twelve since the beginning of European Political Co-operation (EPC) in 1970, including their relations with various categories of outsiders. In doing this we shall base the analysis on two key concepts, neither of which fits easily into the traditional schools of thought about the Community. We have already seen, for example, how the realism/idealism debate is too cramping, despite the useful contributions of Duchêne (1972), De Vree (1987), Pijpers (1991), and others.[4] Equally, although the recent interest of Hoffman, Keohane and Andrew Moravcsik (Keohane and Hoffman, 1991) in the EC has helped to revive neo-functional and neo-institutional approaches to integration theory, this has yet to extend to the special area which is EC external relations, consisting of the interaction between the Commission's diplomacy on behalf of the Community and EPC. Moreover the Harvard approach is highly materialist and rationalist in its stress on 'interstate bargains' (Moravcsik, 1991, p. 75), deals and side-payments between governments who at certain times discover their 'converging preferences'. It does not promise to translate well into the foreign policy field, where past trauma, common values, institutional evolution and ideological earthquakes are more likely to provide convincing explanations of the changing patterns of diplomacy.

   The two indispensable concepts which do not derive neatly from any of the major schools of thought about integration are *actorness* and *presence*. 'Actorness' in the world is something which most non-theoretical observers automatically assume that the European Community possesses, but which on closer examination might be seriously doubted, on the grounds that the EC in foreign policy is solely intergovernmental, and is therefore no more than the sum of what the Member States severally decide. The truth, as those writers who have

---

[4] François Duchêne invented the term 'civilian power' in 1972. For a more recent statement of a broadly idealist position, see Ludlow (1991). Hill (1990) provides an overview of the various approaches.

addressed the problem have pointed out, is that the Community is a genuine international actor in some respects but not all, and that what is fascinating about the history of the last 20 years is to assess the various efforts which have been made to increase the scope of actorness, as well as the consequences in this respect of the more organic changes in the relations between the EC and the rest of the world (Sjöstedt, 1977; Taylor, 1982). 'Actorness' provides us with a theoretical perspective which can incorporate both the internal dynamics of institutional development (in this case CFSP) and the changing nature of the international environment in which it has to operate. In other words, if the EC is less than a state, but more than a conventional intergovernmental organization (IGO), in what ways can it be termed a genuinely independent actor in international relations? This approach enables us to chart the EC's changing role in the world without becoming distracted by the 'is it or isn't it a superpower' red herring (Bull, of course, took the view in 1983 (p. 151) that '"Europe" is not an actor in international affairs, and does not seem likely to become one', but few would follow him so far). Following Sjöstedt, an international actor can be said to be an entity which is (1) *delimited* from others, and from its environment; which is (2) *autonomous*, in the sense of making its own laws and decisions ('sovereignty' could be used here were it not for the spectre of statehood which the term raises); and which (3) possesses certain *structural prerequisites* for action on the international level, such as legal personality, a set of diplomatic agents and the capability to conduct negotiations with third parties.

The second concept, taken from Allen and Smith, is that of western Europe's 'variable and multidimensional presence' in international affairs, which accepts the reality of a cohesive European impact on international relations despite the messy way in which it is produced (Allen and Smith, 1990, p. 20). In other words, it gets us off the hook of analysing EPC in terms of sovereignty and supranationalism, which might lead us to suppose that there was in fact no European foreign policy when common sense and the experience of other states tell us precisely the opposite (Brewin, 1987, is illuminating on the theoretical aspects of this paradox). It is a consequentialist notion which emphasizes outside perceptions of the Community and the significant effects it has on both the psychological and the operational environments of third parties. The presence of the Community is certainly felt in most international organizations, in international economic diplomacy, throughout the European subsystem and its borderlands, in the Third World, and wherever mediated solutions to international conflicts are sought. The extent to which outsiders are puzzled as to whether they should negotiate with the Community or with separate Member States demonstrates the political 'mixity'[5] which characterizes the Twelve's

---

[5] 'Mixity' is essentially a legal term arising out of the 'mixed agreements' signed simultaneously by the Community and its Member States in such areas as the environment and international commodity negotiations (Groux and Manin, 1985, pp. 58–69).

relations with the rest of the world, and therefore the presence of the Community alongside its parts.

## III. External Demands

Before we can make a sensible assessment of the Community's actual and potential capabilities, we need to look at the various functions which it performs, and might need to perform, in the international system. It would be a mistake to attribute collective will or personality to the international system, which is essentially a set of regularized processes that provides its constituent elements with some of the most powerful givens of their existence (Waltz, 1979). Nonetheless, analysts can make judgements about the importance of the Community in the international system, and the world's other major actors certainly have views on what the EC should and should not contribute to the functioning of the whole.

'Functions' in this context is a difficult term to use; there is no implication intended either of clearly demarcated tasks, agreed by the rest of the international community, or of a mechanistic system where each unit repetitively performs tasks without which the whole would not survive. Politics is not so neat or so integrated. But we can assume that within the international states system some actors have an identifiable presence, to the extent that certain things would either not have occurred, or would have been done very differently, without their existence.

On this basis we can divide the analysis into two parts, looking at the four functions which the EC has performed up to the present in the international system, and the six which it might perform in the future.

### EC Functions in the International System up to the Present

*(1) The stabilizing of western Europe.* The EC has not, of course, been the only cause of the peace which has become institutionalized in the region since 1945 (the Cold War paradoxically also takes some credit, together with economic growth), but without the Community such key elements as Franco-German entente and the democratic transitions of Greece, Portugal and Spain would have been much less likely.

*(2) Managing world trade.* World trade is not very effectively 'managed' even through the GATT, but to the extent that it is, the EC is the single most important actor in the negotiating process which produces the various trade regimes. At around 16 per cent (excluding intra-EC trade) it has the biggest share of any state or trading group in world trade, and its weight has become steadily more apparent over the 35 years since 1958, culminating in the dramatic external impact of the Single Market programme after 1985 (Redmond, 1992).

Although the Twelve conduct the major part of their trade with each other, [6] a trend which enlargement would accentuate, there is no chance of the Community ceasing to be, with the USA and Japan, one of the crucial players in world trade politics for the foreseeable future.

*(3) Principal voice of the developed world in relations with the South.* In the 1970s the EC constructed an unusual and imaginative development policy with the first two Lomé Conventions, to the effect that not only did the EC and its Members become easily the most important source of aid in the developed world, but also the rich countries most likely to win trust and exert influence in the South, particularly in Africa, where American, Japanese and Soviet policies were either absent or ineffective. Since then it is arguable that this position has atrophied, partly because of the structural limits on co-operation between very poor and relatively rich states, and partly because of ideological shifts in the 1980s. Nonetheless, the EC remains the principal interlocutor with the poor majority in the UN. With the inclusion of the Lomé system, the Mediterranean preferences, and its agreements with ASEAN and the Contadora countries, the EC enjoys institutionalized relations with at least 90 of the world's poorer countries, who in turn constitute around 80 per cent of the membership of the United Nations.[7]

*(4) Providing a second western voice in international diplomacy.* It may or may not be true that multipolarity provides more stability in the international system than bipolarity (Rosenau, 1969, Part 4A) in which case the development of a collective European diplomacy has served wider needs than its own, but EPC has certainly evolved because of a perceived need to provide an alternative view to that of the United States, both within the western world and on behalf of it. US leadership has served European interests well in many respects, but the gradual changes of historical context during the 1960s and 1970s have highlighted the problems. Accordingly, and channelled largely through EPC, a second and increasingly distinctive western voice has emerged, particularly where there seem to be possibilities of mediating dangerous conflicts between third states. We have now reached the point where even the United States looked first to the EC to manage the reconstruction of eastern Europe after 1989, and to stabilize ex-Yugoslavia (Edwards, 1992; Jorgensen, 1993). That it has not been able to do so does not invalidate the point that the EC has achieved a salience in the international political system which was simply absent in the 1960s.

---

[6] In 1987 41 per cent of the trade of the 12 Member States was with the wider world, and 59 per cent with each other. In 1990 the figure was almost exactly the same (*Eurostat*, 1989 and 1991, 26th and 28th edns, Luxembourg: OOPEC, Fig. 1.16).
[7] By 'institutionalized relations' is meant regular meetings, formal agreements and an EC commitment to assist with future development.

## Conceivable Future Functions for the EC in the Current Flux

Given that the international system is in a condition of transition, without anyone having much idea of the end point, that the Soviet Union has disappeared, and that the United States is in no position to exert worldwide leadership, it is not surprising that a more self-confident and maturing EC should seem capable of extending its global activity. There are six main ways in which it might do so. The EC is potentially:

(i) *A replacement for the USSR in the global balance of power.* If we assume, with traditional accounts of international relations, that there always exists either a balance of power or a tendency towards balancing preponderant power, then we are drawn to the conclusion that there is now a power vacuum in the international system. One of its two major forces, locked together in an antagonistic equilibrium, has suddenly been removed from the scene, with destabilizing consequences which are becoming ever more apparent. On the further assumption that, at least in the short term, the nature of international relations cannot be transformed into a post-power politics, we shall need to think of the EC as a candidate to fill the vacuum. There is certainly no alternative in terms of balancing American strength globally. It would be a mistake to think that this means ineluctable military rivalry. Fortunately grand strategy between similar social systems is more likely to revolve around economics and diplomacy than armed might. But there can be no doubt that even if the EC takes over only some of the roles left vacant by the Soviet Union, then competition and conflict with the USA will increase in proportion.

(ii) *Regional pacifier.* The withdrawal of the Soviet Union's iron fist from central and eastern Europe has created the possibility of serious disputes breaking out between and within the newly liberated states of the region. Since the United States is currently looking to reduce rather than to increase its commitments in Europe, while the EC is becoming ever more ambitious, it falls to the latter to act as mediator/coercive arbiter when the peace of the whole region seems under threat. This has clearly been the general expectation (so far unmet) in the case of Yugoslavia. In institutional terms, it means the Community acting as the motor for the CSCE and for the Council of Europe, taking its legitimacy from the broader constituency of states and citizens represented in these fora, but itself providing the dynamism and capacity to mobilize resources for action that purely parliamentary bodies are unlikely to achieve. The EC also has the capacity to act as a magnet and a model for the countries of eastern Europe. If all persist in wanting to join the Community, then the latter will by definition dominate the international politics of Europe, although it will risk destabilization itself. If, on the other hand, it can achieve a structure in which most countries to the east remain outside but closely tied to the EC, then there is the chance of being able to promote similar forms of international co-operation among the non-member countries.

*(iii) Global intervenor.* Growing out of the previous two potential functions is the possibility of the EC intervening in crises on a global basis. If it becomes a hegemon in Europe, however benign, then the pressures and opportunities which already exist for action further afield are bound to multiply. If relations with the United States deteriorate, then Europe may end up competing with American interventions; if they stay sound, then the Europeans may have to face substituting for a less outwardly-oriented USA. What this means – and it should not be hidden in euphemisms – is that the EC would interfere, on occasions by military force but more often with economic and political instruments, in states or regions where instability seemed likely to threaten European interests and/or the peaceful evolution of the international community of states. At present it seems likely that this second criterion would be judged by the Security Council of the United Nations (where the Europeans have at least a quarter of the votes and two-fifths of the vetoes), but such a legitimization might well not be seen as necessary in the future. In minimalist form an intervention might resemble the limited humanitarian operation of the USA in Somalia in late 1992 and early 1993. In maximalist terms, it might mean the Europeans choosing to take major responsibility for a 'Desert Storm' style campaign, instead of just making up the American numbers.

*(iv) Mediator of conflicts.* The line between forceful intervention and the provision of services to enable third parties to resolve their conflicts is a fine one. But it is easier and more natural at present for the EC to act diplomatically than to exert coercion, even economically. Thus we saw considerable diplomatic effort and creativity in the early stages of the Yugoslavian imbroglio, continued thereafter in harness with the United Nations. Over a much longer period, EPC has made it a major priority to work at narrowing the gap between Israel and the Palestine Liberation Organization (PLO), and eventually it might well be judged to have had some success. If any state or group of states is to achieve much in the area of mediation, then the EC has more claims than most. Between them, its Member States can claim considerable experience in relations with most parts of the globe, they have come through the period of decolonization without incurring too much long-term odium, and thus far they possess the singular advantage of not being perceived as a superpower and potential hegemon. Individual European states carry historical baggage which makes them distrusted in states such as Iran and Iraq; collectively, they represent more of a new beginning, and their claim to neutrality carries more weight.

*(v) Bridge between rich and poor.* As we have seen, the 'privileged' relations between the EC and the poor majority in the international system have deteriorated in recent years, while still leaving the Europeans pre-eminent

among developed states in their concern for the south. The Community now faces an important choice in this respect: whether to accept the impossibility of a special relationship with a very large number of countries at a much lower level of wealth and power, thus allowing the Lomé system to peter out, or whether to make renewed efforts (political and financial) to assist with the relief of poverty and to prevent North–South relations degenerating into mutual hostility or disregard. Nor is this is an academic choice. European decisions on central questions like agriculture, immigration, the budget and the environment, to say nothing of trade, will automatically have profound repercussions for the poor states who look to Brussels for help. It follows that unless the Community is now to be indifferent to the Third World, it should factor these considerations into its overall policy-making process. Concrete and short-term interests certainly must be protected, but internal and external policies are now umbilically connected, and the EC should at least be aware of the trade-offs at stake, not least on such a significant issue for the long-term future of its own external environment.

*(vi) Joint supervisor of the world economy.* The recent dominance of *laissez-faire* thinking notwithstanding, it is more and more evident that the notion of 'a world economy' with attendant management needs is taking hold in the minds of public and private decision-makers. Accordingly, it is increasingly important for governments to find mechanisms whereby such influence as they can exert over the vicissitudes of the market is efficiently co-ordinated. In practice, this means the most powerful economies of the western world joining together in the yearly G-7 summits, in the IMF ministerial meetings and in the Group of Ten meetings of central bankers. The EC states are already powerfully represented in this process, and the opportunity lies before them to increase their weight of influence. With even limited progress towards a single currency, the Europeans will be more likely to make international monetary decisions the preserve of themselves, Japan and the United States. On the trade front, the history of the Uruguay Round has shown how the GATT has become a forum for trials of strength between the EC (strengthened by the Single Market programme) and the USA, while the G-7 will become a G-3, with Canada in the observers' gallery, if the major European states can hold together and develop a common sense of identity. This would mean developing an actorness it does not currently possess in the IMF, World Bank, International Atomic Energy Agency *et al.*, both in terms of institutional recognition and the capacity to act coherently and consistently. If this happens a further issue opens up, that of whether a 'G-3 world' (and such modish simplifications should always be suspect) would mean the EC working in harness with Japan and the US, or whether it would produce tripolar conflict and instability.

## IV. The Capability–Expectations Gap

The above tasks – which the Community will certainly be expected to perform by many influential insiders and outsiders – pose a serious challenge to the actual capabilities of the EC, in terms of its *ability to agree*, its *resources,* and the *instruments* at its disposal. It is arguable, indeed, that the Community has been talked up – as a result of the Single Market and the Intergovernmental Conferences of 1991 – to a point where it is not capable of fulfilling the new expectations already (and often irrationally) held of it. This is true both of the number and the degree of the expectations.[8] Demands, whether for money, preferences or political assistance are flowing in from the Maghreb, southern Africa, central America, Afghanistan and Cambodia, to say nothing of eastern Europe and the pressure to join the EC from at least a dozen neighbouring countries. The extent of the demands is often unmanageable: stability and democracy for eastern Europe, a 'solution' for the Yugoslav crisis, relief for Third World poverty, all loom dauntingly on the horizon. Even with a clear strategy, which the Community demonstrably lacks over at least eastern Europe and the enlargement question, it would be difficult to cope with this flood-tide.

Historical developments such as that of European unity, even leaving aside the obvious teleological problems, are always a slower business than impatient politicians and idealists would wish. The Community does not have the resources or the political structure to be able to respond to the demands which the Commission and certain Member States have virtually invited through their bullishness over the pace of internal change. The consequential *gap* which has opened up between *capabilities and expectations* is dangerous. As with Slovenia and Croatia, and perhaps also the Baltic states, it can lead to excessive risk-taking by supplicant states and/or unrealistic policies on the part of the Twelve. Still, it is possible that this is essentially a transitional condition, brought on by growing pains, and that the general direction of the Community's development will eventually resolve it. To examine this possibility, and to judge how near to comprehensive actorness the EC is, it is worth outlining the theoretical characteristics of a single, effective, foreign policy and then measuring the Community's achievements against them. It is surprisingly difficult to find models of what a proper European foreign policy would mean, practically and constitutionally.

Even the European Parliament's Draft Treaty of Union of 1984, which went as far as it dared, did not spell out systematically what a fully-fledged foreign policy system would look like in the Community context (Bieber *et al.,* 1985).

---

[8] For a rather more optimistic view of the 'challenges' facing the Community, see Rummel (1992, pp. 11–33 and 297–319).

Moreover in practice EPC, and its link with Community external relations, have grown quietly and in piecemeal fashion. Where questions of fundamental change have arisen, especially with constitutional ramifications, they have been quickly slapped down or evaded. But if the Community system evolves further, and if demand for Community actions continues to rise, such empiricism will soon become untenable. A European foreign policy worthy of the name will require an executive capable of taking clear decisions on high policy matters, and of commanding the resources and instruments to back them up. They will need to enjoy democratic legitimacy and also to have a sophisticated bureaucracy at their disposal. Table 1 attempts an outline of these basic powers and associated mechanisms.

It will be seen from the proliferation of 'N's and '?'s in Table 1 that very few of the pieces are yet in place for the EC to acquire the federal foreign policy (for that is what is at issue here), which would give it the external quality of a state (and *ipso facto* superpower status). Indeed, when the requirements are so baldly set down the obstacles to be cleared before this point is reached seem almost insuperable. We can even query the Community's 'regulation of commerce' capability by reference to the Member States' ultimate control over initiating and implementing economic sanctions. Moreover there is still a great deal of differentiation, not to say ambiguity, in the current structure. For instance the Court of Justice has competence over the EC Treaty but not over the CFSP provisions.

And yet ... there is the familiar *sui generis* argument, which stresses that the EC does not need and has not needed to acquire state-like qualities to exert an important influence on the world. Furthermore, for each criterion identified above, it is possible to argue that hidden just below the crude surface judgements are degrees of progress so significant that the point where a qualitative leap becomes possible may at last be at hand.

To say this it is necessary to take the long view, and to assume that despite the current setbacks over Maastricht, the CFSP provisions of the Treaty are likely to hold.[9] They involve some important developments: the concession of the principle of majority voting; the bringing together of EPC and of the external relations of the Communities into the same process and under the same legal umbrella; the acceptance that defence should no longer be a no-go area for the Community. The merging of the EPC secretariat with that of the Council of Ministers is now well in hand. In other words, in many of the categories identified in Table 1, significant change has occurred even if it has not yet produced transformations.[10]

---

[9] At the time of writing, ratification of the Treaty is still hanging in the balance.

[10] 'If ratified, the new treaty will undoubtedly become a major landmark in the history of European integration, and will significantly affect Europe's role in world politics' (Pijpers, 1992, p. 1).

Table 1: The Conditions of a Single Foreign Policy

---

If the EC were to acquire its own foreign policy it would need to possess the following:

*(i)*     *Basic Constitutional Powers*
*over:*

| | | |
|---|---|---|
| (a) | War and peace | (N) |
| (b) | Raising armed forces | (N) |
| (c) | Treaty-making | (N/Y-EC?) |
| (d) | Regulation of commerce (sanctions) | (Y?) |
| (e) | External borders (immigration) | (N?) |
| (f) | Cession or acquisition of territory | (N) |
|     | (but for 'enlargement') | (Y) |

*subject to:*

| | | |
|---|---|---|
| (g) | Democratic accountability at the union level | (N?) |
|     | (cf states) | |
| (h) | Judicial scrutiny | (N/Y-EC) |

*(ii)*    *Mechanisms and Policies*

| | | |
|---|---|---|
| (a) | A single Ministry of Foreign Affairs and | |
|     | diplomatic service, with common missions abroad | (N) |
| (b) | A single intelligence service | (N) |
| (c) | A single set of armed services | (N) |
| (d) | A single development policy | (?50%) |
| (e) | A single cultural policy (?) | (?5%) |

---

*Note:* ('Y' = broadly possesses these powers/mechanisms; 'N' = not yet near; figures in brackets suggest how far down the road the EC has gone in creating a common policy. The judgements – inevitably provocative – assume observation of the CFSP provisions of Maastricht, which leaves the three European Communities intact but changes the title of the 'EEC' to 'EC'.)

These things seem vulnerable to the fate of the Maastricht Treaty. A strong contrary argument, however, is that Maastricht's problems have been largely to do with EMU and with a general perception of technocratic elitism. On this reading most of the CFSP dispositions will survive whatever the fate of the Treaty. The only vulnerable provision is that which enables progress in the area of defence co-operation.[11] Even here, the technical nature of the arrangements for the WEU and its relations with the EC is such (as with the rest of the CFSP) that public opinion is not likely to notice the Community being brought nearer to the threshold of radical change by seemingly innocuous administrative incrementalism.

There is, thus, undoubted potential for a single European foreign policy and some of that potential is already being mobilized. But it is equally true that there is still a large capability–expectations gap, and for two reasons: firstly because a coherent system and full actorness are still far from realization; and secondly because this inconvenient fact has often been ignored, (in Brussels as much as in the 'demandeur' states), in the heady swirl of international transition. Not just in terms of substantive resources – money, arms, room for immigrants – but in terms of the *ability to take decisions and hold to them* – the EC is still far from being able to fulfil the hopes of those who want to see it in great power terms.

## V. Defence Capability

This is most clearly seen in the area of defence, where there has been considerable movement in recent years. In fact, as Bull argued 10 years ago, defence is the key to the development of the Community's place in the world. No doubt there is a circular relationship between the issue of a great new military power emerging on the continent and the general place of force in international relations, but if the Community does not develop the capacity to defend itself and to project military power beyond its borders there will remain a great many things (for good or ill) which it will not be able to do. Conversely if the Community does develop a military dimension, it will have taken an immensely serious step towards transforming itself as an international actor and in consequence also external attitudes towards it.

The defence issue is a different category of problem from that of actorness; the EC could conceivably reach the position of being able to act purposefully and as one while eschewing a military capability. But in that case it would have to face the dilemma of either trusting to other forms of security, and/or leaving in place the individual Member States' armed forces and rights to use them – which course emasculates a collective foreign policy right from the beginning. In this respect, a genuinely European foreign policy cannot simply be an 'add-on' to the existing activities of the states, as some would like to believe. In the military sphere, as in the commercial, there is a zero-sum relationship between what the Member States do severally and what they do collectively. This is the

---

[11] As exposed during the Danish referendum campaign(s), when one major reason for voters fearing the Treaty was the perceived possibility of Danish young people having to fight foreign wars at other people's behest.

classical federal problem. (Dehousse, 1991, chs 1 and 2, although the author is unsympathetic to such an orthodox view, likewise Michelmann and Soldatos, 1990). The cartoon which once showed 12 Prime Ministers voting on whether or not to press the nuclear button pithily summarized the impossibility of having a genuinely intergovernmental defence community (NATO was at bottom a hegemonic defence community, which is why France left its military command structure in 1966 and has not returned). The converse of our initial hypothesis, therefore, does not apply: the EC is unlikely to develop an effective military capacity without also achieving general actorness.

What then, is the position at present in relation to defence? How near are the Europeans to taking on that fabled responsibility for themselves about which the Americans have talked for so long (and so ambivalently)? Leaving on one side the decision-making/federal issue, there are three aspects to the problem – mutual obligation, operational capacity and resources.

*(i) Mutual obligation.* It is strange in a way that the question of an alliance obligation has not been given much attention in the Community, given that diplomatic solidarity, security co-operation and citizenship have all been addressed. The small reason for this is Irish neutrality, while the large one is the desire not gratuitously to damage NATO. Yet it must be assumed that if one Member State were to be attacked the others could not stand aside (excepting dependencies like the Falklands) without undermining the very rationale of the Community. Given this and the extensive net of connections between them, the Twelve clearly constitute more than a 'pluralistic security-community' in Deutsch's original sense of the absence of internecine warfare (Deutsch, 1957), but not an 'amalgamated security community', where one supreme decision-making centre has been established. It would therefore be logical to spell out the *casus foederis* for which unity ultimately exists. This need not conflict with other obligations, whether to NATO, the CSCE or the UN, and does not imply that guarantees will be issued to outsiders, *à la* Britain and France in 1939. If, on the other hand, NATO does crumble away, the Community should in principle have no problem with at least substituting its commitment to a collective defence policy [12] – which could hardly have been said even 10 years ago, such has been the political sensitivity over European defence collaboration.

*(ii) Operational capacity.* When, in 1983–4, the major western states made their ill-fated attempt to interpose military forces between the warring parties in the Lebanon, it was under US leadership and no one supposed that EPC served any function other than that of distant diplomatic chorus. Developments in

---

[12] That is, not 'collective security', which strictly speaking refers to arrangements made to control conflict *between* members of a grouping. This already exists implicitly in the EC, in the sense that the Preambles to the Coal and Steel Treaty and to the Treaty of Rome both make clear the fundamental purpose of building peace in western Europe, i.e. between France and Germany.

recent years in the Gulf and Yugoslavia, therefore, particularly in respect of the WEU and its relation to the EC, have been little short of remarkable, fashionable criticisms notwithstanding (for a robust defence of the EC, swimming against the tide, see Gow, 1992; also Jorgensen, 1993). The WEU's very revival was linked to the desire to get around the block on Community defence discussions, and it has evolved into the position where it is now an inner hub of the EC's foreign policy-making process. Since 1987 it has made possible sophisticated naval co-ordination in the Gulf, on tanker-protection and mine-sweeping tasks, as well as some strategy and policy co-ordination during the pre-war phase of the 1990–1 crisis (Grove, 1990; Van Eekelen, 1990; Salmon, 1992). WEU-COM, a military equivalent to EPC's COREU telex network between foreign ministries, has been set up between members' defence ministries (De Schoutheete, 1990, p. 120). In Yugoslavia the Twelve mandated WEU to organize the first EC monitoring operation,[13] albeit on a very limited scale and increasingly giving way to the UN (Edwards, 1992, p. 176). At the start of 1993 the WEU Headquarters moved to Brussels, anticipating the creation of a CFSP via the Maastricht Treaty. When one adds in the growing institutionalization of Franco–German military co-operation, and the likely spillover into foreign intelligence operations from EPC and from the Trevi process, we can see that there now exists a range of precedents – both practical and political – for the further elaboration of Community operations in the security and defence field.

*(iii) Resources.* There are still, of course, enormous obstacles to the creation of a European defence entity, and the lack of resources is among the first of them. The Europeans have become too used to the American subsidy to be able smoothly to make the transition to funding their own security. Nor is it simply a matter of shifting figures from one balance-sheet (NATO, national) to another. Where several parallel frameworks exist simultaneously it will prove impossible not to incur the costs of duplication. Recently, for example, despite the talk of 'double-hatting' (the same troops being available for NATO and WEU purposes, referred to in the 'Declaration on the Western European Union' attached to the Treaty of Maastricht, section D7) NATO has in principle decided to extend the geographical range for its operations beyond the North Atlantic region, thus making an expansion of responsibilities possible in the long run.[14] Domestic pressures, on the other hand, are all in the direction of defence cuts and the squeezing of resources.

---

[13] The dispatch of monitors to help in the transition to majority rule in South Africa followed in October 1992, but this had nothing to do with the WEU (*EC Bulletin*, 10-1992, 1.5.12). The WEU also co-ordinated naval operations to enforce sanctions in the Adriatic from July 1992, see *The Military Balance*, 1992–93, p. 13).

[14] The decision was of the NATO Council Meeting on 4 June 1992, although it was hedged around with references to the need for unanimity in both NATO and the CSCE (*The Military Balance*, p. 29).

It is always more difficult to reduce costs than to add them on, while the turmoil in post-Cold War Europe, and the US desire to shift the burden, both in Europe and globally, will probably nullify any dramatic 'peace dividend'. Moreover although the Maastricht Treaty talks of the possibility of shifting the operational as well as administrative costs of the CFSP onto the Community budget (Article J.11), its drafters certainly did not have a full-scale European defence policy in mind. Just to mention transferring defence expenditure to the Community level is to realize its continued infeasibility, despite the theoretical economies of scale. It would decisively move the burden of taxation and economic policy-making from the national governments to Brussels. This would be an astounding development, but in practice such things will have to happen before a truly European defence becomes more thinkable. Until then, we have to accept that the Community is a sophisticated alliance, but no more.

The issue area of defence demonstrates a general truth about European foreign policy, namely that there is a dialectical relationship between the substantive and the constitutional. It is not possible to say that either the 'push' of institutional reform or the 'pull' of the pressing need for a particular common policy (here defence) is responsible for such progress as is made towards a common foreign policy. Change occurs in both ways, interactively, as policy needs and the internal dynamics of the Community create new possibilities, each for the other. Just as often, change occurs very slowly or not at all, while a negative spillover is not unknown in which intra-Community problems undermine external policy, or external embarrassments damage internal cohesion and morale. The current excess of expectations over capabilities threatens to cause problems on both fronts.

## VI. The EC-12 as an External Relations System

Given that the EC is still some way from being a full international actor, but that since 1970 it has steadily progressed towards a considerable presence in the world, how can we conceptualize its unique condition? The idea of the 'capability–expectations' gap is a useful starting point: it enables us to see that if the gap is to be closed and a dangerous tension relieved in European foreign policy, then either capabilities will have to be increased or expectations decreased. Capabilities, as we have seen, means cohesiveness, resources and operational capacity. If they are to be increased significantly beyond their present point, then an important political and constitutional leap will probably be necessary (Hill,1991). Lowering expectations means both lowering one's own ambitions in foreign policy and commmunicating the fact to outsiders, so that the limits of European actorness and intentions are clearly visible. Only this will put an end to the apparently widespread view of the EC-as-panacea, a cross between Father Christmas and the Seventh Cavalry.

But, with intelligence and time the capability–expectations gap might be closed, and the concept rendered redundant. Furthermore it is a static concept which cannot do full justice to the complexities of the Community's evolving impact on world politics. More useful is the notion of the *EC-12*[15] *as a system of external relations*. By this is meant both that the Europeans represent a sub-system of the international system as a whole, (perhaps the only functioning regional security arrangement, as envisaged in ch. VIII of the UN Charter) and that they are a system (i.e. not a single actor) which generates international relations – collectively, individually, economically, politically – rather than a clear-cut 'European foreign policy' as such. This system is essentially 'decentralized' in Paul Taylor's term, (Taylor, 1982, p. 41) and consists of three strands (*pace* the CFSP), as illustrated in Table 2.

This conceptualization covers internal and external aspects, decision-making and the Community's impact on the international system. It does not in itself tell us where the Community is going in the world, but it does give a more comprehensive analytical basis for prediction than do other approaches. For it is vital to do justice to the three parallel sets of activities, increasingly intermeshed and easy to confuse in the hurly-burly of political debate, but still essentially distinct, which EC members conduct: their persistently vigorous national policies; their sophisticated co-ordination and common initiatives through EPC; and the highly structured political economy dimension of collective commercial and development policies. It cannot be emphasized sufficiently that there is no evidence to suggest an inexorable (let alone imminent) fusion of the three strands into a single European foreign policy along the lines of a nation-state. Statements to the contrary are usually exercises in wish-fulfilment.[16]

Indeed, the current complexity of the system exists because not only are there three kinds of decision-making involved, but there are also at least three issue areas cutting across them. This means that the debate about 'European foreign policy' has two separate axes: (1) the degree to which policy is conducted on a collective basis; (2) the various issue areas into which policy decomposes in practice. They are expressed diagrammatically in Table 3, with examples.

---

[15] The term 'EC-12' is still necessary, *pace* Maastricht, to do justice to the life which still remains in national diplomacies.
[16] Even Eberhard Rhein, who emphasizes the convergence of EPC with EC external relations accepts that current trends fall short of 'a real European foreign policy … shaped by a single European Foreign Office in a federal system' (Rhein, 1992, p. 46).

Table 2: Parallel Systems of International Relations

| *National Foreign Policies* | *European Political Co-operation* | *External Relations of the ECs* |
|---|---|---|
| Bilateral relations with USA *et al.* | Joint declarations with USA, Canada, Japan; privileged dialogues | Joint declarations; co-operation agreements |
| Membership of IGOs | UN – convergence in voting; common statements | Membership of GATT; observer status in other IGOs |
| Defence policy; arms production | Security co-operation; WEU | 'Consistency' |
| Commercial competition | Commission participation | Common Commercial Policy |
| Domestic politics | European Parliament | European Parliament; bureaucratic politics |
| Embassies | Co-operation in third countries | External delegations |
| Colonial and post-colonial ties | Co-operation on crime and terrorism; links to the Council of Europe *et al.* | Enlargement |

*Note*: The columns contain examples of various aspects of each of the three strands of the system. The rows provide comparisons within the same general issue-area.

Table 3: The Two Axes of European Foreign Policy Actions (with Examples)

| | *Political* | *Military* | *Economic* |
|---|---|---|---|
| National | Greco–Turkish relations | Force de frappe | Export credits |
| Collective | Arab–Israeli policy | WEU/NATO | GATT |

A truly European presence in the world would involve collective policies in all major issue areas, thus bringing economics and politics together, as well as rationalizing the decision-making process. At present there are elements of collectivity throughout, but the degree and extent of states' commitment to co-operate vary considerably. We only have to compare the G-7, where the Commission represents the smaller European states, with the G-5 of the UN Security Council, where the UK and France act independently, to observe the loose character of the system. At present bloc diplomacy is like trying to harness 12 half-broken colts to pull the same carriage.

However the situation is dynamic as well as complex, for there is consider-able interplay between the three strands of activities. What individual states do or do not do in their national foreign policies (as with Germany's aversion to sending troops abroad) sets the limits for collective action. Equally, the common commercial policy, the CAP and now the Single Market lock the Twelve into certain positions in international economic relations which increasingly rever-berate onto EPC – as the very desire for 'consistency' betokens. Indeed the Community is now making definite efforts to increase cohesion, first through consistency, and second through 'linkage' (Wallace, 1976; Kissinger, 1979, pp. 129–30). Although the practice is still kept at bay in the Euro-American dialogue, where anything more than the most delicate allusion to the fact that disagreement in one sector might damage relations in another is still regarded as bad taste, in relations with the Third World, with eastern Europe and with those states made the object of the EC's main political weapon, economic sanctions, explicit linkages are now unashamedly being made.[17]

Not all of these linkages are negative or coercive. There now exist Commu-nity ties and cross-linkages with outside states on an extensive scale, with varying degrees of intensity. Some are simple exchange relationships; some involve EC incentives and assistance in order to build up long-term patterns of friendship and stability. It might well be sensible, therefore, to broaden the conceptualization from that of the EC alone to an image of concentric circles, whereby states like the USA and the EFTAns form the closest ring around the EC, followed by a belt including (say) Japan, the CSCE and ASEAN, and then another constituted by the ACPs.[18]

This concept would have the further advantage of making possible the relaxation of the strict division between members and non-members of the EC.

---

[17] For example, the Commission's suspension on 2 October 1991 of aid programming, under the fourth Lomé Convention, to Haiti, after a military coup there (*EC Bulletin*, 10-1991, 1.3.28).
[18] This would be similar to the 'pyramid of privilege' notion used by analysts of the EC's relations with the LDCs. It even bears some resemblance to the concept of concentric circles boosted by President Mitterrand's New Year speech of 1990, with the notable difference that Mitterrand wanted a European confederation, with non-Europeans confined to the outer orbits (*Agence Europe*, 4 January 1991).

For it is clear that in some respects a *variable geometry*[19] already exists in foreign policy matters, with some states pressing on towards communautarization and others at least as much concerned with national independence or special relationships. Ireland, and Denmark are still fully integrated into defence co-operation via the WEU; France and Germany have a close bilateral relationship only rivalled by that between the Benelux countries; Britain makes no bones about Washington's privileged status in London; the Commonwealth and France's African Community provide preoccupations which do not exist for the other Ten; Italy attempted to develop a central European policy through the Pentagonale/Hexagonale initiatives. In short, there exist foreign policy subsystems (De Schoutheete, 1990) of which some stretch out beyond the Community's membership.

Much of this variability is inevitable. But when it has the effect of undermining EC solidarity on serious issues such as Yugoslavia then the question naturally arises of whether collective action can be *sustained* over time without a further leap into federalist obligations and structures. The stress on 'consistency' since the Single Act can only go so far in creating solidarity. Indeed, the very notion still posits separate strands of activity, which is why it is eschewed in the Maastricht Treaty in favour of proclaiming a Common Foreign and Security Policy. But proclaiming the desirable end-product without providing the means for getting there is insufficient. At present the whole question of the balance of costs and benefits involved in a more fundamental shift of powers, is being evaded.

Ultimately larger political judgements will have to be made about whether something more is required. It may be that some great trauma, internal or external will shock the Twelve into fusing into a single entity, but it is difficult to see anything short of major war provoking a transition to statehood. Given this context, the capability–expectations gap and external confusions will remain embarrassing realities unless a clear decision is made to accept variable geometry and 'multi-institutionalism' (Rummel, 1992, p. 319) as functional in foreign policy. It may be that even the notion of *subsidiarity* would be applicable – although the essentially contested nature of that concept would become even more readily apparent in this highly political field. But variability, including openness to co-operation with non-Member States, is really the only option if (1) the present hotchpotch is deemed unacceptable, while (2) the political impetus does not exist for a jump into federalism.

In some ways the external 'pull' of the international system represents a powerful force acting on the Twelve to acquire the capacity to pursue the tasks

---

[19] The metaphors of variable geometry and the concentric circles are preferred to that of a 'multi-speed Europe', because the latter implies a single destination at which all will arrive in time. I do not share the teleology. Wallace, H. (1985) analyses all the relevant concepts with great clarity.

which loom before them. But external factors alone cannot 'federate' without an internal readiness to do so, and domestic factors in at least four Member-States prevent such a condition coming into being. What is more, although the demands of world politics are increasingly likely to place constitutional questions on the Community's agenda, the decisions they provoke will have to be decisions about the Community's fundamental character, and not just its external face. For instance, despite proliferating arrangements for multinational corps and rapid reaction forces, without political integration even limited military actions in Yugoslavia have proved beyond the EC (cf. NATO; Bonanni, 1993).

The *status quo* in European external policy is clearly unsatisfactory and even dangerous. There is now a large gap between what is expected and what can be achieved. Two measures as a minimum need to be taken to make both internal and external perceptions of EPC/CFSP more realistic and to bring capabilities and expectations back into line. Of these the first and most important is a clear pulling in of the horns, and a signalling that there are certain things that the EC simply cannot or will not do. The emphasis should swing towards long-term attempts to improve the general milieu of international relations, particularly in Europe's own region, and away from precipitate attempts to replace American superpower in particular crises.

The second need is to recognize that 'complex interdependence' applies in foreign policy as well as international economic relations. Variable patterns of co-operation, both within the Community and with outside states, are both inevitable and desirable. The excitements of the last seven years have made the Community too self-regarding, and some assessments of its capacity over-ambitious. Sometimes the language of politics can run ahead of the realities, and if the idea of a 'Common Foreign and Security Policy' is taken too literally, the members of the European Community may well come to regret killing off the dull but accurate title of 'Political Co-operation'.

## References

Allen, D. and Smith, M.(1990) 'Western Europe's Presence in the Contemporary International Arena'. *Review of International Studies*, Vol. 16, No.1.

Barbé, E. and Grasa, R. (1992) *La Comunitat Europea i La Nova Europa* (Barcelona: Fundacio Jaume Bofill).

Bieber, R., Jacqué, J.-P. and Weiler, J. H.H. (1985) *An Ever Closer Union: A Critical Analysis of the Draft Treaty Establishing the European Union* (Luxembourg: OOPEC).

Bonanni, A. (1993) 'L'Impotenza dell'Europa, Gigante senza Stellette'. *Corriere della Sera,* Milan, 6 May.

Brewin, C. (1987) 'The European Community: A Union of States without Unity of Government'. *Journal of Common Market Studies*, Vol. XXVI, No. 1, pp. 1–25.

Bull, H. (1983) 'Civilian Power Europe: A Contradiction in Terms?'. In Tsoukalis (1983).

Dehousse, R. (1991) *Fédéralisme et relations internationales: une réflexion comparative* (Brussels: Bruylant).

De Schoutheete, P. (1990) 'The European Community and its Sub-Systems'. In Wallace, W. (ed.),*The Dynamics of European Integration* (London: Pinter for the Royal Institute of International Affairs).

Deutsch, K. W. (1957) *Political Community and the North Atlantic Area: International Organization in the Light of Historical Experience* (Princeton: Princeton University Press).

De Vree, J. K. (1987) 'Reflections on the Future of Western Europe'. In De Vree, J.K., Coffey, P. and Lauwaars, R.H. (eds.), *Towards a European Foreign Policy: Legal, Economic and Political Dimensions* (Dordrecht: Martinus Nijhoff).

Duchêne, F. (1972) 'Europe's Role in World Peace'. In Mayne, R. (ed.), *Europe Tomorrow: Sixteen Europeans Look Ahead* (London: Fontana/Collins for Chatham House/PEP).

Edwards, G. (1992) 'European Responses to the Yugoslav Crisis – an Interim Assessment'. In Rummel, R. (ed.) (1992).

Gow, J. (1992) 'The Use of Coercion in the Yugoslav Crisis'. *The World Today,* Vol. 48, No.11.

Groux, J. and Manin, P. (1985) *The European Communities in the International Order* (Brussels: CEC).

Grove, E. (1990) *Maritime Strategy and European Security* (London: Brasseys).

Hill, C. (1979) 'Britain's Elusive Role in World Politics'. *British Journal of International Studies,* Vol. 5, No. 3.

Hill, C. (1990),'European Foreign Policy: Power Bloc, Civilian Model – or Flop?'. In Rummel (1990).

Holland, M. (ed.) (1991) *The Future of European Political Cooperation* (London: Macmillan).

Hollis, M. and Smith, S. (1991) *Explaining and Understanding International Relations* (Oxford: Clarendon Press).

Jorgensen, K.E. (1993) 'The European Community's Dilemmas and Strategies in the Balkans'. Paper presented to the ECPR Joint Sessions, Leiden University.

Kahler, M. (1983) 'Europe and its "Privileged Partners" in Africa and the Middle East'. In Tsoukalis (1983).

Keohane, R. O. (1984) *After Hegemony: Cooperation and Discord in the World Political Economy* ( Princeton N.J.: Princeton University Press).

Keohane, R. O. (ed.) (1986) *Neo-Realism and Its Critics* (New York: Columbia University Press).

Keohane, R. O. and Nye, J. (eds.)(1973) *Transnational Relations and World Politics* (Cambridge, Mass.: Harvard University Press).

Keohane, R. O. and Hoffman, S. (1991) *The New European Community: Decision-Making and Institutional Change* (Boulder, Col.: Westview).

Kissinger, H. A. (1979) *White House Years* (Boston: Little, Brown).

Ludlow, P. (1991) *Setting European Community Priorities 1991–92* (London: Brassey's for the Centre for European Policy Studies.

Michelmann, H. J. and Soldatos, P. (eds.) (1990) *Federalism and International Relations* (Oxford: Clarendon Press).

Moravcsik, A. (1991) 'Negotiating the Single European Act'. In Keohane and Hoffman (1991).

Neumann, I. B. and Welsh, J.M. (1991) 'The Other in European Self-Definition: an Addendum to the Literature on International Society'. *Review of International Studies*, Vol. 17, No. 4.

Pijpers, A. (1991) 'European Political Cooperation and the Realist Paradigm'. In Holland (1991).

Pijpers, A. (1992) 'The Treaty of Maastricht and European Foreign Policy'. *Jerusalem Journal of International Relations,* Vol.14, No. 2.

Redmond, J. (ed.) (1992) *The External Relations of the European Community: the External Consequences of 1992* (London: Macmillan).

Rhein, E. (1992) 'The Community's External Reach'. In Rummel (1992).

Rosenau, J. N. (ed.) (1969) *International Politics and Foreign Policy* (revised edn) (New York: Free Press).

Rummel, R. (ed.) (1990) *The Evolution of an International Actor: Western Europe's New Assertiveness* (Boulder, Col.: Westview).

Rummel, R. (1992) 'Regional Integration in the Global Test', and 'Beyond Maastricht; Alternative Futures for a Political Union'. In Rummel, R. (ed.), *Toward Political Union: Planning a Common Foreign and Security Policy in the European Community* (Baden-Baden: Nomos).

Salmon, T. C. (1992) 'Testing Times for European Political Cooperation': The Gulf and Yugoslavia, 1990–92'. *International Affairs*, Vol. 68, No. 2.

Sjöstedt, G. (1977) *The External Role of the European Community* (Farnborough: Saxon House).

Taylor, P. (1982) 'The European Communities as an Actor in International Society'. *Journal of European Integration,* Vol. VI, No.1.

*The Military Balance, 1992–93* (London: Brasseys for International Institute for Strategic Studies).

Tsoukalis, L. (ed.) (1983) *The European Community: Past, Present and Future* (Oxford: Blackwell).

Van Eekelen, W. (1990) 'The WEU and the Gulf Crisis'. *Survival*, Vol. 32, No. 6 .

Wallace, H. with Ridley, A. (1985) *Europe: The Challenge of Diversity*. Paper No.29 (London: Routledge & Kegan Paul/ Chatham House).

Wallace, W. (1976) 'Issue Linkage among Atlantic Governments'. *International Affairs,* Vol. 52, No. 2.

Wallace, W. (1990) *The Transformation of Western Europe* (London: Pinter for the Royal Institute of International Affairs).

Waltz, K. (1979) *Theory of International Politics* (Reading, Mass.: Addison-Wesley).

# Comment on Hill

MICHAEL SMITH

It is a great pleasure to be able to comment on a piece so elegant in its exposition
and apt in its characterization of EC international action as that by Chris Hill.
It is also difficult to take to task an author who gives one's own work such ample
credit! Nonetheless, I think that there are a number of themes which can be
pursued, and on which Hill's assumptions can be tested with the aim of
clarification and development.

Chris Hill's position is essentially this: that there is something special about
foreign policy, in the case of the Community as in the case of the nation-state,
and that it is necessary therefore to assume a sharp disjunction between internal
dynamics and external interests or actions. This is not to say that internal factors
do not matter in the appraisal of Community policies or positions; indeed, the
tension between internal capabilities and external demands or expectations is
central to the argument. The incremental effects of this tension, and of members'
attempts to resolve it in specific circumstances, are the key to an understanding
of how far the Community has advanced. And the key test is defence, an area
in which the Community has been and may well continue to be found wanting.
This is a powerful and parsimonious approach which, as Chris Hill shows,
generates major questions about the Community's role and status.

At the risk of overstating Hill's position, it can be argued that he locates the
issue of the EC's international role firmly within international relations, and that

this accounts for the deficiencies and contradictions he identifies. This may seems obvious and trite, but I wish to suggest that by doing this he is bypassing a number of important alternative assumptions. In particular I want to suggest that the Common Foreign and Security Policy (CFSP) and 'foreign policy' are not as distinctive and different from other policy domains as Hill implies. This leads me to suggest that the issue of collective action, and its relationship to distributional policies, is increasingly one in which the Community's international role is entangled; in other words that foreign policy is no longer as 'different' as it was, and that the test of defence policy is not necessarily the key to an evaluation of the Community's role.

Central to this argument is the impact of the end of the Cold War, and of recession and global restructuring. Hill can be criticized – although he talks much about change – for assuming a rather static and traditional version of international politics and foreign policy. My view is that much has changed, if not been transformed, and that this creates new possible futures for Community policy. In particular, it means that the boundary between 'foreign policy' and internal Community development is very difficult to identify. This in turn leads to two possible scenarios, both of them implied at times by Hill:

(1) The first scenario is that in which foreign policy is *'dissolved' in Europe and in the Community*. The stuff of policy becomes essentially that of distributional politics, rather than the high politics of security traditionally defined, and the linkages referred to by Hill are the core of policy management. The ways in which 'domestic' economic security and welfare concerns are handled become linked inextricably to the external presence and positions of the Community, reflecting the erosion of the clarity implied by the Cold War and the impact of global economic processes.

(2) The second scenario is that in which *foreign policy and international relations are 'internalized' by the Community,* and its growth means that international conflicts become matters of internal order. Whilst high politics is central to this view, it takes place within the boundaries of the EC itself, rather than beyond them. One major implication of the widening of the Community during the 1990s will surely be this process of internalization, and the ways in which issues of external security are transformed into matters of internal order or boundary maintenance. Indeed, the Maastricht Treaty with its emphasis on citizenship in some sense formally recognizes this question. Not only this, but the new salience of migration policies and their links to internal political order have underlined the new political calculus for Community members.

Both scenarios imply a dramatic growth and development, and a far from linear one. Both, in a sense, imply the end of 'foreign policy' as conceived by much of Hill's piece. Importantly, each also means that a focus on collective action is central to the future of Community roles and positions. What versions of collective action can be identified? Will the EC act is a 'union', a 'concert', a 'crocodile' following a leader, or a cacophony? What influences on collective action are likely to be paramount: national policies, coalition policies, institutional bargaining, the context of change? How will collective action be influenced by linkages, differentiation between issue areas, fluctuations in the status and commitment of members? What will be the influence of learning by members, and of the incorporation of new members? These questions and others like them are not the stuff of traditional approaches to foreign policy; rather, they reflect the interpenetration of economic and political systems, and the domestication of security issues, which have been seen as central to the politics of industrial societies in the 1990s. Chris Hill certainly raises these questions, but his approach gives them a different 'spin' and significance from that implied here.

My view is that transformation in Europe has implicitly changed the calculus and bases of collective Community action, and that the boundary assumed by Hill between foreign policy and other areas is highly permeable, if not non-existent. This is not a new insight, but it does challenge the view that foreign policy is both distinctive and the ultimate test of the Community. Quite simply, it may be difficult to determine where the Community ends and abroad begins, and thus to maintain the impressive coherence displayed by Chris Hill in his excellent and provocative analysis. Rather, the stuff of the Community's international role will be that of the identification and enhancement of collective goods, and of the externalities produced by the essentially internal debate about foreign policy and role itself. This is, of course, precisely the area in which the Community can be so infuriating or frustrating for outsiders and for its more assertive members. I sense that Chris Hill and I are not as far apart here as I have implied, but I think it is important to pose the differences of emphasis as clearly as possible so that we can get on with the job of analysing a highly significant and growing area. Debate will no doubt continue!

# 5.
# Journey to an Unknown Destination: A Retrospective and Prospective of the European Court of Justice in the Arena of Political Integration

J.H.H. WEILER*

## I. Retrospective

*Introduction*

In 1982, in the previous anniversary issue of the *Journal of Common Market Studies*, posturing as the legal Daniel in the den of political science lions, I made a plea to a sceptical audience to acknowledge the importance (if not centrality) of the legal paradigm in general, and of the European Court of Justice in particular, to the evolution of the constitutional and institutional architecture of the European Community (Weiler, 1982). I tried to situate a political analysis in a legal context.

In this article, 10 years later, I shall engage in something of a reverse exercise. The importance of the Court as an actor and of law as a context in which

* The first part of this paper is based in part on Weiler (1993, forthcoming) to which Karen Alter, Martin Shapiro and Alec Stone made biting and useful comments for which I am grateful. I am mostly indebted to the continuing dialogue with my friend and colleague, Anne-Marie Burley. All errors of fact and weaknesses of opinion are my own.

to situate political analysis of the Community has become widely accepted.[1] Here, then, a lion in the den of Daniels, I shall try to situate legal analysis in its political context.

## The Court and its Interlocutors – Defining a Perspective for Enquiry

There is more than one way towards an appreciation of the role of the Court of Justice and of judicial process in the evolution of the Community and European integration.

The classical way relates to what lawyers call doctrine, and especially constitutional doctrine: it may be structural doctrine – laying down, in the language of binding rules, a normative framework which purports to govern fundamental issues such as the structure of relationships between Community and Member States; it may be material doctrine, doing the same in relation to, say, the economic and social content of that relationship.

But, of course, from what the Court says (constitutionally) we can learn a lot about what the Court is, or more accurately, what the Court believes itself to be, or, at least, claims to be. In the 'laying down' of binding constitutional doctrine there is, inevitably, an element of constitutional (self)-positioning of the Court itself. When the Court makes those determinations it is implicitly or explicitly placing itself in a power situation as the Community institution with the ultimate authority to make such structural and material determinations.[2]

The content of its constitutional structural and material doctrines – what the Court has said over the years – is so well known a tale (at least in its broad outlines) as to render elaborate description unnecessary. There is really no need for me to repeat, yet again, the story of supremacy, direct effect, human rights, implied powers, pre-emption, and other such well known buzzwords capturing the history of so-called constitution-making by the Court. In structural constitutionalism *Van Gend En Loos, Costa* v. *ENEL, ERTA* and others are cases whose names have transgressed disciplinary boundaries even in Europe and are no longer the reserved domain of the lawyers. And then there is *Cassis de Dijon,* whose fame has spread even further, a case emblematic of the Internal Market philosophy of the Court and which may, or may not, have had a role in shaping the 'new approach to harmonization' and the principle of mutual recognition,

---

[1] Cf. Keohane and Hoffmann (1991): 'Another distinction of the European Community is its legal status: No other international organization enjoys such reliably effective supremacy of its law over the laws of member governments, with a recognized Court of Justice to adjudicate disputes' (p. 11). 'Indeed, of all Community institutions, the Court has gone farthest in limiting national autonomy, by asserting the principles of superiority of Community law and of the obligation of member states to implement [it]' (pp. 11 and 12).

[2] The Court roots this authority in the Treaty of Rome; But it has, of course, considerable power in interpreting the Treaty and being the ultimate arbiter of its meaning. In its recent Opinion 1/91 (not yet reported) it seemed to construe legal principles which even Treaty amendment could not violate.

but is certainly a representative of the material content of the Court's constitution-making.

So, no reiteration of the constitutional doctrine, and not even an elaborate explication of the Court's self-perception implicit in that doctrine. The underlying premise of the doctrinal perspective is fairly evident: self-referential, legal, internal to a possible logic of the Treaty itself; its legitimacy, in the eyes of the Court itself (and of others) indirect – mediated, as is often the case with institutional religious doctrine, through the concept of interpretation.

What, instead, I do want to write about is the *reception* of the doctrine, and especially the reception of the self-positioning of the Court implicit in the doctrine, by other actors in the Community system. I am adopting a perspective in which courts are but one actor – more or less privileged – in a broad interpretative community (and maybe even a series of interpretative communities) and in which the Court's role is understood not simply by what it says but by how (and why) it is received by others.

Under the doctrinal perspective the political institutions of the Community (Commission, Council, Parliament) the governments of the Member States (and other actors within Member States), transnational interests and organizations constitute each, and together, *objects* of the Court's jurisprudence. Under the alternative, actor approach, they are *subjects*, interlocutors, partners to a dialogue or 'multilogue'.

The position of the Court on this view is not, then, a matter of legal determination and then logical deduction from the doctrine but a matter of empirical observation and social and political explanation. Here one must go beyond the self-referential legal universe – though this universe will in itself often be of political importance even if, critically, only as one factor among many in explaining the power or otherwise of the Court. The question of doctrinal content – the interpretative claim made by the Court – is only part of the picture. It must be followed by an enquiry into the 'persuasion pull' and 'compliance pull' which such doctrinal claims can evoke.

In my narrative there will be a time-frame. I think that there is one story to be told about the reception and perception of the Court by other actors in the period commencing with the 1960s (when the Court becomes 'active') and leading up to the entry into force of the Single European Act (SEA) in 1987. The period after that date and leading to Maastricht (1992) is one of transition which suggests that the future may hold in store a very different tale about these relationships.

In the first part of the article I will, therefore, focus on the relationship and its possible causes in that first period. In the second part I shall try to show why, in my view, the future of the relationship of the Court to its interlocutors will unfold in quite a different way.

This is the point to inject, in good lawyerly fashion, a methodological disclaimer. When I speak of 'my narrative' I use the term advisedly. I am offering no 'theory' (at least not explicitly), or 'conceptualization' nor any other grand design. The fact is, that whereas the first doctrinal dimension has been explored endlessly, there is a veritable dearth of systematic, social science *empirical* studies which examine the many facets of the Court as political actor in the Community and on which one can draw. The questions that have been raised in the literature have been haphazard as have been the answers.[3]

This methodological deficiency is not going to be redressed in this article. I will make some factual claims, form some hypotheses, offer some causal explanations. But factual claims and hypotheses will be based on my own experience and observation (hardly systematic) and causal explanation will be no more than personal speculation. *Caveat Lector.*

## *The Court and its Interlocutors – 'Benign Neglect'*

Historically, the European Court of Justice achieved a remarkable relational feat. The opening line of one of the most celebrated articles in the field, Eric Stein's 'Lawyers, Judges, and the Making of a Transnational Constitution', captures this feat superbly: 'Tucked away in the fairyland Duchy of Luxembourg and blessed, until recently, with benign neglect by the powers that be and the mass media, the Court of Justice of the European Communities has fashioned a constitutional framework for a federal-type Europe' (Stein, 1981). Making a federal type constitutional framework involved an aggressive and radical doctrinal jurisprudence, a veritable 'revolution' often in the face of the flailing 'political will' of other Community actors. At times it seemed even at the expense of the power of other actors. The content of this jurisprudence can be summed up, perhaps, in the concept of a 'Community discipline': a set of norms governing many of the relations between Community and Member State legal (and political) orders.

And yet, despite the integrative radicalness of its doctrinal construct, with few exceptions, the Court managed to hegemonize the EC interpretative community, and to persuade, co-opt and cajole most, if not all, of other principal actors to accept the fundamentals of its doctrine and of its position in making the constitutional determinations for the Community.

It did not happen at once, it did not happen uniformly, there have been 'pockets of resistance' but, by and large, it has happened.[4] Both political and

---

[3] There is, nonetheless, a growing political science literature on the European Court. Among the more important contributions, earlier and more recent, from which I have profited are: Burley and Mattli (1993); Garrett (1992); Gibson and Caldeira (1993a, b); Keohane and Hoffmann (1991); Lenaerts (1992, p. 93); Rasmussen (1986); Shapiro (1980, 1992); Snyder (1986); Green, (1969); and Volcansek (1986).

[4] For a comprehensive description of the reception of the constitutional doctrines in the various legal orders of the Member States see, e.g., the excellent Schermers and Waelbroeck (1992).

economic discussion of, say, Community reform 'à la Maastricht' are always set, usually unthinkingly and naturally, against the constitutional structure set in place by the Court. It is not simply the fact of hegemony which is fascinating (and calls for some explanation) but the fact that this has indeed been a relatively *'quiet* revolution' and that the Court has, in fact enjoyed such a lengthy period of 'benign neglect' and not suffered serious challenges to its legitimacy.

In exploring this issue I will focus on three sets of interlocutors: the national (Member State) judiciary, Member State governments and legislatures, and academia – as three communities of which one might have expected a less hospitable reception towards the European Court.

## The European Court of Justice and the National Judicial Branch

The most interesting and, in my view, consequential interlocutors of the ECJ have been national courts at all levels. This is a story of a double acceptance of Community discipline by the national judiciary. One part of the story concerns doctrine: the manner in which, moving and halting, two steps forward and one backwards, the national judiciary, in a process which still continues, has come to accept the constitutional doctrines, structural and material, of the European Court of Justice (Schermers and Waelbroeck, 1992).

But no less important has been the equally growing involvement of the national judiciary in the *administration* of Community law, transforming doctrinal acceptance into processual reality. The two dimensions are equally important: for, after all, what point is there in, say, accepting the principle of supremacy of Community law, if no process exists for its vindication in time of conflict? *Ibi jus ubi remedium*!

The largest number of cases which reach the ECJ do so by way of a Preliminary Reference from Member State courts ex Art. 177 EEC to which the Court responds by issuing a Preliminary Ruling. The importance of this well known procedure cannot be overestimated. It has become the principal vehicle for imposition of judicially driven Community discipline. (For analysis and description, see, e.g., Weiler, 1991). The overwhelming number of Preliminary References arise in the context of litigation before national courts in which individuals seek to enforce, to their benefit, Community obligations against their own governments or other national public authorities.

Although the pattern of usage differs from Member State to Member State and even within Member States (Weiler *et al.*, 1988), it would be a reasonable generalization to suggest that on the whole, since the early 1960, cases which established the utility of the Preliminary Procedure in this context, national courts, typically lower courts, have been willing partners in this use of Article 177 'against' national public authorities.

It is precisely that partnership which is, in my view, so consequential for the overall positioning of the Court even beyond its relationship with national courts. This is so for several reasons.

(1) Viewed from the perspective of compliance it makes all the difference that it is a national court, even a 'lower' (or 'lowly' one), and not the European Court of Justice itself which seeks the Preliminary Reference, awaits the Preliminary Ruling and then uses it in *its* domestic final decision.

When a national court *seeks* the Reference it is, with few exceptions, acknowledging that, at least at face value, Community norms are necessary and govern the dispute. This very issue may be of huge political significance and the subject of controversy among governments or between the Member States as a whole and, say, the Commission.[5] But, the very fact that 'their own' national courts make a Preliminary Reference to the European Court of Justice, forces governments to 'juridify' their argument and shift to the judicial arena in which the Court of Justice is pre-eminent (so long as it can carry with it the national judiciary).[6]

When a national court *accepts* the ruling, the compliance pull of Community law becomes formidable. It is an empirical political fact, the reasons for which need not concern us here, that governments find it much harder to disobey their own courts than international tribunals. When European Community law is spoken through the mouths of the national judiciary it will also have the teeth that can be found in such a mouth and will usually enjoy whatever enforcement value that national law will have on that occasion.

(2) It would be wrong, however, to locate the significance of the partnership between national courts and the ECJ solely, or even principally, in the pathological context of non-compliance and enforcement. As a systemic parameter physiognomy usually trumps pathology. A country's health is probably better measured by indicators such as infant mortality and days lost through sickness than by a review of the latest hospital technologies for dealing with rare diseases and acute medicine. In this context, the relatively high involvement of the national judiciary in the administration of Community law may be said to have a prophylactic effect, to act somewhat like preventive medicine. This involvement helps more than any doctrinal statement of the European Court to render Community law not as a *counter-system* to national law, but as *part* of the

---

[5] In the Demirel decision concerning the treatment of Turkish migrant workers in Germany, that was one of the main issues: the very applicability of EEC law and the jurisdiction of the European Court to adjudicate the case. If the matter were in the hands of the governments of the Member States, there is no doubt in my mind that they would never have risked taking it before the European Court. Indeed, in the Maastricht Treaty, they have attempted to exclude such issues from the jurisdiction of the Court. See Art. L TEU. But the Art. 177 procedure takes it out of their hands.

[6] 'Juridifying' a dispute means that a Member State may have to defend itself before the Court. This implies an inter-statal discourse with its own discipline, language and constraints which can be quite different to the discourse of, say, diplomacy.

national legal order to which attaches the 'habit of obedience' and the general respect, at least of public authorities, to 'the law'. To the extent that national authorities feel constrained by 'the law' in the formulation and execution of policy and in the process of governance (and this will, surely, differ from one Member State to another) the higher the involvement of national courts in the administration and application of Community law, the higher will be the chances that Community norms will be regarded as part of that 'law' to which will attach the habit of obedience (cf. Hart, 1961) associated with domestic rather than international norms. In this respect it may be considered an advantage of the European system that 'everyday' national courts rather than special 'federal courts' administer so much of Community law – in co-operation with the European Court of Justice.

(3) Last but not least, the willingness of national courts, especially of lower courts, to play their role in the partnership will widen the circle of actors, individuals, corporations, pressure groups and others who may build a stake and gain an interest in the effectiveness of Community norms. In this respect we should think, on the one hand, of the relative remoteness of individuals to much of classical international law and, on the other hand, of the huge stake built into federal law in federations when that became accessible to individuals. Without overstating the point, courts are an important vehicle for popular engagement by individual and group interests with and against government. The American reader may wish to contemplate the American polity with a judicial system without any lower federal courts, with state courts indifferent to federal law, and with a Supreme Court with extremely limited individual access. That would be Europe without Art. 177 and the willing partnership of national courts. Some in America (and Europe) might like the idea, but none would deny that it would certainly be a very different polity.

If, then, the overall picture, with all the important exceptions, is one in which the national judiciary accepted both the constitutional reconstruction put forward by the ECJ and also played a willing and keen role in giving that reconstruction reality as measured by the coin of judicial co-operation in the administration of Community law through Article 177, the obvious question is to speculate about the reasons for this willingness of national courts.[7]

*Formalism.* The first possibility, one which might seem the most formal and hence the most naive, but which, in my view has considerable force, relies on the *per se* compliance pull of a dialogue conducted between courts in 'legalese'. Courts are charged with upholding the law. The constitutional interpretations given to the Treaty of Rome by the European Court of Justice carried a

---

[7] I am drawing here mostly on my own speculation in Weiler (1991, pp. 2425–6), cf. Burley and Mattli's (1993) fascinating theory.

legitimacy deriving from two sources: first from the composition of the ECJ which had as members senior jurists from all Member States, and second from the legal language itself: the language of reasoned interpretation, 'logical deduction', systemic and temporal coherence – the artefacts which national courts would partly rely upon to enlist obedience within *their own* national orders. This is not the place to enter into the vexed issue of legal indeterminacy and its compatibility with 'principled' and 'neutral' adjudication. As an empirical observation, legal formalism retains a very substantial power in European jurisprudence and the overall content of the ECJ jurisprudence seemed, (or must have seemed) to reflect a plausible reading of the purposes of the Treaty to which Member States had solemnly adhered.

My claim about the importance of formalism as one explanation for the compliance pull of the Court is re-enforced by the negative reaction of national judiciaries in the face of ECJ interpretations which seemed to do too much violence to formalistic conventions. The initial badly reasoned holding on direct effect of directives encountered national judicial hostility until a better rationale was found.[8]

*Actor interest analysis*. Another explanation expands the definition of the actors involved. As Burley and Mattli have remarkably shown, it is not the national judiciary alone which is responsible for the double acceptance, but a whole community of interests, by individuals, lawyers and courts which developed a stake – professional, financial and social – in the successful administration of Community law by and through the national judiciary and have thus acted as an agency for its successful reception (Burley and Mattli, 1993).

*Reciprocity and transnational 'judicial cross-fertilization'*. There might also be an explanation rooted in the transnational horizontal nature of the process. Apparently it does sometimes matter to courts in one Member State what 'the brethren' in other Member States are doing.[9] One reason why national courts, especially higher courts, but also lower courts, may have been tempted to resist the double acceptance could perhaps be the fear that they would be disadvantaging their national system and their governments in their dealings with other Member States. Accepting Community discipline does, after all, restrict national autonomy. Courts have been sensitive to this issue in the field of international law. Thus, when national courts are satisfied that they are part of a trend, their own acceptance is facilitated. Additionally, holding out against accepting a new doctrine when other similarly positioned courts have committed themselves

[8] Cf. Reaction to the initial Van Duyn decision and the subsequent change of direction in the Ratti, Becker and Marshall cases. For discussion and citation see Weiler (1991).
[9] For an analysis of interstatal court watching in the international law setting, see Burley (1992) and Benvenisti (1993).

might be seen to compromise the professional pride and prestige of the recalcitrant court.

The rhetoric of judicial argument and decision provides ample evidence for both lines of reasoning. We see that transnational reciprocity is employed as a device of both persuasion and justification. National courts have referred to decisions of their counterparts in other countries in a number of critical junctures.[10]

*Judicial empowerment.* Last but not least, normative acceptance of the ECJ constitutional construct and practical utilization through the 177 process by national courts may be rooted in plain and simple judicial empowerment. Whereas the higher courts acted diffidently at first, the lower courts made wide and enthusiastic use of the Art. 177 procedure in many Member States. This is understandable on both a common sense psychological level and also on an institutional plane. Lower courts and their judges were given the facility to engage with the highest jurisdiction in the Community and, even more remarkable, to gain the power of judicial review over the executive and legislative branches even in those jurisdictions where such judicial power was weak or non-existent. Has not power been the most intoxicating potion in human affairs? Even in countries which knew full fledged judicial review, such as Italy and Germany, the EC system gave judges at the lowest level powers that had been reserved within the national system only to the highest courts in the land. Institutionally, for courts at all levels in all Member States, the constitutional architecture with the ECJ signature meant an overall strengthening of the judicial branch *vis-à-vis* the other branches of government. The ingenious nature of Art. 177 ensured that national courts did not feel that the empowerment of the European Court of Justice was at their expense. After all, it is they who held the valve. Without the co-operation of the national judiciary the European Court's power was illusory.

## The European Court of Justice and the National Executive and Legislative Branches

The symbiosis between the European Court and its national counterparts may have been influenced by the similarity of the species. It is far more difficult to explain the relatively low direct level of resistance to the constitutional transformation of Europe by the governments and legislatures of the Member States.

Whereas I hope to have demonstrated that accepting the new constitutional discipline by national courts could be seen for the most part leading to judicial

---

[10] Complete citations from decisions of the various national courts illustrating this point may be found in Weiler (1993, forthcoming).

empowerment, the effect on the Member States' political branches of government could not but be seen, at least at face value, as a weakening. The traditional licence which governments and parliaments enjoy (and often celebrate in the name of the national interest and sovereignty) to bend or break their international obligations was seriously limited by the constitutionalization. Keohane and Hoffmann note in their recent study that 'of all Community institutions, the Court has gone farthest in *limiting national autonomy,* by asserting the principles of superiority of Community law and of the obligation of member states to implement [it]' (Keohane and Hoffmann, 1991, emphasis added).

To be sure, there were 'pockets' of resistance: in the French Parliament, and during the 1975 referendum campaign in Britain. But these must be seen as exceptions to the general rule of equanimity. A survey of the attitudes of MEPs to the European construct is evocative in this respect. The survey demonstrated a high approval rate for the Court. What, however, is most telling for our purposes is to note that many of those MEPs who expressed great scepticism towards, and were critical of, say, the Commission and the European Parliament (on the grounds of enjoying too much power and being too pro-supranational Europe), did not transfer the same discontent to the European Court of Justice. I think the same would be true for national parliamentarians – an anti-marketeer in the European Parliament is not, I think, a different political actor to his or her counterpart in a national chamber.

Judicial appointments by the governments of the Member States to the European Court of Justice in the 1970s and 1980s confirm the same conclusions. This is a period when any misconceptions about the 'least dangerous branch' would have already been dispelled. By this time, governments would have been fully aware of the huge significance of the Court. And yet, most appointees came to the Court with a past reputation of a general accord with the constitutional and material construct of the European Court of Justice. In the process of judicial appointments, the Member States, as far as one can tell in relation to a procedure which is far from transparent, eschewed any possible temptation at obvious 'court packing' or 'jurisdiction stripping'.

The burden of the evidence available for the period leading up to the SEA and Maastricht, is then that the Court's structural and material constitutional construct and the Court's hegemonic role in defining that construct, unpalatable as they may have been in individual decisions and contested rather strongly by individual Member States on an *ad hoc* basis, were eventually accepted by both the executive and legislative branches of the Member States.

That this should have been so is not self-evident. To be sure, we have already seen the impact on the perception of the ECJ resulting from the integration of the national judiciary into the administration of Community law. But the limits of this impact on national actors – especially governments – must be carefully drawn. The involvement of the national judiciary may explain a basic, if grudging, compliance pull of Community law and its inclusion under the domestic canopy of respect for the 'rule of law'. But forced respect for the rule of law cannot explain why governments will not have acted vigorously to change and even neutralize an uncomfortable or dangerous actor – by reducing the powers of the Court, trimming its jurisdiction and, if necessary, controlling its personnel. After all, in the same period, the Member States objected to the most fundamental decisional rules of the Treaty and unceremoniously overturned them with the 1966 Luxembourg Accord.

What, then, can explain the relative deference accorded the Court and its output by the political branches of Member State government?

I would suggest the following possible, mutually reinforcing, lines of explanation.

*Formalism.* The pull of formalism has a role in this arena too. In this context the formalistic claim is that the judicial process rests 'above' or 'outside' politics, a 'neutral' arena in which courts 'scientifically' interpret the meaning of policy decided by others. As noted above, the European tradition tends to overemphasize somewhat the formal nature of law and its alleged neutrality. The point about formalism is that its extra-legal impact is conditioned as much, or even more, by perception as by reality. Even if we fully understand some of the fictions of neutrality, the subjective belief in the apolitical and neutral nature of the judicial process is, in fact, the reality that counts.

*'Non-partisanship'.* Beyond the pull of formalism, even when the judicial process was perceived as being, in larger or smaller part, integrationist, 'political', policy driven, with varying degrees of resultant indeterminacy and concomitant judicial discretion, *it was not inter-state politics.* The Court has been scrupulously non-partisan and non-favouratist towards this or that specific Member State or group of Member States. To that extent the Court was, and was perceived to be, neutral. This perception was helped by the composition of the Bench with its virtually even national distribution, by the nature of the judicial process and mostly by the even spread of judicial deserts in which *there were no permanent and fixed Member State winners and losers.* The Court may have been perceived as a wild card or an unruly horse but not as partisan to the interests of this or that Member State.

*Interest analysis.* One could object, however, that even if the Court was not partisan to any individual Member State, its structural and material jurisprudence affected dramatically, and arguably adversely, the position of all the Member States *qua* Member States and that neither the pull of formalism nor the inter-statal neutrality can explain the relative equanimity and overall accept-ance of the constitutional jurisprudence.

In the first place, it is overstating the case to say that there was no reaction. In certain areas of jurisprudence, such as external economic relations, the States did react to countermand the potential consequences of judicial decision making (Weiler, 1985). But this reaction tended to be local and never reached the stage of a more general drive to delegitimate the Court and/or substantially recast its role through, say, Treaty amendment. Could it be that the Member States developed an interest in the new judicial *status quo* and that a stake was created in maintaining rather than challenging judicial authority? Whence this interest?

There are two ways to narrate the structural and material jurisprudence of the European Court. The classical way has been 'confrontational' and 'pathologi-cal'. It presents such emerging structural doctrines as direct effect, supremacy and implied powers or material doctrines in the area of free movement in a conflictual setting which pits the interest of this or that Member State against that of the Community and then demonstrates how these doctrines 'compel', 'constrain', 'bend' and 'subject' the Member State to a Community discipline. To use the medical metaphor again, the context is an illness – a Member State attempting to escape its Community obligations (that is the confrontational pathology) – and the structural and material doctrine is the medicine, the remedy. It is this narrative which can explain not only the localized resistance of this or that Member State to this or that judicial outcome, but also explain our expectation of a more generalized political resistance to the Court. The United States government, for example, is known to exclude or seriously limit the jurisdictional reach of its own judicial system and courts in relation to some of its trade agreements. The reasons for this USA practice are complex, but clearly one aspect is the government's wish not to have its hands tied by its own courts.

But it is possible to analyse the same structural and material constitutional jurisprudence in a political-dialectical fashion. On the whole, in the pre-SEA/ Maastricht period, the Court interfered little in the decisional process of the Community, except for a great insistence on respect for institutional arrange-ments – leaving a relatively free hand to the political organs to strike their bargains.[11] By contrast it  intervened, through its structural and material jurisprudence rather boldly in the post-decisional phase – creating a legal apparatus which would make these bargains stick. The judicial message was: you are free to bargain, but agreements reached (through legislation) must be respected. This analysis would suggest a strong interest on the part of the Member States to uphold the judicial construct, given their obvious interest in

[11] In some areas it allows Community institutions a freer hand than Member States acting unilaterally. It did intervene, however, quite aggressively to make sure that bargains were not struck outside the Community framework.

making bargains stick. As I have often argued, the fact the Member States, in the period under discussion, had jointly and severally virtual control over decision-making, would not only make the constitutional revolution digestible but would actually create an interest by the Member States in, say, supremacy, since, arguably, delicate bargains would be disrupted if Member States could disregard and violate them at will, and the Community as a whole would be disrupted if the way of responding to such violation would be classical international law devices such as reprisals, countermeasures, trade wars and the like to which we have become accustomed in other arenas such as EC–USA trade disputes.[12]

These two narratives can, thus, be recast as follows:

> Narrative 1: structural jurisprudence as a constraint on the freedom of action of individual Member States, the imposition of a Community discipline *vis-à-vis* the Member States, creating a common Member State interest in resisting the judicial move and an expectation of Member State dissatisfaction and counteraction.

> Narrative 2: structural jurisprudence ensures that bargains struck in the decisional process will stick, thereby creating a common interest in upholding the judicial doctrinal moves and an expectation of support for the Court.

To say that both narratives have their truth is to undermine their falsifiability: resistant Member State behaviour could be attributed to the first narrative, supportive, to the second. Still, both narratives do have their truth.

There is one important line of cases which cannot be explained by the second narrative: The jurisprudence of the Court concerning the internal market which derives from a direct interpretation of the relevant Treaty Articles and of which the *Cassis de Dijon* case law is the most well-known trademark, though clearly not the only line of cases. In that line of cases the Court 'decimated' classical mechanisms of state protectionism by non-tariff barriers and other forms of protectionism and national discrimination. It cannot be said that in the *Cassis* line of cases, and others like it, the Court was simply making a bargain, struck in 1957, stick. But what could be said is that the *Cassis* line of cases actually accorded and accords with Member State and Community interests. Although annoying to this or that Member State in concrete situations, the internal market jurisprudence, on this reading advanced their collective agenda.

One should be careful not to exaggerate any extrapolation of this argument. It is clearly true that in the long run, a court's jurisprudence cannot consistently stray too far from the overall political *Weltanschauung* of the polity. But it is worth remembering that in the Community, the governments of the Member

---

[12] For the most recent formulation of my theses in this respect see Weiler (1991).

States do not hold a monopoly over the definition of that *Weltanschauung*, and that the Court's jurisprudence itself has a role in defining it. It is also clearly false that a Court can never, even in critical areas and on sensitive issues, depart from that *Weltanschauung*. The single market jurisprudence of the European Court of Justice should be read as charting a *via media* between these two polls.

*Transparency*.[13] There is one additional possible explanation to the equanimity of reception by Member State political actors. At the moment in which the constitutional foundations were put in place the material province of Community law was rather narrow and socially and politically non-controversial. *Van Gend en Loos*, the case which ushered forth the new legal order, concerned tariff re-classification of imported chemicals – not an issue which would excite public sensibilities. There is, I believe, much truth in this proposition, but it has to be taken with caution. In the first place, even some of the early cases – such as *Costa* v *ENEL* which introduced supremacy in 1964 – were socially sensitive. *Costa* concerned the ability of the Italian state to nationalize public utilities, hardly a side issue. Even more so, by all accounts the Common Agricultural Policy – of huge importance to internal French and German politics – was a centre-piece of the Community legal order. It does not strike me as plausible that the French government would not assess the implications of direct effect and supremacy in such a politically sensitive area. Elsewhere I have argued for a different variant to the perception paradigm. The Member States felt less threatened by constitutionalization because they took control of the decisional process through the *de facto* veto of the Luxembourg Accord. As I shall argue below, it is the (re)introduction of majority voting in the post-SEA era which drove home the radicalness of the constitutionalization and which may, among other reasons explain why attitudes to the Court may be changing. Nonetheless, what is clearly true of the first period is that the jurisprudence of the Court 'enjoyed' a low visibility in terms of general public opinion and that the character of its case law was typically not the stuff to hit the front pages of the popular press. This, too, as we shall see, is something that is changing.

## The European Court of Justice and Academia

Finally, though of more limited political significance, the place of the European Court among academics is of some interest.

In the first place academia is, at times, a barometer to wider currents of elite public opinion. The process of European integration has from its inception been an elite driven phenomenon. Given the importance of judicial federalization, one could have expected the development in academia of a classical 'counter

---

[13] I am indebted to Karen Alter for her illuminating comments on an earlier draft in relation to this point.

majoritarian' type critique of the Court which tends to emerge in the face of judicial activism. Although the Community has had many critics over the years, a focus on legal and judicial Europe is conspicuous in its absence. This is true for political science, economics and law.

Academia is important in another way. In Continental Europe at least, the law professorate has an influential place in legal discourse. *La doctrine,* the synthetic view of legal norms, is a quasi-source of law and has an importance far greater than in, say, the USA. Academic legal writing is elemental in shaping it: as a collectivity the legal professorate is the custodian of *la doctrine.* Non critical integration of European constitutionalism into doctrine could help its legitimation within the profession.

The overall response, of academia – political science, economics and law – to the judicially-driven constitutional revolution has ranged from indifference and equanimity to celebration. Among scholars working on European integration, very few critical voices emerged in the period under consideration. It is a phenomenon which merits some reflection.

The lacuna among non-legal academics was not an outcome of analysis by political scientists and economists on the role of law and of the Court and a dismissal of them as irrelevant. There is simply no indication of this analysis and conclusion in the literature. I do not think either that an explanation can be summarized on the premise of the 'primacy of politics' or the 'primacy of economics'. After all, a turn to law and the Court by political scientists and economists was common in examining national polities.

The reason for the scarce politological literature about the Court should be sought in the intellectual background and formation of those who turned to examination of the European integration phenomenon as a whole. Two intellectual traditions served as background to Community observers and theorists: international relations and federalism.

The most common background was in international relations (IR), and by the 1950s whatever school of IR one belonged to, the function, power and importance of *international law* and, say, the International Court of Justice, were – not altogether without reason – dismissed as marginal and irrelevant. Is it possible that this baggage 'prejudiced' observers from even looking at the legal paradigm and at the Court as potentially important? As for the federalists, comparative federal experience suggests that there is some mutuality in the strengthening of central institutions in federal polities. All branches, executive, legislative and judicial tend to strengthen (not necessarily at exactly the same pace) at the expense of their counterparts at constituent unit level. The story of European integration from the late 1950s to the mid-1970s – the period in which European integration received the greatest academic attention – defied the comparative federal experience. The political institutional and decision-making processes were undergoing their deepest crisis and moving in a typically non 'federal' direction, whereas this was the 'heroic' and most 'federal' period for the law and courts. Perhaps the non-legal academic profession assumed that the political disintegration of that period would have been coupled with a reduced role for law and the Court – as was the experience with other transnational integration experiences – and just abandoned the field as not worthy of serious attention. It is a common feature of politological writing of the period to analyse the decline of the political institutions of the Community without even mentioning the Court.

If we turn to the legal academy the picture is interestingly different. Among those who turned to Community law and legal integration as a subject of research, the role of law and the Court has, if anything been overemphasized. This is reflected by titles such as *Political Integration by Jurisprudence* (Green, 1969) and *Integration Through Law* (Cappelletti *et al.*, 1986). It has been overemphasized in overstated claims about the importance of law in the overall process of European integration and the simplicity of the integration models explicitly or implicitly relied upon.

Even more interesting was the almost unanimous non-critical approach and tradition developed by European Community Law scholars towards the Court of Justice. Studies of the Court tended to be, as Shapiro scathingly but aptly put it in relation to one typical example:

> Constitutional law without politics ... [presenting] the European Community as a juristic idea; the written constitution as a sacred text; the professional commentary as a legal truth; the case law as the inevitable working out of the correct implications of the constitutional text and the [European Court of Justice] as the disembodied voice of right reason and constitutional theology... (Shapiro, 1980)

Criticism of the Court, when it appeared in the legal literature, was usually of two kinds: Either constitutional or administrative law professors fulminating at the encroachment of their turf by the newcomers and arguing, typically from a crude 'national sovereignty' basis, against the EEC usurper or critics from within the European law fraternity which, to continue the Shapiro theological metaphor, were in the Lefevre or Satmar corner, castigating the Court for any deviation from the strictest integration orthodoxy.

The few exceptions can be regarded as the proverbial exception that proves the general rule and their work was generally received with scepticism in Europe (cf. Rasmussen, 1986).

The reasons for the non-critical legal approach are, as with the other disciplines, also rooted in the background and formation of the legal professorate who turned to European integration. A great many of the first generation of professors came to Community law from international law. The international legal order was, from the 1950s until the 1980s, in deep crisis prompted by the Cold War which induced failure of the United Nations and most other major institutions. Academic international law suffered from a particularly acute spell of its perennial deep-seated insecurity (when compared to its domestic counterpart) and its practice was more than usually uncomfortable with the twin medicines of apology and rationalization. In some ways, Community law and the European Court of Justice were everything an international lawyer could dream about: The Court was creating a new order of international law in which norms were norms, sanctions were sanctions, courts were central and frequently used, and lawyers were important. Community law as transformed by the European Court of Justice was an antidote to the international legal malaise.

Secondly, with only a few exceptions, even in the national Member State public and private law traditions, from which other professors were drifting into Community law in the 1960s and 1970s with its expansion into new fields such as environmental protection and the like, there was no powerful critical tradition either on the Continent or in the UK and Ireland. The critics from without became more or less silenced, simply swamped by the general acceptance of the integration construct around them, and also unable to keep up with the increased technical proficiency in Community law which was necessary to make one's critique effective.

Additionally, in a period in which the Community was shown to be suffering from a 'democracy deficit' rooted principally in the non-accountability of the Council of Ministers directly to a parliamentary chamber and to the empowerment of the executive branch of the Member States through their reincarnation as the principal legislator when wearing their Community hat, it was easy to defend the Court as a 'bulwark' against excessive power in the hands of the Council and Commission.

Finally, no critical symbiosis developed with sister disciplines. There was no helping hand from the economic and political science flank since, as mentioned above, they simply neglected the legal phenomenon of European integration: Even in the best political science and economic works of the time, including those with considerable critical bite, when law and the Court were mentioned at all, treatment was descriptive, very often by a lawyer brought in to graft a legal chapter onto a political science volume (cf. Henig, 1980).

## Conclusions to the Retrospective

The relationship of the European Court of Justice, an actor with a powerful vision and remarkable influence in shaping key dimensions of the evolving Community, to its principal interlocutors may be described as an extended honeymoon:

- With its all important national judicial counterparts, it has been, on the whole, a story of courting and eventual consummation of a mutually empowering relationship.
- With national political organs it has been an even more remarkable story of power made acceptable to these organs by, at times, the politeness of convivial indifference, at times, the legal masks of judicial neutrality and the Rule of Law, at times, the seductiveness of calculated self-interest.
- With academia it has been either love scorned or rapture based on conquest and domination rendered felicitous by ignorance.

## II. Prospective

*Introduction*

That, then, concludes the narrative of the reception and acceptance of the Court by its three interlocutors. The honeymoon is, I think, at an end, and though no divorce is predicted, it will be the ups and downs of a mature marriage which henceforth will characterize the relationship.

There is not a year in the history of the Community where some enterprising academic could not, with credibility, convene a conference or write a paper on the theme: 'The Community in Change – Future Perspectives'. The changes I shall focus on in the post-SEA and Maastricht period are those which in my view are likely to rock the boat in the relationship between the European Court of Justice and the three sets of interlocutors we have dealt with.

My thesis is simple enough: it is not the Court which has changed or is changing in a way which will affect its perception. If anything, the Court has become somewhat more 'prudent' in its jurisprudence (Koopmans, 1986). Instead, it is the environment, political and social, and the conditions in which the Court operates which will become consequential. The Court will, I shall argue, be called upon to adjudicate disputes which, inevitably, will subject it to public debate of a breadth and depth it is unaccustomed to. For reasons I shall explain, its overall visibility is bound to grow and it will be judged by a media and public opinion far more informed than before. The adoration and adulation by academia is also, thankfully, likely to weaken.

In relation to many of these elements there is nothing the Court will be able to do, since, I shall argue, the new environment will often place it in a 'no win' situation.

The following are, then, the principal considerations affecting and constituting the new environment for judicial activity.

## Limits to Competences of the Community

The most fundamental change in the interaction of judicial decision-making in the new political environment relates to the issue of competences, the dividing line between Community and Member State sphere of activities. (I am drawing here on Jacqué and Weiler, 1990.)

The student of comparative federalism discovers a constant feature in practically all federative experiences: a tendency, which differs only in degree, towards controversial concentration of legislative and executive power in the centre/general power at the expense of constituent units. This is apparently so independently of the mechanism for allocation of jurisdiction/competences/powers between centre and 'periphery'. Differences, where they occur, are dependent more on the ethos and political culture of polities rather than on mechanical devices.

The Community has both shared in and differed from this general experience: It has shared it in that the Community, especially in the 1970s, had seen a weakening of any workable and enforceable mechanism for allocation of jurisdiction/competences/powers between Community and its Member States.[14]

This occurred by a combination of two factors.

(1) Profligate legislative practices especially in, for example, the usage of Art. 235.[15]
(2) A bifurcated jurisprudence of the Court which, on the one hand, extensively interpreted the reach of the jurisdiction/competences/powers granted the Community and, on the other hand, has taken a self-limiting approach towards the expansion of Community jurisdiction/competence/powers when exercised by the political organs.

To make the above statement is not tantamount to criticizing the Community, its political organs and the Court. This is a question of values. It is a sustainable thesis that this process was overall beneficial, in its historical context, to the evolution and well-being of Community, Member States, its citizens and residents.

The interesting thing about the Community experience, and this is where it does not share the experience of other federative polities, is that despite the massive legislative expansion of Community jurisdiction/competences/powers and the collapse of constitutional guarantees against that expansion, there had not been any political challenge or crisis on this issue from the Member States other than on an *ad hoc* basis.

---

[14] For a full analysis of this Community phenomenon, see Weiler (1991).
[15] For analysis and empirical data see Weiler (1985).

This was so mostly for the simple and obvious fact of consensus decision-making in the pre-Single European Act era. Unlike federal states, the governments of the Member States themselves (jointly and severally) could control absolutely the legislative expansion of jurisdiction/competences/powers. Nothing that was done could be done without the assent of all national capitals. This fact diffused any sense of threat and loss of power on the part of governments.

This era has now passed with the shift to majority voting in the post-SEA period. Governments of the Member States no longer have the 'veto guarantee' and thus have taken a new very hard look at the question. Limiting the competences of the Community has become one of the most sensitive issues of the Maastricht construct. The Treaty on European Union introduced formally not only the principle of subsidiarity into the Community legal regime,[16] but also set severe limits on Community legislative action in some of the new fields such as culture, public health and the like.[17] Public opinion in the Member States has also become far more sensitive to this issue.

In this new climate the Court's earlier 'hands-off' attitude to expansive Community competences will no longer work. Whether it likes it or not, it will be called upon, with increasing frequency, to adjudicate competence issues. And here the Court will be put into a 'no win' situation: Whatever decision it will take in this vexed field, it is likely to earn the displeasure of one or more powerful constituencies.

I will draw now, by way of hypothetical examples, four typical 'competence'-related scenarios which will illustrate the new political environment.

*Scenario 1: The outer reaches of Community jurisdiction.* The Commission has now before the Council a controversial draft directive proposing an almost total ban on all advertising in the Member States for tobacco products.[18] The proposal has evoked considerable controversy as evident by the heated debate in the European Parliament, the constant revisions by the Commission and the postponement, by Council. The Commission, which proposed Art. 100a as the basis for its proposal, justifies it as a measure necessary to ensure elimination of barriers to trade in media carrying tobacco advertisements and as a means to eliminate distortion to competition in the market. Its opposers claim that it is a health measure, for which the Community has no competence, masquerading as a Single Market provision. There is disaccord among the Member States about the substantive merits of the total ban and about the competence of the Community to enact such a ban. This example illustrates perfectly how the issue

---

[16] Art. 3b TEU.
[17] See, e.g., Arts. 128, 129 TEU.
[18] Commission's Amended Proposal for a Council directive on the approximation of Member States' laws, regulations and administrative provisions on advertising for tobacco products (OJ C 129/5 of 21.5.92).

of competences is almost always intricately involved with the substantive content of any proposal. Often, substantive opposition will be masked as opposition to the principle of Community jurisdiction and *vice versa*. Critically, in the pre-SEA period consensus among the Member States would be necessary for adoption. Once such consensus were achieved, the issue of competences would be diffused.

Imagine then that the proposal is adopted by majority vote and reaches the Court with a challenge claiming that the Community exceeded its jurisdiction, a claim supported by some Member States and powerful economic actors (the tobacco lobby), opposed by other Member States and the equally powerful anti-tobacco public forces.

The intricacies of jurisdictional and substantive issues are daunting. To approve the measure would represent an expansive reading of Article 100a in an era where the political climate opposes, in principle, such expansive readings. The Court might draw considerable 'flak' and its credibility as an effective guarantor against profligate Community legislation might be damaged. By contrast, to strike down the measure, even in part, will give rise to vocal complaints of the Court succumbing to the interests of big business and being insensitive to social issues.

There is no need to conceptualize the example – it speaks for itself. If I am right in my prediction that this type of issue is likely to arise with increasing frequency, it will become apparent that the Court will increasingly find itself in visible controversy.

*Scenario 2: Subsidiarity.* I do not wish here to go beyond what is necessary to achieve the objectives of this article, by adding more waste to that growth industry, academic Subsidiarity commentary. Adjudication of Subsidiarity issues is likely to put the Court in the same 'no win' situation outlined above.

Art. 3b TEU provides:

> The Community shall act within the limits of the powers conferred upon it by this Treaty and of the objectives assigned to it therein.

> In areas which do not fall within its exclusive competence, the Community shall take action, in accordance with the principle of subsidiarity, only if and in so far as the objectives of the proposed action cannot be sufficiently achieved by the Member States and can therefore, by reason of the scale or effects of the proposed action, be better achieved by the Community.

> Any action by the Community shall not go beyond what is necessary to achieve the objectives of this Treaty.

Whereas the prevailing view, influenced in part by German constitutional theory, was that subsidiarity was not a justiciable concept, in the conclusions to the Edinburgh Summit the European Council pronounced that:

> [t]he principle of subsidiarity cannot be regarded as having direct effect; however, interpretation of this principle, as well as review of compliance with it by the Community institutions are subject to control by the Court of Justice, as far as matters falling within the Treaty establishing the European Community are concerned.

Issues of subsidiarity are likely to reach the Court, if at all, when there is disagreement between a majority and minority of Member States. As regards the first paragraph of Art. 3b, the issue before the Court would present itself in precisely the manner of the tobacco draft directive given above and with the same political consequences. The second paragraph – subsidiarity in the strict sense – is, in my view, justiciable and should be so (Jacqué and Weiler, 1990). Given, however, the open-textured nature of the provision, the appropriate criterion for judicial review would be reasonableness and excess of jurisdiction. The Court should not simply substitute its view of the matter for that of the majority in Council, but decide whether, in the circumstances, the Council decision could reasonably be considered to accord with subsidiarity. In most cases the answer is likely to be positive.

But it is likely that here too, substance and constitutional limits will be intricately connected, in a sensitive political context. Each time the Court affirms a measure, it will be charged as weak on constitutional limits. When it annuls, it will be accused of being political, ideological and worse. My own view is that if the Court avoids subsidiarity issues put before it on the grounds that they are 'political', it will not only lose credibility as a guarantor against Community jurisdictional excesses, but this task will be taken on by national supreme courts at huge cost to the constitutional architecture of the Community. But this does not mean that in deciding subsidiarity issues the Court will not pay a political cost as well.

*Scenario 3: Legal bases.* The question of legal basis for Community legislation is a sub-species of the general competences issue. Here the issue is not simply whether or not the Community may act, but what is the appropriate legal basis. In the pre-SEA period this mattered little. When in doubt there was a regular usage of the catch-all Art. 235. By contrast, since 1987, under renewed Community majority voting, the legal basis means a lot: it will determine the decisional process with the intricacies of majority voting and parliamentary involvement. The intricacies of the decisional process will, in turn, determine substantive outcomes. Once more, the mixture of constitutional principle and substantive content will render these controversies, of which there have been quite a few already, increasingly explosive. A decision on a legal basis will often determine whether and with what content a decision will emerge. If say, the Court in our hypothetical tobacco directive example were to decide that Article 100a is an inappropriate legal basis and that, instead, the Community may only act on the basis of, say, Art. 235, the measure in its current form will be doomed with the same political outcome.[19]

*Scenario 4: Competences and the national courts.* The fundamental constitutional architecture of the Community as elaborated by the European Court was based, I would argue, on a subtle unstated 'Socio-legal Contract' between the ECJ and its national counterparts. The heightened sensitivity to competence issues is not likely to stop at the door of national courts. Sooner or later, 'supreme' courts in the Member States would realize that the 'socio-legal contract' announced by the Court in its major constitutionalizing decisions, namely that 'the Community constitutes a new legal order ... for the benefit of which the states have limited their sovereign rights, *albeit within limited fields*' (emphasis added) is at stake, and that although they (the 'Supreme' courts) accepted the principles of the new legal order – supremacy and direct effect – the question of who adjudicates the limits to the field is one on which a battle may be fought. The position of the European Court has been emphatic: it alone can strike down a Community measure for whatever reason, including lack of competences. But whereas national supreme courts have all accepted explicitly the basic constitutional principles of supremacy and direct effect, there has not yet been a full ventilation of the 'Kompetenz–Kompetenz' issue and it is not clear whether at least Courts such as the German, Italian or Irish highest courts will cede that power so easily.

## Visibility

Implicit in the analysis of the competence issue is another consideration – the growing visibility of the European Court of Justice beyond the circle of practitioners and cognoscenti. The increased visibility is another sign of the maturing of the system and derives, in my view, from the following causes:

(1) A general new awareness of the Community resulting from the Maastricht Debate, the first veritable Community-wide debate on the Community in its history.

A recent pioneering public opinion survey conducted through the Eurobarometer is instructive in this regard (Gibson and Caldeira, 1993a). In a Community wide survey in 1992, 34.5 per cent [20] of *Eurobarometer* respondents had

---

[19] See, e.g., Case 45/86 *Commission* v. *Council* [1987] ECR 1493 for an account of this issue.
[20] The comparable figure for the US national high court was 58 per cent. For the Commission 51.2 per cent, for the Community as a whole 81.4 per cent.

some cognizance of the European Court (63.4 per cent in Denmark, 22.7 per cent in the Netherlands) though of a non-profound nature. The learned authors of the survey conclude that '[t]hese data suggest that the Court has become more of a public institution, one that no longer works in virtual anonymity and obscurity (Gibson and Caldeira, 1993b). Excluding 'inattentive respondents' (those who registered no awareness of the Court) the results become even more remarkable. The authors of the survey, apparently using standard social science techniques in this field, developed a measurement of diffuse public support or otherwise for the Court.[21] This is not the place to reproduce the intricate techniques and the prudent analysis of the survey. One of the general conclusions of its authors is 'that the European Court of Justice has substantial but still very limited legitimacy' in the general public. 'Overall' they add, 'the European Court of Justice seems to have more enemies than friends within the mass publics of the European Community' (p. 15).

These pioneering studies will, in time, be scrutinized, hopefully repeated, and the interpretation subjected to critical review. Much of the current diffuse public attitude towards the Court is possibly conditioned by general attitudes to the Community rather than by the specificity of Court decision-making. The timing of this particular survey, in the height of the Maastricht debate, will have had its impact too. By citing some of their more dramatic conclusions I take no position except to indicate that as public visibility grows, so will public awareness, and with it, the Court will, willy-nilly, be thrown into public debate and also be used by politicians in their own arenas. The results demonstrate too another lesson of Maastricht: support by elites and public and statal institutions is not necessarily an indication for the mood in the street.

(2) The visibility of the Court has grown not simply as a result of the Maastricht-related general higher visibility of the Community, but also because of the growth in the number of cases before the Court which are of a character to capture media and public attention. The logic of the Single Market *strictu sensu* have brought before the Court cases such as the British Sunday Trading and the Irish Abortion cases. This is the stuff of headlines even in the popular press. Delors' famous prophecy of the elevated percentage of social legislation which will emanate from Brussels is also likely to contribute to the number of such high-visibility cases.

---

[21] Thus, to give but a couple of examples, one question read: 'If the European Court of Justice started making a lot of decisions that most people disagree with, it might be better to do away with the Court altogether'. Another read: 'The political independence of the European Court of Justice is essential. Therefore, no other European Institution should be able to override court opinions even if it thinks they are harmful to the European Community'.

## Case Load and Judicial Burden

In the first part of this article I retold the success story of the Court *vis-à-vis, inter alia,* national courts. This success has had a cost, the principal one of which has been a dramatic rise in the workload of the European Court of Justice, a growth which has not peaked and is likely to grow with the entry of new Member States. In 1988, 373 cases were brought before the Court, in 1989, 401 (385 ECJ, 16 Court of First Instance). In 1990, 443 (384, 59) and in 1991, 440 (345, 95). There are more cases today pending before the European Court of Justice than there were when the Court of First Instance was created and so many cases transferred to it. The average waiting time for a case is now 24.2 months which is longer than the average waiting time when the Court of First Instance was established.

This increase in the workload of the Court has had, in turn, three adverse effects (I use here Jacqué and Weiler, 1990).

(1) The time lag for Court decisions, be it under Art. 177 but also under all other heads of jurisdiction, is, in my view, unacceptable. Given that in 177 proceedings the Preliminary Reference and Ruling are only a stage in the principal judicial proceedings before a national court, the conclusion is that the invocation of Art. 177 becomes a serious time drain on the litigants undermining in a pragmatic sense the principle of effective remedies.

(2) But it is not only the time delay itself which is problematic in relation to this increase. Even if rearrangement of the working procedures of the Court would bring about a reduction in the time delay, the very fact of a large number of decisions, even if given in timely fashion, is, beyond a certain point, harmful. The corpus of decisions of the European Court of Justice constitutes a remarkable chapter of judicial excellence and creativity. Nonetheless, judges are human. There can be no question that, at a certain point, the number of cases will negatively affect the ability of the Court to address cases with sufficient deliberation. The quality of decisions is bound to suffer.

(3) Finally, it is not only the Court that is likely to suffer from the increase in the case load. The European Court of Justice is the highest judicial organ of the Community. It thus plays, like all other 'supreme' courts, a dual role. On the one hand it is, of course, the ultimate guardian of the administration of justice in the sphere of application of Community law. But, on the other hand, it is also responsible for overseeing and directing the judicial evolution of Community law. As such its judgments are designed to be read, interpreted, discussed and ultimately internalized by all legal actors within the Community who have a contact with the Community legal order. Such is the case with the jurisprudence of courts like the Supreme Constitutional Courts of Germany, Italy, the House of Lords, the Supreme Court of the United States and all similar courts.

However, as the experience of other supreme courts clearly demonstrates (Tunc, 1978), at a certain point when the quantity of cases surpasses a certain level, the ability of a supreme court to play this double role is called into question. Beyond a certain number of cases (and it is not possible nor necessary to give a precise figure) the ability of the legal community to follow and digest appropriately the jurisprudence of its high courts begins to diminish. The specific gravity of each decision is diluted and the supreme court's status at the apex of the judicial pyramid self-destructs. There are some signs that the European Court of Justice might already be facing this dilemma.

The only long-term solution to this problem is, in my view, the creation of regional Circuit Courts which will take the principal burden away from the Court of Justice, a radical redefinition of the role of the Tribunal of First Instance and the transformation of the Court of Justice into the Constitutional Court of the European Community (Jacqué and Weiler, 1990). Until this or some other solution is found, a negative effect that these practical aspects may have on the quality of dialogue between the European Court and its national interlocutors cannot be excluded. A significant and rising delay in the administration of justice, a possible decline in the quality of judgments[22] and a dilution of the specific gravity of decisions are all counter-indications to a continued healthy relationship between the European and national jurisdictions.

## The Cost of Effectiveness

Another development which is likely to have an impact on the relationship between the Court and its national counterparts, as well as political organs within the Member States, derives from the new strategies for ensuring the effectiveness of Community law. Maastricht itself provides for financial penalties for Member States who fail to comply with ECJ decisions to be determined by the Court itself in an action brought by the Commission. Additionally, the Court itself, in cases such as the *Francovich, Emmott* v. *Minister for Social Welfare, Marleasing,* and *Factortame* as well as others going in the same direction (Snyder, 1992), has developed a new strategy for rendering it more difficult for Member States to evade their obligations under the Treaty.

This jurisprudence illustrates perfectly the dilemma of the Court. There is little doubt that a high priority must be given to ensuring uniform compliance with Community law in the different Member States and that the judicial strategy adds an important dimension in this direction. But the recent line of cases represents a potential encroachment of Community law and the authority of the European Court into procedural matters which hitherto were within the

[22] One cannot but note the far greater degree of legal craftsmanship which characterize some of the decisions of the Court of First Instance compared to some recent decisions of the European Court of Justice. The time factor must be of some importance in this regard.

almost exclusive province of national courts. In the past the European Court was always careful to present itself as *primus inter pares* and to maintain a zone of autonomy of national jurisdiction even at the price of non-uniformity of application of Community law. If the new line of cases represents a nuanced departure from that earlier ethos, the prize may be increased effectiveness, but the cost may be a potential tension in the critical relationship between European and national courts.

## A Changing Academic Environment

Several changes in academic practices and processes are also contributing to a more critical environment for Court studies.

(1) There is, on the one hand, both in Europe and the US, a renewed and growing interest by political scientists in the Court of Justice, and, on the other hand, a growing number of Community Law lawyers, even sitting judges, whose writings situate the Court in its political, social and economic contexts.[23] 1994 will even see the appearance of a new legal journal, *European Law In Context,* dedicated to a non-doctrinal approach to EC legal research. These new directions are broadening the scope of judicial studies; the Court is being subjected to empirical investigation, to critical theorizing, to public attitude surveys and to a general demystification of the Community judicial function. In other words, the Court is finally receiving the attention from social scientists which its importance in the European structure merits.

(2) The growth of Community law and its heightened profile resulting from the 1992 psychosis and the Maastricht debate has removed it from the province of the closed circle of Community law experts – a category which no longer exists – and extended it into the circles of national substantive law experts. One cannot be an 'expert' in, say, Member State labour law or environmental law, without gaining proficiency in the concomitant European Community law. One effect of this transformation of the field has been the importation of a far more critical apparatus to the treatment of Community law and its Court. It is critical because the Community law importation will be judged against pre-existing substantive standards and also because these national fields have often developed their own critical tradition and the practitioners do not bring to the study of the EC and its court the exuberance of the first generation of Community lawyers.

## Conclusions to the Prospective

I have identified five areas in which recent developments would suggest a different, politically more volatile, environment for the Court. There are signs

---

[23] See, e.g., Lenaerts (1992). Lenaerts is a judge on the Court of First Instance.

that the effects of this volatile environment are already showing.

- In the political arena, in the context of the delicate competence issue, one merely has to consider, by way of example, the fierce attack by Chancellor Kohl on the Court in October 1992: 'If one takes the Court of Justice ... it does not only exert its competencies in legal matters, but goes far further. We have an example of something that was not wanted in the beginning. This should be discussed so that the necessary measures may be taken later.'[24] Far more ominous and dangerous was a suggestion, attempted to be tabled by a Member State at the Edinburgh Summit which suggested curtailing the reference powers of national courts to the European Court of Justice. It is, of course, more significant that the proposal did not gain support, but as a possible harbinger of things to come it is illustrative. The express attempt at judicial exclusion from the two Maastricht non Community 'pillars'[25] should be read as a illustration of the same type of reticence *vis-à-vis* the Court.
- In the sphere of general public opinion one may recall the tentative conclusions of the *Eurobarometer* study alluded to above.
- In the academic literature, there is a growing amount of hard hitting, irreverent, 'bottom line' oriented, and at times highly questionable legal writing about the Court (Coppel and O'Neill, 1992).

More examples could be given and should be treated, in my view, as a sign of things to come. To be sure, the general authority and support the Court enjoys is not about to be overturned. But, across a broad range, its decisions are likely to be subjected to a far greater measure of critical political, popular and academic scrutiny than in the past.

All of this should not be read as a prophecy of doom, or a programmatic warning. On the contrary, these are developments which should, in great part, be welcomed as natural and healthy. Natural, since, if anything, it is really the early period which was anomalous in allowing the Court, even if tucked away in the fairyland Duchy of Luxembourg, to be blessed with benign neglect by the powers that be and the mass media, in the face of its critical centrality to the European construct. Healthy, since it is far better that institutions such as the Court which exercise considerable power, be subjected to the scrutiny of other institutions, academia, the media and general public opinion.

Interesting days ahead.

---

[24] *Europe*, 14.10.92 No 5835. See too, 'Die leise Übermacht', *Der Spiegel*, p. 102.
[25] Art. L TEU.

# References

Benvenisti, E. (1993) 'Judicial Misgivings Regarding the Application of International Norms: An Analysis of Attitudes of National courts'. *European Journal of International Law,* Vol. 14, p. 159.

Burley, A.-M. (1992) 'Law Among Liberal States: Liberal Internationalism and the Act of State Doctrine'. *Columbia Law Review*, p. 1907.

Burley, A.-M. and Mattli, W. (1993) 'Europe Before the Court: A Political Theory of Legal Integration'. *International Organization*, Vol. 1.

Cappelletti, M., Weiler, J.H.H. and Secommbe, M. (eds.), (1986) *Integration through Law*, Vols. I–V (Berlin/New York: de Gruyter).

Coppel, J. and O'Neill, A. (1992) 'The European Court of Justice, Taking Rights Seriously?'. *Common Market Law Review*, No. 29, p. 669.

Garrett, G. (1992) 'International Cooperation and Institutional Choice: The European Community's Internal Market'. *International Organization*.

Gibson, R.O. and Caldeira, G.A. (1993a) 'Compliance, Diffuse Support and the European Court of Justice: An Analysis of the Legitimacy of a Transnational Legal Institution'. Paper presented to the 1993 Annual Law Society Association Meeting, Chicago, 27–30 May.

Gibson, R.O. and Caldeira, G.A. (1993b) 'The Legitimacy of the Court of Justice in the European Community: Models of Institutional Support'. Paper presented to the Annual Meeting of the Midwest Political Science Association, Chicago, 15–17 April.

Green, A.W. (1969) *Political Integration by Jurisprudence* (Leyden: Sijthoff).

Hart, H.L.A. (1961) *The Concept of Law* (Oxford: Clarendon Press).

Henig, S. (1980) *Power and Decision in Europe* (London: Europotential Press).

Jacqué, J.-P. and Weiler, J.H.H. (1990) 'On the Road to European Union – A New Judicial Architecture'. *Common Market Law Review*, No. 27, p. 185.

Keohane, R.O. and Hoffmann, S. (1991) 'Institutional Change in Europe in the 1980s'. In Keohane, R.O. and Hoffmann, S. (eds.), *The New European Community: Decisionmaking and Institutional Change* (Boulder, Col./Oxford: Westview).

Koopmans, T. (1986) 'The Role of Law in the Next Stage of European Integration'. *International and Comparative Law Quarterly,* p. 925.

Lenaerts, K. (1992) 'Some Thoughts about the Interaction between Judges and Politicians'. University of Chicago Legal Forum.

Rasmussen, H. (1986) *On Law and Policy in the European Court of Justice* (Dordrecht/ Lancaster/Boston: Martinus Nijhoff).

Schermers, H.G. and Waelbroeck, D. (1992) *Judicial Protection in the European Communities* (5th edn) (Deveneter/Boston: Kluwer).

Shapiro, M. (1980) 'Comparative Law and Comparative Politics'. *South California Law Review,* No. 53, p. 537.

Shapiro, M. (1982) 'The European Court of Justice'. In Sbragia, A.M. (ed.), *Euro-Politics: Institutions and Policymaking in the 'New' European Community* (Washington: Brookings).

Snyder, F. (1992) 'The Effectiveness of European Community Law: Institutions, Processes, Tools and Techniques', *Modern Law Review,* Vol. 56, p. 12.

Sorrentino, F. (1970)   *Corte Constituzionale e Corte Giustiza delle Communità Europea.*

Sorrentino, F. (1982) 'La tutela dei Diritti Fondamentali nell'Ordinamento Communitario ed in Quello Italiano'. In Cappelletti, M. and Pizzorusso, A. (eds.), *L'Influenza del Diritto Europeo sul Diritto Italiano.*

Stein, E. (1981) 'Lawyers, Judges and the Making of a Transnational Constitution'. *American Journal of International Law,* Vol. 75, pp. 1–27.

Tunc, A. (1978) *La cœur judiciaire suprême – une enquête comparative* (Recherches Pantheon-Sorbonne, Université de Paris I).

Volcansek, M.L. (1986) *Judicial Politics in Europe* (New York/Berne/Frankfurt: Peter Lang).

Weiler, J.H.H. (1982) 'The Community, Member States and European Integration: Is the Law Relevant?' responding to Hoffmann, S. 'Reflections on the Nation-State in Western Europe Today', *Journal of Common Market Studies*, special anniversary issue, No. 39.

Weiler, J.H.H. (1984) 'Attitude of MEPs Towards the European Court of Justice – Some Interim Results'. *European Law Review*, 169.

Weiler, J.H.H. (1985) *Il Sistema Communitario* (Bologna: Il Mulino).

Weiler, J.H.H. (1991) 'The Transformation of Europe'. *Yale Law Journal*, No. 100, p. 2403.

Weiler, J.H.H. (1993) 'A Quiet Revolution: The European Court of Justice and its Interlocutors'. *Comparative Political Studies* (forthcoming).

Weiler, J.H.H., Dehousse, R. and Bebr, G. (1988) 'Primus inter Pares, the European Court and National Courts: Thirty Years on Cooperation'. (The Florence 177 Project), Interim Report (European University Institute, mimeo).

# Comment on Weiler

ZENON BAŃKOWSKI

The development of the EC as a new legal order challenges traditional thinking about law. It decouples law and state; it institutes an order which is neither national nor international law. It illustrates rapid legal development by a judiciary of diverse background; it shows the importance of fundamental principles in legal development. It develops a legally-oriented concept of a transnational free market. It increasingly incorporates a human rights tradition. Joseph Weiler gives an analysis of the role of the European Court of Justice (ECJ) in this process. He looks at the 'remarkable feat' that the court performed; how it managed to start the process of creating a constitutional structure for Europe. Now, when we talk of the Community and its past or future, we do so within the context of the framework which the court has largely created. This framework for 'Community discipline' was the result of radical interpretation of the Treaty. Yet, according to Weiler, for a long time the court was able to perform this role in a relatively unimpeded way. He charts the reasons and suggests that this will no longer be so. The process that the court is engaged in will be more public and more contested. Weiler is careful to point out that he offers no grand theory, as there have not been enough empirical studies to raise the possibility of such theories. Ten years ago he ventured into this conference to present a legal perspective within a largely political discourse. He now feels it is necessary to put the legal into a political context. All this is important if we are to be able to theorize adequately the present momentous events. I do not myself wish to offer any grand theory, but Weiler's incisive and thoughtful work enables us to see how legal theory has passed these developments by. As yet, legal theory in European countries remains locked in paradigms which presuppose the nation-state or the direct link from international to municipal law. The development of European law has outrun the development of European legal theory.

*Inter alia*, he looks at the academy. Though there was much cogent analysis, there has been no real critical analysis of the court. For various reasons, that part of the academy concerned with this area was ideologically predisposed to believe in the ideal the court was driving towards. Now the framework of European law has been established and driven deep into national jurisdictions. The implications of this are that those dealing with European law now come from all parts of the academy – we are all European lawyers now. A substantive lawyer in any of the countries of the EC cannot afford to ignore the European dimension. It is, as Weiler says, shaping the national law as well. These are the conditions for a critical analysis of the court.

But what of legal theory? Is the same the case here? What are the implications for legal theory of the new and emerging normative order? We might also say that we are all European legal theorists now. By this I do not mean to say that we have to be more open to European theorists. We do of course, but that would have been true whether or not the EC existed. Rather the existence of such an entity as the EC means we have to revise our traditional theories to accommodate it. It gives us a test bed for our theories and a means of developing them in more fruitful ways. I want briefly to look at two areas where further work would be useful.

## I. State and Sovereignty

Let me start with what I think is perhaps the most important effect the EC has on legal theory (MacCormick, 1993). It decouples law and state. It forces us to revise our ideas of sovereignty upon which traditional legal theory is based.

Does it? On one view of it, it does not. The traditional view of sovereignty can accommodate this new entity. I will illustrate this with the legal system of the UK. Many have said that going too far with the EC would mean loss of state sovereignty – the sovereign state's power would be curtailed. The *Factortame*[1] case might be thought to highlight this. Here the European Court of Justice ruled that regulations made under the Merchant Shipping Act 1988 were invalid. They restricted fishing against EC fishing quotas in British waters to boats substan-

---

[1] *R v Secretary of State for Transport, ex p Factortame* [1991] 3All ER 769 (Case C221/89) CJEC.

tially British owned. However, sovereignty is not necessarily compromised. We can view this case simply as one where Parliament has delegated some of its law-making power to community organs. Thus the rules are binding ultimately by virtue of the fact that the UK Parliament has assented to this delegation. So the fact that UK legislation can be derogated by Community organs does not imply that the UK state, as personified by Parliament, is not sovereign. For that derogation is by virtue of the sovereign state. It can, technically, always repeal the act (European Communities Act, 1972) by virtue of which that derogation was made.

But can it? Is that a real possibility in the political world as it now is? Many would say that it is not. But even that would not pose a problem. For then we could say that it is the EC that is sovereign and that the UK Parliament acts by virtue of it. Either way the coupling of law and state is not endangered. But should it be?

According to Weiler, one of the reasons that the ECJ was so successful was that it was able to implicate the national judiciaries in its constitution making. For him this can be seen in the way that the most common pathway of cases to the ECJ is by a preliminary reference from the national courts under Art. 177. What this does is make the national courts partners in the task of the ECJ. In seeking the reference, the national court is acknowledging in some way that it is Community norms that are at issue here. This also widens the circle of actors for whom the European norms become not something remote but part of their actual practice. Also the ECJ gets its legitimacy both through the fact that it is composed of senior jurists in the Member States and that it works through the national law. But what are the implications of that? Weiler says that it makes them able to see EC law not as 'counter to national law' but as part of it. For Weiler it is important that much of Community law is administered not by a special system of Community courts but by the national courts. This also means that the legitimation that attaches to national law also attaches to Community law.

However, on this way of looking at it, it does not make Community law part of the national system, but its acceptance is explained by its being inextricably connected with it. Thus, one does not have to see any particular system as being sovereign. One might think instead, of many systems intermeshing and inter-connecting with no particular one being privileged. As MacCormick says, it is the curse of foundationalism that makes us think that there must be one foundation which is the basis of all the law (MacCormick, 1993). And this is precisely what the notion of sovereignty in legal theory forces us to do. For it forces us to look at normative ordering from one perspective, that of the sovereign nation-state, and to ignore all the other forms of normative ordering that occur in our everyday life. The growth of the EC demonstrates this more than the other normative orderings because it so clearly threatens the 'sovereign state' view. Politically this has important consequences. For it moves us away from looking at sovereign states, supreme in their own territory. We can look instead at various interlocking systems over the same territory and perhaps dealing with the same people. There is not one normative space but many. Furthermore normative and territorial space are not coincidental. Here two developments in legal theory are germane. Systems theory, especially in the version of Teubner (1993), helps us look at how these interconnections might work. This is particularly useful for looking at the way that the interconnections work. Particularly interesting is his *unum actum* theory where the same act has different meanings in differing normative systems. In this way communication between the systems occurs. Institutional legal theory, seeing as it does normativity mapped in institutional clusters, is also useful here (see MacCormick and Weinberger, 1986). For this enables us to get beyond the system view which seems always to lock us in one system. With it we can get 'a view from nowhere', enabling us to map all the systems and their interconnections without privileging any.

## II. Visions of Unity

What I now turn to is an examination of the normative system that is the EC. What visions and ideals does it have? What are its ideological presuppositions? Weiler gives us a clear picture of how the EC normative order has developed. He is surely right when he rejects the view that to understand this framework one needs only to study the doctrine of the court, that the other actors can be seen as objects of the jurisprudence of the ECJ. For him, it is all these actors together that might be said to constitute the constitutional framework. It is their 'multilogue' which constitutes the system. But this, and his article therefore, do not explain why it is that this happened. Rather it is a description, hermeneutically nuanced, of its happening. Positioning and doctrine, as he says, are both necessary to constitute the framework. Systems then, are interpretivist from the start. The interpretive community is itself constituted by interpretation, by the reciprocal interaction of positioning and doctrine.

I now turn to some of the problems with the 'unity' that might be ascribed here. The phrase 'common market' is significant. Unless given the specific economic meaning of a non-segmented market, it is a contradiction. For the point of the market is to make atomic individual action possible. There is nothing common, in the sense of communal, about it. Thus the more it gets 'common', in the sense of communal, the less, some would argue, is it a market (van Roermund, 1991). Weiler gets at some of these problems in an interesting manner (Weiler, 1991). He contrasts two visions of the EC. The one is a vision of the market, the other a communitarian vision. The former will transform Europe into a single market and therefore (insofar as a state is necessary) into a single state; the latter sees a limited or shared sovereignty in a growing number of fields. It celebrates a sort of interdependence, the community's interest is one interest among the national interests. Nation and community live in an uneasy alliance. What it means in the EC context is, according to Weiler,

> It is not State *or* community. The idea of community seeks to dictate a different type of intercourse among the actors belonging to it, of self-limitation in their self perception, of a redefined self interest and hence redefined policy goals. (pp. 433–4)

Better to understand some of the problems arising from this we may turn to the typology of legal orders given by Kamenka and Tay (1975). Using the work of Tonnies and Pashukanis, they have picked out ideal types of social-legal order, namely *Gemeinschaft*, *Gesellschaft* and bureaucratic-administrative, and have identified three forms of, or elements in, regulation of modern societies.

In *Gemeinschaft* law, justice is substantial and expressive of the organic community. There is no distinction between public and private, between political moral and legal issues. All are one in the community but differentiated by status.

*Gesellschaft* law is different. It arises out of, and constitutes, atomic individualism. The community is not seen as an organic whole, rather it is the sum of individual bearers of rights, all standing equal before the law and all pursuing their own interests. Contract is the paradigm form of such a law. There is a distinction between the public and the private, between the moral and the legal. This type of law is best expressed in individualistic, *laissez-faire* societies; the individual interest being just one competing and sometimes overriding interest among many.

In bureaucratic-administrative law, the concern is neither with an organic community nor one composed of the sum of a mass of competing interests but rather with policy regulation. The point here is not the adjudication of disputes between individuals, the *Gesellschaft* concern, but rather with the regulation of an activity. It is a managerial directive type of regulation concerned with the fulfilling of a particular concern, the public good, the public interests, and not with the status or rights of individuals.

This type of organization, according to Kamenka and Tay, predominated mainly in the societies of the former Eastern Europe where the 'social technical norm' predominated. Quite clearly the 'market' vision of unity falls into the *Gesellschaft* view. The community vision is somewhat more difficult to place. In many ways it fits into the bureaucratic-administrative type. And if this seems to negate community, it must be remembered that this, to proponents of the *Gesellschaft* idea, is precisely what the visions of community of the old communist countries degenerated into. Something like the community of the corporate state. This then is why Margaret Thatcher so virulently attacked that 'community' view of the market since it embodied that 'socialist' vision of community.

If we take the 'multilogue' approach of Weiler, we see that different actors have differing views of this vision. The question becomes: how can an organization which was set up as a common *market*, whatever the reasons for that, express another more communitarian view? Can you express, in market terms, something that seems to go beyond the market? How can you produce what seem to be substantive rights, from the formal rights and duties needed to run the market? Thus the formal rights and competences that are needed to set up the framework and possibility of the market, clash with the more substantive policy issues that are also used to found rights. This then is why we get, in the reasoning of the ECJ, substantive points dressed up in formalist terms. This is not hypocrisy. The Court is trying to come to terms with all the views in the multilogue. This is why Weiler is right when he says that the clashes will get greater not because of the formal competences that are being discussed. Rather, it will be an effect of the particular substantive issue. Take Scenario 1 and the ban on tobacco advertising. Is this really a case of unfair competition and therefore within the competences of the organs? Or is it a substantive issue of health policy? The latter is one that fits the bureaucratic-administrative typology – state intervention in private rights. The former fits the *Gesellschaft* typology – making the market framework. The Court, swayed by both visions, nevertheless, will have to start from the original vision of the *market*.

The effect of this will be to lead to more clashes. Why? We have here, as we saw, an interpretive community being constituted. Who are the objects of that jurisprudence? It is not the actors that Weiler mentions, for they help constitute that jurisprudence. The 'habit of obedience' is mainly given by the citizens of the Community. As the framework of 'Community discipline' gets more developed and more pervasive it impinges upon them as well. They are not part of the interpretive community as yet but are being more and more constrained by the EC. The question then naturally arises: by what power is that interpretive Community doing what it is doing? Is not the Court arrogating to itself powers beyond the formal law? Are not the officials and Community organs doing the same themselves? Have we not now got the tyranny of the official, even though they are trying to help? This then, is the democratic deficit.

Secondly, one seems to get into a situation where what seem fundamental rights are translated into economic rights. Thus in the tobacco case one might say that the right to health is translated into the right of free competition. In

*Grogan*,[2] questions about the right to life are seen only in terms of the right to free movement of labour (Phelan, 1992). So we get the translation of fundamental rights into economics. Thus the universality of fundamental rights is being transmuted into the contingencies of economics.

There is an opposing view to this. These so-called fundamental rights are contingent and substantive. What are called economic rights are in fact related to keeping the market going as an efficient and fair entity. These might lead one further into substantive rights than one thought but then so be it. The Court now has a well-formulated jurisprudence and mode of reasoning (Begoetxchea, 1993). But they precisely show how it is not merely formal considerations that play a part but also policy directed visions of what is good for the Community.

The challenge for legal theory then is to marry these principles into a vision of a polity, even though there will inevitably be internal tensions. How to understand an order where the sovereign state has no longer such sway, where group identity counts, where there are many normative systems intersecting with no one being especially privileged? The problem is not altogether new. How to combine market visions with communitarian visions? How to achieve this without collapsing into the bureaucratic administrative systems of the old Eastern Europe or the soulless vision of fully-fledged market capitalism? The events in Europe in the last few years have ensured that this process is no longer something that we can ignore. Which vision of the community will prevail is not clear. What is clear is that we have only just begun working on the legal theory of Weiler's community vision and beyond.

## References

Begoetxchea, J. (1993) *The Legal Reasoning of the European Court of Justice* (Oxford: Clarendon Press).

Kamenka, E. and Tay, A. (1975) 'Beyond Bourgeois Individualism: The Contemporary Crisis in Law and Legal Ideology'. In *Feudalism, Capitalism and Beyond* (Canberra: ANU Press).

MacCormick, D. N. (1993) 'Beyond the Sovereign State'. *Modern Law Review,* pp. 1–18.

MacCormick, D.N. and Weinberger, O. (1986) *An Institutional Theory of Law* (Dordrecht: Reidel).

Phelan, D. R. (1992) 'The Right to Life of the Unborn v Promotion of Trade in Services: The European Court of Justice and the Normative Shaping of the European Union'. *Modern Law Review,* pp. 670–89.

Teubner, G. (1993) *Autopoiesis in the Legal System* (Oxford: Blackwell).

---

[2] Case 159/90, *Society for the Protection of the Unborn (Ireland) Ltd v Grogan and Others* [1991] 3 CMLR 849.

Van Roermund, B. (1991) 'The Common Market and Legality'. Paper given to IVR World Congress, Göttingen.

Weiler, J. H. (1991) 'Problems of Legitimacy in Post 1992 Europe'. *Aussenwirtschaft*, pp. 411–37.

# 6.
# The New Regionalism and Developing Countries

## I. Introduction

The purpose of this article is to outline the salient components of a modern, 'state-of-the-art' approach to the analysis of regional economic integration (REI), and to consider the light it throws on policies of regional integration among developing countries in the present context of policy reform. In the light of that discussion, the article goes on to discuss some topical aspects of the bearing of the new regionalism and of some elements of newer analytical approaches for the main concerns of the European Community with regional economic integration. Its empirical focus is, for that reason, on Africa, but the discussion has a wider application.

A number of the most recent re-evaluations of regional integration among developing countries are based essentially on orthodox customs union theory and focus almost exclusively on discriminatory trade policies. They do not take any account of other important ingredients of the theory of international integration, and thus neglect many of the benefits that should form part of a state-of-the-art evaluation of the case for REI among appropriate partners. The neglected ingredients add weight to the orthodox case which, in any event, is not irrelevant, even in an era of policy reforms that emphasize outward-looking trade policies.

* I am indebted to Rolf Langhammer and André Sapir for comments on an earlier draft of this article.

© Basil Blackwell Ltd 1994, 108 Cowley Road, Oxford OX4 1JF, UK and 238 Main Street, Cambridge, MA 02142, USA

## II. New Approaches to Regionalism

The term 'the new regionalism' may be employed in either of two senses. Firstly, it has been used to refer descriptively to the new-found or rediscovered enthusiasm for REI that has recently been evident in Europe, Africa, and North and South America. This phenomenon has been partly fuelled by GATT failures. But is partly attributable to the EC's own initiatives aimed at establishing a Single European Market (SEM) and an economic and monetary union, and the perceptions and responses of other countries – notably the US – to those developments.

But the term may be used in an alternative sense to refer to state-of-the-art theoretical analyses of the effects of REI, many ingredients of which have themselves been partly stimulated by these developments. This is the new regionalism on which this article concentrates. The analyses in question fall into two main categories. The first and largest category consists of studies that evaluate regionalism in terms of the interests of the blocs themselves. Although many of these studies are purely academic, a large and growing number are driven by the institutional policy concerns of the European Community or international agencies, and some of these are frankly forensic and justificatory. The second stream of theorizing about regionalism, though also prompted by contemporary developments, is not concerned with evaluating REI from the standpoint of the internal interests of the blocs themselves, but instead with a consideration of the multilateral dimension of regionalism in its impact on the world trading system and on world welfare (Krugman, 1992; Bhagwati, 1992). The two dimensions are not, of course, unrelated. Unlike the first stream of analyses, the second has little empirical content and might be designated as oracular. Stimulating and provocative as it may be, it will not be further considered in this article.

A survey of the analytical literature of regionalism of the past five years or so prompts the reflection that, although it contains much that is important, much of what is important is not new, and much of what is new (and apparently paradoxical), is not important. For instance, the significance of transactions costs was emphasized by Jacob Viner; of public goods by Harry Johnson; and long before Krugman (1988) drew attention to the significance of economies of scale for comparative cost theorizing on integration, Grubel, Kojima and Meade had identified the problems. Likewise, Kindleberger dealt with important aspects of TNCs in integration as long ago as 1959.

In certain instances, the new approaches represent attempts to deal with crucial omissions of the orthodox static analytical framework. But much of what is sometimes put forward as unorthodox in respect of impacts and gains represents to an extent a revival, rediscovery, re-emphasis, or novel juxtaposition of matters dealt with in earlier theorizing. That should not surprise. The 'state-of-the-art' in economics rarely embodies revolution. Nevertheless, significant new policy perspectives and implications do arise partly from the combined thrust of current analytical appraisals which attempt to take these and other factors into account, and partly from the relative weight which is attached to the various effects as compared with those considered by orthodox analysis.

In relation to advanced countries, the implications of recent new approaches have on the whole been perceived as reinforcing the traditional benefits of REI in a variety of policy domains, and thus to strengthen the case for regional integration – or, as in Europe in the last decade, to strengthen the case for closer integration.

By contrast, the balance of recent 'Northern' policy-oriented appraisals of REI among developing countries and, significantly, the one sponsored by the World Bank and CEPR (de Melo *et al.*, 1992), have been unsympathetic or hostile. Part of the reason for this difference may lie in the fact that these appraisals focus largely on conventional trade policy considerations, whereas appraisals for blocs of advanced countries are based on much broader considerations. To put the matter another way, unlike the case for advanced countries, most recent attempts to evaluate regionalism among developing countries take little or no account of the considerations stressed by state-of-the-art analyses. Forming a correct view of the appropriate role for regional arrangements among developing countries is not made any easier because for most third World blocs, actual or prospective, good empirical evidence is lacking on the significance of most of the unorthodox effects to which newer analyses, hitherto geared to advanced country blocs, have typically given great weight.

Two principal features characterize newer approaches to the analysis of regionalism among advanced countries from the standpoint of the blocs themselves: firstly, their analytical models rest on less restrictive assumptions than those of their predecessors; and secondly, and partly for that reason, they identify a range of non-orthodox sources of benefit.[1]

The essence of the newer approaches (which originated in and for advanced countries), could be expressed in the following ways: they perceive the potential gains from REI or regional economic co-operation (REC) (taken here to include integration, co-ordination and harmonization) as coming from two sources. The first is the gains from overcoming the costs associated with market distortions and barriers that result from government policies. These costs are not limited to the traditional static allocative costs of tariffs (on which earlier trade creation

---

[1] How far treatment of the new approaches to REI constitutes a progressive, rather than a degenerative research agenda in the methodological sense is a question that will not be pursued here. Some relevant material will be found in Bensel and Emslie (1992). But in any case, as with the post-neo-functionalism of political science, it seems clear that some of the newer economic analyses lack predictive content and are essentially descriptive or taxonomic in nature.

and trade diversion-centred analysis focused) and of equivalent quantitative restrictions. A feature of newer approaches is the emphasis given to the impact of integration on production via the effect of regional integration on cross-border direct investment and investment creation and diversion. The new approaches also emphasize administrative efficiency, and transactions costs. It should be underlined that most of these costs (in the European context these have been termed 'the costs of non-integration'), together with the corresponding gains from overcoming them by integration, may arise even when significant differences in 'comparative advantage' are lacking. The second source of potential gain arises from policy co-ordination. Gains can be anticipated from this source where there are economies of scale in the operation of the public sector, and/or significant external repercussions are involved in the use of policy instruments or in the development and operation of infrastructure.

Two other considerations find an important place in newer approaches. The first is the renewed emphasis on the point that it is a necessary condition of actually securing the potential benefits of REI that its gains should be acceptably distributed. If the market cannot itself be relied upon to bring this about, it is emphasized that some form of regional policy will almost certainly be a condition of long-term cohesion – as indeed has been recognized in the case of the EC.

Secondly, emphasis is given to the importance of 'credibility'. If this is lacking, the behaviour of crucial actors – in particular that of investors on which production integration depends – is unlikely to be constructively influenced, and the 'regional problem' is likely to be made worse. Credibility and the related attention given to enforcement mechanisms constitute elements of a state-of-the-art approach which has important implications for the traditional perceptions of the political classes in developing countries concerning which countries might constitute appropriate partners for them. It has implications too for a hitherto major stumbling block of Third World groups, namely, the difficulty of ensuring that all benefit.

Both the Cecchini Report (CEC 1988) and a number of the studies produced in connection with the Canada–US free trade area (CUSFTA) initiative (see, for instance, those contained in Whalley and Hill, 1985), are examples of state-of-the-art approaches to the evaluation of potential gains from market completion in regional integration schemes. A central feature of these analyses is that they rest on theories of international trade which encompass scale economies, product differentiation and imperfectly competitive behaviour. At the same time, they each incorporate substantial elements of an industrial organization approach. In such a framework, additional sources of potential efficiency gains from integration must be taken into account, over and above any that may derive from what is loosely termed 'comparative advantage'. These include, notably, reductions in oligopolistic margins and gains from reducing 'X-inefficiency'. Further sources of 'unorthodox' gains arising from reductions in transactions and administrative costs were addressed in the Cecchini Report. In general, the report emphasized the major significance of a variety of non-tariff barriers which impede not only trade, but also production and investment integration. Elaborate empirical studies were commissioned to quantify their costs.

Despite its important contribution to the state-of-the-art discussion, the Cecchini Report can be criticized for several crucial omissions.[2] Firstly, it did not address distributional aspects of market completion. This is a deficiency which others have subsequently attempted to remedy (Neven, 1990). Secondly, it failed to treat dynamic effects adequately. One approach to quantifying these has been put forward by Baldwin (1989). Thirdly, although the report recognized the importance of competition for capturing the potential unconventional gains that it identified and quantified, it neglected to consider the significance in this connection of the behaviour of TNCs (Robson, 1993). In view of the dominant role in trade and production of TNCs in the EC, and their ability through internalization to circumvent the operation of the market, this is a potentially serious omission. The implications of regional integration for foreign direct investment (FDI) itself in the context of 1992 and more broadly have been the subject of considerable attention in several sources (Gittelman, 1992; UNCTC, 1990).

In another important policy domain, namely that of monetary integration, newer evaluation criteria that look beyond those of traditional optimal currency area theory have been much in evidence. Their application can be seen in the analyses of the costs and benefits of integration undertaken by the European Commission (CEC, 1990) and by others (see, e.g., Gros and Thygesen, 1992; Cobham and Robson, 1992; de Grauwe, 1992). In this policy domain, however, attempts at quantification of benefits have been few (CEC, 1992).

### III. The Structural Context and Performance of Regionalism Among Developing Countries

Many arrangements for REI among developing countries (DCs) have been established in Africa and Latin America, since the initial enthusiasm for bloc formation in the early 1960s.

The structural context in which developing country initiatives took place was then, and continues to be, very different from those of the EC, EFTA and North America. For instance, in Africa, intra-regional trade intensity is relatively low and external trade dependence is correspondingly extremely high;

---

[2] The Cecchini Report was not concerned with the external effects of the SEM. As far as developing countries are concerned, this aspect has been considered by Koekkoek et al.(1990).

exports consist mainly of agricultural and mineral products; transactions costs are relatively high; market size is small in relation to the minimum economic size for many industrial products; very large disparities exist between levels of income and development of countries in relevant regions; frontiers are permeable, and 'informal' trade is of great significance in many countries; major distortions impede the working of the market system. The inference that has been drawn from orthodox theory is that countries with such characteristics form neither optimal trading blocs nor optimal currency areas.

It is in fact the case that hardly any of the African trade blocs have been successful. Most blocs have been incapable of generating immediate, significant and tangible benefits in terms of trade expansion or faster growth. The protectionist and inward-looking bias of most arrangements partly explains their inability to generate net benefits. In these, and in certain other cases also, badly chosen sequencing, instruments and structures have contributed to their ineffectiveness. Nor surprisingly, their failure to produce tangible benefits has eroded real political support for them during the past decade or so. (A cynic might term much of the support as 'acts of piety rather than commitments to specific action' – as Marjolin once characterized certain early EC initiatives!) In the few cases where benefits were demonstrably significant, such as in the East African Common Market (or for Latin America in the Central American Common Market), and even where they were not, the distribution of gains, and in particular, the perceived lack of benefits derived by less developed partners, has been an acute source of stresses. Suitable compensation schemes have been difficult to devise. Distributional stresses, in combination with political differences on the role of the state, have in some cases, as in East Africa, produced break-up. In others, more commonly, the institutional arrangements have formally continued, but there has been a widespread failure to implement crucial aspects of the agreements, in some cases from the outset. A further problem is that the national policy responses to the financial crises that originated in the oil shocks also widely produced distortions and severe interferences with markets. The effect of the distortions was to render market-driven integration largely ineffective – and indeed – inappropriate.

Arrangements for monetary integration have been rather more successful. During the 1960s and 1970s, African unions experienced low inflation accompanied by a generally better growth performance than other similar countries lacking unions. The unions also appear to have contributed to promoting economic integration in the form of expanded trade and cross-border investment flows during that period. Relative performance in the 1980s is more difficult to evaluate and remains a controversial issue.

Several recent statistical and econometric studies have attempted to appraise the growth and other measurable effects of past REI initiatives. The most notable include studies of trade blocs throughout the world (de Melo *et al.*, 1992), and of the impact of the African monetary unions (Devarejan and de Melo, 1987, 1991; Guillaumont *et al.*, 1988).[3] Their results are consistent with earlier appraisals based on qualitative, industrial and institutional studies.

Analysis of the historical record of regionalism may suggest a variety of lessons for the future. But past performance as such is unlikely to be a good basis for prognosis unless it is the case that the crucial current external and domestic policy contexts, constraints and concerns and those in prospect are sufficiently similar to those of the past. In fact, both the domestic and international contexts are in significant respects different from the context of the first and largely unsuccessful wave of regional initiatives.

The first difference is that the policy reforms adopted during the past decade in many Latin American and African countries have involved a crucial emphasis on trade liberalization and on outward-looking policies.

The second important difference is that the world trading environment in the future promises to be strongly influenced by the success and the practices of the EC and those of the emergent trading bloc of North America. Even if an Asian bloc should not be established, producing a triad of major regional blocs, the potential impacts on developing countries as a whole of the North American Free Trade Area (NAFTA) and US initiatives towards Latin America and, more especially, of the completion of the SEM, can be expected to be considerable, and to have a significant bearing on the weight of the case for integration among developing countries.

The third important difference is that 'the new regionalism' promises to direct the attention of policy-makers to domains of integration that were not central to the concerns of the original initiatives.

## IV. Regionalism Among Developing Countries in the New Context

How far do the sources of benefit stressed in the new thinking on REI affect the merits of the case for regional integration among developing countries in the present policy context? Has the new thinking any implications for the specific character and thrust of integration among suitable partners? In this connection,

---

[3] It is beyond the scope of this article to go into these studies, but three points should be borne in mind in considering their significance; first, the evaluations rest in part on broad cross-country comparisons and regressions, whereas what is relevant is how the actual experience of the Member States themselves compares with what it would have been without integration; second, for most blocs of developing countries it should not be surprising if attempts econometrically to go beyond cross-country regressions to allow for an unspecified integration effect are apt to find an absence of significant effects because they assume implementation which, in the real economy, as noted, has rarely occurred: thirdly, the measures of trade impacts look only at recorded trade and take no account of informal and clandestine trade which in Africa accounts for much cross-border activity.

it should not be assumed that the factors stressed in newer approaches, which have been elaborated mainly with advanced countries in mind, necessarily have a similar importance in developing countries.

In forming a view on the role of REI among developing countries, in addition to the material already mentioned on the EC and CUSFTA, note should be taken of a number of recent surveys that have specifically discussed the issue. (See, in particular, World Bank, 1989; *Journal of Common Market Studies*, Special Issue, June 1992; World Bank and CEPR, 1992, 1993; *Economic Journal*, November 1992.) The last two surveys however, either treat Africa and Latin America rather superficially, or, in the case of the *EJ* policy forum, not at all.

The progress of structural adjustment and the character of the process, including its emphasis on outward-looking policies, pose a number of questions for regional integration among developing countries. In that context, are the benefits of integration increased or diminished? Are the prospects of workable integration advanced or retarded? What changes in existing arrangements are needed to exploit such possibilities as will be created?

Few, if any, convincing arguments can be made for the proposition that the new policy context in any way reduces the potential benefits to be derived from well-formulated arrangements for REI among suitable partners. On the contrary, insofar as the adoption of structural adjustment programmes (SAPs) is concerned, these should in principle be expected to make the pursuit of economic integration easier and its benefits greater in several ways. The administrative reforms that are involved, by reducing unnecessary bureaucratic constraints on the working of the market, should enable the private sector to trade and invest more easily. The usual accompanying fiscal and structural reforms should at the same time increasingly help to ensure that market-driven integration does in fact serve the interest of participating countries by basing it firmly on efficient investment and production structures in the member states. The difficulties that SAPs have presented for certain established blocs may seem to contradict this view. But such difficulties have resulted from a failure of SAPs – hitherto purely country-specific in nature – to give any weight to the regional dimension.

Yet despite the lack of any analytical or empirical foundations for supposing that the policy reform context reduces the potential benefits from regional integration, several important studies undertaken in connection with appraisals of the new enthusiasm for regionalism nevertheless contend that with outward-looking policies and trade liberalization, any gains from trade creation through market integration among developing countries must be negligible (de Melo and Panagariya, 1992). *A priori*, it is difficult to see why this should be so, though such a view might well be justified for certain countries or groups. But in any case, it should not be forgotten that in state-of-the-art analyses that address the

European context, gains other than trade creation gains have been claimed (CEC, 1988) to be several times more important than those conventional ones. There are indications that some at least of these other gains are of similarly great importance for blocs of developing countries.

The message from the World Bank–CEPR conference is nevertheless unequivocal. Despite the current enthusiasm for REI in the south, it urges that any attempt to promote South–South integration in the future should be resisted. Unilateral liberalization is its recommended strategy. This is the orthodox view reasserted in an orthodox perspective. Integration is identified with tariff-preference-based trade expansion to the neglect of other significant aspects of integration and sources of benefit.

The proposition that developing countries should not be encouraged to go *just* for their local markets on the basis of trade preferences is indisputable but banal. In the context of the revolution in the attitudes of most African governments today, and of the SAPs that affect most of them, it is also a man of straw. In any case the arguments in favour of REI that stem from the newer thinking have a much broader foundation. Thus the fact that less developed countries (LDCs) may not be optimal trading areas or optimal currency areas in terms of the categories of orthodox analysis does not justify the inference that the potential gains from integration are small if there are other significant sources that orthodoxy neglects. Those emphasized by newer approaches in connection with the real economy have already been briefly mentioned. They may usefully be spelt out at this point.

In the first place, apart from the static allocation effects of REI, on which the 'World Bank approach' is formally founded, there are administrative, efficiency (via increased competition) and transactions cost savings to consider, all of which have been much emphasized for the EC. In its case, they were thought to be several times larger than orthodox TC gains. A growing number of studies point to the conclusion that the costs of non-integration in relation to these matters are apt to be even more important in Africa where they contribute greatly to market fragmentation and avoidable costs and inefficiencies. For instance, the cost per ton/kilometre of unilateral transport policies in West Africa (involving road blocks for enforcement) has been put at considerably more than the cost of transport itself! (Badiane, 1992). It takes 28 days for a heavy goods vehicle (HGV) to make the round trip from Mombasa to Bujumbura. Settling payments through African banking systems (outside the monetary unions) can take 4–6 months.

Secondly, although scale economies in themselves fail to provide a justification for REI (Robson, 1987b), where such economies arise in the provision and operation of goods and services, notably infrastructure, whose products are only to a limited extent tradeable internationally, different considerations apply.

In these cases substantial gains can be expected from regional co-operation. In practice, such gains can only be procured by regional, as opposed to 'global' co-operation. Interstatal roads, railways, ports, telecommunications and water supply and energy are cases in question, if credibility, which means security, can be guaranteed. Certain well-recognized aspects of research, education, public health and the environment constitute other areas where the advantages of rationalized production and administration on a regional basis are not disputed even by 'regio-sceptics'.

Thirdly, there is a range of public activities that typically gives rise to significant external repercussions, partly in the provision of public goods, but more particularly in the use of policy instruments. In these cases also, regional integration or harmonization or co-ordination can yield potential benefits. At the level of policy instruments, taxation instruments and policies and a variety of supervisory activities in financial market regulation and in transport are in question. In its own case, the EC has accepted the need for fiscal harmonization as a preliminary to opening its internal frontiers to unrestricted trade. In Africa, most internal frontiers are already substantially open, or more accurately, highly permeable, but outside existing blocs no prior harmonization has been attempted (Berg, 1985; Robson, 1987a). The outcome for many countries has been major fiscal losses and the growth of much 'directly unproductive and rent-seeking activity' (Bhagwati, 1982). Although fiscal competition (like currency competition through parallel currencies) continues to find a few supporters among analysts of integration strategies in Europe, the argument in favour of any such 'market' approaches to harmonization and integration among developing countries appears to be even more misplaced than it is for Europe.

Yet there has been a widespread disposition to argue in their favour. For instance, Deardorff and Stolper (1990) say of illicit trade, that 'smuggling in African circumstances is an unequivocal blessing for the economies, the people, and ultimately perhaps even for the governments'. In a strictly limited sense this cannot be denied. Smuggling in Africa can sometimes be considered to be a healthy reaction to bad situations caused by bad policies. But the crucial objection is that it is a third-best solution as compared with the outcomes to be realistically expected from different degrees of co-ordination. Moreover, evaluations that view it favourably take no account of the tax revenues which are lost, although it is true that smuggling is not simply motivated by tax avoidance considerations (Berg, 1985) and that currency distortions play a large part.

There are, in short, many areas in the three general fields enumerated, where good arguments of principle exist for supporting regional integration initiatives, based in part on unconventional benefits. The integration policies required to secure them do not, for the most part, depend on cost-raising protection and would not therefore be inconsistent with World Bank doctrine. At the same time, for a variety of practical reasons bound up with the impact of organizational, managerial and information costs, many could not be implemented other than on a regional basis.[4] Of course, an insufficient degree of similarity in political and social preferences might rationally rule out integration in certain domains on a regional basis, even when there are solid economic gains to be anticipated. The issues, well explored in the academic literature, have recently made a dramatic entry in public debate in Europe in the debate on subsidiarity in connection with the Maastricht Treaty.

A further different reason for giving REI some weight in developing countries has been articulated in certain World Bank circles less hostile to REI. This sees a role for regional market protection in the context of outward-looking policies – in Africa at least – as a transitional means of supporting SAPs. The argument, which is essentially a variant of the training ground argument, is that the costs of adjustment will be reduced if firms are first exposed to competition from other firms in the region before they are exposed to the full force of world competition. Some of the evidence for the training ground argument, utilizing as an indicator Spearman rank correlation coefficients between the absolute growth of intra- and extra-regional growth of manufactures, is assembled in Table A.1 of Langhammer and Hiemenz (1990).

If policies of REI are being evaluated practically, and *ex ante*, a crucial question is whether the size of the potential benefits would justify the costs of negotiation. In many parts of Sub-Saharan Africa (SSA), much of the work of negotiation has already been undertaken for a number of aspects of policy. That consideration would argue for giving some weight to trying to reap the benefits by building on what exists, though there can be no doubt that, in Africa in particular, a major rationalization of existing organizations and institutions concerned with integration is urgently needed. In the past, aid has often served to disguise both the costs of a failure to rationalize institutions and those of the non-integration of economies.

This article has so far been focused on South–South integration. But an important aspect, both of recent developments, and of academic analysis, has been a consideration of North–South integration. This is perhaps the single novel feature of the new regionalism in practice. A free trade area (FTA) covering the whole of North America, incorporating Mexico, Canada and the United States currently awaits ratification. Other free trade arrangements are in

---

[4] This does not apply to non-tariff obstacles to market integration that take the form of quantitative restrictions on trade and currency controls. These can and should be relaxed on a non-discriminatory, not a regional basis. To do so would in any case usually favour intra-regional trade since regional products are usually good substitutes, whereas quantitative restrictions are commonly biased against them and favour imports from the rest of the world.

prospect between South American blocs (and perhaps individual countries), and the United States. A number of unorthodox potential advantages can be urged in favour of such kinds of arrangements for developing countries. Increased credibility is one of the most important of these. Experience of the arrangements for monetary integration in francophone Africa which have survived for 40 years would certainly lend support to this proposition. This source of potential gain, however is almost certainly dependent on the arrangements in question yielding significant benefits which would not otherwise be obtainable. This could reasonably be expected to be the prospect of the case for an FTA with the US, where guaranteed access to a large market, encouraging inflows of FDI to less developed partners to serve the US market, is both a powerful inducement for initial entry and a strong assurance of later adherence to the rules. Where non-tariff barriers exist in potential major markets of developing countries that REI can be expected to overcome or reduce, the orthodox proposition that unilateral liberalization is the first-best trade policy may not be valid.

The World Bank–CEPR report recognized the merits, on such grounds, of SSA integration with the EC, but did not see that as a feasible goal. On that assumption, it advocated that integration efforts in Africa should be discouraged on the grounds that they would divert attention from efforts to integrate SSA with the world economy.

For SSA countries, entry to the EC is certainly not an option. But to discourage intra-SSA integration on that ground is questionable, neglecting as it does a number of significant sources of potential benefit of the kinds already outlined. Regional integration initiatives aimed at securing many of these would not entail cost-raising discrimination, although once-for-all adjustment costs would often have to be incurred.

A further important reason for questioning the view from the World Bank that SSA integration should be discouraged, resides in the external implications of the initiatives already discussed that are being taken in regional blocs of advanced countries to overcome the costs of market fragmentation. If Africa does not respond with policies to reduce its own costs from non-integration, it will be relatively less well placed in the future to compete in attracting inflows of foreign investment and technology and cross-border investment on which it will continue to depend heavily for development. Beyond that, African countries need to prepare the ground that will enable them to take full advantage of longer-term developmental opportunities that can be expected to present themselves if wage convergence in Europe prompts a further shift of labour-intensive production from the EC's periphery to developing countries. Regional economic integration may be the most practicable way to minimize the costs of African market fragmentation that is necessary on these counts. It may thus be a precondition for, rather than an obstacle to, integrating SSA more effectively with the world economy. The arguments in favour of certain kinds of regional monetary arrangements, in that case, mainly to ensure macroeconomic stability, are similarly telling.

The importance of REI for development anywhere in the world should not be exaggerated. Integration cannot be a substitute for good domestic policies and does not render them any less necessary. But the arguments that favour its pragmatic retention as a policy tool in developing countries, in part as a means of reinforcing good policies, appear to be more compelling than those that simply argue for its blanket rejection on orthodox trade-based considerations. In the end, however, only convincing empirical evidence of the wider benefits of REI can decide the issue, and at present that is lacking. This is equally the case however for many aspects of the reform programmes which are currently advocated by international agencies.

## V. The Implications for Development Assistance Policy: The Role of the EC

To turn in conclusion to development assistance policy in the new context of policy reform and analysis, several broad issues are posed by regional initiatives. There is, first, the basic issue of whether REI initiatives should be supported, and if so what kinds? There is, secondly, the issue of whether development assistance can be made more effective by taking the regional dimension into account. In relation to the EC's specific concerns, there are two main immediate aspects. Firstly there is the question of how to implement those parts of the Lomé Agreement that provide for support for regional co-operation. Secondly, in pursuance of the consensus at the Maastricht Africa Conference of July 1990 that the EC should play a leading role in promoting economic integration in Africa, there is the question of what kinds of initiatives the Community should put forward in meetings of the donor community. A third question for the longer term is whether, in light of the strong thrust towards regionalism in trade policy towards Latin America, and signs of its possible emergence in Asia, the EC should not consider the case for moving towards reciprocity when the trade policy provisions of Lomé V are negotiated. Improved market access to Europe for ACP countries on such a basis might well ultimately offer gains to both side, and for Africa, provide a basis for giving greater credibility to policy reform and regional integration in Africa.

It has been suggested in this article that there is no theoretical reason for supposing that regionalism in trade policy among developing countries need be other than beneficial purely in terms of trade creation, so long as it is coupled with a significant degree of trade liberalization that is a normal requirement of SAPs. The other benefits from market unification through regionalism that are stressed in newer approaches can only reinforce the practical benefits that could be anticipated in appropriate cases. Likewise, modern analysis suggests non-traditional benefits from forms of regional monetary co-operation and integration, notably as a means of producing macroeconomic stability. No convincing empirical evidence has been adduced to support the view that such policies would be harmful. If that is accepted, the real issue for the EC concerns the kinds of regional arrangements that should be supported.

The principal reappraisals cited in this article that deal specifically with developing countries (de Melo and Panagariya, 1993; Langhammer and Hiemenz, 1990; Langhammer, 1992) take the view that, among developing countries certain limited regional arrangements have merit. They see these, however, mainly in terms of *ad hoc* co-operation for such purposes as regional transportation, research, the environment, etc. The objection to confining support for regional arrangements to such areas on an *ad hoc* basis and discouraging any multipurpose arrangement – existing or proposed – that possesses a continuing institutional basis, and centring on market unification, is twofold. Firstly, if confined to such limited fields the machinery for addressing constructive policy reforms and co-ordination to secure the many unorthodox gains from integration would be lacking. Secondly, within such an *ad hoc* framework, it is likely to be difficult if not impossible to take care of the issue of the distribution of costs and benefits except at the price of introducing unacceptable sectoral distortions.

A state-of-the-art based approach would of course equally support co-operation and integration in those areas, but provides grounds for supporting its extension to many others. It also has specific implications for the kinds of wider regional arrangements that might be aid-supported. A state-of-the-art analysis suggests that in relation to market integration, trade and production, significant gains – the unorthodox gains – hinge on the elimination of a variety of *non-tariff* barriers (NTBs) (in the broadest sense) to market integration and to cross-border investment. These unorthodox gains could be several times larger than the orthodox trade co-operation gains to be anticipated from discriminatory tariff reductions. Although the European analysis and conclusions cannot simply be transposed to Africa – if only because there, unlike Europe, the trade creation gains have as yet hardly been exploited – there can be little doubt that if REI is to be supported in Africa and certain other developing regions such as the Caribbean, a major emphasis should be given to encouraging regional initiatives that seek to reduce the barriers that permit market fragmentation to persist. They are bound up mainly with transactions costs, monetary and payments obstacles, entry barriers, uncertainty and lack of credibility. Beyond this, in African conditions, there are many indications that initiatives to harmonize fiscal structures and banking regulations, and to promote integration in infrastructure co-ordination and in agricultural policies promise to be fruitful as a means of reducing transactions and other avoidable costs and to promote allocational efficiency. Meeting once-for-all costs of adjustment for such purposes is usually considered an appropriate area for aid.

A further issue derives from the emphasis placed in the newer thinking on the need for credibility. It is this which partly justifies the proposition of the new regionalism that integration by developing countries with advanced countries is to be recommended. If reforms are undertaken by African countries that contribute to market completion, in macro and micro policy fields, what means can be devised to establish confidence in their durability?

There may be an important new role for the EC to assume in development assistance in this field, not least at the level of macroeconomic policy and monetary co-operation and integration. The issue of support will in any case arise for the two existing African monetary unions if EMU is established, and the French franc disappears. In that connection Guillaumont and Guillaumont (1989) have discussed the possibility of a partial generalization of the franc zone arrangements to certain other countries through the creation of an ECU zone. In a similar context, a recent report of the African Development Bank suggests that aid to underpin exchange-rate stability and convertibility in and perhaps beyond the existing Common Monetary Area of Southern Africa, might be an efficient and cost-effective form of assistance for development policy through regional integration.

In terms of the criteria of orthodox optimum currency area theory, the existing unions would be viewed as anomalies and any extension would make matters worse. However, as with trade-related analysis, recent thinking on monetary integration evaluates regional arrangements by reference to broader criteria. Its significance for Africa in terms of the promotion of macroeconomic stability is reviewed in Cobham and Robson (1992).

It should not be overlooked that credibility has important implications for one of the principal problems confronted by existing Third World trading blocs, namely the distribution of costs and benefits. In the past, polarization has undoubtedly been encouraged by a lack of credibility. If that can be overcome, less developed areas in such blocs can be expected – as in Europe – to be able to exploit more effectively the competitive advantages that their lower wage and other costs give them.

A second issue is whether, in the interests of making development assistance more effective, the regional dimension needs to be specifically taken into account. The need to co-ordinate EC development assistance aid to increase its effectiveness is recognized by the Commission (CEC, 1992), but the difficulties of doing so in relation to project aid are considerable. One reason is that, as has been aptly said, 'all donors want to coordinate, but no-one wants to be co-ordinated' (Whittington and Calhoun, 1988). The constraints are the resource and adjustment costs (for their own sensitive industries) that donors are prepared to accept, and their separate and sometimes inconsistent objectives. These considerations apart, the purely technical obstacles to co-ordination must not be underrated. Similar difficulties are not absent in relation to policy reform assistance, but may be less acute in that area. There are several areas of policy reform where the regional dimension could usefully be given weight without provoking major donor resistance.

Firstly, development assistance policy could usefully take more account of the fact that important instruments of policy have already been integrated in African blocs that currently incorporate half the countries in Sub-Saharan Africa. This institutional background can and has constrained the efficiency of country-specific structural adjustment programmes, notably by making it difficult for countries unilaterally to introduce desirable reforms in the structure of taxation, or of money and banking. Since many of these limitations show every sign of enduring, a co-ordinated regional approach within and between agencies (perhaps underpinned by an extension of co-financing) would have merit by helping to speed desirable policy reforms and facilitate structural adjustment, in particular by enabling much more reliance to be placed on the most suitable policy instruments. The implementation of such a co-ordinated approach might point to the introduction of an element of regional conditional-ity into aid programmes. The potential gains from support for regional reform programmes are disregarded in the negative appraisals that have recently appeared (de Melo and Panagariya, 1993; Langhammer and Hiemenz, 1990; Langhammer, 1992).

Secondly, there are numerous cases in which country-specific development assistance initiatives had damaging indirect impacts on existing regional co-operation and trade flow patterns through the neglect of their regional repercus-sions. A notable example is in price and marketing policy reform in agriculture. Again, this is an area where the encouragement of a broader and more co-ordinated approach to reform could be beneficial (Dioum, 1992).

The mutual interaction of SAPs and REI, and the case for taking the regional dimension into account in development assistance policy is discussed and supported in a study undertaken by Coussy and Hugon (1991) for the French Ministère de la Co-opération et du Développement.

Thirdly, there is the question of the significance of new approaches and of the policy reform context for Lomé IV, which is the EC's unique and distinctive contribution to development co-operation policy. In its trade aspects, the successive Lomé arrangements have not yet significantly benefited SSA countries. The advent of the SEM is unlikely to improve the situation. Steps to encourage regional co-operation, so as to secure non-orthodox benefits, could contribute to relaxing supply-side constraints, and help to minimize any exacerbated problems of market access that might derive from the SEM.

In connection with Lomé IV, support for certain regional monetary initiatives is already under consideration, although the agreement has no specific monetary co-operation provision. In recommendations that have recently been made to the EC in this field (Cerruti and Hugon, 1993), it is pointed out that to underpin such initiatives, changes in the way that STABEX support is provided would be desirable.

Fourthly, if the EC wishes to promote REI in Africa, post-apartheid South Africa presents it with a new opportunity. In this connection, the EC's stance on trade and assistance to a post-apartheid Republic of South Africa is what is at issue. If the RSA should be accorded Lomé-like status, at least for trade, the incentive for Southern African production integration would be enhanced. That could also improve the region's ability to compete against third parties in the European market.

A final area in which there is a need for EC initiative is in relation to assistance for policy-oriented research. If new approaches to the analysis and evaluation of regionalism are to be properly taken into account by policy in and towards Africa, the Caribbean and elsewhere, empirical research is needed in a number of areas. In particular some attempt, however indicative, needs to be made to quantify the costs of market fragmentation, and of other forms of non-integration beyond the trade policy arena, and to identify what constitute the crucial obstacles to action being taken to overcome them if the potential mutual gains from doing so are substantial. Work of this kind could help to throw more light on the relative merits of the 'World Bank approach' as compared with a regional alternative for specific cases. The EC's own work gives it a head-start in their area. An exercise on the scale of the Cecchini Report is no doubt out of the question for Africa, but at least a SPEC-like programme might be considered. This idea raises one particular difficulty because, unlike the case of Europe (and perhaps the Caribbean), the specific geographical constituencies to which it should be addressed are not wholly clear. Further work on 'natural partners' might help here.

## References

Badiane, O. (1992) 'Regional Integration in West Africa: The Importance of Country Macroeconomic and Sector Policies'. Mimeo (Washington: International Food Policy Research Institute).

Baldwin, R. (1989) 'The Growth Effects of 1992'. *Economic Policy*, No. 9, October, pp. 3–54.

Bensel, T. and Emslie, B.T. (1992) 'Rethinking International Trade Theory: A Methodological Appraisal'. *Weiltwirtschaftliches Archiv*, Band 128, Heft 2, pp. 116–41.

Berg, E. *et al.* (1985) *Intra-African Trade and Economic Integration*. Vols I and II (Alexandria: E. Berg and Associates).

Bhagwati, J.J. (1982) 'Directly Unproductive Profit Seeking (DUP) Activities'. *Journal of Political Economy*, Vol. 90, pp. 988–1002.

Bhagwati, J. (1993) 'Regionalism and Multilateralism: An Overview'. In Melo, J. de and Panagariya, A. (1993), pp. 22–51.

Brown, D.K., Deardorff, A.V. and Stern, R.M. (1992) 'North American Integration'. In 'Policy Forum: Regionalism in the World Economy'. *Economic Journal,* Vol. 102, No. 415, November, pp. 1507–18.

Cerruti, P. and Hugon, P. (1993) *'La coopération monétaire et l'ajustement structurel en Afrique sub-saharienne'* (Paris: LAREA).

Cobham, D. (1991) 'European Monetary Integration: A Survey of Recent Literature'. *Journal of Common Market Studies*, Vol. 29, No. 4. June, pp. 363–84.

Cobham, D. and Robson, P. (1994) 'Monetary Integration in Africa: A Deliberately European Perspective'. *World Development,* Vol. 22, No. 3.

Commission of the European Communities (1988) 'The Economics of 1992: An Assessment of the Potential Economic Effects of Completing the Internal Market of the European Community'. *European Economy*, No. 35, March.

Commission of the European Communities (1990) 'One Market One Money'. *European Economy*, No. 44, October.

Commission of the European Communities (1992) 'Development Cooperation Policy in the Run-up to 2000'. Discussion paper, SEC (92) 915.

Coussy, J. and Hugon, P. (1991) 'Intégration régionale et l'ajustement structurel en Afrique sub-saharienne'. *Etudes et documents*, Ministère de la Coopération (Paris: La Documentation Française).

Deardorff, A. and Stolper, W. (1990) 'Effects of Smuggling under African Conditions: A Factual, Institutional and Analytical Discussion'. *Weltwirtschaftliches Archiv*. Band 126, Heft 1, pp. 116–41.

De Grauwe, P. (1992) *The Economics of Monetary Integration* (Oxford: Oxford University Press).

Devarejan, S. and Melo, J. de (1987) 'Evaluating Participation in African Monetary Zones: A Statistical Analysis of the CFA Zones'. *World Development,* Vol. 15, pp. 483–96.

Devarejan, S. and Melo, J. de (1991) 'Membership in the CFA Zone: Odyssean Journey or Trojan Horse?' In *Economic Reform in Sub-Saharan Africa* (Washington, D.C.: World Bank), pp. 25–33.

Dioum, B. (1992) 'Intégration et coopération au niveau du secteur agricole'. Mimeo, for EDI Seminar on West African Integration.

*Economic Journal* (1992) 'Policy Forum: Regionalism in the World Economy'. Vol. 102, No. 415, November, pp. 1488–1529.

Gittelman, M. (1992) 'Transnational Corporations in Europe 1992: Implications for Developing Countries'. *CTC Reporter*, No. 29.

Gros, D. and Thygesen, N. (1992) *From the European Monetary System to European Monetary Union* (London: Longman).

Guillaumont, P. and Guillaumont, S. (1989) 'The Implications of European Monetary Union for African Countries'. *Journal of Common Market Studies*, Vol. 28, No. 2, December, pp. 139–54.

Guillaumont, P. and Guillaumont, S. (1992) 'Les instruments anciens et nouveaux de l'intégration économique; leçons politiques de l'expérience africaine. *Etudes et documents de CERDI*, E.92.07. Clermont-Ferrand.

Guillaumont, P., Guillaumont, S. and Plane, P. (1988) 'Participating in African Monetary Unions: An Alternative Evaluation'. *World Development*, Vol. 16, No. 5, pp. 569–76.

Johnson, O.E.G. (1987) 'Trade Tax and Exchange-Rate Coordination in the Context of Border Trading'. *IMT Staff Papers*, Vol. 34, pp. 548–64.

*Journal of Common Market Studies* (1992) (Special Issue) 'Regionalism and the Integration of the World Economy'. Vol. 30, No. 2, June 1992.

Killick, A. (1991) 'The Developmental Effectiveness of Aid in Africa'. *African External Finance in the 1990s* (Washington, D.C.: World Bank).

Koekkoek, A., Kuyvenhoven, A. and Molle, W. (1990) 'Europe 1992 and the Developing Countries: an Overview'. *Journal of Common Market Studies*, Vol. 29, No. 2, December, pp. 111–32.

Krugman, P. (1988) *EFTA and 1992*. Economic Affairs Dept., EFTA, Occasional Paper, No. 23 (Geneva: EFTA).

Krugman, P. (1993) 'Regionalism vs. Multilateralism: Analytical Notes'. In Melo, J. de and Panagariya, A. (1993), pp. 58–79.

Langhammer, R. (1992) 'The Developing Countries and Regionalism'. *Journal of Common Market Studies*, Vol. XXX, No. 2, June, pp. 211–31.

Langhammer, R. and Hiemenz, U. (1990) *Regional Integration among Developing Countries*. Kieler Studien (Tübingen: Mohr).

Mansoor, A. and Inotai, A. (1991) 'Integration Efforts in Sub-Saharan Africa: Failures, Results and Prospects'. In *Economic Reform in Sub-Saharan Africa* (Washington, D.C.: World Bank), pp. 217–32.

Melo, J. de and Panagariya, A. (1992) *The New Regionalism in Trade Policy* (Washington, D.C.: World Bank and CEPR).

Melo, J. de and Panagariya, A. (1993) *New Dimensions in Regional Integration* (Cambridge: Cambridge University Press).

Melo, J. de, Montenegro, C. de and Panagariya, A. (1992) 'Regional Integration Old and New'. Policy Research Working Paper WPS 985 (Washington, D.C.: World Bank).

Neven, D.J. (1990) 'EC Integration Towards 1992: Some Distributional Aspects'. *Economic Policy,* No. 10, April, pp. 13–62.

Robson, P. (1987a) *Intégration, développement et equité: l'intégration économique en Afrique de l'Ouest* (Paris: Economica).

188 PETER ROBSON

Robson, P. (1987b) *The Economics of International Integration* (London: Allen & Unwin).

Robson, P. (1993) *Transnational Corporations and Regional Economic Integration* (London: Routledge).

Robson, P. and Wooton, I. (1993) 'Transnational Corporations and the Theory of Regional Integration'. *Journal of Common Market Studies*, Vol. 31, No. 1, March, pp. 71–90.

Sapir, A. (1992) 'Regional Integration in Europe'. In 'Policy Forum: Regionalism in the World Economy', *Economic Journal*, Vol. 102, No. 415, November, pp. 1491–506.

United Nations Centre for Transnational Corporations (UNCTC) (1990) *Regional Economic Integration and Transnational Corporations in the 1990s: Europe 1992, North America, and Developing Countries* (New York: United Nations).

Whalley, J. and Hill, R. (eds.) (1985) *Canada–United States Free Trade* (Toronto: University of Toronto Press).

Whittington, D. and Calhoun, C. (1988) 'Who Really Wants Donor Coordination?'. *Development Policy Review*, Vol. 6, No. 3.

World Bank (1989) 'Intra-regional Trade in Sub-Saharan Africa'. Mimeo Report No. 7685.

World Bank (1989) *Sub Saharan Africa: From Crisis to Sustainable Growth: a Long-Term Perspective Study* (Washington, D.C.: World Bank).

World Bank (1990) *The Long-Term Perspective Study: Background Papers, Vol. 4: Regional Integration and Cooperation* (Washington, D.C.: World Bank).

World Bank (1991) *Economic Reform in Sub-Saharan Africa: A World Bank Symposium* (Washington, D.C.: World Bank).

World Bank–CEPR (1992) Conference on New Dimensions in Regional Integration. See Melo, J. de and Panagariya, A. (1992, 1993).

Yamazawa, I. (1992) 'On Pacific Economic Integration'. In 'Policy Forum: Regionalism in the World Economy', *Economic Journal*, November, Vol. 102, No. 415, pp. 1519–29.

# 7.
# Trade Blocs and Multilateral Free Trade

DEEPAK LAL

## I. Introduction

Economists' attitude to trading blocs – whether they be common markets or regional free trade areas (FTAs) – has been ambivalent. This follows from the classical case for free trade, as modified by the modern theory of trade and welfare (see Corden, 1974). This states in its static version that free trade is in the interest of each country because it expands its feasible set of consumption possibilities by providing, in effect, an indirect technology for transforming domestic resources into the goods and services which yield current and future utility to consumers. The dynamic version incorporates investment in line with a country's comparative advantages, which minimizes the present value of the resource costs of its future demand. The modern theory, moreover, does not necessitate a commitment to *laissez-faire*. Except for the so-called optimum tariff argument (when a country can influence its terms of trade), most arguments for protection can be shown to be arguments to deal with so-called domestic distortions in the working of the price mechanism. They require domestic public interventions, but not in foreign trade. From this perspective – as the relevance of the optimum tariff argument is likely to be limited (see below) – the ideal policy for each and every country is unilaterally to adopt free trade in its own self-interest, as Britain did after the repeal of the Corn Laws. The case for trading blocs must therefore at best be a second best one.

Such a case is ultimately based on the judgement that irrespective of the theoretical case in favour of unilateral free trade, most countries are mercantilist, looking upon foreign trade as a zero-sum game. The negotiating mechanisms underlying the promotion of multilateral free trade even under GATT are implicitly mercantilist. Mercantilists view trade as a war, and the various GATT rounds with their 'concessions' to economic virtue are like multilateral disarmament.[1] If in this contest some countries decide to disarm amongst themselves, and that on balance does not hurt others (that is if the arrangements are net trade creating), then the resulting trading bloc is to be blessed. This in essence is the rationale of GATT's article XXIV allowing exceptions to its MFN rule and the principle of non-discrimination which is the cornerstone of the multilateral trading system constructed under its auspices since the Second World War.

Most economists agree that the net effects of the two major trading blocs which are currently emerging – the European Community (EC) after the completion of the Single Market, and the North American Free Trade Area (NAFTA) – are likely to be net trade creating (see, e.g., Krueger, 1992a). But there are two remaining and serious worries. The first is that rather than being a step towards multilateral free trade, such blocs will lead to a retrogression. This arises from the new interest groups created who benefit from the trade diversion which accompanies any discriminatory preferential trading arrangement. They will oppose any further movement to an open multilateral trading system. The second is that the concentration of scarce political capital and energy on promoting regional trading blocs will divert the attention of traditional supporters of the global system towards these second best schemes. Further, given the inevitable trade frictions that will arise between large regional trading blocs – with those left outside, such as the East Asian newly industrializing countries (NICs) and Japan trying to form their own defensive blocs – the whole multilateral trading system built up since the Second World War could unravel. In this context it is the US endorsement of regionalism which is most worrying. As Wolf notes: 'The shift in US thinking towards FTAs, and more generally toward bilateralism as a principle, rather than a shamefaced expedient, is momentous. As the progenitor and most enthusiastic upholder of the unconditional MFN principle, the US may well doom the GATT system in its present form by this defection' (Wolf, 1989, p. 93).

But is GATT, particularly its largest Uruguay Round, worth saving? There have been a considerable number of academic, and other, commentaries about the defects of GATT, from which it has been ably defended by Bhagwati (1991). More serious is the danger of a trade war between rival trading blocs if the

---

[1] See Ludema (1991) for a game-theoretic analysis which shows that despite the free-rider problem, the GATT bargaining techniques and procedures based on the most Favoured Nation (MFN) rule, will, if side payments are allowed, result in free trade.

Uruguay Round collapses. The World Bank's *World Development Report 1991*, estimated that this could lead to a loss of 3–4 per cent of world output.

One great paradox of the 1980s is that, whereas developing countries are finally coming around to accepting the economists' case for the unilateral implementation of free trade, the developed countries, which in the past have been the major votaries of multilateral free trade, have been gradually turning their backs on their professed principles through various forms of creeping administrative protection such as non-tariff barriers like voluntary export restraints (VERs) and anti-dumping actions. Stoeckel *et al.* (1990) have estimated on the basis of their world trade model that a 50 per cent reduction in these non-tariff barriers and in the much lower current tariff barriers would result in an increase of world income of over 5 per cent. This is the prize offered by multilateral trade liberalization.

But, instead, the current prospect is of a strengthening of regional trading blocs at the expense of the multilateral trading system (see Lawrence and Schultze, 1990; Schott 1989). This growing impatience with the multilateral trading system is unlikely to lead to the 1930s-type collapse of the world trading system as many observers fear. A more likely outcome is by analogy with the gradual erosion of the first liberal trading order established in the second half of the nineteenth century.

The great Age of Reform began with the repeal of the Corn Laws in 1846, and culminated in Gladstone's 1860 Budget, the first of a series which unilaterally freed the UK's trade. Subsequently, with the Cobden–Chevalier Treaty of 1860, and a string of other tariff treaties, all of which for the first time incorporated the MFN principle, the 'dream of universal free trade appeared to be approaching reality' (Kenwood and Lougheed, 1971, p. 76). The peak of this liberal free trade order was probably 1870. From 1880 onwards there was a revival of protectionism. During this free trade period, along with the international integration that ensued there was also a movement towards national integration through the formation of the Zollverein in Germany in 1834, and the unification of Italy in 1861. World trade boomed, growing at an annual rate of over 4 per cent per annum between 1850–70 (see Rogowski, 1989, p. 22).

Similarly in the quarter century after the Second World War, the second great liberal economic order was created under American leadership through successive multilateral GATT trade rounds. Simultaneously, the movement towards European integration parallelled the movement towards national integration in the nineteenth century. In the peak period of this second Golden Age, world trade grew at an annual average rate of about 9 per cent (Rogowski, 1989, p. 89) – twice as fast as in the nineteenth century's Golden Age. The OECD countries and those developing countries which adopted relatively outward-oriented trade policies saw dramatic increases in their standards of living. The major problem it seemed was to convince the remaining developing countries to reverse their inward orientation – a task on which I have spent much of my professional career. Just as they seem to be coming around, and with the unexpected collapse of the autarkic system of central planning in communist countries, leading to their rushing to be integrated with the world economy, another universal free trade order seemed to be on the cards. But as in the 1880s, a gradual slide towards protectionism gained momentum in the 1980s. However, there were two major differences. Whereas the UK, which had led the nineteenth-century march to free trade, remained constant to its principles, it was the then newly industrializing countries – the US, Germany and France – which revived protectionism. Today it is the NICs – and those who aspire to this status – who are converts to free trade, whilst it is Europe and the US – the leaders of the post-war free trade movement – who are turning inwards. Secondly, unlike the nineteenth century where the instrument of protection was the tariff, today's new protectionists increasingly use various forms of administrative protection whose common feature is a quota. This is more damaging both to their and world economic welfare, as quotas on foreign trade – unlike tariffs – break the link between domestic and foreign prices, and effectively prevent specialization according to a country's emerging comparative advantage, on which its long-run prosperity ultimately depends. The current movement towards regional trading blocs is a culmination of this trend towards what is called 'managed' trade.

It could be argued that the trading blocs being formed, in particular the bilateral free trade agreements currently in favour in the US, are merely replicating the commercial treaties the UK signed to promote free trade in the nineteenth century. But there is an important difference. Whereas the nineteenth century treaties all embodied the MFN clause and hence were non-discriminatory, the current FTAs are based on bilateral reciprocity, are discriminatory and go against the GATT MFN rule. To protect the preferences granted to the partners they set out complex rules of origin to prevent non-members shipping goods to partners with high external trade barriers through those with lower ones. (See Krueger, 1992b for an analysis of the protectionist content of rules of origin in FTAs). Though it is possible to have FTAs which are GATT plus, and are on a conditional MFN basis (to avoid the problem of 'free riders' with the unconditional MFN rule, which has exercised many politicians – see Schott 1989), the purpose of the FTA route being pursued by the US as Krueger (1989) notes is that they 'at best provide assurances to American trading partners that protectionism will go no further with them' (p. 197).

So why, given the unprecedented prosperity that the multilateral liberal international economic order has delivered to its participants, are the major architects of the order turning their backs on it? There is a complex web of reasons, and only a few can be highlighted.

The first is that, 'historically, FTAs have been the economic policy of the uncompetitive and the foreign policy of the weak. The shift of the UK to a full-blown policy of imperial preferences in the 1930s was an admission of both political and economic decline. Equally, the discriminatory policies of the EC have their roots not only in fear of competition (initially from the US, now from the Far East), but also in the limited number of instruments of foreign policy available to it. Should one interpret the movement of the US in the 1980s toward a trade policy based more on discrimination as a tacit admission of its relative economic and political decline? The answer, unfortunately, is "yes"' (Wolf, 1989, p. 92).

The second is that, historically, largely due to the interactions of its factor endowments and mass democracy, the US is naturally protectionist. From the Stolper–Samuelson theorem we would expect protection to be in the interest of the scarce factor of production. In the US this is unskilled and semi-skilled labour. In a mass democracy, however, labour is likely to have a disproportionate influence on the polity, if for no other reason that raw labour is the factor of production most evenly distributed amongst the voting public, and hence its interest will tend to be reflected in public policy.[2] The surprising fact therefore is not the US's current lurch to protectionism, but the nearly three decades after the Second World War when it was a free trader (see Rogowski, 1989).

The third reason is that, with the integration of world capital markets, trade imbalances are now the other side of the coin of imbalances on the capital account. As is well known, the US trade deficit is the mirror image of the surplus on its capital account, which in turn reflects the imbalance between domestic investment and savings. This imbalance has been aggravated by the burgeoning fiscal deficit, in turn caused by an expansion of age-related middle-class social entitlements (see Lal and Wolf, 1986). The constant trade friction with Japan, because of its trade surplus, cannot be cured through trade-related measures, because this surplus is merely the counterpart of the deficit on the capital account due to the Japanese proclivity to save more than they invest. It is also ironical that Japan-bashers, whilst railing at unfair Japanese trade practices,[3] fail to note that indirectly it is Japan which has financed both investment and the social entitlements that the Americans are unwilling to pay for themselves.

---

[2] This alludes to the theory of endogenous tariff determination, which marries the so-called specific factors model of trade theory with the median voter type theorem of political scientists. See Mayer (1984), Findlay (1990), Lal (1989).

[3] It is a common misperception that Japan is more closed than the UK or the EC. Rogowski (1989) notes:

> No less an authority than the U.S. International Trade Commission has concluded that Japan's average tariff level is lower than that of either the United States or the European Community. In 1982, Japanese non-tariff barriers in manufacturing industry were estimated at between 5 and

Last but not least are the academics who, in the 1980s, have tried to construct a so-called 'new' trade theory, which seeks to justify selective protection and industrial policy.[4] Here again there are parallels with the 1880s. In the free traders' Black Book, to the names of List, Hamilton and Carey must be added those of Krugman, Helpman and Grossman, amongst others. It has been known since John Stuart Mill that a country with some monopoly or monopsony power in its foreign trade could (in the absence of foreign retaliation) garner more of the potential cosmopolitan gains from trade for itself by levying the optimum tariff to improve its terms of trade. With foreign retaliation the welfare outcome is uncertain for the country initiating the trade war, though the cosmopolitan gains will naturally shrink (see Johnson, 1958). The 'new' trade theory has provided a sophisticated variant of this optimum tariff type argument, whereby a country can, through a 'strategic' trade policy, cause profits in oligopolistic world markets for certain high-tech commodities to be shifted from foreign to home producers (see Baldwin, 1992). Though theoretically valid, as is the classical terms of trade argument for protection, its practical relevance is equally limited, largely because of the threat of retaliation, as well as (until recently) the altruistic concern in the OECD for the welfare of poor developing countries. Thus Whalley (1985) estimated that the optimum tariff for both the US and EC, assuming no retaliation, is 150 per cent. However, if the world's trading blocs simultaneously imposed their optimum tariffs, all would lose and world GNP would fall by over 3 per cent.

Nor are the arguments for a type of infant industry protection being made on the basis of the 'new' trade theory any more cogent. It is argued that countries can create a comparative advantage in high-tech industries which purportedly have high fixed costs due to initial R&D expenditures, dynamic scale economies due to learning by doing, and technological externalities. But as with the more traditional Hamilton-List arguments for protection to deal with domestic distortions, the first best policy for this case is also some domestic tax-subsidy scheme, as the modern theory of trade and welfare has shown.[5]

---

7 percent; those of the European Community were 20 percent, of the United States 34 percent.
... Protection continues in a few sectors deemed to be strategically or politically essential e.g. advanced electronics and rice, but it is consistently overrated by Western politicians and journalists. (p. 106, n60)

[4] There have been three intellectual protectionist waves since the Second World War. I have discussed the first two in Lal (1983, 1985). The latest is discussed in Lal (1992a, 1993).

[5] In Lal (1993) I also deal with the industrial policies of the Far Eastern super growth performers, which have mesmerized various observers. I argue that these were meant to deal with the agency problem in capital-intensive industries when there was insufficient agglomeration of private wealth, to allow for a small group of shareholders in each capital-intensive firm to hold sufficient shares to monitor the management. Keeping an outward orientation, whilst promoting certain industries through credit subsidies

Hence, the 'new' trade theory does not in my view provide sufficient reasons for the US or EC adopting industrial policies and various forms of selective protection. Nor does it provide a case against the traditional multilateral trading system and in favour of bilateralism and regional trading blocs. Nevertheless, with theorists of this kind filling influential posts in the Clinton Administration, it would not be surprising if they gave intellectual succour to the growing protectionism in the US.

If there is every likelihood that the world is moving towards regional trading blocs, what are likely to be the effects on world trade and, in particular, on the welfare of developing countries?

Again analogies with the late nineteenth century are instructive. Kenwood and Lougheed (1971) note that the effects of protectionism were offset by many other trade-creating forces, such as the continuing decline in the costs of transport, so that world trade continued to grow 'steadily between 1870 and 1914, averaging some 3.4 per cent annually over the entire period, and was growing faster than total world production which averaged 2.1 per cent per annum' (p. 86). Krueger (1992a) reaches a similar judgement about the prospects for world trade in the near future. The protectionist pressures have so far been offset by declining costs of transport and communications, and increased specialization in intra-industry trade, in effecting world trade, which has continued to grow faster than world GNP. The real long-run danger is that increasing trade frictions between rival trading blocs could lead to an intensification of trade barriers between them, which could over time erode the multilateral trading system. As Krueger (1992a) notes: 'It would not be the case that any major country *decided* to abandon open, multilateral trade in favour of its own trading bloc, the shift would happen gradually in response to increased trade frictions' (p. 16).

Finally, there is a more ominous parallel with the later nineteenth century – of particular concern to developing countries. The slow unravelling of the nineteenth century liberal economic order was also accompanied from the 1880s by a fresh burst of imperialist expansion. Africa was carved up by the European powers, the US seized the Philippines, then intervened politically in numerous Central and Latin American countries, the British added Burma and Malaya to their eastern empire. The reasons for this imperialist expansion are too complex to adumbrate, and remain controversial (see Roberts, 1990, pp. 754–5 for a succinct summary). But one aspect was the idealism of those who saw themselves as the custodians of a superior civilization and sought to transfer

---

to firms which met their export targets, was a way to create wealthy industrial groups who would have a personal stake in monitoring the management of their firms. The outward orientation and export targets implied that the firms would be efficient, because exports cannot be willed by governments. This enabled their emerging comparative advantage in relatively capital-intensive industries to become effective, as they moved up the ladder of comparative advantage.

it to more benighted lands and climes. Kipling's famous poetic exhortation to the Americans captures this spirit:

> Take up the White Man's burden –
> Send forth the best ye breed –
> Go, bind your sons to exile
> To serve your captives' need;
> To wait in heavy harness
> On fluttered folk and wild –
> Your new-caught, sullen peoples,
> Half-devil and half-child.

There is a contemporary movement of idealists in the West – the global environmentalists – who might trigger another round of imperialism in the name of saving Spaceship Earth. Already the North American Free Trade Area agreement has come under attack because of the supposedly lax environmental controls in place in one of the partners, Mexico. Austria recently banned imports of hard wood in order to save the rain forests, but had to reverse course when Malaysia and Thailand threatened a trade war. Environmentalists are reportedly lobbying Washington against the confirmation of a Clinton appointee, who as Chief Economist of the World Bank, had the temerity to make the obvious economic point that countries differed in the extent of their local pollution and absorptive capacity of their environment, hence some might have a comparative advantage in producing 'polluting' goods. The desire of the Greens to green GATT by setting up global environmental standards for the production of all commodities is resonant of past attempts to legislate universal labour standards, by putting tariffs on goods produced by labour which did not meet them (see Lal, 1981, for a critique of this pauper labour argument). These attempts to discriminate against goods because of the way they are produced is completely at variance with the principle of comparative advantage and the multilateral trading system which embodies it. The Greens in America, worried that imports of goods produced in countries with lower environmental standards will undermine the domestic standards in their own countries, 'are building a formidable popular coalition around the argument that the removal of trade barriers prevents the Untied States from pursuing whatever environmental policies it deems appropriate' (*Economist*, 1993, p. 25). A US trading bloc whose rules could be more readily dictated by the Greens would presumably be more favourably viewed by them than promoting multilateral free trade under GATT.

More ominous is the Greens' desire to dictate environmental policy to the rest of the world. This currently is based on attempts to ban trade in goods which harm the so-called global commons, or promote global warming and the depletion of the ozone layer – which supposedly threaten life itself.[6] It is this last factor which could in time provide a pretext for direct or indirect imperialism. If developing countries do not adopt the requisite policies (despite trade bans) to control their noxious emissions, continue to degrade their eco-systems, and fail to control their burgeoning populations, what are the bets on the emergence of a green variant of the nineteenth-century's white-man's burden?

These are still straws in the wind. But the diversion of intellectual and political support from GATT towards the creation and strengthening of regional trading blocs, makes it harder to fight this growing dirigisme, and incipient green imperialism.

## References

Baldwin, R.E. (1992) 'Are Economists' Traditional Trade Policy Views Still Valid?' *Journal of Economic Literature*, Vol. 30, No. 2, pp. 804–29.

Bhagwati, J. (1991) *The World Trading System at Risk* (Princeton: Princeton University Press).

Corden, W.M. (1974) *Trade Policy and Economic Welfare* (Oxford: Clarendon Press).

*Economist* (1993) 'The Greening of Protectionism'. 27 February, pp. 25–8.

Findlay, R. (1990) 'The New Political Economy: Its Explanatory Power for LDCs'. *Economics and Politics*, Vol. 2, No. 2, pp. 193–221.

Johnson, H.G. (1958) 'Optimum Tariffs and Retaliation'. In Johnson, H.G. (ed.), *International Trade and Economic Growth* (London: Allen & Unwin).

Kenwood, A.G. and Lougheed, A.L. (1971) *The Growth of the International Economy 1820–1960* (London: Allen & Unwin).

Krueger, A.O. (1989) 'Comment'. In Schott, J.J. (ed.), *Free Trade Areas and US Trade Policy* (Washington, D.C.: Institute of International Economics), pp. 197–9.

Krueger, A.O. (1992a) 'The Effects of Regional Trading Blocs on World Trade'. Paper presented at the conference on 'NAFTA, the Pacific and Australia/New Zealand', University of Texas at Austin, Austin, Texas, 1–2 October, 1992.

Krueger, A.O. (1992b) 'Free Trade Agreements as Protectionist Devices: Rules of Origin'. Paper presented at a conference in honour of John Chipman, Minneapolis, September.

Lal, D. (1981) *Resurrection of the Pauper Labour Argument*. Thames Essay No. 28 (London: Trade Policy Research Centre).

Lal, D. (1983, 1985) *The Poverty of 'Development Economics'* (London: Institute of Economic Affairs/ Cambridge, Mass: Harvard University Press).

---

[6] The scientific basis of the fears surrounding global warming and the ozone hole is controversial to say the least. I have surveyed the available evidence in Lal (1990), whilst Lal (1992b) takes a cool look at green imperialism!

Lal, D. (1989) 'The Political Economy of Industrialisation in Primary Product Export-ing Economies: Some Cautionary Tales'. In Islam, N. (ed.), 'The Balance Between Industry and Agriculture', Vol. 5 *Factors Influencing Change* (London: Interna-tional Economic Association, Macmillan).

Lal, D. (1990) *The Limits of International Co-operation*, 20th Wincott Memorial Lecture (London: Institute of Economic Affairs).

Lal, D. (1992a) 'Industrialisation Strategies and Long-Term Resource Allocation.' In Iwasaki, T., Mori, T. and Yamaguchi, H. (eds.), *Development Strategies for the 21st Century* (Tokyo: Institute of Developing Economies).

Lal, D. (1992b) 'Green Imperialists'. *The World in 1993* (London: Economist Publica-tions), p. 16.

Lal, D. (1993) 'Does Openness Matter?'. In Siebert, H. (ed.), *Economic Growth in the World Economy* (Tübingen: Mohr).

Lal, D. and Wolf, M. (eds.) (1986) *Stagflation, Savings and the State* (New York: Oxford University Press).

Lawrence, R.Z. and Schultze, C.L. (eds.) (1990) *An American Trade Strategy – Options for the 1990s* (Washington, D.C.: Brookings).

Ludema, R. (1991) 'International Trade Bargaining and the Most-Favoured-Nation Clause'. *Economics and Politics*, Vol. 3, No. 1.

Mayer, W. (1984) 'Endogenous Tariff Formation'. *American Economic Review*, Vol. 74, No. 5, pp. 970–85.

Roberts, J.M. (1990) *The Penguin History of the World* (Harmondsworth: Penguin).

Rogowski, R. (1989) *Commerce and Coalitions – How Trade Affects Domestic Political Alignments* (Princeton: Princeton University Press).

Schott, J.J. (ed.) (1989) *Free Trade Areas and U.S. Trade Policy* (Washington, D.C.: Institute of International Economics).

Stoeckel, A., Pearce, D. and Banks, G. (1990) *Western Trade Blocs* (Canberra: Centre for International Economics).

Whalley, J. (1985) *Trade Liberalization Among Major Trading Areas* (Cambridge, Mass.: MIT Press).

Wolf, M. (1989) 'Comment on "Is There a Case For Free Trade Areas?"'. In Schott, J. (ed.).

# 8.
# The European *acquis* and Multilateral Trade Rules: Are they Compatible?

STEPHEN WOOLCOCK

## I. Introduction

In recent years there have been important developments in regional integration, both within Europe in the shape of the deepening of EC integration and the conclusion of the European Economic Area, and in North America with agreement between the US, Canadian and Mexican administrations on a North American Free Trade Area (NAFTA). These developments in regional integration have coincided with the continued failure to reach agreement in the GATT Uruguay Round negotiations. As a result concern has been expressed that the creation of regional 'blocs' threatens fundamental multilateral principles, such as most favoured nation (MFN) status. Indeed some observers believe that the GATT is already dead.

Others are more relaxed about the impact of regional integration and indeed argue that regional approaches to liberalization offer a faster and possibly more effective means of addressing the challenges of increased economic interdependence than multilateral rules. Regional integration and free trade agreements are clearly a fact of life. The key question is therefore whether they are or can be made compatible with a multilateral trading system.

This article considers whether the *acquis* of European integration, that is the system of rules which goes to make up the European Community and its relations with neighbouring countries, is consistent with the multilateral rules of the GATT and the OECD. The focus is on the shape of the rules. A full assessment of the compatibility of European integration with multilateralism would also have to look at how the rules are applied and the impact of regional agreements on trade and investment flows. These tasks are beyond the scope of this short article. But a comparison of the shape of the rules is important at a time when the EC's work on the Internal Market and the extension of the *acquis* to include EFTA countries in the European Economic Area (EEA) coincides with the GATT Uruguay Round as well as work in other fora such as the OECD.

This article argues that the challenges facing the European and multilateral liberalization efforts are similar. Both must find ways of dealing with increased economic interdependence. This means that both must find means of coping with the barriers to trade and investment created by domestic or national policies. The article concludes that the EC and multilateral *acquis* have, on balance, been mutually supportive. It argues further that concrete liberalization has resulted from European integration, so that there has been a net beneficial effect for third parties even if there remains some doubt about how the EC might use the reciprocity provisions included in a number of the Internal Market directives. Regional integration in general and European integration in particular are seen as resulting in increased codification of regulatory policies. This codification has reduced the discretionary power in the hands of national governments or regulators. As integration deepens, the coverage of EC codification increases. This is beneficial for indigenous producers because it provides for a more certain, stable climate for business and investment. It is especially beneficial for third country companies because discretionary power has often been used to protect domestic industries.

The article also shows the role of the EC as a regional hegemon shaping approaches to trade and investment within the whole of Europe. Much the same could be said of the US role in North American free trade agreements. As European and other approaches to market integration proceed they also set important precedents. If these diverge or develop in such a fashion as to make future multilateral agreements impossible, then regional integration could well threaten to undermine multilateralism. This article therefore considers whether the European approach to integration has to date been compatible with multilateral approaches and what indications there are concerning future trends.

## II. A Common Challenge

The growth in international trade and investment has increased interdependence to the point at which multilateral commercial diplomacy now faces the challenge of dealing with different domestic policies that have been the substance of EC integration for some time. As a result GATT and other multilateral organizations are having to address important new areas, such as services, competition and environmental policies, as well as seek to resolve the more familiar problems of tariff and non-tariff barriers.

Tariffs remain on the European and multilateral agendas. The EC had removed internal tariffs by the late 1960s and the EC/EFTA free trade area of 1972 removed tariffs between the EC and EFTA countries in industrial and some agricultural products. The European Economic Area (EEA) agreement, signed in Oporto on 2 May 1992, will remove further tariffs and effectively extend the entire EC *acquis* to the whole of western Europe (Council, 1992). The Europe Agreements, the interim association agreements with Poland, Hungary, the Czech Republic and Slovakia concluded in 1992 will remove tariffs within ten years. During the course of these Interim Agreements there remain exceptions in sensitive sectors, such as steel, textiles and agriculture where tariff quotas will remain for some time (Interim Agreement, 1992). At the multilateral level tariffs, at least between the OECD countries, have been reduced to an average of less than 5 per cent and the GATT Uruguay Round, if agreed, will reduce these even further. Tariff peaks in sectors such as textiles or integrated circuits will, however, remain and tariff levels in some newly-industrializing or developing countries are likely still to be high, sometimes reaching prohibitive levels.[1]

Completing the task of removing non-tariff barriers (NTBs) to trade is also a common challenge for European integration and the multilateral system. The treaties establishing the EEC addressed technical barriers to trade (under Art. 30–36 EEC), national subsidies (Arts. 90–93 EEC) and public procurement (measures having an equivalent effect to quantitative restrictions under Art. 30–36 EEC). But these were not sufficient. Secondary legislation was introduced in the 1970s in an effort to implement the treaty provisions, but this also failed to create a genuine internal market. Procurement contracts were still placed almost exclusively with national suppliers, national technical regulations grew faster than EC efforts to introduce common regulations and standards, and Community controls of national subsidies proved ineffective during the economic recessions of the 1970s.

The GATT efforts to deal with NTBs, by means of a series of Codes during the Tokyo Round of trade negotiations, were even less successful. As a result both the EC and the GATT were faced with the challenge of completing the job of removing such NTBs during the 1980s. The EC responded with its Internal

---

[1] Regional integration agreements in other parts of the world are also contributing to a reduction in tariffs. For example, the Treaty of Asuncion of March 1991, establishing the Mercusor Free Trade Area covering Uruguay, Paraguay, Brazil and Argentina aims to eliminate duties, charges or other restrictions by the end of 1995. The North American Free Trade Area will also remove tariffs between Mexico, the USA and Canada by the end of a 10-year period, or 15 years for some sensitive products.

Market programme and a tougher approach to the use of EC competition policy to control national state subsidies. The GATT responded by making another attempt to deal with NTBs such as subsidies, technical barriers to trade, and government purchasing in the Uruguay Round which began in 1986.

Increased interdependence and the growth in the services sector meant that a new set of NTBs with a more indirect effect on trade forced their way onto the agenda before the problems caused by the existing NTBs could be resolved. These new NTBs generally fall into the category of national regulatory policies, such as those in the field of financial services, telecommunications, the environment or the professions. The main objective of such regulatory policies are legitimate national policy objectives, such as protecting the environment, but they can have important indirect effects on trade and investment.

The EC was again the first to address this type of regulatory barrier to trade. The first directives on banking and insurance, for example, were adopted in the 1970s. But as with the efforts to deal with NTBs such as procurement, these proved ineffective. National regulatory policies were therefore one of the main targets of the EC's Internal Market programme. The Uruguay Round included services and thus the same NTBs resulting from national regulations in financial services, transport, telecommunications and other services. The Uruguay Round also included investment issues. Given the nature of the service sector, market access often depends on the ability to invest in the host market. There is therefore a particularly close link between trade in services and investment. Multilateral efforts in the OECD in the shape of the work on a strengthening of the Code on the Liberalization of Capital Movements (and Invisible Transactions) and of the National Treatment Instrument, were also highly relevant to the effort to liberalize trade in services.

Another area in which there was – and continues to be – a common challenge is that of enforcement. For regional or multilateral liberalization to be credible there has to be a perception that agreed rules are being effectively implemented and enforced. In the EC or EEA this means directives must be implemented and enforced and EC competition policy pursued vigorously. In the GATT or OECD it means the establishment of effective dispute settlement procedures.

Further new issues have been forced onto the multilateral agenda, even before the Uruguay Round has been concluded. These include structural impediments (SIs) and trade and environment, trade and competition questions. Structural impediments to trade have been forced onto the agenda through the US–Japan Structural Impediments Initiative. These are impediments that result from structural characteristics of an economy rather than any direct action by government. They take the form mainly of an absence or lack of effective competition or market transparency. Unlike NTBs they do not require governments to stop doing something, such as subsidizing exports or favouring

domestic suppliers of goods, but require positive action through active competition policies or regulatory reform of open markets. The EC is developing an
active competition policy which has begun to find application in removing SIs.
At a multilateral level the only action in this area has been the inclusion of
monopolies in the OECD surveys of restrictions on investment. If the challenges
are the same, are the approaches to dealing with these challenges similar at the
European and multilateral levels?

## III. Compatibility: Exemptions for Customs Unions

Existing multilateral rules in the shape of GATT Art. XXIV recognize that
regional arrangements can lead to 'increased freedom of trade' through 'closer
integration between economies' (GATT,1986a). Countries not involved in
regional arrangements have consistently criticized the effectiveness of this
provision. In the 1970s the US was critical of EC enlargement. Today the main
criticism comes from Japan. This has led to the inclusion of Art. XXIV in the
GATT Articles negotiating group of the Uruguay Round.

At issue is whether the criteria contained in Art. XXIV should be tightened.
The exemption from the GATT MFN and non-discrimination rules for customs
unions and free trade agreements is conditional upon: (i) the regional agreements resulting in duties or regulations which are 'not *on the whole* ... higher
or more restrictive than the general incidence of duties and regulations'
applicable in the constituent parties; and (ii) 'that duties and other restrictive
regulations of commerce are eliminated with respect to *substantially all trade*
with the constituent territories of the union or at least with respect to substantially all trade in products originating in such territories' (emphasis added).
Preferential agreements which do not satisfy these conditions can still be
concluded, provided they are endorsed by two-thirds of the Contracting Parties
of the GATT (Art. XXIV(10)).

The EC has always claimed that the establishment of the EEC, all enlargements of the EC, the current EEA agreement with EFTA and the Europe
Agreements with the Central and East European Countries (CEECs) are all
consistent with Art. XXIV. Only once has the two-thirds support been sought
in the case of the establishment of the European Coal and Steel Community,
which clearly did not satisfy the 'substantially all trade' condition. Earlier
enlargements were criticized by the United States, and more recently Japan has
emerged as the main critic of the EC's compatibility with Art. XXIV. On each
EC enlargement or free trade area, a GATT working group has been established
to consider the compatibility of the extension of the EC with Art. XXIV. The
broad criteria used, such as 'substantially all trade' and the 'general incidence'
of duties and restrictions, have made definitive rulings on compliance impossi-

ble. Examination under Art. XXIV has, however, helped focus debate on the level of compensation required for third parties. In these debates the EC has argued that the GATT Art. XXIV(5)(a) criteria provide for 'internal compensation', in which increases in tariffs or regulation in some sectors are possible provided they are compensated by lower tariffs in others. Here the EC makes a similar argument to the one it has made in the Uruguay Round for the 'rebalancing' of reductions in agricultural subsidies in some sectors with increased subsidies in others. The EC has also tried to claim 'reverse compensation' from its trading partners for reductions in tariffs or regulation in new members of the EC. The EC's trading partners have opposed both internal and reverse compensation and argued for sector-by-sector assessments of the impact of EC enlargements. (Report on Unfair Trade Policies, 1993).

Although not well publicized, the interpretation of Art. XXIV was included in the Uruguay Round negotiations, in the negotiating group on GATT Articles. This pitched those seeking tighter criteria, such as Japan, against the EC; the US having toned down its criticism of Article XXIV because of its move towards regional integration. Although progress was slow in the GATT Articles group the draft final act of December 1991 included provisions which could tighten somewhat the criteria of Art. XXIV (Devuyst, 1993). These propose that the 'general incidence of duties' should be measured by the weighted average of (tariff) duties and that there should be no reverse compensation. On a further point of contention concerning the length of Interim Agreements, the Dunkel text suggests that 'a reasonable length of time' (the wording in Art. XXIV) should be interpreted as 10 years (GATT, 1991). Adoption of the Dunkel text will thus represent a modest improvement, but there remains considerable scope for differences over how to measure the general incidence of regulatory restrictions on trade. The EC will probably be able to argue that its agreements with EFTA and the CEECs still comply, but others will still be justified in contending that exclusion of sensitive sectors means that substantially all trade is not covered. The exclusion of agriculture from the EEA is a case in point, but the enlargement of the EC to include the EFTA countries will mean that the EC will become more compatible with Art. XXIV.

The Uruguay Round negotiations on a General Agreement on Trade in Services (GATS) also considered customs unions and FTAs. In Art. V the draft GATS uses wording similar to that in the GATT (Draft Final Act, 1991). A customs union or FTA will be consistent with the GATS if: (i) its coverage is 'substantial in terms of sectors, volume and the modes of supply (i.e. cross border and local establishment)'; (ii) the agreement results in the elimination of 'substantially all discrimination' within the territories concerned; and (iii) the agreement does not 'raise the overall level of barriers to trade in services' for third countries. It is easy to see that without tighter criteria the scope for different interpretations will be as great in services as in GATT.

The OECD also has provisions on the role of regional agreements. Article 10 of the 1961 Code on the Liberalization of Capital Movements, the basis of the OECD liberalization work on investment, provides a general exemption from the strict most favoured nation (MFN) requirement of the Code for customs unions (OECD, 1992a). In other words the EC and other customs unions, are able to remove more controls on investment among their members than with regard to other OECD countries. Interestingly there is no reference to FTAs in the Code and the equally important OECD National Treatment Instrument (NTI), adopted in 1976 and revised in 1984 and 1991, does not even contain an exemption for customs unions (OECD, 1992b).[2]

The general nature of the criteria for compliance in the GATT, GATS and OECD means that the EC has had no major problems justifying its position that it complies with the multilateral provisions for customs unions and FTAs. What is more the further the EC moves towards integration the easier it is to satisfy the criteria of 'substantially all trade'. Nor is the compliance of the EC seriously challenged. Third countries have been more interested in using Art. XXIV to get adequate compensation. If the final act of the Uruguay Round includes the draft provisions on Art. XXIV there could be some tightening of the criteria, but it does not seem likely that they will be tight enough to cause the EC too much trouble arguing that it complies.

## IV. Is the *acquis* Compatible?

The formal conformity of European integration with GATT Art. XXIV or the equivalent GATS and OECD provisions tells us little about its real impact on the multilateral trading system. The secondary legislation which goes to make up the EC *acquis* is more important. The complexity of the *acquis* poses a methodological problem. On the one hand, it is impossible in a short article to cover the whole EC *acquis*. On the other hand, an assessment of the compatibility of the EC *acquis* with the multilateral system requires an understanding of the detail. This section therefore illustrates the impact of European integration by considering a number of examples: namely technical barriers to trade, public procurement and investment/services.

[2] The 1990 Review of OECD instruments on investment produced a draft agreement on a strengthened, binding OECD National Treatment Instrument. This included an exemption for customs unions, but the strengthened instrument failed to be adopted due to opposition to its provisions extending binding rules on national treatment to sub-federal authorities. On the other hand, a weaker procedural decision agreed in 1991 provides for the accession of the EC as a whole to the agreement, which would presumably mean that actions taken inside the EC would be no more subject to OECD monitoring than actions of sub-federal authorities in federal states. To date, however, the Council has failed to act on the European Commission's proposals to accede to the instrument.

## Technical Barriers to Trade

Technical barriers to trade resulting from national technical regulations pose a challenge to both European integration and the multilateral system. The challenge is threefold. First, the desire to protect the environment or health results in a constant stream of obligatory national technical regulations which can, unless monitored and controlled, easily constitute barriers to trade. Second, there are national voluntary standards which can favour national producers. Third, conformity assessment, with either obligatory regulations or voluntary standards, can discriminate in favour of national companies or industries.

The GATT addresses the first part of this challenge by requiring national treatment of technical regulations. The 1979 Code on Technical Barriers to Trade negotiated during the Tokyo Round requires foreign suppliers to be treated no less favourably than national suppliers (GATT, 1986b). National treatment is unintrusive in the sense that it allows countries to set whatever level of regulation they wish, provided national and foreign suppliers are treated equally. This is important because it prevents overt discrimination, but experience in the EC and the GATT has shown that national regulations can and are crafted in such a way as to benefit the local industry. The GATT Code has, as a result, proved to be pretty ineffective.

The EC as signatory of the 1979 Code complies with the GATT *acquis*, but internally the EC goes further than national treatment. By the 1970s experience in the EC had shown that a simple prohibition of discrimination, as provided in the Treaty of Rome, was not enough. Environmental and health policy measures, covered by a general exemption under Art. 36 EEC provided a means of introducing national regulations which distorted competition. The EC therefore first sought to harmonize national regulations and when this proved too slow shifted to the 'new approach'. The 'new approach' required harmonization of minimum essential requirements, but over and above this there was to be mutual recognition of national regulations. This means that once a non-EC product has been accepted in one Member State, it can be sold throughout the 12 Member States of the EC and, with the implementation of the EEA, all 17 members of the EEA. This represents an advance on the GATT national treatment requirement.

The International Standards Organization (ISO) and the International Electrotechnical Commission (IEC) are the multilateral bodies in the field of voluntary or technical standards. The ISO/IEC has proved to be slow in drawing up international standards. As a result national standards have grown far more quickly and thus opened up the probability of covert trade barriers. The more the pace of international standards-making falls behind national standards-making, the greater the scope for national standards to become barriers to trade. This has also been the challenge facing European integration. In contrast to the international level, however, European standards- making has been revitalized by the Internal Market programme. The EC has also introduced legislation to help ensure European standards are not undermined by new national standards. For example the EC's so-called Information Directive (189/83) effectively puts a hold on national measures until there has been an assessment of whether European measures are needed (Council Directive, 1983). This has the effect of checking the growth of incompatible national standards. The issue for the international community is whether there is an effective check on the growth of European standards.

In an effort to strengthen co-ordination on international standards-making, the provisions on technical barriers to trade in section G of the draft final act of the Uruguay Round (GATT, 1991) contain a code of good practice for standards-making bodies. A code resulted because some non-European contracting parties (CPs) were not in a position to accept an agreement which bound private/ industry controlled standards bodies to comply with any multilateral agreement. The European standards-making institutions, at both the national and European level, comply with the draft GATT Code. In 1990 there was also an understanding between the European standards institutions in the CEN/CENELEC and ISO/IEC that CEN/CENELEC would provide the international body with information on its work schedule and thus provide other ISO members with an opportunity of commenting on any proposed European standard and/ or initiating work at the international level. This represents a non-binding form of the EC Information directive at the international level. The practice in CEN/CENELEC is also to consider first what ISO/IEC standards are available before embarking on work on European standards. Some European national standards-making bodies, such as the British and German, oppose any implicit European preference through standards-making, and go out of their way to ensure that international standards do not suffer at the expense of European standards. As a result there are more ISO standards embodied in European standards than any other member of the ISO. In October 1990 the European Commission proposed, in its Green Paper on the Development of European Standards, a stronger, more centralized organizational structure for European standards. If this had been adopted it would arguably have strengthened European work at the expense of international work. But opposition from national standards-making bodies succeeded in blocking the proposals.

For conformity assessment as for technical regulations, the GATT requires national treatment. This means that a foreign supplier should not be treated any differently from national suppliers when it comes to testing for conformity with technical regulations or voluntary standards. In its policy statement of 21 December 1989 entitled 'A Global Approach to Certification and Testing', the

EC confirmed its compliance with this provision (Council Resolution, 1990). When an EC Member State accepts type approval or a manufacturer's declaration of conformity for EC origin products or services it must also be accepted for non-EC origin products. The EC also accepts mutual recognition of foreign conformity assessment, but for mandatory testing this has to be agreed by the EC as a whole rather than at national level. This is important because some Member States have had mutual recognition agreements with third countries for some time. Before extending such bilateral agreements to the EC level there is a reciprocity test based on 'mutual benefit'. In other words when the third country does not provide equivalent recognition for all EC products the EC may not recognize that country's test result. For non-mandatory requirements, such as those required by professional bodies, it is open to the bodies concerned to conclude mutual recognition as they wish.

This brief discussion of technical standards illustrates the degree of detail that must be considered in assessing the compatibility of the EC *acquis* with that of the GATT. It suggests that the EC *acquis* does conform with the GATT in that it offers national treatment for technical regulations and conformity assessment. In the field of standards-making real efforts have been made to ensure European standards do not conflict with international standards, and proposals that might have resulted in a strengthening of European standards at the expense of international standards were not adopted. The looseness of the multilateral rules makes compliance relatively easy, but lack of progress in tightening the multilateral rules cannot be put down to the EC alone.

Reciprocity raises its head in the area of conformity assessment no doubt in part because the EC, in general terms, offers third countries better than the national treatment offered by the multilateral rules in the field of technical barriers to trade.

The EEA extends the whole EC *acquis* on technical regulations to the EFTA countries that accede to the EEA. Everything, from the harmonized regulation for cars to the new approach directive for toys, will be applied by the EFTA countries. This extension of the *acquis* helps ensure EEA complies with the Art. XXIV requirement that substantially all trade is covered. In standards-making the EFTA countries are already members of CEN/CENELEC and, by virtue of the 1990 Memorandum of Understanding between the EFTA and EC bodies, also subscribe to European Organization for Testing and Certification (EOTC) which oversees conformity assessment. The integration of the EC and EFTA on technical barriers to trade illustrates the dominance, at least within the European region, of the EC *acquis*. This is clearly visible in the Europe Agreements with the CEECs. These neighbouring countries have little option but to adopt the west European rules. Even the international bodies such as the ISO are dominated by Europeans. Thus although the EC *acquis* is compatible with the current multilateral rules, the EC poses a challenge to the multilateral system in that it represents a regional and partial global hegemon in the field of technical barriers to trade.

## Public Procurement

Both European integration and the multilateral system face the challenge of reducing or eliminating local preferences in public contracts. With contracts equivalent in value of 9–10 per cent of GDP at stake it is clear that removing such preferences would contribute to trade liberalization. Within the EC the Treaty of Rome contains a prohibition of measures having an equivalent effect to quantitative restrictions under Arts. 30–36 (EEC) which include discriminatory application of public contracts. In practice this prohibition of overt buy-national policies did little to open markets because of the close links between purchasers and suppliers and the continued existence of covert national preferences.

The EC and other regional integration agreements have both shaped and been shaped by developments in the GATT. The EC introduced a code on common contract award procedures in the early 1970s. This covered government contracts for supplies and works (construction). The intention was to provide greater transparency and consistency in the granting of contracts. The approach adopted by the EC was essentially the same as that used in the subsequent GATT Government Purchasing Agreement (GPA) agreed at the conclusion of the Tokyo Round in 1979 (GATT, 1986b). The positive impact of the EC precedent was offset by the exclusion of utilities from the EC directives which also resulted in their exclusion from the GPA. The GPA proved to be little more effective than the EC directives, primarily because there was no effective system of compliance.

Negotiations in the GATT have also shaped the EC. For example, the coverage of EC directives has been partially determined by the GPA in the sense that the (lower) thresholds agreed in the 1979 agreement were incorporated in the EC directives. This interaction between, on the one hand, the EC and other regional agreements and, on the other hand, the GATT, has continued throughout the 1980s and up to the current phase of negotiations on a revised and strengthened GPA. The extension of coverage of the EC directives to include the utilities, energy, telecommunications, water and transport as well as all service sectors, opened up the way for their wider inclusion in the GATT. Japan was the only CP to include some telecommunications and railway purchasing in its offer for the 1979 GPA.

Recent developments in European integration have therefore contributed to multilateral liberalization in the sense that of introducing comprehensive multilateral (i.e. EC) regulation of contract award procedures. Without this precedent it is doubtful that the GATT negotiations would have succeeded in widening the coverage of the GPA. More importantly, the seven EC directives on procurement introduced since 1989 included provisions on compliance. Given the decentralized nature of purchasing decisions, central compliance or enforcement is infeasible. The EC therefore introduced provisions granting private parties the right of action when they feel they have been discriminated against (bid protest). The introduction of compliance measures within the EC cleared the way for the EC to support the introduction of equivalent measures in the GATT. The draft revised version of the GPA produced in early 1992 included a bid protest/compliance provision. In accepting such a legalistic or adjudicative approach to compliance, the EC moved towards the approach used in North America, which has long relied on private actions. This is the approach used in the Canada–US Free Trade Area (CUSFTA) and the North American Free Trade Area (NAFTA).

Apart from the legal requirements of the directives, European integration has contributed to the liberalization of procurement practices by undermining the credibility of national champions. Before the EC's Internal Market (IM) programme, preferential access to national procurement markets was an important prop for national champions. The IM resulted in competition across the EC and thus undermined the viability of national champions' strategies. Henceforth companies would have to have a European and or international presence in order to compete. This resulted in the creation of cross border alliances and mergers, and a weakening of the close identification with specific national champions which had influenced national preferential purchasing.

The EC approach to liberalization is comprehensive in that it covers public and private purchasing entities and all forms of contract including supplies (goods), works (construction) and services. Liberalization within the EC (and the EEA) also exceeds that of the GATT. Even if all the objectives of the negotiations on an improved GPA are achieved, GATT will still cover less than the EC. As a result the EC included reciprocity provisions in three of its seven procurement directives. In the directive on procurement of utilities this consisted of a 3 per cent price preference and 50 per cent rule of origin provision, that would be applied in cases where the bidder came from a country which did not meet the EC objectives on reciprocal access (Council Directive, 1990). The directives on services procurement by government agencies and utilities contain a reciprocity provision similar to that used for financial services, see below. The target of these reciprocity provisions was statutory state and federal Buy-America provisions in the US and preferential practices in other countries. The reciprocity provisions were seen as negotiating chips. Policy statements at the time the directives were adopted made clear that they would not be applied to any country which offered reciprocal benefits within the new GPA. As such the reciprocity provisions were seen as levers in multilateral negotiations rather than as an instrument of aggressive unilateralism.

Another implication of the comprehensive EC approach is that it is unlikely to find application at a multilateral level. Within the EC a balance of benefits was achieved by regulating all forms of procurement, even to the extent of including private entities in the EC regulation. Such an approach does not seem feasible at the multilateral level, even with the existing, limited number of signatories of the GPA. The GATT has traditionally sought a balance of benefits by means of the more limited request and offer approach. With request and offer, balance is sought by negotiations on the basis of a set of national bids. This is a less integrationist, less intrusive approach and has found application in FTAs such as the NAFTA. As in the case of technical barriers to trade the EC *acquis* is compatible with the existing multilateral provisions and is also developing in parallel with extensions of the GATT regulation. But the EC *acquis* is incompatible with the GATT *acquis* in the sense that represents a much deeper form of integration than the intergovernmental approach of the GATT.

### Services and Investment

The growth in trade in services and international investment has accentuated the need for both European integration and the multilateral system to provide a framework for liberalization. All trade and investment is linked, but trade in services is especially closely linked to investment. In many service sectors establishment of a subsidiary, or as is more frequently the case today, the acquisition of a local presence is essential for effective market access. For example, access to the retail banking markets can effectively be achieved only through the establishment of a branch or subsidiary. Therefore the ability to invest or the 'right of establishment' is a vital element in market access for many services sectors. The OECD, EC and the GATT have therefore all addressed the linked issues of trade in services and investment.

The OECD work on investment began in the 1960s with the Decisions on Codes on the Liberalization of Capital Movements and Current Invisible Transactions (OECD, 1987). These Codes contained an obligation to remove restrictions on investment but, given that many countries retained investment controls, liberalization was to be achieved progressively. The OECD approach combined an obligation to liberalize with specific reservations (negative list). The reservations were then subject to clarification and review by the Committee on International Investment and Multinational Enterprises (CIME), made up of member government representatives. Despite the fact that the only means of enforcement was peer pressure during reviews, the Code made a real contribution to the liberalization of capital movements including investment. Member countries of the OECD retained reservations on general investment controls, such as those used by Canada, France, Spain, Portugal and most Scandinavian countries, as well as sensitive sectors such as financial services, energy and air and sea transport, where most countries wanted to retain national control. But progress has been made over the years in removing these. In 1984 the Code on the Liberalization of Capital Movements was strengthened to include essential liberalization required for the right of establishment.

A further OECD instrument of growing importance to the liberalization of investment and services is the National Treatment Instrument (NTI). This was introduced in the 1976 Declaration and Decisions on International Investment and Multinational Enterprises (OECD, 1992b). It adopts the same approach as the Codes in that exceptions are first listed, clarified and then subject to a review. An important distinction from the Codes is that the NTI contains no binding obligation to liberalize. This means that new exceptions can be introduced. Attempts to make the NTI binding in 1990–91 failed, due to a reluctance on the part of the US Congress to bind the states of the US to comply. In 1986 the NTI was extended to include coverage of monopolies and reciprocity provisions. These are not prohibited but like other exemptions they must be notified and are subject to review. The EC Member States have participated in these OECD liberalization efforts. As other OECD countries each retains some reservations and exceptions, some more than others. But there has been a general liberalization especially during the 1980s.

Investment and services have only recently become the focus of work in the GATT. The United States has sought to include them since the beginning of the 1980s and, with the support of the EC and other OECD countries, succeeded in including the two topics in the Uruguay Round. GATT has, arguably, always covered certain aspects of investment policy. For example, in 1984 a GATT Panel Report found that the actions of the Canadian FIRA (Foreign Investment Review Agency) were contrary to the national treatment provisions of Art. III (GATT). The applicability of the GATT to investment was clarified during the course of the Uruguay Round negotiations on Trade Related Investment Measures (TRIMs).[3] The draft final act (GATT, 1991) contains a draft agreement on TRIMs which confirms that GATT provisions preclude a range of investment performance requirements such as local content requirements (Art. III GATT) and export requirements (Art. XI GATT). If this agreement is finally adopted as part of the Round, the EC will have few difficulties complying. There are no EC-level investment performance requirements, but local content requirements are maintained by some Member States, for example, Britain and France have local content requirements for Japanese car manufac-

---

[3] The narrow definition of trade related investment measures resulted from developing country opposition to the inclusion of investment and represents a compromise.

turers. Although these are informal requirements they will have to be removed
to comply with the spirit of the GATT agreement.

The more important multilateral agreement is the draft General Agreement
of Trade in Services (GATS) included in the draft final act of December 1991.
This seeks to liberalize trade in services by requiring compliance with the GATT
national treatment, non-discrimination and MFN principles. The GATS approach incorporates both positive and negative list approaches, compared to the
OECD Code which uses the negative list approach only. With the GATS, a
particular activity, such as banking or architectural services, is covered only if
it is included in the positive list binding the contracting party to provide national
treatment and non-discrimination. In addition to this positive listing, the GATS
has a negative list of exemptions. The GATS also differs from the OECD Code
in that it will, in all probability, not include an unqualified MFN obligation. In
the OECD even countries that have lodged reservations or exemptions can still
benefit from the liberalization of countries which have not lodged reservations.
In the GATS negotiations leading OECD countries, led by the US, have been
unwilling to accept that 'free riders' should benefit from such an unqualified
MFN rule. As a result reciprocity has figured more in the negotiations. Finally
the GATS includes a set of sectoral annexes which interpret the application of
the general agreement to each sector. These cover sectors such as financial
services, telecommunications and maritime transport.

How does the EC *acquis* compare with these approaches? Within the EC Art.
58 (EEC) grants an unqualified right of establishment to EC companies. But, as
in many other aspects of the EC, it has taken more than a simple treaty provision
to ensure effective right of establishment. Secondary legislation was needed in
the form of, for example, the first directives on banking and insurance adopted
during the 1970s. Even these had little impact, and banks and insurance
companies stuck to their national markets. It was not until the more ambitious
second directives, such as the Second Banking Co-ordination Directive (SBCD),
adopted as part of the IM Programme in 1989, that cross border investment in
financial services really began. Paradoxically, these second Directives were
designed to enable the cross border provision of services which should theoretically obviate the need for investment in the target market (Woolcock *et al.*,
1991).

As in the case of technical barriers and procurement, the EC approach to
investment and services is at once more intrusive in national sovereignty and
more comprehensive in its coverage than the GATT or GATS. Rather than offer
national treatment it offers home country control. This means that a supplier
from country *A* can supply services in country *B* according to the regulatory
rules applied in *A* (single passport), subject to country *A*'s regulation complying
with the common minimum essential requirements. The OECD and GATS

approaches offer only national treatment, which means the supplier from *A* must be treated no least favourably than the home country supplier in *B*, but the supplier from *A* must still comply with *B*'s regulations in all respects. This can mean that one market is less open than another. For example, within the EC a US supplier established in Britain can, in theory, supply a service across all borders to customers in any other Member State of the EC. An EC supplier established in a US state may not, however, supply services to other states unless it complies with the local state regulations. In other words host state control prevails in the US system.[4]

The EC approach has also had a spill-over effect. For example, the adoption of the SBCD in 1989 led to pressure for equivalent agreements in insurance and investment services. This has meant that the EC approach is once again comprehensive in its coverage. Difficult sectors such as telecommunications were approached in the EC in a similar way to that used in the multilateral liberalization efforts. The EC has first sought to improve transparency, just as the OECD instruments had. It then separated the regulatory and operational functions of telecommunications, and then liberalized enhanced or value-added services. The final stage of liberalizing basic network services is still to be achieved. This approach is the one recommended in the telecommunications annex of the GATS. It is also the approach used in the CUSFTA and the draft NAFTA.

Although the EC did not initiate the trend towards a greater liberalization of investment that occurred during the 1980s it added considerably to the momentum of liberalization. The initiative came from individual countries. The example of capital controls illustrates what has been a general phenomenon. In the late 1970s a number of OECD countries, such as Australia, Canada and especially Britain and the US, liberalized capital controls unilaterally. This was followed by the decision, taken in 1988, to remove all capital controls within the EC. EC liberalization then had a knock-on effect on the EFTA countries which made radical moves to reduce or remove their long-standing controls (OECD, 1992c).

In the services sector the EC ac*quis* was also extended to the five EFTA signatories of the EEA. Once again EC liberalization was comprehensive in contrast to the more progressive approach in the OECD and the more selective GATS approach. The Internal Market programme in services gave impetus to the GATS efforts, including  areas such as telecommunications where EC policies were chipping away at national regulation. The comprehensive nature of liberalization within the EC again led to pressure for reciprocity provisions to ensure that EC suppliers of services would have equivalent access to third

---

[4] Individual states in the USA have introduced reciprocal agreements which have begun to erode this effect of the US banking laws.

country markets. Perhaps the most important example of EC reciprocity was the provision added to the SBCD. This set a precedent for reciprocity measures in all financial services directives, as well as for public services contracts. The initially vague wording of the SBCD provision gave rise to concern among the EC's trading partners that it would be used restrictively. After some uncertainty within the EC, the policy that emerged was essentially one of reciprocal national treatment. The EC Commission would act only when third countries do not offer national treatment. Having said this there remains scope for reciprocity to be applied more generally, such as when there are no 'equivalent competitive opportunities', but in such a case the Council of Ministers and not the European Commission would have to act. Given the differences that generally prevail among the Member States' governments, there seems little likelihood that there would be a qualified majority in favour of any aggressive use of this or other reciprocity provisions. The EC has also accepted that any use of this reciprocity provision would be subject to GATT dispute settlement.

On balance, therefore, the actions by the EC have contributed to the efforts to liberalize investment and services. The EC *acquis* complies with the existing multilateral rules and the coverage of the EC is more comprehensive than the multilateral liberalization efforts. Once again the EC employs a more potent instrument of liberalization than national treatment, in the shape of home country control. This is unlikely to be acceptable at a multilateral level and thus raises doubts about the future compatibility of the EC with the multilateral approaches. The request and offer, national treatment, host state control approach used in other regional integration agreements, such as NAFTA, would seem more likely to continue to provide the model for multilateral approaches.

## V. Conclusions

Trade and investment policy is becoming more and more intrusive in national policies. This is illustrated in the above examples of some of the important challenges facing European integration and multilateral trade diplomacy. These examples suggest that a detailed study of the development of secondary legislation in the EC and the GATT and other multilateral bodies is needed before judgements can be made on the compatibility of the European and multilateral *acquis*. Formal compatibility of the EC with the provisions for customs unions in the GATT, GATS or OECD is not an adequate test. It is therefore important to look at the detail.

The detailed cases considered above suggest that, in general terms, the EC conforms with the existing multilateral rules as far as these go. Given the similarities in the challenge faced by both the EC and the multilateral efforts at liberalization, there is not surprisingly a similarity in approaches adopted. In each case one can find examples of how the EC and multilateral approaches to liberalization have developed in an interdependent fashion. The principles behind GATT and EC rules on technical barriers to trade are the same. Rules setting out the procedures to be followed when placing public contracts are also common. Even the approaches to opening difficult areas such as telecommunications are the same.

European integration has also resulted in the European countries moving towards a greater acceptance of rules-based, or adjudicative methods of resolving disputes. The traditional view in Europe was that trade disputes should be resolved through negotiation. The establishment of the EC *acquis* based on the supremacy of EC law has meant that governments and interest groups have come to accept that intra-European disputes should be resolved through adjudicative means. Like the rest of the EC *acquis* this will be extended to the EFTA states through the establishment of an EFTA court on the ratification of the EEA. The EFTA countries managed to prevent the ECJ having jurisdiction over all intra-EEA disputes. Having accepted adjudication within Europe, it was harder to argue against a strengthening of GATT dispute settlement provisions based on more adjudicative methods. This is illustrated by the radical shift in EC policy of GATT dispute settlement. At the launch of the Uruguay Round in Punta del Este, the European Commission was given a mandate by the Member States of the EC to oppose a stronger GATT dispute settlement based on more adjudication. By 1991, however, the EC had endorsed Section S of the draft final act of the Uruguay Round which contains just that (GATT, 1991).

European integration has contributed to multilateralism thus far but there are a number of ways in which it could threaten the future well-being of the multilateral system. The most immediate threat comes from the reciprocity or third country provisions in many areas of EC legislation. It is not just the shape of the rules but how they are used. By definition reciprocity provisions provide scope for discretionary action. The question is whether the EC will use these in an aggressive or protectionist manner. Experience to date suggests that the EC will not use reciprocity provisions in an aggressive fashion to open third markets. This contrasts with the ever more aggressive use of such means by the United States, where they are seen as more effective than the frustrating, slow multilateral negotiations. Whether the EC position is due to support for multilateralism or the inability of the EC Member States to agree on such a common approach is a moot point. The inertia of the EC decision-making suggests that there is a greater danger of reciprocity measures being used to justify protection. For example, the adoption of the utilities directive introduced a European preference rather than an obligation to negotiate for the removal of other countries' preferences. The latter is the aggressive approach embodied in the 1988 US Omnibus Trade Act provisions on public procurement. On balance, however, the jury is still out on how the EC will use its reciprocity provisions.

Another potential threat to multilateralism can be found in the growth of the EC as a regional hegemon. The examples above illustrate the power of the EC *acquis*. The EEA adopts, with very minor exceptions, the whole of the EC *acquis*. The Europe Agreements with the CEECs set out the expectation that these will also adopt the *acquis*. The implication of this is clearly that countries neighbouring the EC find multilateral rules and GATT discipline over EC trade policy a poor second best to having a closer link with the EC. Thus even if the EC is moving towards acceptance of a more rules-based international trading system, it is unlikely to diminish the attraction of membership or association for countries neighbouring the EC. The net effect is that the EC becomes a regional hegemon within Europe.

The EC may be a regional hegemon but it is not a global hegemon. Individual countries – above all the United States, but also Japan – also have a major impact on the international trading system. Other regional groupings also exist in competition with the EC. The most important among these is NAFTA, assuming the agreement signed in 1992 is ratified. NAFTA is based on intergovernmental agreement. The approach to resolving conflicts between national interest and international liberalization is the traditional one of national treatment, in which countries have sovereign rights to determine national regulation. This contrasts with mutual recognition and home country control in the EC which undermine national sovereignty. In NAFTA a balance of benefits is achieved through request and offer methods in which parties seek to find an overall balance of benefits. In the EC balance of benefits is more often achieved by liberalizing everything. Of these two models for liberalization NAFTA conforms much more closely to the existing multilateral approach. The loss of sovereignty involved in the EC approach makes it an unlikely model for future multilateral agreements. This is not to say that multilateralism cannot learn much from experience in European integration. But the European *acquis* is not about to be adopted at a multilateral level.

On balance therefore European integration appears to have contributed to the process of multilateral liberalization. Whether this will continue to be the case depends on what use the EC makes of reciprocity and whether it will be possible to reconcile the European model of liberalization with that of the dominant intergovernmental approach in the rest of the world.

# References

Council of the European Communities (1992) *Agreement on the European Economic Area* (Luxembourg: OOPEC)

Council of the European Communities (1983) Directive laying down a procedure for the provision of information in the field of technical standards and regulations (Information Directive), 83/189/EEC, 28 March.

Council Directive (1990) 1990/531/EEC.

Council of the European Communities (1990) Resolution on a global approach to conformity assessment, (90/C10/01), 21 December.

Devuyst, Y. (1992) 'The EC's Common Commercial Policy and the Treaty of European Union – An Overview of the Negotiations'. *World Competition*, December, Vol. 16, No. 2.

Interim Agreement on trade and trade related matters between the EEC and ECSC and the Czech and Slovak Federal Republics, *Official Journal of the European Communities*, L 115, 30 April 1992.

GATT (1986a) *The Text of the General Agreement on Tariffs and Trade* , July (Geneva: GATT).

GATT (1986b) *The Texts of the Tokyo Round Agreements*, August (Geneva: GATT).

GATT (1991) 'Draft Final Act Embodying the Results of the Uruguay Round of Multilateral Trade Negotiations' (Dunkel Text), 20 December, unpublished.

OECD (1987) *Introduction to the OECD Codes of Liberalisation* (Paris: OECD).

OECD (1992a) *Code of Liberalisation of Capital Movements*, 1992 Edition (Paris: OECD).

OECD (1992b) *The OECD Declaration and Decisions on International Investment and Multilateral Enterprises, 1991 Review* (Paris: OECD).

OECD (1992c) *Foreign Direct Investment: Policies and Trends in the OECD Area During the 1980s* (Paris: OECD).

*Report on Unfair Trade Policies by Major Trading Partners* (1993) Industrial Structure Council, Uruguay Round Committee, Subcommittee on Unfair Trade Measures (Tokyo: MITI)11 May.

Woolcock, S., Hodges, M. and Schreiber, K. (1991) *Britain, Germany and 1992: The Limits of Deregulation* (London: RIIA/Pinter).

# 9.
# Corporate Strategies and European Challenges Post-1992

ALEXIS JACQUEMIN

and

DAVID WRIGHT

## I. Introduction

According to the 1987 Cecchini Report on the cost of non-Europe (Cecchini, 1987; Emerson *et al.*, 1988) the potential gains from completing the Internal Market rely on three expected effects, in addition to direct cost saving through lower real trade costs: greater production efficiency achieved through the enlargement of the market; reallocation of resources between enterprises and activities; and reduction in monopoly power. The Report also underlined several conditions for these effects to materialize at micro and macroeconomic level. One is the assumption that economic agents will change their behaviour, knowing that adjustment to the new conditions will give rise to major costs.[1] The purpose of this article is firstly to explore the extent to which European

---

[1] From a macro perspective, it was argued that completion of the Internal Market will produce increased interdependence between Member States, since it is based on an expansion of intra-Community trade and free movement of people and capital. 'Observation of economic factors shows that any inconsistency in macroeconomic objectives between highly interdependent countries or any external disequilibrium in one of them is frequently resolved by downward adjustment, the correction being made through recessionary rather than expansionary measures' (p.221). It was added that 'early 1988 sees a weakening of the world and European business cycle and a much higher level of European exchange rates against the US dollar and other currencies linked to it. ... These trends hold out obvious dangers' (p. 9).

industry and the business community have already been influenced by the perspective of the Single Market. Secondly, we shall examine the business expectations and priorities for Europe post-1992.

## II. European Industry and Anticipatory Corporate Strategies

It is clear that the task of completing the Single Market is not a one-off decision but a gradual process. As suggested by the 1992 EC Report on the state of completion of the Single Market, it can be compared to the building of a house, with different teams of workers following the plan set out in the White Paper. Admittedly the pace of work has speeded up since 90 per cent of the White Paper has been implemented, compared with 75 per cent in 1991; this progress includes the opening-up of public procurement in the services sector, the finalization of certain technical harmonization measures and the liberalization of some transport services.

But in certain areas, such as industrial property and company law, the objectives have not yet been fully achieved. Furthermore, effective implementation beyond the formal transposition of legislation cannot be guaranteed by the Commission given that the prime responsibility for administering the Single Market rests with national and local administrations. With the slow-down in growth and new protectionist temptations, the risk is that some countries could express resistance to existing legislations, with 'subsidiarity' and 'national self-interest' as a pretext for opposition. They could also hamper the adoption of some far-reaching measures such as the creation of an open market for energy or the deregulation of some public monopolies.

In spite of those uncertainties, European industry has largely anticipated the Single Market. The EC has seen five years of steady growth during which company profits and investments have reached an all-time high. During the 1985–90 period, EC industrial output increased at an annual average rate of 3.8 per cent. Since investment increased at a higher rate than consumer goods, it was producers of capital goods who benefited most, with an average increase in output of 4.4 per cent. As shown in the 1991–92 *Panorama of EC Industries* (CEC, 1991), among the prime beneficiaries are the manufacturers of machines for processing plastics, the aerospace industry, machine tools, the printing and publishing industry, and textile machinery. As far as consumer goods are concerned, the most notable successes are consumer electronics and car manufacture; by contrast, food industries experiencing huge restructuring are characterized by fairly weak growth.

Behind these global trends a set of corporate strategies, including internal organization, has been developed to safeguard and reinforce competitive advantages in the European market with a leverage effect for moving on to the world market. Corporations are trying to concentrate on their main product lines and withdraw from other activities. A justification of this *intra-industry* specialization is given by econometric studies, which show that firms' profitability in their core activities is far greater than that in their diversified activities. European firms are also looking to extend their geographical market. They thus prefer to concentrate on their top-grade products, and extend their geographical diversification, as an alternative to product diversification in a limited geographical area. After 1992, it can be expected that the typical large EC company will pursue its efforts to increase its brand strength in search of market leadership, and to replace multiple regional or national locations by Euro-centralized production and selling structure with more destinations.

Indeed the lowering of intra-EC trade barriers, linked with more flexible and less costly transportation and distribution conditions, induces parent companies to relocate and to concentrate their existing European network, selling off or rationalizing subsidiaries. These subsidiaries were mainly set up as a device for playing as 'insiders' within captive national markets (telecommunications, pharmaceuticals, electrical engineering), and will be less relevant in a more integrated continental market.

A complementary move relating to foreign direct investment is also observed. Given that the Single Market will be more and more an integrated system based on trans-European networks in terms of transportation, transmission of information, transfer of technologies, norms and standards, non-EC firms have a growing interest in being located within the system. This suggests a tendency to complement exports by direct investment, even in the absence of, say, tariff barriers, as such direct investment allows a more complete exploitation of the benefits of the system; furthermore, the specificity and the often sunk cost character of these investments create a more irreversible commitment to the European market than do exports. For example, we have observed that during the period 1980–90, there has been a strong positive correlation between direct investment and exports, in the case of the Japanese and the US manufacturing operations (Buigues and Jacquemin, 1993). At the sectoral level, US and Japanese investment has led principally to the consolidation of their strong positions in high-growth, 'strategic' activities that will be very sensitive to the removal of their non-tariff barriers. A clear implication is that, in the 1990s, these multinationals will be major players in the Single Market.

European restructuring is achieved through external as well as internal operations, mergers and take-overs being one possible route. The corresponding reallocation of capital among firms leads to three distinct effects that, in some sectors, could generate efficiency gains: a change (increase or decrease) in the total output of industry, a new distribution of output among firms and a reallocation of productive assets (physical capital, patents, management skills, etc.) among firms. The current merger wave in Europe presents characteristics potentially important for the post 1992 patterns of industrial structure.

- Existing data suggest that the total number of mergers and acquisitions involving at least one of the top 1000 EC firms has been steadily increasing until recently; generally the market share of the merging firms is large relative to that of the non-participating firms, reflecting an effort to acquire or to reinforce leadership.
- Horizontal mergers and acquisitions, in contrast to conglomerate operations, are the most frequent and generally are not limited to financial transactions; this partly corresponds to the fact that firms try to reinforce their specialization in the activities in which they perform best and dispose of assets related to activities in which their competitive position is weak.
- National transactions have for a long time comprised the majority and often correspond to an effort to strengthen the positions of national champions in the home market; however, in recent years, the percentage of transnational transactions has been dominant.
- Mergers and acquisitions are concentrated in a few industries, such as the chemical sector (economies of scale), food products (high non-tariff barriers), the defence industry (fear of competition), and on the whole have risen significantly less quickly in growth sectors than in the rest of the industry.

Studies suggest that a large percentage of these mergers and acquisitions are not successful. The main reasons appear to be that too high a price is paid for the acquisition, the potential of the acquired business is over-estimated, and the process of integration after the acquisition is inadequately managed.

Joint ventures and other types of co-operative arrangement are also an important way of anticipating the Single Market. Indeed firms respond to increased competition by forming alliances. In certain circumstances, these operations promote synergies through complementarity, making it possible to disseminate technological information more widely, and to reduce the time required to bring a new product or process onto the market; they also ensure that risks are more widely distributed among the partners; they facilitate entry, especially for small and medium-sized firms. This is most often apparent in co-operative agreements in high-tech activities (information technology, new materials, biotechnology).

However, obstacles to the conclusion of co-operation agreements and their stability have appeared. In addition to the difficulties of finding a partner able to make a balanced contribution, setting up a management structure to minimize the running costs of co-operation, and ensuring full and fair use of the proceeds, there is also a set of regulatory and political obstacles to co-operation in Europe. Differences in company law, social legislation, standards and tax systems, for instance, are often considerable. Completion of the Internal Market will remove only some of these obstacles to co-operation. Co-operative agreements in the Community present some interesting characteristics.

- There has been a significant increase in the number of agreements over the last 10 years, especially through the setting up of joint ventures; these operations are mainly intended to improve R&D, production and market ing activities.
- Agreements between Europeans are difficult to forge and non-European partners are often preferred; reservations about co-operation are expressed, above all, by strong national companies who do not wish to alter the terms of their competitive position (regarded as favourable) *vis-à-vis* their European rivals, and who are more attracted by agreements with more distant American or Japanese partners; thus, in the formation of joint ventures, partners from non-member countries are more sought after than Community partners.
- Most of the reported co-operation occurs in a small number of industries; some are characterized by a high technological content (telecommunica tions and computers, aeronautics, electrical machinery), but others (chem- icals, metals, paper) correspond to mature or declining sectors and often include leading domestic competitors.

To conclude, the 1992 Single Market is largely shaped by corporate strate- gies. These exploit the opportunities offered by the dynamics of Schumpeterian competition, and tend to create sustainable competitive advantage compatible with increased actual and potential competition in the product and factor markets. But there are also signals according to which liberalization alone may be insufficient to reap the full benefits of the 1992 programme: perverse redistributive effects could materialize, and various private and public strate- gies emerge with the aim of slowing market processes, promoting collusive behaviour and resegmenting pan-European markets. Credible micro- (and not only macro-) policies at the Community level must then play a major role, including the implementation of measures agreed in Brussels by the Member States.

### III. Challenges and Business Priorities for Europe Post-1992

As we have seen in the previous section, the business community has largely anticipated the creation of the Single Market. But simultaneously the perception is that there is still important work to be done to capture its full potential, which is the essential first step for improving long-term competitiveness in global markets. Recent research by the Cellule de Prospective (Forward Studies Unit) of the European Commission throws light on these post-1992 issues (Jacquemin and Wright, 1993). This study is based on reports made by the 12 national institutes selected by the Forward Studies Unit, specializing in medium and long-term prospective analysis. Each was requested to provide a comprehensive forward-looking overview of the main socio-economic, socio-political and socio-cultural shaping factors that will govern the future, with particular attention paid to the expected role of corporations. In collaboration with McKinsey, the Forward Studies Unit has also investigated what the business world perceives as its European priorities in the post-1992 period.[2] The objective of this approach was to secure two types of input. Firstly, the business world was asked to express quite openly its aspirations and priorities for post-1992 Europe. Secondly, a series of general themes, reflecting a summary of some of the major shaping factors identified by the institutes were used to prompt firms to describe their own vision of the future. The following considerations were based on the results of this analysis.

The national institutes' reports have expressed in various ways the perspectives of an ambitious European project. Through different national traditions and histories, the European Community is moving from an era of narrowly-defined and self-contained commercial bargains, to an era of potentially unlimited overlapping common interests. Project 1992, with its mythical dimension, has worked and built much more than a free-trade area. It took off after 1986 when the Single European Act provided the legal basis for overcoming the principle of national vetoes that had long paralysed the Community's rule-making, with the effect that policies have really changed in the domain of freedom of movement of people, goods, services and capital.

The essential role played by firms in responding to these challenges and the opportunities offered by the large Internal Market is well recognized. As we have seen, the business community has been the main engine of the integration process through its internal and external restructuring and its cross-border co-operative agreements, mergers and acquisitions. But, if European integration has been and continues to be principally about economics, the national institutes have shown that social, cultural and political dimensions are becoming more

---

[2] Three research techniques were used: (1) Four seminars brought together representatives of the Commission's Directorates General, the Forward Studies Unit, and McKinsey & Co. to consider the future of the automobile industry, railways, banking and telecommunications services, as examples. (2) Seminars and interviews conducted by McKinsey & Co. highlighted attitudes among industrialists in the various countries under study. (3) Meetings with a broad cross-section of 30 chairmen and/or senior executives of European firms in different sectors of the economy, most of them members of the European Round Table, led to direct dialogue with some of the leading protagonists in the European Single Market.

and more important. The Maastricht ratification debates underline this shifting emphasis even further.

Internal and external phenomena analysed by the reports require new options and new processes. Internally, it appears that 1992 cannot simply be a policy of deregulation aimed at the gradual dismantling of the Welfare State established in post-war Western Europe: accompanying common policies based on deliberative democracy are necessary, insofar as the objectives of the proposed action cannot be adequately achieved by the Member States. Even from a viewpoint of pure industrial competitiveness, there is no substantial market mechanism without political and social regulation where the concept of *public good* is asserted.

External pressures also point towards the need for a more ambitious Community. The disintegration of the rest of the Continent and the liberated economies of eastern Europe have made the need for political integration in western Europe stronger than ever. The multiplication of regional trading agreements and, beyond, the challenges from countries such as the United States and Asia call for a Europe respected throughout the world. The combined size of the EC countries makes them a major economic actor on the world scene, but the challenge is to be strong politically to assert a socio-cultural identity, to promote partnership, and to change from being an environment-*taker* to one of being an environment-*maker*. It is important to note here that, in general, European business focused on different external Community issues from those emphasized by the national institutes. What was mainly mentioned by business and industrial leaders were the globalization of financial markets, the expansion of international trade, the importance of helping eastern Europe to develop, and the growing role of Japan. Broader socio-political issues such as migration or the North–South divide were relatively neglected.

To illustrate this, it is interesting to note that in the European Round Table of Industrialists' publication, *Reshaping Europe* (September 1991), most, but not all, of the issues raised tended to focus on internal Community issues. Of the nine major priorities listed, only one and a half are externally rated. Likewise, in the report itself, the developing world, the Lomé Convention and the Mediterranean are covered in only six paragraphs. Much more emphasis is placed on a wider Europe and in particular the development of eastern Europe, a result that is mirrored in our own findings.

Another issue where the view of the national institutes and business diverge to some extent is that of Economic and Monetary Union. In general, EMU is seen in a somewhat positive light by the national institutes, although they do not underestimate the difficulties of achieving economic convergence, a single currency or an independent Central Bank. The views of business, however, are more varied and less positive. Some companies are unambiguously in favour, believing that the foreign exchange transaction costs saved will increase company profits. Others are sceptical, doubting that such a system can work, given the diversity of European economies. Particular caution, even veering towards hostility, was mentioned by some German interviewees. The dangers of a two-speed Europe were also mentioned. Prior to the crisis in the EMS, a third strand felt comfortable with the status quo on the grounds that those companies felt that they had an advantage over their competitors within the ring fence of the present system. We do not want to level the financial playing field, they argue, our Treasury department outperforms those of our rivals!

Overall, it appears that, given its objectives, its constraints and its horizon, the business community cannot be the main engine for a major qualitative jump in the next phase of European construction, relying as it does on a grand political vision. On the contrary, the business community seems to hope that the European authorities, especially the Commission, will do the minimum necessary, and leave more room for market mechanisms. In this perspective, the Commission will be recognized, not through the affirmation of ambitious new designs, but as investing in the tangible and measurable rather than philosophic, quixotic, or even the cultural and external. In responding to the concrete needs expressed by its citizens and the Member States' governments, and by demonstrating clearly that adequate answers must be found at a pan-European level, the Commission must demonstrate the capacity to provide policy-efficient answers that rigorously respect the subsidiarity principle.

Should we be surprised by these conclusions? Not really. The genius of those who invented Europe in the 1950s (Monnet, Schuman, Spaak and Adenauer), was precisely to promote tangible measures of obvious mutual interest and let greater political integration follow naturally from those practical steps. This method has been explicitly expressed in the Preamble to the Treaty of Paris establishing the European Coal and Steel Community in 1951, in which it is said that the goal is: 'To create ... the basis for a broader and deeper community among peoples long divided by bloody conflicts; and to lay the foundations for institutions which will give direction to a destiny hence forward shared'. But the Preamble also recognizes that: 'Europe can be built only through *practical achievements* which will first of all create real solidarity, and through the establishment of common bases for economic development' (emphasis added).

Two reflections are therefore possible. On the one hand it is undoubtedly true that the demands for increasing competitiveness on Europe's business world will meet a message of caution; do not open up any more Pandora's Boxes; give us time to take in what is already on the table. These messages are less positive, less dynamic than those the Commission solicited in 1984–5, when the business world provided the essential turbo-charge for the Single Market programme. The replies overall are also tinged, inevitably, by our poor economic situation.

Clear priority is given by the business community to the effective implementation of the Single Market. For the Commission this implies a change of emphasis from a legislative to a management strategy. The perception is that implementing the Single Market is the crucial issue, so much so that no new vision should be introduced before the 1992 Single Market programme has been firmly and fully achieved. Most business people also consider that the Single Market will be a reality and that it will be necessary to accept the corresponding increased competition. But, for Europe post-1992, it is more a necessity than an energizing theme, all the more so because the adjustment costs are already there, while some of the benefits are still expected. The transition period is critical and new obstacles and uncertainties have already emerged, including the temptation, in the name of subsidiarity, towards some 'renationalization' to limit transnational competition. In our context of fragility, the view is then that clarifying Europe's strategies around a set of concrete projects is necessary. The Community has a great deal to digest and must consolidate its results, define its essential binding, non-negotiable interests, and agree on well-identified issues, before launching another crusade.

Several specific and practical projects in certain key areas of economic development emerge from the enquiries. At the internal level, the development of trans-European infrastructure and networks, including telecommunication services and railways; improved flexibility in the labour market and training systems to meet business needs; reinforced competitiveness on the part of European technology. At the external level, a *Marshall Plan* for eastern Europe and, going beyond a macro-economic approach, the building up of a managerial capability with concrete results benefiting European industry; better access to foreign markets and reciprocity at the world level. The question of an improvement in European education systems is also relatively important for the business community. However, the extension to broader social issues, including the perspective of participation in a new social contract, creates a suspicion of interventionism and a fear of higher costs for business corporations. Several other themes praised by the national institutes are considered with some scepticism by the corporations.

- Potential European leadership through sustainable development is doubtful. Firstly, it is not very likely that Europe could acquire such leadership. It will be very difficult to generate a prime-mover advantage, given the dynamism of some Japanese and American corporations in this domain. Furthermore, there are the added difficulties of finding the capital required for huge investments, and the time lag for achieving the bottom-line benefits. Secondly, business people fear that the external competition, mainly from eastern Europe and Asian countries, could exercise some form of *environmental dumping* (competitors having access to the

EC market despite their lower environmental standards) and force re-
location. In general, many companies seem to take a reactive rather than
a proactive stance towards environmental protection. Even though intentions are good, many have no policy and approach the problems unsys-
tematically, on an *ad hoc* basis.

- The search for more stability and security at Community level is viewed
  with suspicion. Apart from some specific problem areas such as nuclear
  prolification, the attitude is that increasing uncertainty and risk are in-
  inherent in a process of liberalization, and such a situation is preferable
  to a system of protection for weak players. Of course, in weak countries,
  the position is less clear-cut, and pleas for help in transition are made.
- The positive value of European diversity is not denied but the implications are controversial. Too much diversity could maintain fragment-
  tation, while a more homogeneous market created by breaking down
  intangible barriers may enlarge the level playing field. Let market forces
  determine the appropriate level of diversity.

Given the importance of small and medium-sized enterprises (SMEs) in
Europe, it is important to gain some insight into their expectations. Inquiries
made within the framework of the 'shaping factors' study and based on a series
of interviews with British, German, French and Spanish SME associations
provide interesting viewpoints (Löser, 1992). Three messages are especially
relevant in the light of the information coming from the large companies.
Firstly, as in the case of big business, SMEs attach the greatest importance to the
completion of the Internal Market and they warn the Community authorities
almost unanimously 'not to invent new things, first get Europe 1992 working.'
Secondly, Europe post-1992 is perceived as an opportunity *and* a threat. On the
one hand, no single national government would ever have had the courage to
enforce deregulation in a way Europe 1992 does, since it means challenging the
vested interests of thousands of established companies and their employees. On
the other hand, the Internal Market appears as a threat for European SMEs who
work only in a protected local market, with little or no export experience. SME
owners are strong individualists who like to remain their own boss. The dynamic
entrepreneurial characters among them know that in order to exploit the new
market opportunities rapidly they need partners and co-operative agreements.
In some cases they accept them (preferably for less than a 50 per cent stake), but
the large majority remains sceptical and attitudes are changing only slowly. So
SMEs must rely strongly on self-financing or on credit, and they complain
vigorously about banks being too prudent, basing their lending too strongly on
security and preferring clearly to do business with larger companies. Thirdly,
there is some scepticism towards EC R&D programmes which, in terms of total

spending on R&D are 'a drop in the ocean anyway'. They benefit primarily the large companies and the money set aside for the SMEs would be not much more than 'cosmetic balancing'. The procedures to win EC finance are also too complicated, thus contributing to frustrations over the Community. There is also the fear that an EC industrial policy would benefit mostly the big companies and therefore distort competition.

To conclude, there is no radical choice to be made between a new vision and pragmatism. Rather it means asking how the Commission can be the architect of progress, responding to both the direct, pragmatic requirements of European business and the long-term, ambitious challenges emerging from the shaping factors outlined by the national institutes and which correspond to the qualitative political and institutional leap created by European Union. One implication is that such a difficult juggling act requires an improvement in the dialogue, organization and consultation procedures between European business and the European Commission, a subset of wider problems of communication, transparency and democratic structure that the EC must face up to in the 1990s.

## IV. Conclusion

In conclusion, it is useful to emphasize that our studies also suggest a wide consensus expressed by the business community and national institutes, around a European model of society. Reference is made to core values where the dynamics of the market economy combine with the solidarity of social cohesion. This vision does not draw on the old ideas of social engineering and large-scale government intervention, but expresses the need for a new paradigm.

This can be made more explicit by using the famous distinction proposed by Hirschman (1971), between two types of mechanism to ensure the functioning of an organization or a society: Exit and Voice. In 'Exit' social change is ensured through a decentralized and anonymous mechanism that secures victory for the most efficient. Winners are rewarded with growth, and losers are obliged to disappear. Results worked out by the market are considered natural and legitimate, including international, national, regional, and personal redistribution of resources. In 'Voice', the process of social adjustment rests on a collective consensus that establishes solidarity of existing interests and determines the general direction of change. The consequences of change are themselves tempered by effective redistribution between winners and losers. Outcomes of market mechanisms are not automatically regarded as legitimate and can be politically modified. Each of these types leads to perverse effects in an extreme form. In the Exit type, transmitted information is poor, the mechanism is brutal, and the probability of reconciliation of conflicting social interests is low. In addition, there is the risk of a *dual society* developing, in which a significant proportion of the population becomes peripheral and marginalized, and in which the legitimacy of the winning circle is as much based on a strategy of domination as on initial efficiency. In the Voice type, on the other hand, the desire for consensus and equitable compensation is liable to undermine the inducement to creativity, initiative, experimentation and diversity. Defence of group interests and acquired rights easily deviates toward corporatism and protectionism. Growing and paralysing interventionism creates inefficiencies, even in the social sphere.

The problem is then not to choose between Voice and Exit but to combine their virtues whilst avoiding their vices. Nor does it come down to a radical and irreversible choice between public and private initiative, thus freezing the abilities of each; rather it should raise the issue of the difficulty of implementing mobility in respective areas according to appropriate modalities. For instance, deregulation of spheres mismanaged by the state is undoubtedly desirable. This, however, does not imply a return to a utopian free market but a change of regulation: delegation of functions, grants for public services, or transfer of assets to the private sector must be matched with institutional rules and alternative forms of social control. If the public authorities renounce the monopoly of determining social welfare, it would nevertheless remain a privileged player among the participants in the games of social and economic relations. It would take on only what is strictly necessary but it would safeguard pluralism, avoid replacement of public monopolies by private cartels, and ensure effective redistributive transfers.

The European project could then be the benchmark for the building-up of such a *social market economy* where dialectic relations and not opposition are developed between market mechanisms and social cohesion, competition and co-operation. But this project, related to the *Soziale Marktwirtschaft* model is fragile. The prospect of a very considerable loss of jobs over the next five to ten years has dangerous implications for social stability and the economic sustainability of 'Eurocapitalism'. From that point of view, dialogue between the European authorities and industry must be improved on both sides in order to identify energizing guidelines that generate a consensus and enable the Community to move forward.

### References

Buigues, P. and Jacquemin, A. (1993) 'Foreign Direct Investments and Exports in the Common Market'. In Mason, M. (ed.) *Does Ownership Matter?* (Oxford: Oxford University Press).

Cecchini, P. with Catinat, M. and Jacquemin, A. (1987) *The European Challenge* (Wildwood House).

Commission of the European Communities (1991)  *Panorama of EC Industries* (Brussels: CEC).

Emerson, M. *et al.* (1988) The *Economics of 1992*. (Oxford: Oxford University Press).

Hirschman, O. (1971) *Exit, Voice and Loyalty* (Cambridge, Mass.: Harvard University Press).

Jacquemin, A. and Wright, D. (eds.) (1993) *The European Challenges Post-1992: Shaping Factors, Shaping Actors* (London: Edward Elgar).

Löser, P. (1992) 'A Snapshot of European SMEs'. Working document, Forward Studies Unit, Commission of the European Communities.

# 10.
# Towards Monetary Union in Europe – Reforms of the EMS in the Perspective of Monetary Union

NIELS THYGESEN*

This article reviews a number of options to reform the EMS in the light of the currency turmoil of 1992–3. While greater flexibility – wide fluctuations margins and frequent small realignments – may now seem attractive to some countries, notably the United Kingdom, steps in this direction are likely to lead to increased instability and divergence while postponing for a long time advances towards monetary union. If anything, the fluctuation margins and the Basle-Nyborg Agreement of 1987 providing mechanisms for the short-term defence of exchange rates, need to be tightened up. The article also discusses the scope for strengthening monetary co-ordination in the European Monetary Institute which is to start on 1 January 1994, respecting the principle that monetary sovereignty should remain ultimately in national hands until the start of full monetary union and the set-up of the European Central Bank.

Over the weekend of 31 July–1 August 1993, the EC monetary authorities found themselves unable to defend the existing EMS against the strong speculative pressures on several currencies and they agreed as a last resort to widen

* The author is grateful for comments by the discussant Andrew Hughes-Hallet. Subsequent developments of the paper owe much to the work in a study group organised by the Association for Monetary Union in Europe for the European Parliament. The author would also like to record the influence of several years of collaboration with Daniel Gros, while assuming sole responsibility for remaining errors of interpretation and judgement.

fluctuation margins to +/–15 per cent. The central rates were preserved. Although this step marks a clear step in the opposite direction of what is recommended in the present article – prepared about two months before the dramatic developments – the author has chosen to make only minimal factual corrections to the analysis and proposals in the belief that the issues addressed under the heading of reforms in the EMS will have to be faced sooner or later, if Member States wish to revive the EMU process.

## I. Introduction

Two major and interrelated upsets to the process towards monetary union occurred in the course of 1992–3: (1) several countries experienced far greater difficulties than anticipated by governments in getting the Maastricht Treaty ratified; and (2) a major crisis in the European currency markets in September 1992, followed by recurrent periods of turbulence, made the European Monetary System (EMS), viewed as the essential stepping stone to monetary union which the EMS was seen to shadow increasingly closely, look very vulnerable – indeed, as potentially incapable of surviving. Two currencies left the system and no less than four realignments took place in less than five months. Fluctuation margins were widened dramatically to +/–15 per cent on 2 August 1993. Both of these events – popular disaffection with the objective of monetary union and a single currency and a breakdown of co-operation between national monetary authorities – have raised serious doubts about the feasibility of the timetable for moving towards full monetary union foreseen in the Treaty signed in Maastricht in February 1992 (henceforth 'Maastricht'). The purpose of the present article is to discuss whether the approach to monetary union remains viable and, if so, how monetary unification could be resumed, possibly with a revised timetable.

Only nine Member States out of the 12 had ratified Maastricht within the time-frame foreseen as end-1992. Denmark voted 'No' by a small margin on 2 June 1992, but this result was reversed in a second referendum on 18 May 1993 after the Edinburgh European Council had granted Denmark significant exemptions in four important areas; one of them was to accept that Denmark already now exercises its option, granted in a special Protocol in Maastricht, not to join the third stage of Economic and Monetary Union. The United Kingdom, which had already obtained this particular exemption in Maastricht along with a freer status in relation to some of the provisions applying in the second stage, ratified on 2 August 1993. Although German ratification has been challenged in the Constitutional Court of the Federal Republic, it now seems a safe assumption the Maastricht will be ratified by all 12 in the course of 1993. This implies that the new provisions of Maastricht can enter into force before the date of 1 January

1994 when some of them may prove essential to the resumption of monetary unification. The alternative scenario in which the new provisions remain unusable after 1 January 1994 will not be discussed further in this article.

The following sections are organized as follows: Section II looks at a number of specific reforms of the EMS, bearing in mind the differentiated requirements and starting points of the Member States (and of the prospective new entrants in the EC). Section III attempts an overall evaluation of the scope for reforms; it explores, in particular, the limits of the so-called indivisibility doctrine, according to which national monetary sovereignty can be effectively shared only in the final stage of monetary union, since this doctrine poses the main challenge for the European Monetary Institute (EMI), the precursor of the European System of Central Banks, in convincing financial markets that the transitional arrangements are robust and deserve credibility. Section IV offers some tentative conclusions.

## II. Paths of Reform in European Monetary Unification

### Individual Floating

Having watched the main elements which brought forward the 1992–3 crisis in European monetary arrangements, it is tempting to ask – encouraged by the analysis of many North American observers – why not revert to *individual floating* for a period to accommodate the real or perceived difference in the environment for monetary policy within the EC? Feldstein (1992) advocated this option forcefully in words that may now be close to the official UK position:

> Even defenders of monetary union recognise that the loss of flexible nominal exchange rates makes it more difficult for countries to respond to shocks to demand that create local unemployment. A single European currency precludes adjusting national monetary policy and interest rates to offset shocks to demand that are greater locally than in the EC as a whole.

Feldstein does allow for the high probability that the option of flexible exchange rates will not appeal to several smaller countries in the EC which have come to appreciate the advantages of a very tight exchange rate link to the Deutschmark (DM) and do not think that they could produce policies of their own which are on average superior to what they could achieve by abandoning German leadership. The prescription for floating would apply only to the major EC countries, including the largest of them, Germany.

The reason why this option is regarded as undesirable by EC policy-makers outside the UK is not just that it might for a long time close the road to monetary union. More importantly, it would deny also the reasons why the EMS was formed in 1978 and the lessons from its gradualist experience which has built up over nearly 15 years.

The Treaty of Rome stated (Art. 103) that economic policies and hence, ultimately, the exchange rate of Member States were a matter of common concern. This principle, retained in the same article in Maastricht, would itself put severe constraints on the extent to which a Member State would be allowed to rely on movements in its exchange rate to accommodate differences in performance and/or policy preferences. This principle in the Treaty was violated in the early years of the post-Bretton Woods period (1972–8) and the response in 1978 was the creation of the EMS, designed to constrain movements in the strong as well as in the weak currencies in the face of fundamentally similar shocks to all the European economies, i.e. US policy shocks or changes in the price of imported energy. The Germans were primarily concerned over the prospect of a trendwise weak US dollar triggering an unwarranted strong appreciation of the DM against all important EC trading partners – a concern not far removed from those of the 1990s. Other EMS participants feared the implications of the mirror image of this scenario: excessive devaluation of their weaker currencies and consequently additional inflation. The EMS was set up to contain the potential for additional divergence between the performances of the European economies which intra-EC exchange rate changes had revealed in the 1970s.

In short, the emerging view was that unless exchange-rate stabilization was made an explicit policy objective, currency instability would persist. Even firm and apparently parallel monetary policies in two countries could not be relied upon to be sufficient to achieve an indirect objective of a stable exchange rate between their currencies, as demonstrated by the adoption in the mid-1970s by nearly all of the main industrial countries of a policy of designing policy consistently in terms of broadly similar monetary aggregates. Exchange rates were never less stable than in the early years thereafter.

There is no inclination in the main EC countries to have to relearn this early post-Bretton Woods experience. Admittedly, with the low inflation now prevailing in the EC, and a stronger commitment to maintain it more permanently, the risk of a repeat of the currency instability of the 1970s may look remote. Nevertheless, the events of 1992–3 have shown that such a repeat cannot be excluded. Once formal policy commitments weaken and national elections are approaching, with the prospect of significant policy shifts in the modified environment, the exchange rate can move far in a short time.

Currency fluctuations of the size experienced in some years in the 1970s and in 1992–3 would be seen, and rightly in my view, by Europe's business community, trade unions and policy-makers as highly undesirable and as incompatible with the realization of a well-functioning internal market in goods and services. The benefits of a single currency which had begun to be regarded as marginal towards the end of the long period of a stable EMS because the standard of comparison was so close to monetary union[1] suddenly loom much larger. With renewed instability all transaction and information costs related to exchange-rate changes rise towards earlier observed levels. At the same time, transition to a floating rate environment could not provide national governments with an additional policy instrument. Dissolving the EMS would remove an apparent constraint, but at the cost of introducing additional uncertainty in the ability to forecast the effects of other policy instruments, notably fiscal policy. One advantage of a monetary union and an EMS that has come to shadow it closely is that the effects of change in budgetary policy become more predictable than in looser exchange-rate regimes.

Whatever the validity of the general arguments against a significant reversal to floating, the fact that the EMS has been loosened and that two important currencies are currently floating and at least one of them – sterling – is unlikely to return soon to any system, implies that the proposal by Feldstein and others to allow floating as a temporary solution while targeting monetary policy to domestic objectives, is being adopted by some – voluntarily or by the force of circumstances. The question then becomes whether individual floating of one major currency could still be viewed with equanimity by the others, or whether changes in the value of that currency should be constrained by a more formal monitoring procedure than simply building on the revised Art. 103 and its multilateral surveillance provisions. This is where the idea of examining the suitability of the target zone proposal as a regime intermediate between a continuing EMS and individual floating comes into its own.

## Target Zone

The target zone proposal was advanced in its most elaborate form in Williamson (1985) and subsequently expanded in Miller and Williamson (1987) into a more comprehensive scheme for international policy co-ordination by bringing in rules for fiscal policy as well as exchange- and interest-rate policy. The basic idea, however, goes back at least another decade,[2] and it is interesting to reflect that it was used as a framework for discussing how the then joint float management (the 'snake') between five EC currencies could be extended to comprise all or most of the EC's then nine currencies. The analysis and the reasons why the target zone ideas was not put into practice appear just as relevant in 1993 as 17 years earlier.

[1] By the late 1980s intra-EMS exchange rate variability – measured by the standard deviation of monthly changes in bilateral rates – had been reduced to about one quarter of what had been observed in the five-year period just before the EMS (1974–8). See Gros and Thygesen (1992), ch. 4, particularly pp. 101–10.
[2] Ethier and Bloomfield (1975) is one early reference. Williamson (1977) and contemporaneous articles also applied the concept to IMF surveillance and to his ideas for reviving European monetary integration.

The then Finance Minister of the Netherlands, Wim Duisenberg – currently chairman of the Committee of EC Central Bank Governors – submitted a letter to his colleagues in July 1976. This was shortly after massive depreciations of the lira and of sterling which had greatly weakened the competitive position of participants in the snake (and a few months after the exit of the French franc from the snake). Duisenberg complained about the absence of an effective EC framework for co-operation on exchange-rate issues. More specifically, he proposed a mutual surveillance procedure inspired by the IMF guidelines for floating centred on a set of mutually agreed target zones for the three main floating currencies (lira, sterling and the French franc) and – presumably – for the snake as a whole. The target zones would be defined in effective exchange rate terms; they would imply no positive obligation for a country to keep its exchange rate within the zone through interventions or domestic policy measures ('soft buffers'), only a presumption that no steps would be taken to push the rate away from the target zone. The latter would from time to time be reviewed and central rates realigned. Exit from the zone would trigger discussions of closer policy co-ordination.

This subtle, but minimalist plan never materialized, though it may have inspired some of the ideas that went into the EMS one or two years later.[3] It failed for several reasons: it was considered too vague by those policy-makers who were getting ready for the more ambitious EMS, and too open-ended by the Germans who feared they might be drawn into large interventions in support of currencies that had not themselves accepted real obligations. Finally, idealists objected on the grounds that the target zone proposal would create additional asymmetries and consolidate a two-speed monetary Europe.

The similarities with the current debate on reforming or reviving the EMS are indeed striking. Informed public opinion in the United Kingdom now appears to think the system should be made more flexible, possibly by extending more freedom to participants in realigning and in waiving their obligations than was available even in the early and most 'permissive' EMS period (1979–83). In this spirit, *The Economist* (8 May 1993) proposed 're-entry' of sterling along lines similar to those of the Duisenberg Plan.

If the UK were to seek to attach sterling to other European currencies in such a way – no doubt updating the proposal by presenting it in terms of sterling's exchange rate *vis-à-vis* the DM or the ECU rather than the effective rate and by focusing on wide fluctuation margins more than on the other two dimensions of flexibility: frequent central rate changes and only negative obligations to

---

[3] The EC Monetary Committee and the Governors' Committee did introduce, in 1977, more regular consultations on exchange-rate issues. And the notion that there should be an exchange-rate related trigger for closer policy co-ordination survived in the form of the supplementary indicator of divergence – which has not, however, been much used in the EMS. For a fuller account of the Duisenberg Plan, see Gros and Thygesen (1992) pp. 39–41.

support the zone – would other EC Member States be interested in accepting it? The balance of the arguments suggests the answer to the question is No, while raising doubt whether the UK could even serve her own interests by 'participating' on these terms.

The core of the matter is that the target zone proposal in one of its more flexible variants appears in today's perspective as no more than a framework for monitoring a deviant currency and preparing its entry. This type of framework will be used anyway when the time comes to consider on what terms re-entry for the lira and sterling could take place. The competent EC bodies will need to examine at that point whether market exchange-rates for currencies which floated from September could be maintained within the EMS at the level established in the market. This judgement would focus on the competitiveness of their economies, i.e. on whether they have improved sufficiently or not since 1992. There is no need to revise the operations of the system itself, only its rules of entry.

The point may be seen by some as almost purely semantic. But it is not. If the UK wishes to give the impression that it is again 'participating' in European monetary integration, a form of words could no doubt be found. The danger lies in the precedent such a position would set to other potential entrants and in the general impression it would create that the whole process of European monetary integration had drifted into such an agnostic and confused stage that even proposals which were rejected 17 years ago at the bottom of the European disintegration of the 1970s as being too vague could be entertained. The difference between, on the one hand, a group of countries that try with some joint determination to peg their currencies as a strategic element in maintaining low inflation and, on the other hand, a potential participant in the club wishing to adjust its exchange rate regularly to avoid disequilibria more continuously, is basic and cannot readily be accommodated within the same system, as has been recognized recently by Williamson (1993) who distinguishes sharply between these two views of the exchange rate. One emphasizes its role as a nominal anchor in an anti-inflationary strategy; from time to time that may produce misalignments. The other stresses the need to prevent disequilibria from arising in exchange markets and hence foresees regular small realignments.

There remains one residual appeal of the target zone approach even to those who prefer to use their exchange rate as a firm nominal anchor: the approach could still put constraints on the behaviours of outsiders and hence be less destabilizing also to the cohesion of the first group clustering around a common nominal anchor. The major question for this group is whether a target zone arrangement for sterling could in practice provide better protection against further large currency movements and, particularly, additional competitive advantage for the UK economy, than simply individual floating for sterling.

This must be unlikely, if the target zone is wide and flexible and if departure from it cannot be subjected to sanctions by the countries that have joined the first group. If so, the disadvantages of appearing to provide a general alternative to their approach to monetary union will be decisive in determining their attitude to the far-reaching flexibility sought by the United Kingdom.

Another question is, whether it would serve UK interest in any meaningful economic sense if sterling were to be accepted within a soft arrangement. Credibility effects, allowing lower long-term UK interest rates than if sterling were to float individually, would be unlikely, as the markets would perceive that the trend inflation rate had not been affected in any appreciable way relative to what the UK could achieve anyway by her own efforts. It would be more than difficult to envisage that the UK authorities could expect intervention support, if the target zone were to be wide and subject to regular revision; such support could, of course, not even be imagined if the zone was only to be defended by negative obligations not to take steps that would push sterling away from the zone. And if there were to be positive obligations to defend the zone, the UK authorities would have to expect to provide the defence by unilateral interest rate hikes, though the latter could presumably be much more modest than was required in the (wide) EMS band of September 1992. If the hypothesis advanced in the previous section, *viz.* that the depreciation of sterling has overcorrected any previous misalignment, is true, any subsequent appreciation of sterling may be easier to handle under individual floating than in a modified target zone system.

In short, the UK would appear to have no well-defined economic gains in prospect from obtaining a target zone arrangement with the EMS countries. There might be political gains. 'Rejoining' on a new basis could be presented to domestic opinion as a pragmatic reintroduction of an exchange-rate objective to reinforce domestic objectives of low inflation and as a partial victory over a European system which had become overly rigid and too intolerant of a country wanting to pursue a monetary policy better attuned to domestic conditions than a replica of policies in other EC countries. But there should, in case other EC countries accept the implications of this argument, be expression of a firm determination that what is being put in place is a specific and temporary arrangement for the United Kingdom rather than a general reform of the EMS, converting it to more flexibility.

*Reforms within the EMS*

Having argued that neither individual floating nor target zone arrangements for those currencies that may request them would be desirable paths of EMS reforms, it must be asked whether there exist reforms which appear at the same time economically desirable and politically feasible? This will be discussed in the following under three headings: (1) the width of fluctuation margins, (2) an updating of the defensive mechanisms of the Basle-Nyborg Agreement, and (3) the role of realignments.

*Margins of fluctuation.* Prior to August 1993 the EC currencies fell into three distinct categories: seven currencies[4] observed the normal margins of 2.25 per cent (and have done so continuously since the start of the EMS in 1979), two (escudo and peseta) observed margins of 6 per cent (used also by Italy 1979–89), while three were individually floating. It was hard to conceive that a common prescription could be made for these diverse groups; in any case the theoretical arguments for choosing the width of the margins and the accumulated evidence of the EMS experience both warrant more careful examination.

Historically the width of the normal margins dates back to the European response to the widening of margins against the US dollar from +/– 1 to +/– 2.25 per cent which was introduced by the Smithsonian Agreement of December 1971. Since that step implied that the exchange rate between two EC currencies could change by as much as 9 per cent if they were to switch position between the ceiling and the floor of their respective margins against the US dollar – a degree of variability which was considered excessive in 1972 – the participants in the snake chose to put each others' currencies on a par with the dollar in terms of predictability. This simple and logical response has now survived the floating of the dollar in 1973, the transition to the EMS in 1978–9, the subsequent tightening of that arrangement in the course of the 1980s, the liberalization of capital movements, and the formulation of a treaty in 1991 setting out a blueprint for the transition to full monetary union in which the margin would by definition be reduced to zero. Given the increasingly arbitrary character of the margins, this attachment to a figure chosen more than 20 years ago is surprising.

The Delors Report on EMU (para. 57) did propose that the standard margins be narrowed to, say, +/– 1 per cent at the beginning of stage 2. This proposal was supported by the European Parliament and in various reports by private groups, though without any particular analytical underpinnings. The idea of narrowing margins as a general prescription never won favour among officials. When the Danish government proposed early in the 1991 Intergovernmental Conference on EMU that margins be narrowed for all participants to ± 1.5 per cent from the start of stage 2, no other government supported the idea. EMS participants appear to have preferred, on the one hand, to accept wider margins as a transitional arrangement available on demand and, on the other hand, to retain the option to move unilaterally to narrower margins when individual circumstances permitted, as the Benelux countries have done *de facto* in recent years.

If one examines the target zone literature where the choice of margins is at times explicitly discussed, a trade-off emerges between the removal of part of

---

[4] Counting the Luxembourg franc as a separate currency.

the residual autonomy available to a participant in the EMS contemplating a narrowing, and the benefits in terms of improved credibility of the central rates as the monetary authorities signal their decision by words or actions to move to narrower margins. While agreeing on the objective – to manage their currency with as little tension as possible at short-term interest rates a minimum distance above (and ideally just below) comparable German rates – countries observing the normal margins appeared for a while to interpret this trade-off in different ways. The Benelux currencies were managed – for some time in the late 1980s for the Netherlands, since the spring of 1990 for Belgium – within unilaterally narrowed margins against the DM. They were rewarded with near-complete convergence of their short-term rates with German ones in 1991–2 and at times in 1993 by a fall to levels slightly below them. France and Denmark by contrast wanted to retain the freedom of action of the normal margins. As long as there is (nearly) full confidence in the markets that the central rate will continue to be observed and that present margins will be defended, a strategy of retaining the normal margins while using short-term interest rates to keep the DM exchange rate as close to the floor as possible should, in principle, enable short-term interest rates to move around a lower average level than the 'Benelux strategy' can deliver; the currency at the floor will be expected to revert towards the central rate, hence allowing for an appreciation discount to be incorporated into the yield on short-term assets denominated in the currency. The size of the discount should rise with the width of the margins – provided the credibility of the central rate is unrelated to the width of the margins and to the position of the currency inside them.

These are, however, strong assumptions. France tested the limits of policy autonomy inside the normal margins in late 1991, well before the currency turmoil of 1992, and succeeded temporarily in keeping the French short-term rate below the German level. But France lost more than FFr 50 billion through interventions in support of the franc over the October 1991–January 1992 period; apparently the French policy was seen as unduly aggressive by market participants since it created fears that a devaluation might be in preparation. Once such fears arise, the 'honeymoon effect' identified by Krugman within a credible target zone disappears and interest-rate differentials have to widen in favour of the weak currency. France decided the outflows were enough and raised short-term rates relative to Germany by approximately 50 basis points in early 1992; until the political uncertainties over ratification of Maastricht set in with the first Danish 'No' and the announcement of the French referendum in early June, the French franc was maintained near the centre of the band. There is little doubt, judging from both actions and policy statements at the time, that France was attracted by the idea of shifting to a Benelux strategy of narrower margins. The currency turmoil since June 1992 made the adoption of such a policy infeasible, but it will reappear.

Denmark and Ireland have shown a more permanent readiness to make full use of the margins than has France; they could hardly be tempted to opt for a unilateral narrowing of margins. Following the end of January devaluation of the punt, the Irish currency moved to the top of the margins; relatively high interest rates were maintained in order to facilitate the reflow of capital. With the uncertainly surrounding the exchange-rate policy of major non-EMS trading partners of both Denmark and Ireland (Sweden and the United Kingdom), these two EMS participants seemed comfortable with the normal margins. For Denmark there is an additional complication, viz. that Denmark has announced an opt-out from the third stage of EMU, so that steps aimed in that direction have little domestic appeal despite the Danish economy's relatively strong perform-ance with respect to the Maastricht convergence criteria.

A tentative conclusion prior to August was that only France was likely to join the Benelux countries in maintaining (announced or unannounced) narrow margins *vis-à-vis* the DM.

The official report of April 1993 already suggested that more flexibility, including wider margins, rather than less, may be in store. The official reports advocate a continuation of the practice in the EMS since the start of leaving the decision regarding fluctuation bands to the national authorities; though the Governors' report adds that 'experience with operating the EMS has shown that the width of the fluctuation band must be regarded as a matter of common concern', and that the decisions 'should be preceded by close consultation taking due account of the same factors as those considered when the sustaina-bility of the parity grid is examined' (Section IV. 1). Remarkably, the text makes no reference to the provisions of Art. 109 J, 1, according to which a currency must have observed the normal fluctuation margins for at least two years without devaluing in order to qualify for the final stage of monetary union. It is possible, of course, that the official committees thought that no Member State needed to be reminded of this point, but the omission is still an indication of the extent to which the officials were – already before the crisis of the summer of 1993 – trying to separate reforms in the EMS from the progress towards monetary unification which they were supposed to facilitate.

Whether countries should be given the choice of wider than normal margins must depend on the experience with such margins and their expected contribu-tion to sustaining the system in the future rather than on tradition and established rights. The wide margins were initially offered to Italy in 1978 with the following provision:

> In terms of exchange-rate management the EMS will be at least as strict as the 'snake'. In the initial stages of its operation and for a limited period of time

member countries not currently participating in the snake may opt for somewhat wider margins around central rates. (Annex to the Conclusions of the Presidency of the European Council of 6 and 7 July 1978 in Bremen)

Italy chose this option because its inflation rate in 1978 was still well into double figures and some 7–8 per cent above that of Germany. Though the lira probably started life in the EMS from a comfortable position of some undervaluation after the massive depreciation of the 1970s, it was in retrospect a prudent strategy on the part of both Italian and other EC authorities to grant the temporary exemption of the wide band which could – and did – prevent Italy from having to realign more frequently than other participants. It also protected the lira against the need to face discontinuities in market exchange rates at the time of realignments; the latter were never, in the nine cases of devaluation *vis-à-vis* the DM, so large as to prevent the new fluctuation margins from containing the previous market rate.

It may well be asked whether the 11 years from the start of the EMS to January 1990 when Italy narrowed the margins to the normal level was not an unduly long transition period. The initial turbulent phase of the first four years in the EMS when no inflation convergence got underway, the relatively slow subsequent convergence and the fact that Italy gave priority to removing her controls on capital flows over the narrowing of margins help to explain why the process took so long.

Spain joined the EMS in June 1989, also with a wide band. The country had only become a member of the EC three and a half years earlier, leading to very rapid integration of goods and services markets. Massive capital inflows had been observed and the peseta appreciated nominally; real appreciation was much stronger, since inflation was still running at a rate about 4 percentage points above that of Germany, while the current account showed a large deficit. It was understandable that there was some uncertainty as to whether the exchange rate was in equilibrium. In any case, with inflation clearly above the EMS average, high interest rates were required. The peseta was near the top of the wide band for most of the more than three years after entry, but abnormal rates did not explode the system since they were in part offset by the expectation that the peseta would revert towards the centre of the margins. Somewhat similar comments apply to Portugal; the authorities had stabilized the escudo for about a year and a half before they took it into the EMS in April 1992, while also asking for a wide band. The latter no doubt helped the Iberian currencies in reconciling the need for very high interest rates – by EC standards – and the desire for a stable exchange rate with the main trading partners.

The UK authorities took sterling into the EMS in October 1990, also opting for the wide band (which had been refused in 1978). The UK's situation was not dissimilar to that of Spain, excess inflation being the most obvious source of policy divergence with the narrow margins group. But, as recession proved to be deeper and more protracted than expected, inflation was temporarily reduced to a rate well below the German one and the UK economy came to look more like some Continental economies, such as France and Denmark, with a need to keep interest rates as low as technically possible for domestic reasons. Efforts in this direction, political pressures for additional monetary ease and a marginally higher sensitivity to the decline in the US dollar than that observed for other EMS currencies drove sterling to the bottom of the +/– 6 per cent band in the summer of 1992, which could not in these circumstances provide much of a buffer. Sterling was divergent from August and higher interest rates were not considered a viable option. Having borrowed heavily in international markets to bolster resources for intervention, the UK authorities gave up their defence of the currency and embarked on an aggressive lowering of short-term interest rates causing a fall in sterling of approximately 20 per cent relative to its EMS central rate.

The common element in the experience of the Iberian currencies and of sterling with the +/– 6 per cent band is that, although the extra flexibility provided some additional monetary autonomy while the currencies were strong, it did not protect them in any significant sense in the currency crisis of 1992. On the contrary, the fact that these currencies had so far to fall and did move rapidly towards the floor of the band may have accentuated speculative pressures against them, because markets interpreted these moves as a signal of a possible devaluation. Obviously this issue is one that requires careful study of the comparative efficiency of interventions in the wide and in the narrow band, but the burden of proof would appear to be on those who believe that the wide band was helpful.

Even if this turns out not to be the case, a preliminary examination of the data suggest a +/– 6 per cent band might still be regarded as useful in more normal times than during the exceptional economic and political turbulence of 1992. One should not expect to continue to fight yesterday's battles.

The present exchange-rate constellation should prove easier to defend than the one prevailing in the summer of 1992 because the earlier weak currencies have overadjusted and are now more likely to move up rather than down while the present weakness of the DM is widely perceived by market participants. The currencies presently in the wide band or the two potential entrants, lira and sterling, which might want to ask for it, could be more in need of the upward flexibility provided by the wide band than of the buffer provided by an exceptional scope for weakening.

If such a scenario is realistic it would, however, be preferable that the required flexibility be used while the presently floating currencies are still outside the system. That would cause less tensions with (and among) the currencies which have remained in the EMS and avoid any undue pressure on the new entrants to lower interest rates faster than their domestic situation warrants to observe their renewed exchange-rate commitment.

A desirable scenario prior to August would have been one in which the lira and sterling had shown stability in the markets for some time, possibly around somewhat higher levels than today, before entering straight into the normal margins. As regards Spain and Portugal, discussions could begin in late 1993 as to a narrowing of their margins; at that time the results of the Spanish elections should have been fully digested by the financial markets. Again this recommendation hinges on the belief that the present exchange rates in the two Iberian countries does not reflect any lack of competitiveness, rather the opposite. The markets are more likely to be impressed that the period of devaluations has come to an end if the two countries were to narrow their margins than if they stay with them. Such a change would also show that the two countries should be considered serious candidates for monetary union later in the 1990s, as is their – not unrealistic – wish. In short, in the course of 1994 the wide margins could be eliminated for those that presently use them, Italy would have come back also with the normal margins while the United Kingdom – for whom maintaining candidacy for monetary union currently holds no attraction - still has a floating exchange rate.

There is, incidentally, nothing in the situations of the preferences of the four EFTA countries which are currently negotiating for membership of the EC to suggest that they would require or welcome having the option of entering the EMS with a wide band. Austria has pegged tightly to the DM for more than a decade, while the three Nordic countries all chose a narrow band when they announced their unilateral peg to the ECU in 1990–1. All four have stated explicitly that they have accepted the provisions of Maastricht which apply to EMU and to transition towards it.

*Updating the Basle-Nyborg Agreement.* This agreement, negotiated in 1987 as a response to the speculative attacks preceding the realignment of January that year, made explicit an emerging consensus among central bankers. The EMS was to be defended, in a world of increasing capital mobility, by a mixture of three types of mechanism. First, currencies should be allowed to move inside the margins in response to market pressures. Second, interventions could be used to stem undesirably strong fluctuations; for that purpose the use of the Very Short Term Financing mechanism was made more easily accessible to debtors. Third, if pressures persisted, short-term interest-rate differentials should move to abate the tensions. If that still did not work, a realignment might have to be resorted to. The latter point is not explicitly mentioned in the official text,[5] which is in itself significant. At the time the governors were anxious to be seen to regard realignments as a last resort only to be used in exceptional circumstances, since many of them regarded the January 1987 realignment as basically superfluous. Several Governors expressed the view that, if a realignment did become inevitable, it should be sufficiently small to permit continuity of market exchange rates, implying that realignments should at a maximum be twice the width of the margins, of 4.5 per cent, assuming that the weak currency would go to the top of the new margins. Avoiding jumps in market exchange rates around realignments was seen as strategically important in deterring future speculative attacks, since no immediate gains would then be made by speculators.

For a long time the provisions of Basle-Nyborg worked very well. The provisions were put to the test in early November 1987 in an almost textbook – like fashion, particularly since short-term interest rates were moved in opposite directions by Germany and France which effectively checked speculation. The Agreement also survived well the complete removal of capital controls in eight EC countries by 1988–90, the accommodation of two important new currencies and the narrowing of the band for the lira in January 1990. In retrospect, it is amazing and encouraging that a simple rule book could suffice for five years. A careful historical analysis of how several periods of moderate tensions were handled would be instructive, also as an antidote to the gloom surrounding the recent performance of the EMS.

However, in the September 1992 crisis the Agreement did become inoperative. Movements inside the margins did not provide an initial protective buffer, but appeared to trigger further large flows as exchange rates moved rapidly towards intervention limits. Interventions became very large and had to carry the main burden for longer than could be sustained, prompting the Bundesbank to invoke its initial understanding with the German government that even the presumed mandatory interventions could be suspended, as happened for the operations in support of the lira. Most would say that the main departure from the spirit of Basle-Nyborg was the failure to use the final short-term defence by moving short-term rates in a decisive fashion. But this could hardly have been done without prior institutional changes in the UK and Italy to protect the domestic financial markets better against the spill-over effects of very high money market interest rates targeted at speculators. Finally, when realignments came, they were not exactly small, they were improvised rather than negotiated, and two countries felt compelled to leave the system altogether.

The breakdown in the regular official machinery was also evident in the

[5] Press communiqué of the Committee of Governors of 18 September 1987, reproduced in Gros and Thygesen (1992) p. 99.

absence of any formal meeting by the EC Monetary Committee or the Ecofin Council prior to the Italian devaluation in September and the very casual approach to the subsequent three realignments in November (peseta and escudo), January (punt) and May (peseta and escudo). This violated an earlier tradition in the EMS back in the early 1980s when realignments were equally large. They were then typically accompanied by domestic measures to underpin the shift in resources in the devaluing countries, the most notable example being that of France in 1983 (and Belgium in 1982). It is when a government is negotiating to obtain a devaluation, typically trying to achieve a maximum figure that it is most sensitive to peer pressure in the Ecofin Council. It becomes much less sensitive when the currency has been devalued or has given up its commitments altogether. The EC countries are now faced with the task of trying to influence *ex post* the domestic adjustment that should have been decided at the time of the realignment. In the specific environment of 1992, that would have implied peer pressure on Italy and the UK to accelerate budgetary consolidation in the light of the substantial devaluations they were obtaining. A major boost to competitiveness enables a country to contemplate faster budgetary retrenchment. Symmetrically, countries that have not devalued should be prepared to accept more of a cyclical weakening of their budgets than they would otherwise have done. Neither the sequence of events in the currency market, nor the convergence requirements of Maastricht have been conducive to this kind of constructive dialogue.

Although both the rules and the spirit of Basle-Nyborg were shown to be inoperative, the recent official reports are not necessarily wrong in presenting the view that the system remains basically sound and that most of what needs to be done in the future could be achieved if the rules are adhered to. Outside turbulent periods that is still likely to be entirely adequate. But a capacity to handle turbulence is also essential to the survival of a system. What reforms could be envisaged to make the EMS more robust?

There are two types of mistake an exchange-rate system must attempt to avoid. The first is to defend rates that are perceived by markets to be misaligned. The second is to give in to speculative pressures when rates are in good correspondence with fundamentals. In an earlier incarnation the EMS handled the former challenge quite well by regular realignments while the second pitfall hardly materialized. With Basle-Nyborg emphasis shifted to avoiding the second challenge, while the first faded into the background for a time due to better convergence. It reasserted itself in 1992. With the massive realignments that have taken place there could be an extended period of grace, as the devaluers gradually lose some of their gains in competitiveness. With the degree of inflation convergence currently in prospect it is unlikely that the formerly weak currencies will become overvalued for some time. During that period emphasis on meeting the second challenge could make a decisive contribution not only to preserving the cohesion of the present EMS participants but also to making it a pole of attraction for those who are currently outside.

The three elements in the short-term defences need not be changed, but the balance between them needs to be adjusted. In particular, some mechanism needs to be introduced to ensure that interest-rate responses are triggered early in response to external pressures. One way, as discussed above, is to discontinue the wide margins and to encourage their further unilateral narrowing. This would have the double effect of (1) signalling greater determination to maintain the exchange rate, and (2) requiring more rapid use of the two other defence mechanisms.

Since the experiences of 1992–3 have demonstrated that interventions cannot in practice be unlimited it may be thought that the transition from these to interest-rate changes in the graduated series of responses has become more rapid. However, a greater awareness of limitations to interventions has also tempted markets to test the resolve of the national authorities trying to defend their currency. Announcing limits to interventions could be outright destabilizing, particularly if the national authority managing the weak currency is thought to be unwilling to use interest rates actively, because then the next response has to be a realignment. It would be preferable to design mechanisms that offer incentives for the central banks to modify interest rates so as to check the need for intervention.

Two proposals have recently been formulated in this spirit, by Peter Bofinger and Graham Bishop respectively (Collignon *et al.*, 1993; Bishop, 1993). Bofinger's proposal is to suspend the requirement that a debtor central bank repurchase its own currency acquired by the creditor central bank in interventions. At present, the time limit within which repurchase has to be made is three and a half months (extended from two and a half in the Basle-Nyborg Agreement), except for the relatively modest amounts under the debtor quotas in the short-term facility. This provision has been central to the functioning of the EMS in the past; because a debtor central bank knows that it must repurchase its currency not very far into the future it has to generate a private capital inflow – or the government must borrow – to enable it to do so. This is an incentive to raise interest rates which would weaken with an extension of the credit period.

The Bofinger proposal could harden the reluctance of creditor central banks to intervene at all, because they would risk being stuck with the increase in reserves for a long time. So a prior question is how they could still be obliged to intervene. If the obligation existed, the creditor central bank would have an incentive to give a greater weight to external pressures in designing its interest rate policy. By swift management of interest rates the creditor central bank could minimize the interventions which have now become too onerous. But in so doing it would lose much of its monetary autonomy. The Bofinger scheme would create a more symmetric system by increasing the pressure on the creditor central banks. Precisely for that reason its implementation would be resisted by the Bundesbank, at least as long as the German monetary authorities see themselves as cast permanently in that role.

The Bishop scheme is explicitly asymmetric in that it is foreseen that a country which has lost a large amount of reserves through the intervention of other EMS central banks also loses its monetary autonomy. When reserves corresponding to a certain percentage of the domestic money supply – 15 per cent of M2, to be specific – have accumulated as balances with other EMS central banks, the creditors take over and presumably raise interest rates or take other measures to restore confidence in the debtor's economy. This prospect obviously gives the debtor a strong incentive to avoid being put into such a position of dependence – in short to take action early of the type that would otherwise be forced upon him later. This approach will appeal to those monetary authorities who see themselves as trendwise creditors, but hardly to the debtors. It may not even appeal to a large creditor central bank, because the task of assuming responsibility for another country's monetary policy at a time when political integration is only moderately advanced can become very burdensome for the creditor. It is an advantage in such a framework to have an international institution to oversee policy adjustments and take the political flak, rather than to project individual foreign central banks into such a visible role. It must remain an open question whether even the creditor central bank will feel encouraged to take on the task.

Both the Bofinger and Bishop plans, appealing as they are in pure logic, seem unlikely to enlist sufficient political support to materialize. The proposals may also make inadequate use of the emerging multilateral framework which will become an increasingly significant feature for the next few years as the EMI begins to operate. Hence there is a case for a third approach which remedies these weaknesses.

One element in the September 1992 crisis already noted in passing in Section II was that both strong and weak currency countries strongly resisted drawing the money supply and interest-rate implications required for interventions to fulfil a stabilizing purpose. The Bundesbank has prided itself on having proved able to sterilize 90 per cent of the interventions undertaken within a short period of time. Some of the weak currency countries similarly made an effort to sterilize fully; it is difficult, for example, to see any trace of the dramatic outflow from the UK in the monthly UK money supply figures for 1992.

It is a well-known property of a fixed exchange-rate system that the higher the degree of combined sterilization of interventions the more unstable the system becomes. If all participants succeed in sterilizing completely, stabilization would hinge only on the so-called portfolio effect: as additional volumes of financial assets denominated in the weak currency are held reluctantly, an increasing premium return is required which dampens activity in the deficit country and conversely in the surplus country. Empirical work by Dominguez and Frankel (1993) and others suggests that this effect is modest, because even in turbulent periods interventions are small relative to the total size of the stocks of financial assets denominated in the respective currencies. Nearly fully sterilized interventions can therefore go on for a long time, because they reduce only marginally the tensions which prompted them.

This is the problem which the Bofinger and Bishop proposals address, though in ways that are likely to meet maximum resistance. If repurchase obligations for the deficit country were removed, as proposed by Bofinger, sterilization would become harder in the longer term for the surplus country which is accordingly likely to resist by intervening less and trying to push the burden of adjustment back onto the deficit country. If monetary autonomy is lost by the deficit country automatically once it has lost an important part of its reserves, the deficit country may resort too quickly to the instrument it can control, *viz.* devaluation.

A more acceptable device might be one in which sterilization practices in both the surplus and the deficit country are monitored collectively on a continuing short-term basis. After 1 January 1994 the EMI is the institution designed to manage collective action. Its potential for discharging this task would be enhanced if a significant number of participating national central banks were to use the provisions of Maastricht[6] to entrust to the EMI the task of managing their foreign exchange reserves, in which case the EMI would itself undertake the interventions. No specific norms would be set for the degree of sterilization; discretionary judgements would be made from day to day as to whether the need for intervention was accelerating, in which case the degree of sterilization would be reduced, or decelerating in which case no change in recent practice would be required. The scheme would be designed to speed up the transition from sterilized to non-sterilized interventions in circumstances where the gradualist approach of Basle-Nyborg is blocked and a risk is perceived that the deficit country will be tempted or forced into a devaluation not warranted by fundamentals.

The proposed scheme would be facilitated if the EMI were also to be empowered through bilateral contracts to manage domestic money market operations of the participating central banks. Such a pooling of operations was suggested during the work of the Delors Committee by Lamfalussy (1989) in order to make all operations by each central bank more transparent to other participants while presenting a more common front to market participants. In the

---

[6] Art.6.4 of the Protocol of the EMI Statute.

© Basil Blackwell Ltd 1994

Lamfalussy proposal only operations were to be pooled, while no transfer of decision-making authority was to take place. The proposal did not meet with favour among the national central bankers, perhaps surprisingly since it was a minimalist proposal that could nevertheless have improved the efficiency of the operations and not only in an international sense. Preoccupied as the discussion was with the detailed blueprint for ultimate monetary union with a European system of central banks combining centralized decision-making with decentralised implementation of policy, the idea of early centralization of operations did not fit in very well. The experience of the 1992 currency crisis justifies a reconsideration of this reluctance. But in order to prevent speculative attacks from succeeding when they are basically seen as unwarranted, some pooling of authority is now required.

As in the case of the proposals by Bofinger and Bishop, the present proposal will be met with the objection that monetary sovereignty is transferred to an unacceptable degree. The following sections takes up briefly the limits of the principle of the indivisibility of monetary policy.

*Realignments.* If the revised combination of defensive measures already contained in the Basle-Nyborg Agreement proves insufficient, the issue is of how realignments, which may then become inevitable, should be handled. The questions centre on two issues which are, however, interrelated: What size of realignments should be permitted? Who should take the decision?

Given the two types of 'errors' which an exchange-rate system may commit – trying to defend basically misaligned rates and giving in to speculative attacks not justified by fundamentals – the responses to the two challenges should be different. In the former case, realignments should be sufficiently large to stop for a long time any expectation that it will be followed by another. A recent example of a successful large realignment is that of the 10 per cent devaluation at the end of January 1993 of the Irish punt, which arguably became misaligned as a result of the sharp depreciation of sterling, the currency or Ireland's dominant trading partner, and a rapid decline of UK interest rates. Subsequently the credibility of Irish exchange-rate policy was rapidly restored as expressed in terms of the simple test proposed by Svensson (1990) for currencies in the target zone. Currently Irish short-term interest rates are slightly below German rates, a result that would hardly have been attainable following a smaller devaluation triggering expectations of more to come.

A sizeable realignment should, as was the case in the pre-1987 EMS, be accompanied by domestic measures designed to improve performance in terms of the Maastricht budgetary criteria. Such a realignment is accordingly a decision of high politics and could only be taken by the Ecofin Council.

Should the possibility of a small realignment of the type envisaged in Basle-

Nyborg (and carried out in January 1987) remain as an option throughout stage 2? A mini realignment would serve a different purpose from a large one. It would be designed as one additional and ultimate response in a chain of events in which the traditional short-term defensive instruments, even when revamped as suggested above, had proved inadequate to stem speculation which is basically seen as unwarranted.

Ideally this type of realignment should be superfluous if the other defences work well and participation in the EMS is confined to currencies that are not misaligned. The mere fact that realignments remain a possibility over the next few years is itself an invitation to speculation. By insisting on the retention of this form of continued flexibility, the more stable currencies in the EMS are storing up trouble for themselves. In order to limit this cost, realignments among these currencies should explicitly be restricted in the way that was implicit in Basle-Nyborg, i.e. to changes in central rates that do not cause any jumps in market exchange rates. Furthermore, in order to protect the credentials of participants wishing to join the final stage of monetary union they should be confined to cases in which one or two currencies become divergently strong so as not to disqualify a country which has trusted its own initiative.

In these circumstances a mini revaluation would appear only as a final response in monetary management. Since no domestic adjustments outside the monetary area would be required – that would not make sense given the small size – the question arises whether the decision could not be taken by the central bankers rather than by the Ecofin Council. This ideas was discussed at times in the late 1980s, but it was dismissed not only by the political officials, but also by the central bankers themselves. Careful analysis is now required whether the strong attachment to stable exchange rates demonstrated over the past six years by all countries which have observed the normal margins has not changed the balance of the argument in favour of leaving the decision to the machinery of central bank co-operation in the EMI.

### III. The Limits of the Principle of Indivisibility of Monetary Policy

During the work of the Delors Committee the most difficult task was to define how the transition to monetary union was to take place. It was obvious that the starting point in the EMS was one in which monetary authority rested ultimately in national hands. The EMS is a system of rules, but relying in the end on the will of independent states to let their central banks co-operate. The incentives for them to do so were becoming visibly stronger than before in the course of the 1980s as economic performances began to converge and capital controls were removed. But the mere fact that realignments could occur made it obvious that in the end there was an escape route. The lack of central bank autonomy in several Member States increased the likelihood that policy conflicts between countries would escalate quickly to the political level and create a public debate which would encourage market expectations that the system was becoming vulnerable. For a long time period to the 1992 crisis these two elements receded into the background and central bank publications were able to offer a rosy picture that voluntary monetary co-operation was quite adequate to the task. Many central bankers would have preferred to leave matters like that and to adopt a very slow gradualist approach to monetary integration. They feared that forcing the pace towards monetary union would stir up political antagonisms, putting their regular task of managing the EMS at risk.

The European Council in 1988 asked the Delors Committee, consisting largely of central bank governors (1) to study how EMU could be realized, and (2) to propose concrete stages leading towards this objective. In meeting the former of these challenges, the Committee outlined an advanced form of monetary unification with a federal central banking institution, issuing a single currency as soon as possible after the definitive locking of intra-union exchange rates. Bini-Smaghi *et al.* (1993) have aptly termed the inspiration for this blueprint of monetary union 'national', in the sense that monetary policy in the union could be analysed in terms familiar to large individual countries, rather than as an advanced form of international policy co-ordination. All monetary conflicts would be fully internalized inside the union.

This was clearly a system qualitatively very different from that of the existing EMS, even on an optimistic assessment of the state of monetary integration at the end of the 1980s. Accordingly, there was a long road to travel to the final stage and it is obvious from the nature of the proposals that the central bankers initially assumed that the transition would have to take a long time-span. As the subsequent political debate preparing and negotiating the Maastricht Treaty began to set dates not too far into the future, the vagueness and the fragility of the preparations for the transition stood out even more clearly than before. Paradoxically, the more the transition was telescoped into a few years, the less substantial the concrete provisions for transition became. Symbolically, the European system of central banks was no longer to be set up at the start of stage two to begin the transition from co-ordination of independent national monetary policies of the formulation and implementation of a common policy in the final stage – only a temporary and preparatory EMI which looks like an only slightly modified Committee of Governors. It is possible to argue that the nomination by the European Council of a full-time EMI President, the requirement that the members of its Council exercise their collective functions without receiving political instructions, the possibility that national central banks will delegate some of their tasks to the new institution and, above all, the intended preoccupation of the EMI with planning for policy in the final stage will all tend to give the EMI a higher public profile and greater authority as mediator/co-ordinator for the central banks than the Committee of Governors. But it is clear that *de jure* there will be very little the EMI can do to impose its authority. It will have to work by persuasion.

Is it possible to envisage a transition in which monetary authority is somehow shared between the national level and EMI? The Delors Committee deliberated long on this issue, but efforts to develop specific proposals under the heading of 'gradualism and indivisibility' had to be abandoned – not only because there were disagreement on the substance, but also because any precise description of a division of responsibilities would have been very difficult to draw up. It is obvious that there should be no doubt in financial markets as to who is responsible for any particular decision, but would that necessarily preclude the attribution of some clearly defined policy functions to the EMI? Could, for example, as was proposed by some members of the Delors Committee, two important instruments of monetary management – one external, interventions in third currencies, and one 'domestic', changes in a European-wide reserve requirement – be assigned to the EMI while leaving other instruments in national hands?

It is tempting to argue the case for such a division of responsibilities, but by now this is rather unproductive. The Germans – and some others – have indicated their firm opposition to any intermediate stage between the decentral-ized framework of the present and the federal model of the final stage and the transition and the role of the EMI. Nothing can change that as a legal reality. But still the environment within which policy-making nationally or collectively takes place can be modified in ways that shift the incentive in voluntary co-ordination strongly towards collective action and management so that *de facto* the system begins to operate as a closer substitute for a common monetary policy.

Two changes in the environment appear central. The first which is occurring is to make the national central banks more independent of their respective governments. This will at the same time make them more dependent on each other. In Maastricht the argument was that initiatives of this kind should be delayed until the final days of the transition to EMU, but since then several modifications in the status of the central banks have occurred or are under way, most significantly in France. The risk that incipient policy conflicts would quickly escalate to the political level has in the past severely constrained voluntary central bank co-operation in the EMS. The most dramatic event in the 1992 crisis was the public policy conflict between Bundesbank and the UK Treasury.

The second change in the environment for central bank co-operation will come about as the EMS tightens up without excessive flexibility of exchange rates (in the form of wide fluctuation margins or regular realignments) and becomes more symmetric. When the decision to dismantle capital controls fully was taken in 1988, the challenge of near complete capital mobility promoted reflections on how to share monetary policy more efficiently in the long term and pushed the monetary authorities into tighter co-operation at that time. Notably, interest rate convergence became stronger than in the past. Leadership in monetary policy began to be more widely shared among the participants as the relative financial weight of Germany declined. But this process was reversed by the shock of German unification and the exceptional need for the Bundesbank to maintain high interest rates in its aftermath. Leadership shifted back to Germany, not because it had a superior economic performance as in the mid-1980s, but because of the need to conduct the tightest monetary policy in the EC. This phase now appears to be over. As German interest rates decline in recession and the German stability performance is no longer superior to that of several other Member States, the anchor function will widen to comprise all the countries conducting stable exchange rate policies – whether this development is planned or not. Germany will obviously continue to exercise the influence that its financial weight accords, but that is inevitably smaller than corresponding to the role in the past. In this process the German attitude to even tighter forms of monetary co-operation should change and the limits of the doctrine of the indivisibility of monetary policy will be explored. As financial markets change their evaluation of Germany's economic prospects – as already seems to happen during the recent period of surprisingly strong interest rate convergence – Germany will see her own interest in being less averse to testing new initiatives and procedures such as those advocated in the previous section for sharing monetary sovereignty. In this process the growing independence of the central banks of partner EMS countries will be major determinant of the speed. Other countries are now showing their capacity of anticipating this new opportunity.

## IV. Tentative Conclusions

Although the present state of monetary integration and  the prospects for resuming the advance towards monetary union are seen as unpromising and uncertain by more observers, and official proposals for reforms are extremely bland, there may nevertheless be some grounds for the apparent complacency and lack of initiative.

One element is that there is little risk of a repeat of the massive adjustments of 1992–3. Weak currencies have, if anything, overadjusted and now appear more likely to rise than to fall. Those countries that maintained their central rates appear determined to continue. There is no need to prepare to fight anew yesterday's battles and good reason to resist any future attacks in the market.

The alternative of a reversal to a much more flexible exchange rate is unattractive; continued convergence of inflation rates at a low level will make this gradually more evident.

There is a problem of how to reintegrate the presently floating currencies. The strategy that seems best is to wait until they have stabilized in the market, and then invite them back at agreed central rates and with observance of the normal fluctuation margins. Specially arranged margins would not help the new entrants and they could destabilize the system for the regular membership. On the contrary, those countries that can do it, should be encouraged to narrow their margins.

The Basle-Nyborg Agreement of 1987 worked well until 1992 and is in need primarily of a change of emphasis in the short-term defences. Interest rate coordination must become the prime tool, but interventions are also necessary, provided their effects are to some extent allowed to work their way through to domestic money supplies and interest rates. Two recent proposals to this effect by Bofinger and Bishop are discussed, but are considered for different reasons, unlikely to win political favour because they will be seen as unfairly burdensome or risky by either surplus or deficit countries. A third proposal is to monitor sterilization of interventions closely through the EMI in stage 2.

A reform of Basle-Nyborg in a direction of more symmetry should be tailored to the new reality that there is no longer an obvious tendency for Germany to retain the leadership role in the EMS. The anchor function will be broadened to include those countries that are prepared to accept a very tight EMS and take steps to make their central banks more independent. These developments will ease the constraint on the process of monetary unification imposed by the doctrine that monetary authority is indivisible.

The decision to widen fluctuation margins taken in early August was a major retrogressive step, though certainly preferable to a total suspension of the EMS. The central rates remain, as do all the more technical provisions. The +/–15 per cent band is now the normal band in the sense of the Maastricht Treaty. It is theoretically possible, provided intra-EC exchange rates remain fairly stable – which seems plausible given the intention of most monetary authorities to stabilize them by more direct means, above all a firm continuing commitment to low inflation – that participants could move directly from the present wide margins to very tight ones, or directly to the final stage of EMU. This is not likely, however. A more plausible scenario is one in which the national authorities will one by one return to the earlier margins, a road already taken by the Netherlands. Then all the issues discussed in this article will again become relevant, possibly already in the course of 1994.

# References

Bini-Smaghi L., Padoa-Schioppa, T. and Papadia, F (1993) 'The Policy History of the Maastricht Treaty'. Paper presented at a conference 'The Monetary Future of Europe', organized by the Centre of Economic Policy Research in la Coruna, Spain, Bance d'Italia, February.

Bishop, G. (1993) 'Is There a Rapid Route to an EMU of the Few?' *Economic and Market Analysis*, 11 May (London:Solomon Brothers).

Collignon, S. *et al.* (1993) *The EMS in Transition*. Study prepared for the European Parliament, July (Paris: Association pour l'Union Monétaire de l'Europe).

Committee of Governors of the Central Banks of the Member States of the European Community (1993) 'The Implications and Lessons to be Drawn from the Recent Exchange Rate Crisis', Basle, 21 April.

Committee of Governors of the Central Banks of the Member States of the European Community (1993) *Annual Report 1992*, Basle, April.

Dominguez, K. and Frankel, J.A. (1993) *The Effects of Foreign-Exchange Interventions* (Washington, D.C.: Institute for International Economics).

Ethier, W. and Bloomfield, A.I. (1975) 'Managing the Managed Float'. *Princeton Essays in International Finance*, No. 112 (Princeton: International Finance Section).

Feldstein, M. (1992) 'Does European Monetary Union Have a Future?'. Paper presented at a conference 'The Monetary Future of Europe', organized by the Centre of Economic Policy Research, La Coruna, Spain, December.

Gros, D. and Thygesen, N. (1992) *European Monetary Integration: From the European Monetary System to European Monetary Union* (London: Longman).

Lamfalussy, A. (1989) 'A Proposal for Stage Two Under Which Monetary Policy Operations Would Be Centralised in a Jointly-Owned Subsidiary'. Collection of Papers Annexed to the *Delors Report* (Luxembourg: OOPEC).

Miller, M. and Williamson, J. (1987) *Targets and Indicators: A Blueprint for the International Co-ordination of Economic Policy* (Washington D.C.:Institute for International Economics).

Monetary Committee of the European Community (1993), 'Lessons to be Drawn from the Disturbances on the Foreign Exchange Markets', Brussels, 13 April.

Svensson, L.E.O. (1990), 'The Simplest Test of Target Zone Credibility'. *NBER Working Paper* No. 3394, Cambridge Mass., June.

Williamson, J. (1977), *The Failure of the World Monetary Reform* (London: Nelson).

Williamson, J. (1985) The Exchange Rate System (Washington, D.C.: Institute for International Economics).

Williamson, J. (1993) 'Exchange Rate Management'. *Economic Journal*, Vol. 103, January, pp. 188–97.

# Comment on Thygesen

ANDREW HUGHES HALLETT

## Some Counterarguments

It is fascinating to read such an authoritative discussion of the options for reform in the European Monetary System (EMS). Naturally that has been the issue uppermost in many minds since the events of September 1992. The European Commission has recently accepted a report which reached the same conclusion as this article; namely, that a reform of the existing mechanisms was neither necessary nor desirable, but that it was important to make the existing regime function more effectively. So Thygesen's article is more than timely; it supplies much of the reasoning which might have led to that conclusion. Indeed, while Thygesen would be the first to say that he was writing in a personal capacity, it would be hard to imagine that the views of an ex-member of the Delors Committee on Monetary Union with a continuing affiliation with the European Parliament's Association for Monetary Union would not correspond fairly closely to official thinking.

I find the article to be rather alarming for the very partial nature of the analysis which the authorities would have used to reach their conclusions. And I use the word partial in both senses. The analysis is *incomplete* because it systematically ignores the fact that the exchange rate regime, and hence the underlying financial and policy variables, may have important real effects. It therefore also ignores the implications for fiscal policy when *(relative)* mone-

© Basil Blackwell Ltd 1994, 108 Cowley Road, Oxford OX4 1JF, UK and 238 Main Street, Cambridge, MA 02142, USA

tary positions cannot be adjusted in a world with significant asymmetries in structures, preferences or shocks, and where governments still feel accountable to their electorates and wish to resolve disequilibria as and when they occur. That means official policy cannot take account of the kind of fiscal divergence which we have seen (between Germany and the others over the past three years; and between Italy, Belgium, Ireland on one side, and Denmark, France and the UK on the other, for the past 10 years). Nor can it take account of the lack of credibility in fiscal policies, and hence expenditure patterns, which a tighter and more uniform EMS regime would imply. Forward-looking firms/consumers are never going to invest/spend very much in economies which show no growth, however credible their anti-inflation policies.

There are four points here: (1) the real effects of the financial/exchange rate regime which occur directly through competitiveness, crowding-out, credit effects, debt servicing, savings, etc.; (2) the indirect effects via induced policy changes with real consequences; (3) the lack of fiscal co-ordination (both between countries and between the fiscal and monetary policies themselves) caused by applying a uniform monetary policy to an asymmetric world; and (4) the lack of the fiscal/expenditure credibility when a tight monetary regime renders the associated fiscal expenditures either unsustainable or too limited for what is required. All of these have real effects, and all of them are jointly dependent on the exchange rate regime. Yet none of them is accounted for in this evaluation of the EMS mechanism, although several are recognized in the text. To dismiss them as either unimportant or irrelevant is to store up trouble for the future in the form of *increased* instability and overshooting in other variables.

The analysis is also *partial* in the sense that it allows objective economic reasoning to be guided by certain preferences or value judgements. If the conclusion is to be that the ERM regime (or a version with even narrower bands) *is* best, and if the reason is that the credibility and stability of a 'no realignments' anti-inflationary strategy is preferable even at the cost of ruling out small realignments designed to cure local disequilibria (I am doing no more than rephrasing the argument of Section II, p. 249 here), then that conclusion could only have been reached by imposing an objective function which has price stability alone among its arguments, not output growth or employment stability. Now it is quite possible to argue that the underlying premise is wrong anyway: exchange stability does *not* ensure price stability because, although it is a necessary condition, it is clearly not sufficient. The US, as a collection of regional economies, has not yet achieved price stability; and even the 'tying one's hands' model of Giavazzi and Pagano shows that, as fast as the high inflation country gains credibility and lower inflation by fixing its exchange rate, the other country gains higher inflation. There is therefore a difference between *relative* and *absolute* discipline.

However, that is not the real point. What matters here is that, even if we agree that adopting price stability as the sole objective means that we must maintain an unrevised or tightened ERM system, who is to say that that objective is the right one? That is a value judgement, if not a political statement. Why should I not care about unemployment? Europe's high and rising unemployment is socially irresponsible, economically inefficient, and a fiscal luxury we can ill afford. Yet if I were one of Ireland's 25 per cent unemployed, or Spain's 20 per cent or Italy or France's 11–12 per cent, I would be resentful of this continuing disregard. And if I were employed, I would be resentful of having to pay increasing taxes or face the higher interest rates of the associated debt overhang. In other words, one has to ask whether fiscal indiscipline, driven by the need to repair the costs of having imposed an inappropriately restrictive set of preferences, as if they were an analytic truth, would not cause more instability or overshooting, through a lack of policy co-ordination *internally*, than a system which recognizes both aspects of the policy problem? Or to make the point more dramatically, the German hyperinflation of 1922–23 may have demonstrated only too clearly the damage which price instability will cause. But it was Brüning's deliberate deflations in the 1929–32 period, designed to prevent inflation reappearing, which caused the unemployment, the change in voting patterns and hence Europe's tragedy – not the inflation itself.

I argue that everyone is entitled to make their own value judgements; and the policy-makers should not seek to determine what our preferences 'ought' to be, even if implicitly by their choice of regime. Instead they should identify what the preferences are and design regimes which best serve those preferences. From that perspective, the argument that the 1987–92 ERM should not be revised, that the bands should even be tightened, and that the burden of proof must lie with those who wish to stay outside to demonstrate why they should be allowed to do so, really does look like an attempt to turn the clock back and fight yesterday's battles all over again.

The counterargument to this would be that the choice of (monetary) regime has no real effects. However that cannot be the case here. There may be theoretical models which produce a complete separation between real and monetary variables, but none is ever mentioned. Nor is one implied, since the repeated references to competitiveness (whether determined by nominal exchange rates or relative prices) shows some concern for real effects. Nor would such a model have been believed anyway. If German unification has proved anything, it is that monetary spillovers can have very real and very large spillovers in the form of deflation, and that changing the regime can radically alter those spillovers. I therefore find it highly significant that this article, while arguing in detail why the UK would *not* find it in its own interest to stay outside the 'new' EMS, and why the remaining members would not want to accept the UK staying outside, never makes *any* mention of the apparent UK recovery since 1992. It may be that the two events are not totally connected; but they cannot be totally unconnected either – look at the changes in investment, and compare the changes in growth or inflation rates. The supreme irony is that, while being vilified for its actions, the UK is the only EC country which is putting any locomotive power (small as it may be) back into the European economy. Indeed if the other countries continue their present course, it is they who will destroy what 'growth without extra inflation' there is. The other irony is that this is not the first time that this has happened. I wonder if the policy-makers realize that this article (with a suitable change of names and dates) provides an exact and almost complete rerun of the arguments which raged around Britain's decision to leave the Gold Standard in September 1931 – down to the details of inflation credibility, priorities, the relative importance of deficits, the separation of real and monetary effects, etc. Well now we know the outcome of that episode. Britain was able to enjoy half the slump of those who stuck with the regime unrevised, which was fortunate considering the call on resources and political stability which was necessary later.

Having made the point that a proper welfare analysis is necessary, I should also point out that economic systems' characteristics are important as well. If all economies were the same and shared the same goals, then they would not need fixed exchange rates since they would all adopt the same policies and respond in the same way to changing circumstances. Hence, if it is necessary to fix exchange rates, it must be either because the policy-makers are incompetent or because economies are not all the same and it is necessary to constrain them away from their 'private' optima for the sake of the common good. The arguments above stress that those constraints can be imposed *only* insofar as they are incentive compatible. The ERM regime makes no such claims, and in the event clearly proved not to be incentive compatible despite its success in producing inflation convergence. The problem was therefore on the real side and I see nothing in this discussion which would persuade markets that incentive compatibility has been re-established. So, while I agree with Thygesen that the crucial elements are not to allow fundamental misalignments, and not to give in to speculative pressure when there are no misalignments, how do you demonstrate that there are and never will be any misalignments in a world with asymmetric shocks and asymmetric responses? Narrowing the bands, deciding not to revise the system or to allow periodic realignments to accommodate fundamental changes, or pursuing monetary credibility to the potential exclusion of 'expenditure credibility' is hardly going to persuade the markets that the system will generally yield benefits for everybody. Incentive compatibility therefore has to be made an explicit component of the system; or, put another way and in contrast to the claims made here, the burden of proof must be placed on those who argue that an unrevised ERM is best, to show that the UK or any other country would benefit (and continue to benefit) *on its own criteria* by rejoining. One simply cannot expect to sustain the system by forcing those who believe they need an option on realignment, or a looser system, to justify their wishes according to someone else's criteria.

Hence, whether one accepts Thygesen's judgements and conclusions must turn on whether you think the regime is supposed to serve the community of interests or the interests of the Community. If it is the latter, it is not clear how, in an asymmetric and developing world, the policy-makers' aim to defeat the markets for ever since misalignments will probably appear sooner or later (even if policy-makers could determine exactly what the equilibrium exchange rates are, which I doubt). But if it is the former, they may well be successful because they will have to treat markets as constraints on what they do. If you follow this line, and recognize the real effects of the exchange rate regime, then you realize that the process leading to monetary union is not really about monetary policy at all – although it obviously involves that. It is at least as much about fiscal policy; the degree of activism necessary, the size of the interventions and their sustainability, and the choice of fiscal regime and its co-ordination with monetary policy. Given the inflation and monetary convergence since 1987, it seems almost inevitable that the system's crisis in 1992 was due to the sharp fiscal contradictions within the system. It therefore makes little sense to try and redesign the system while abstracting from those aspects of the system – although I can see that if you do so, you will inevitably end up recommending that no substantive revisions need be made!

Those are the features of particular interest to the markets and the doubters in the run-up to monetary union. Yet, even if price stabilization were the sole objective, some consideration of the supporting (fiscal) policies and relevant economic characteristics is still required. If one represents the economies in question by a system of equations, then a fixed regime merely renormalizes that system on a new set of endogenous variables. The question of interest is, which variable will take the place of the exchange rate as endogenous? The EC's One Market, One Money publication lays great stress on wage/price flexibility, which implies wages have to vary to equilibrate the (policy constrained) system rather than to satisfy the aspirations and needs of the workforce. To some extent France has followed this prescription, and a political judgement has been delivered on that. An alternative is to endogenize interest rates via a reaction function – as Germany and the UK had done with generally unacceptable results. Another possibility is to allow unemployment to float freely, as Spain and Ireland have done. The last possibility is to allow fiscal policy to take up the slack via some reaction function, although there is no guarantee that the interventions (or changes in interventions) will prove either technically feasible or sustainable. Italy's fiscal position illustrates some of the difficulties which arise there. But one thing is certain: all that happens with a fixed exchange rate scheme is that the uncertainties or instability in the system get transferred onto other variables. The question then is, do those instabilities get bigger or smaller, and do they get more damaging or less damaging in the process? That is a matter of the parameters of the system (for the first question) and of society's welfare or priority function (for the second question). It is not something to which an unambiguous answer, or an answer which applies to all economies or in all circumstances, can be given on a first principles basis.

So my complaint is that the work simply has not been done to justify an unrevised ERM regime across the range of policy objectives which actually apply, across the different economic structures in the system, and across the policy responses that would have to be used. If the job is done with a lexographic ordering of one objective (price stability) above all others, then inevitably one regime will appear best. But that is to prejudge the issue. However it seems equally likely that, if the assessment were done on a wider basis, some EMS structure would still emerge as best. But it would almost certainly be a more flexible EMS because it would not be possible to persuade all of the markets all of the time of the virtues of one set of fixed rates in an asymmetric and changing world – unless realignments are allowed to correct fundamental misalignments. Hence the more flexible EMS would be asked to balance mild pressures for change against less frequent but much larger changes or overshooting in other variables. Flexibility in that very restricted sense is just a matter of an insurance policy. I do not count on making a claim on an insurance policy when I take it out; but when the downside risks are very large, it is certainly handy to have one should the need arise. Since we cannot control the random shocks in any economy it seems just as reckless not to have the insurance of an option on realignment as it would be to drive a car without insurance. And, should a misalignment ever appear in an economy without such an insurance policy, the markets would certainly demonstrate that 'those who try to make revolution impossible, actually make it inevitable' in order to save their own skins.

# 11.
# Round Table Discussion

## The Future Research Agenda

DAVID MAYES*

In my view there are two most important contributions that should be made to framing the research agenda. The first is to try to break free from the shackles of viewing the process of integration separately from the viewpoint of each social science discipline in turn. The process is inherently complex and multifaceted, and needs to be analysed coherently with the benefit of ideas from all of these disciplines. It requires an interaction between economics and politics, social policy and indeed geography and environmental science. This does not imply that any individual researcher should possess the whole range of capabilities, nor that all or indeed most research projects should be multidisciplinary, merely that much of the most interesting and the least developed research runs along the borderlines. Clearly my prejudices about the ordering of importance reflect my background as an economist.

The second essential ingredient, to my mind, is to pull together the intellectual and empirical contributions from the different European countries and, I should stress in the present context, from outside Europe. One of the main barriers to integration comes from differences in culture and economic and social institutions. This is reflected not just in difference in tastes but behaviour-

* David Mayes is Co-ordinator of the ESRC's Single European Market Initiative, 'The Evolution of Rules for a Single European Market', and gratefully acknowledges the financial help of the ESRC in preparing the contribution.

al responses, either individually through the corporate governance of firms, or systemically through the legal framework or the mechanisms for co-ordination, consensus, co-operation and social dialogue. These differences apply also to academic traditions. Because of the sheer size of the European economy, it plays an important role in the development of the global economy and system of operation. Its preoccupation with internal issues has led to external difficulties. Again, this does not imply that all projects should be multinational, merely that this particular interface is weak, in part because it is more difficult to finance research across borders. Current emphases lie on finance for networks and realization of these differences, rather than on joint projects to address them.

An agenda can be approached in more ways than one. There are over 2,000 people doing research in this area of whom we have heard, and probably many others we do not know. Any attempt to set out the agenda for them would be on the long side, to say the least. All I can do here is to point to a few prejudices.

In a sense I have an agenda set out for me for the next five years or so through the Single Market initiative. We have identified four main research questions for this programme:

- Will the Single Market lead to a widening of economic and social disparities within the Community?
- Will closer integration in Europe worsen economic relations with the rest of the world?
- Is the concept of competition among rules a means of achieving convergence or a device for dealing with continuing diversity?
- Will the Single Market assist the broadening of the Community?

Some 25 projects involving around 100 researchers in the UK and other European countries are addressing these questions. The main projects are listed in the Appendix Table.

Although progress has been good and we have published a long list of papers already, we are a long way short of providing adequate answers. So no doubt there will be some similarity between the research agenda agreed for 1993 and that for 1992.

The theme of the evolution of rules for a Single European Market provides a helpful framework for bringing together different ideas in a way essential for our understanding of the processes on which this part of Europe has embarked. It looks at the way in which rules are set, implemented, enforced and changed. Much of our work thus far has been on the setting and influencing aspects. This includes the work by Jeremy Richardson and Sonia Mazey, already in the process of publication, on the lobbying process (see Appendix Table). Christopher Brewin has been looking at the influence, or lack of it, from third countries; Mick Moran has been examining the way in which the rules are being set and influenced in the case of the professions; and Simon Bulmer is exploring regulatory institutions in more detail. On the social front, Michael Gold has been investigating how the social dimension is being set and influenced.

All of these have produced interesting new insights: Mazey and Richardson explain how the process of effective influence works with a Commission keen to take a 'technocratic' view of the optimal approach to problems, with a small and rather fragmented organization; Brewin shows the motivation by EFTA countries for application for full membership of the EC; and Gold explores the sources of the clash between the Anglo-Saxon and Continental traditions in labour market and workplace regulation.

There is a second strong set of studies on the concept of implementation – one of which is a major project on legal implementation led by the Institute of Advanced Legal Studies working with the European University Institute in Florence, which has parallel teams in each of the Member States. Some of their work on foodstuffs, a key area of EC regulation, has been recently published.

There has been less output thus far on the subject of impact, although we are looking at a number of industries – airlines, insurance, retailing, pharmaceuticals and motor cars, for example, and indeed looking at impact in the context of labour markets. There is a great deal of difference in this area in the way in which people from different disciplines use the same sorts of terms; what economists tend to mean by implementation and what lawyers mean by implementation shows this clearly. There is considerable difference over whether implementation is enabling change or achieving it. Economists tend to feel that something has been implemented when it actually happens and there is an observable change in behaviour. There is no single market until it actually behaves like a single market – it does not matter what the rules say. If people are not behaving as if there is a single market, even if they are allowed to, then the single market has not come into being.

The next stage in the research tackles enforcement and compliance. This is a rather weak area of knowledge at present and one that will be developing considerably because it is very much crucial to the success of the Single Market as suggested by the Sutherland Report.

The process of change, the 'evolution', is also an area where work is currently limited, but one where we will be trying to achieve something which will be theoretically interesting as well as looking at the practice of what is going on. The process of evolution is not clearly articulated; this is therefore something I am trying to improve on, in the case of the firm, with my colleague Duncan Matthews. The evolution of rules is firmly on our research agenda.

This whole element, the theoretical underpinning, has emerged rather strongly from the current conference in the discussions of theories of integration in the political context. I do not think that in this case economists have in their tool kit a set of theories of integration which allow them to argue that we should not worry about the extent of underdevelopment in the political dimension because they have a satisfactory alternative approach. As far as the economics agenda is concerned, there are many different means which are used to look at the subject of integration, but they are not normally expressed in terms of a generalized theory.

Turning now to items ahead in our research agenda, we are in the process of developing a second phase of the study (which was agreed in March 1993). Most of the obvious categories for the agenda in terms of issues are fairly straightforward and will be generally agreed – whether they relate to the inability to provide satisfactory advice on eastern Europe, the widening of the EC, to the issues which have been raised on Economic and Monetary Union, or the environment. All I want to do here is explore two of these in some detail to give an idea of the way in which the thinking might progress.

The first of these is 'cohesion'. In my view this is one of the issues crucial to whether the Community can hang together in terms of its current objectives, or whether it will fail to achieve such a degree of integration. Much work has been done on questions of nominal convergence, and that is really what the Maastricht Treaty articulated fairly clearly; whether it did it rightly or not is a different matter. Much less work has been done, however, on issues of real convergence, and still less on the concept of social cohesion. You will notice that in some of the recent remarks from the Commission, the order of the words has been altered to 'social and economic cohesion', to try to change our view of their importance.

The problem with cohesion is that it is not just a simple objective concept – it is a subjective one. It really depends on how various parts of the Community and groups within them view the way in which the process is developing. So it does not matter whether, on objective criteria, circumstances have greatly improved. Unless people view this as being a benefit which stems from the Community, and they feel that the Community is doing as much as they anticipated (and more than can be achieved from alternative regimes), cohesion will not be achieved. This gives rise to many questions about regional policy, the behaviour of the periphery and indeed a whole range of non-spatial issues relating to minorities, questions of identity and the definitions of border. Lastly, it refers to questions of migration and I think that there will be much research directed towards that particular subject because the whole thrust of the Internal Market in terms of the four freedoms of movement of goods, services, capital and labour is made inoperative because of the lack of mobility of labour. We heard, in this conference, the idea that the US was not an optimal currency area because of the lack of labour mobility there. Yet in the US system there is an order of magnitude of mobility of labour much greater than in the Community.

At the same time there are very considerable concerns about the nature of immigration from outside the Community and the way in which that will develop. These pressures may lead to the creation of new frontiers at a stage when we are trying to abolish the existing ones within the Community.

On the economic side, a very helpful assessment by Rory O'Donnell has tried to show the way in which, although many of the previous ideas in regional economics have been largely demolished in terms of what one can achieve with policy, a set of new ideas is now emerging relating to indigenous growth, to the effectiveness of localized policies, to the focus on human capital, to the matching of local institutions and local interests, and to the clustering of activities. These, coupled with foci of technology in particular regions do give rise to a whole series of issues which may well lead to some promising developments. Indeed, these are not unrelated to ideas of subsidiarity either. Iain Begg, Melanie Lansbury and I are developing a series of analyses in this field, funded by a grant from the Leverhulme Foundation. Earlier in the conference we had a discussion about issues of fiscal federalism, and it will be interesting to see what will appear from that Commission document. It was suggested that the Commission now thinks that with a Community budget of 0.2 per cent of GDP, they will be able to achieve what the MacDougall Report in 1977 expected would have required the spending of 5–7 per cent of Community GDP in the then EEC of nine Member States. Since then, Greece, Portugal and Spain have joined, increasing the importance of the issue of cohesion. If, by spending very small sums of money, it is possible to achieve the sorts of cohesion objectives which have been discussed, then this is something very different from anything we have seen before, and will go a long way towards solving the problems of convergence that face the EC. In the meantime, I remain to be convinced that satisfactory answers yet exist.

My second concern to be put on the agenda is that insufficient attention is being paid to the lessons which can be learned from integration in other parts of the world. There is not so much a tendency for the focus of integration in Europe to become introspective, as for a feeling to develop among integrationists that this is *the* way forward, and there is little need to look at the way in which some of the same issues are being dealt with elsewhere. Let me take competition policy by way of illustration. In the Community we are trying to divide responsibilities between the Commission and the Member States, when in fact they have very different structures for the implementation of competition policy and indeed quite different attitudes towards these policies. If we look at what is happening with closer economic relations between Australia and New Zealand, they feel that they need similar policies right down to the last detail, so that they can achieve a cultural structural similarity in the way the system works. This is in nice contrast to the situation with NAFTA. In that case they are approaching integration from the other end of the spectrum with a private access system to the courts in Canada and an officially generated investigation system in the USA. This approach entails very clear cultural separation, although by states geographically next to each other. We ought also to look at this in eastward terms, because the Commission has been developing a competition policy very similar to that which is being applied in the west. It is by no means clear that one should apply the same sort of competition policy in the face of the problems of transition as for the problems of a mature mixed economy. Certainly I think that we will find that the aims of competition policy and cohesion overlap the most, and may indeed conflict. The work of Ash Amin and Tim Frazer at Newcastle is already exploring this.

Let me in conclusion draw attention to two other papers presented at the conference. Niels Thygesen suggested that we have real problems explaining the transition to stage 3 of Economic and Monetary Union and that we need to explore in greater depth how a multi-speed system might work. This raises some important issues of political economy as the longer-run benefits are usually described as being 'microeconomic' while the costs of transition are 'macroeconomic'. It is easy therefore for the losers and beneficiaries to belong to different interest groups and, since the costs appear before the benefits, the process can be halted when the costs appear high, hence never reaping the benefits. This discussion of different interests has been explored widely in the conference. If benefits and costs do not accrue in a symmetric manner it becomes difficult to take positive decisions. As with the reform of the CAP, if French agreement is required, some form of benefit from the change must be apparent to them. Second, Alexis Jacquemin made clear the role of firms in shaping the market and the importance of global issues in how they go about achieving this. Thus it is not only European issues which affect behaviour in Europe, but issues relating to how they deal with the global market. We are clearly now seeing how the rule-setting process is responding to this, and I think this particular game is a long way from being played out.

All this discussion is very much issue-driven, and some sort of balance is needed between being able to address the issues of the rest of the decade and increase ways of analysis, if we are to maintain our academic credibility. As I said earlier, what we are working on in the present ESRC initiative is an evolutionary framework, and the way in which economists have been dealing with these subjects offers a number of contributions towards tackling problems of integration. We have learned a lot from game-theoretic approaches, particularly where they can explain changes in the number of players, as shown by the work of Smith and Venables in the background papers to the Cecchini Report. But there are obvious limitations, because the rules of these games are clearly so artificial that they are only an aid to thought, and not an explanation of behaviour. We are at last making progress in the theory of where firms locate although, again, this has tended to be a rather artificial exercise, one which makes gross and unreal assumptions about the various parts of a geographical spectrum. There is still a lot of mileage in the way in which bargaining theory is developing, and there is a great deal more to come from theories of globalization.

This really sounds like a shopping list, a whole series of separate items. My impression is that a 'shopping list' is exactly the way in which economists are approaching the subject, and they have much to learn from other approaches which are trying to bring some of the ideas together within a single coherent framework. What I would like to see on the research agenda is some coherence in the different approaches during the coming decade, and particularly the development of some *theory* of integration, whether it be economic integration, political integration or some other form. Although I have advanced this idea at the end of my presentation, I would like to see it at the head of the research agenda.

Further details of the projects in progress referred to are obtainable from David Mayes at NIESR, 2 Dean Trench Street, Smith Square, London SW1P, 3HE, UK.

## Appendix: List of Projects

European Cohesion: Competition, Technology and the Regions

Participation of Non-Member States in Shaping the Rules of the EC's Single Market

Competition Between Metropolitan Regions in the Single European Market

The Legal Implementation of the Single European Market at National Level

The Future of Public Procurement in Europe: Rules, Public Choice and the Single European Market

The Interaction of Trade, Competition and Technology Policy in the Single Market

Human Resource Regimes and the Single European Market

A New Strategy for Social and Economic Cohesion after 1992

1992: The Stimulus for Change in British and West German Industry

The Implications of the Evolution of European Integration for the UK Labour Market

The Harmonisation of EC Securities Market Regulations

Regulatory Institutions and Practices in the Single European Market

The Free Movement of Workers and the Single European Market

Environmental Standards and the Politics of Expertise in the Single European Market

Lobbying in the EC: A Comparative Study

Regulation and Competition in the European Air Transport Industry

Rules for Energy Taxation in the Single European Market
The Consequences of Finnish Membership of the EC for the Finnish Food Industries
Comparative Competition Policy
The Evolution of Rules for a Single European Market
The Competitiveness of Spanish Industry in the 1990s: Unleashing the Potential
The Role of the Firm in the Evolution of Rules for a Single European Market
The Implications for Firms and Industry of the Adoption of the ECU as the Single
    Currency in the EC

# Theory and Practice in European Integration

### WILLIAM WALLACE

I hope that we will all agree that interdisciplinary work is absolutely essential
in understanding the complex processes of European integration. Lack of co-
operation between the different disciplines – history, sociology and social
anthropology, as well as political science, economics and law – has been a major
obstacle to reviving the theoretical and conceptual debate.

We need most of all to focus on the relationship between theory and practice.
I want to suggest some areas where theory is useful and where there is a clear
need for research which integrates theoretical insight and empirical work. First
– and here I agree with what David Mayes has just said – bargaining theory is
highly relevant to understanding the intergovernmental dimension of the
Community process. Policy-making in the Council of Ministers and the spreading network of Council committees is a continuous negotiating game. This is
Helen [Wallace's] territory more than mine; I look forward to seeing the book
on the Council of Ministers on which she and Fiona Hayes-Renshaw are now
working (H. Wallace, 1989, 1990).

Second, I think there is rather more to be gained in terms of theoretical
insights into European integration from drawing on the literature of domestic
and comparative political science than from the literature of international
relations. That is because what we are looking at in western Europe, I would
argue, is better understood as a semi-developed political system than as a highly
interdependent regional international system. The work of Karl Deutsch on
nationalism, social communication and political community has stood the test
of time much better than that of most early theorists of European integration

(Deutsch, 1966; Deutsch *et al.*,1957). He focused on the interplay between the national and the international, between state-building and community-building – his passionate concern stemming from his own youthful experience in inter-war Czechoslovakia of the painful consequences of the disintegration of the Austro-Hungarian multinational state. Deutsch has a great deal to say about the problems of national identity and community, to which we are now returning: how such concepts as legitimacy and authority strengthen or weaken within political communities, the growth (or decay) of assumptions about mutual security, the conditions for popular acceptability of redistribution of resources to others within what people regard as a political community, and so on.

The work of a number of sociologists and social anthropologists, from Ben Anderson to Anthony Smith and Ralph Grillo, is also extremely valuable, and ought to be required reading for all those interested in European integration (Anderson, 1991; Smith, 1991, 1992; Grillo, 1980). With the break-up of the socialist successor to the Austro-Hungarian empire, questions of identity, nationalism, multiple loyalties and shifting perceptions of relevant communities are again posed by developments in central and eastern Europe.

That leads me into a third area, which is the whole overlap between political science and sociology; including the developing literature on the concept of 'civic society', much of which has been addressed to the problem of social and political transition in central and eastern Europe (Keane, 1988). There is a great deal of comparative work to be done here: on the shifting boundary between the 'public' and the 'private' in western and in eastern Europe, the indications of the weakening of civic society in western Europe at the same time that west European governments are funding projects to strengthen civil society in eastern Europe, the impact of the processes of formal and informal integration on national political communities and on civic participation. I have also learned a lot from other sociologists examining patterns of convergence and divergence in European societies: from Hartmut Kaelble, for instance, and his study of the social history of western Europe (Kaelble, 1990), and from Colin Crouch, who is both teaching a new course at Oxford University on the development of European society and writing a book on the same theme.

Fourth, there is some interesting work under way in the field of political geography on which we ought to draw. When Europe is changing shape, when its extent and boundaries are actively contested, historical and psychological mapping – mental maps – are valuable aids to understanding. I have learned much from Michel Foucher of the *Observatoire de Géopolitique* in Lyons, who is just completing a volume on the political geography of Europe – which will also be available in English in 1994. John Salt (at the University of London) and others have provided some fascinating insights into the development of European elites: the emergence of a European social space across which business elites, administrative and intellectual elites move easily and regularly (Salt, 1986). The other side of this development, on which so far as I am aware much less work has yet been done, is the extent to which this western Europe-wide social space exists *only* for the elites, with the broader mass publics much less caught up in this web of integrative activities and still living, therefore, in a series of separate – largely national – social spaces. This is not just the predicament of the socially excluded, of whom Brigid Laffan was talking in her comment; it is probably also the experience of most blue-collar workers (and of a great number of women, working in safe but poorly-paid public sector jobs) who thus see 'Europeanization' as a process which brings few gains for them. There is some useful and relevant sociological work also on demographic change and its implications for European societies, and on the links between demographic change and migration, of which we should all be aware.

Fifth, we need to grapple with the whole concept of the state. Kenneth Dyson's study of *The State Tradition in Western Europe* seems to me to have been unjustly neglected (Dyson, 1981). Some of the underlying tensions within the European Community have stemmed from the different concepts of the states held by both major and minor EC members – French assumptions distinct from German, Spanish from Greek, the British and the Belgians deeply confused about the state in very different ways. The political entity which these governments and national administrations have created not surprisingly represents a rather unstable compromise between these different concepts of the state and of state action, which comes out at one level in disputes over competition policy and industrial policy and at another level in arguments over sovereignty and over the division of powers between different levels of government.

What has now been created in the European Community is a constitutional system which has some state attributes, but which most – or all – of its constituent governments do not wish to develop into a state, even while expecting it to deliver outcomes which are hard to envisage outside the framework of an entity which we would recognize as a (federal) state. Take the position of the European Court of Justice: a constitutional court, in effect, which operates outside the framework of an established state order. The concept of a common foreign policy, and *a fortiori* a common defence policy, is a contradiction in terms without at the same time conceptualizing a state framework to provide authority, legitimacy and accountability. Similarly a common currency, and the monetary controls and economic management authority needed to accompany that, implies a state-like framework within which to operate – as Karl Otto Pöhl, the former President of the German Bundesbank, and others have repeatedly argued. Border control and policing, like a single currency, diplomacy and defence, have been central functions of the nation-state, as nineteenth- and twentieth-century Europe understood the nation-state. The retreat from a federal objective for the European Community, while retaining a constitutional agenda which implied the need for a federal state-framework, has left a shadowy area at the centre of EC construction which substitute concepts such as 'democratic deficit' and 'subsidiarity' – which themselves make little sense without a clearer definition of the constitutional framework within which they are to be placed – have failed to illuminate. I am increasingly fascinated by questions of sovereignty and statehood, along with shifting patterns of identity and community, in the light of the post-Maastricht confusion over the shape and structure of an institutional European order.[1]   I hope many others are now working on these questions as well.

Part of the current contradictions of the debate over a European institutional order, after all, stem from the underlying crisis of the nation-state across western Europe. The integration of the central functions of government into one authoritative, legitimate, and (at least in principle) accountable entity which was the achievement of the late nineteenth-century model of the nation-state has now given way to a progressive disintegration, with authority, functions and even loyalties ebbing away to other levels above and below. The disintegration of Belgium, regarded 100 years ago as a model nation-state, is the most advanced: but regional challenges, made more plausible in the alternatives they offer to centralized states by the existence of the broader framework of government which exists at the EC/NATO/WEU level, are also apparent in Italy, Spain, and Britain, while the addition of five new – and poor – states to the German Federation has exacerbated the problem of maintaining an agreed balance between Bund and Land.

This erosion of nation-state pre-eminence in western Europe in the face of the establishment of broader political, security and economic communities poses immense problems in turn for those former socialist states which are trying at the same time to re-establish their sovereignty and to come closer to an integrated western Europe. I remember hearing a group of leading Bulgarians talking about their efforts to rebuild an independent national economy, only a few days after hearing some Swedish officials admitting the sense that their government had lost control of the national economy as Swedish companies pursued strategies aimed at a wider European market: two states with very similar sizes of population, but radically different understandings of the relationship between independence and integration. There is an underlying question here about our understanding of the technological, economic and social dynamics of informal integration. It may well be – as some of us have argued elsewhere – that the integrated nation-state should be seen as an historical phenomenon, the development of which depended crucially upon the nationally integrative

---

[1] I have published two discussions of this set of issues in the British context: W. Wallace (1991,1992).

forces of nineteenth-century technology and industry: railways, the telegraph, large-scale factories requiring disciplined labour. The dynamics of technological and economic change, and associated social changes, now operate to undermine the territorial integrity and autonomy of European nation-states.

Good theory comes out of good empirical work. We cannot build theory without the accumulation of case studies which support or modify the hypotheses advanced. We are faced with an extremely complex policy process within integrated western Europe, not all of which takes place within the institutional structures of the European Community, strictly defined. Students of European integration have too often accepted the assumption that Europe is a 'civilian' power, neglecting to look at the gradual evolution of co-operative and integrated defence structures within NATO and its overlapping European groupings. Western European Union, the Eurocorps, are beginning to take substantive shape alongside the various NATO standing groups and the NATO Rapid Reaction Force; there is room for careful study of how far patterns of interaction in the defence field are beginning to converge on those in other areas, and how far they remain distinctive. Apart from the excellent work at the Europa Institute in Edinburgh, few either in the academic field or in national parliaments have paid any attention to the remarkable developments in police co-operation over the past 15 years, to consider what that tells us about the evolution of a European policy system (den Boer and Walker, 1993).

Opt-outs from the Maastricht Treaty, inner groupings like the Schengen Agreement, the spreading network of association agreements across central and eastern Europe, and the prospect of a succession of further negotiations for enlargement, all increase the complexity and untidiness of the structures for formal European integration. Don Puchala's imagery of the study of European integration as a process in which a small group of blind men were attempting to describe those parts of the elephant which they could get close enough to touch describes accurately what we face today: an extremely disaggregated policy process, operating often under differing structures and rules from one sector to another, partly outside the European Community itself, with only the twice-yearly European Councils of heads of government to hold it loosely together. We need a large number of careful studies of what different parts of this lumbering elephant feel like if we aspire to describe the whole and how it moves (Puchala, 1972).

Lastly, we need to look at the interaction between the evolution of the European political system and developments within the wider global system. There has after all been from the outset a close relationship between the two; the integration of western Europe took place under the sponsorship and security guarantee of the United States, the limited and ultimately unsuccessful integration of eastern Europe under the hegemony of the Soviet Union. The collapse of the Soviet Union, and the downgrading of Europe in American foreign policy priorities, has radically altered the external context for European integration – with the potential either to force more integrated policies or to lead to disintegration. The proposed North American Free Trade Area (NAFTA), together with current American rhetoric about 'bloc-to bloc' bargaining in international economic relations and with the shift towards bilateralism in US–Pacific relations, carry implications for the future pattern of European external relations – implications which will become more radical if the GATT structure weakens further, or if the US military commitment to Europe slips far below its anticipated 100–150,000. The complex game in which the USA, the European Community and the industrialized east Asian states are now engaged about rule-making and advantage-seizing in international trade is also likely to feed back into EC policies and policy competences. There is a good deal in the – overwhelmingly American – business school and economic literature on the creation of comparative advantage, the use of government to help multinational companies compete in global markets, the competitive negotiation of rules over airline regulation (or aircraft manufacture), which is of direct relevance to how European governments and companies, individually and collectively, will define their interests in the post-Cold War world. My personal research agenda will be mainly concerned with this external dimension over the next two years.

That is a huge agenda. If we are to make progress on the reconstruction of theory, we will need to work together, across universities and disciplines: developing hypotheses, testing them through case studies, drawing on as wide a range of related insights as possible.

## References

Anderson, B. (1991) *Imagined Communities* (revised edn.)(London: Verso).

Den Boer, M. and Walker, N. (1993) 'European Policing After 1992'. *Journal of Common Market Studies,* Vol. 31, pp. 3-28.

Deutsch, Karl W. (1966) *Nationalism and Social Communication* (2nd edn) (New York: MIT Press).

Deutsch, Karl W. *et al.* (1957) *Political Community and the North Atlantic Area* (Princeton, N.J.; Princeton University Press).

Dyson, K. (1981) *The State Tradition in Western Europe: A Study of an Idea and Institution* (Oxford: Martin Robertson).

Grillo, R. (1980) *Nation and State in Europe: Anthropological Perspectives* (London: Academic Press).

Kaelble, H. (1990) *A Social History of Western Europe 1880–1980* (Dublin: Gill and Macmillan).

Keane, J. (1988) *Civil Society and the State* (London: Verso).

Puchala, D. (1972),'Of Blind Men, Elephants and European Integration'. *Journal of Common Market Studies,* Vol. X, pp. 267–84.

Salt, J. (1986) 'High-Level Manpower Movements in Northwest Europe and the Role of Careers: An Explanatory Framework'. *International Migration Review,* Winter 1986, pp. 951–72.

Smith, A. D. (1991) *National Identity* (London: Penguin).

Smith, A. D. (1992) 'National Identity and European Identity'. *International Affairs,* Vol. 68, No.1, pp. 55–76.

Wallace, H. (1989) 'The Best is the Enemy of the "Could": Bargaining in the European Community'. In Tarditi, S. *et al., Agricultural Trade Liberalization and Economic Perspective in the European Community* (Oxford: Oxford University Press).

Wallace, H. (1990) 'Making Multilateral Negotiations Work'. In Wallace, W. (ed.), *The Dynamics of European Integration* (London: Pinter).

Wallace, W. (1991) 'Foreign Policy and National Identity in the United Kingdom'. *International Affairs* Vol. 67, No. 1, pp. 65–80.

Wallace, W. (1992) 'British Foreign Policy after the Cold War'. *International Affairs* Vol. 68, No. 3, pp. 423–42.

# New Directions in Legal Research on the European Community

ANNE-MARIE SLAUGHTER BURLEY

## I. Introduction

American lawyers, particularly academic ones, are routinely accused by their European counterparts of confusing law with politics. Yet such confusion may be precisely what is wanted when commenting on the evolution of research on European law for an interdisciplinary journal. To begin in fine Continental tradition, I see three categories of such research, with various possibilities for further inquiry in each. Let me outline them briefly and then discuss each in more detail.

First is old-fashioned comparative law, comparing and contrasting the substantive evolution of an area of Community law either with different national laws of Community Member States or, increasingly frequently, with the evolution of that area in the United States. This is a well-travelled path among European and US lawyers, and one that I will argue is a useful point of departure for political scientists. Second is 'interactive' or 'contextual' theory, a growing school pioneered by Weiler that seeks to locate the activities of the European Court of Justice (ECJ) and the national courts in a broader political context. The focus here is on how the Court does and should interact with political bodies. Third is analysis of the Community as a paradigm of policy co-ordination among liberal states, either from an institutional or intergovernmental perspective, and thus of the Court as a uniquely successful international judicial organ. From this perspective, the Court is an example of vertical relations among a supranational judicial body and national judicial bodies in liberal states. My aim in this brief space is to describe potential new directions for research in each of these three areas.

## II. Comparative Law

The purpose of comparative law, as a discipline unto itself, is normally to shed light on one's own legal system by viewing it through the lens of another. Comparative legal studies in the Community, however, also fulfil a more straightforward informative function; as a nascent legal system, the Community can both use other systems as a model and as a caution, be inspired by their example and learn from their mistakes. This is not the kind of scholarship generally published in the *Journal of Common Market Studies*; it is more likely to grace the pages of the *Common Market Law Review* or the *European Law Review*. For the political scientist student of law, however, this literature can provide a mirror for other phenomena political scientists seek to study, helping to crystallize and pinpoint precise areas of difference.

In short, comparative law is a guide to comparative context, a window onto those areas in which the interaction between legal institutions and political, economic and social forces produces different results. Comparative federalism is an obvious subject, as is comparative antitrust law. The one offers a primer for nation-building, mapping the different possibilities for relations between a central authority and its component parts; the other a blueprint for a national economy on the basis of competition policies as central to political as to economic order. Future areas to watch are comparative administrative law, with particular emphasis on enhanced transparency and accountability in governance,[1] what we in the United States would call 'equal protection' issues and environmental law. Challenges in these areas may convince the Court to reshape some of its federalist or 'pre-emption' doctrine, causing new 'jurisdictional

---

[1] Compare Shapiro (1993), arguing that the evolution of requirement for giving reasons, from a simple check against arbitrary decision-making into fully fledged substantive judicial review is likely to take the same path in the United States as in Europe. Such a claim questions the differential impact of different legal systems *per se*, arguing essentially for the autonomy of legal logic. Shapiro would nevertheless be the first to admit the impact of different political, economic and social factors on the development of streams of legal doctrine.

mutations' to permit something of the 'laboratories for the nation' approach that the U.S. Supreme Court has recently encouraged again regarding state experimentation in social and economic policy.

## III. Interactive Theory

The subject here is the Court as catalyst: of integration, of disintegration, of equilibrium. The Court affects political processes. But to what extent? And how? How is it in turn affected by them? These are ultimately empirical questions, but they require informed theorizing to generate hypotheses that can be systematically tested. Does law act through its power and aura as the voice of legitimate authority? Or as the vehicle for judicial and professional interest groups at both the national and supranational levels? Does it lead or follow political will? It undoubtedly does both, but can we specify precisely how? Interactive theorists have laid the foundation for analysis of the ECJ and the national courts at least as quasi-political actors, whether self-consciously or not, and for an interpretation of specific decisions and the trend-lines of individual doctrines from a broader political perspective. The law may be insulated, but it is not isolated. The following is a discussion of three sub-strands of this category of scholarship.

(1) The first sub-strand of interactive theory draws most heavily on traditional legal and political theory concerning the role of courts in conjunction with other political institutions, drawing on concepts such as Ely's reinterpretation of American judicial review in light of pluralist political theory, Hirschman's voice and exit, Dahl's theory of federalism, and various theories of political legitimacy. Here Weiler has made his name, along with others such as Stein, Bieber, Cappelletti and other participants in the massive study sponsored by the European University Institute, *Integration through Law* (Cappelletti *et al.,* 1985–). They have been subtly encouraged by many of the judges themselves. The result, consonant with these origins, is a blend of both analysis and prescription.

Weiler has argued that the Court has not been plagued with what is described in the US literature as the 'counter-majoritarian difficulty', but agrees that the Court is now in for attack. From an admittedly Americano-centric perspective, I strongly suspect that it will not escape challenge to its democratic credentials. If so, we may expect European versions of what have become familiar struggles in the history of the US Supreme Court. First, I suspect that scholars and critics of the Court will rediscover American legal scholar Bickel's theory of the 'passive virtues', the techniques for *not* deciding controversial political questions before the public and their political representatives have reached at least minimum consensus.[2] Time also to peruse the progressive ideology animating Justices such as Frankfurter, a leading practitioner of the passive virtues, who believed strongly in the organic whole of the governmental processes and the risk of judicial disruption of those processes on the basis of inadequate perception and appreciation of highly complex political and economic processes.[3]

Frankfurter, Bickel and other giants of the 1950s such as Wechsler, who propounded a theory of judicial review guided by 'neutral principles' (Wechsler, 1959) or Hart and Sacks (1957), progenitors of the 'legal process' school (which sought to restore democratic legitimacy by paying enormous attention to *which* court should decide), were all products of an era in which a Supreme Court boasting a majority with the mores of 1900 consistently sought to block the construction of the social welfare state of the 1930s (and before). They appreciated the dangers of such judicial activism, not only to the populace, but above all to the legitimacy of the court. I predict that their diagnoses of the problem and prescriptions for its solutions will enjoy a renaissance in Community legal scholarship over the next decade.

Another possibility within this category of scholarship, for which Weiler has already laid the ground in his article, 'Eurocracy and Distrust' (Weiler, 1986), is the potential reconceptualization of the Court not as the engine of integration but as the protector of minority rights, where the minorities are national populations. In other words, if the *real* democracy deficit, as Weiler argues, is the weakened control by *national parliaments,* then the ECJ could perform the historic judicial role of protecting minority rights by consciously reversing course and supporting national governments as 'transitional minorities' in the emerging political Community. This would be a more activist stance but one, if the diagnosis of the problem is correct, equally supportive of long-term integration.[4]

(2) A second sub-strand of 'interactive theory' draws not on domestic legal and political theory *per se*, but rather on integration theory. With co-author Mattli I have published an analysis of the success of the Court from a neo-functionalist perspective (Burley and Mattli, 1993). We argue that the original neo-functionalist theory, in which economics acted as a relatively autonomous sphere sheltered from the prevailing political winds, allowing private actors to pursue their own interests in a dynamic process marked by spillover and the upgrading of common interests, may have fallen short as a theory of economic integration, but is remarkably successful as a description of the evolution of Community law. We apply neo-functionalism as a political theory of legal

---

[2] See, generally, Bickel (1986).
[3] For a description of this philosophy as it influenced Frankfurter, see Hockett (1992).
[4] For an elaboration of this argument, see Burley (1993, pp. 81–91).

integration, one that analyses the interaction between the 'Court' and the political branches of the Community in explicitly interest-based terms, but also one that recognizes the importance of maintaining the autonomy and legitimacy of law as a practice distinct from politics.

From this perspective, the next set of questions on the agenda concerns the continuing interaction, or perhaps we should say competition, between the ECJ and the national courts. The 1989 *Nicolo* decision of the French Conseil d'Etat set the stage for a new round.[5] Our thesis was that for the judges of the ECJ, and for the scholars and practitioners whose convictions and interests are united in support of continuing integration, the strengthening of EC law has been at one with the strengthening of the supreme EC court. The continuing application of doctrines such as 'acte claire' on the part of national supreme courts threatens this identity of interest. It seems possible for instance that, having now fully accepted the supremacy of Community law, some national courts in some countries may nevertheless seek to appropriate the interpretation and application of that law within the national jurisdiction as a way of maintaining their own power. This possibility seems particularly likely in light of the growing 'juridification' of national politics documented by a growing comparative literature on European judicial politics (Stone, 1993).

(3) A third sub-strand of interactive theory is rational choice analysis of the ECJ, pioneered by Garrett and Weingast (Garrett and Weingast, 1991; Garrett, 1992). They argue that the Court performs the necessary functions of monitoring compliance with interstate bargains and filling in gaps in the interstate contract. The Court may also be relied upon to generate useful ideas. This analysis denies the possibility of any autonomous judicial power that is not derived directly from the will of the Member States. Thus, the Court would not be worth the costs it imposes on individual Member States unless 'it faithfully implement[s] the collective internal market preferences of [Community] members'. They then seek to demonstrate that virtually all the major EC decisions have been consistent with the preferences of at least France and Germany.

I suspect that the next subject for rational choice analysts is likely to be the construction of formal models of the internal politics of the Court itself. If rational choice theorists were to admit that the Court is on occasion seriously out of step with Member State preferences, then they would have to formulate a rational choice explanation of why Member State governments do not try more aggressively to change the political composition of the Court or to subject it to more direct and stringent political controls. 'Rule of law' explanations will not wash among these theorists; they are instead likely to be more receptive to

---

[5] In Re Nicolo. 1990 Recueil Dalloz-Sirey, Jurisprudence 135, 63 *La Semaine juridique* II, No. 21, 371 (1989), 25 *Revue trimestrielle de droit européen* 786 (1989). *Conseil d'Etat* (Assemblée) 20 October 1989.

explanations focusing on the impact of the alternation of political parties in national government. In other words, should a Conservative government in Britain appoint an aggressively anti-European judge, its Labour successor would have licence to appoint an aggressively pro-European judge. The danger of direct political control in such a system is even more apparent.

All three of these sub-strands of interactive theory are also likely to be interested in the comparative analysis of different acceptance rates of European law among different Member States and different types of national court systems within one country. What drives these differences? The relative autonomy of the national court system? The executive's attitude toward the Community? Differences in national constitutions? A comparative study of national receptivity rates for European law would seem a natural next step.

## IV. The ECJ as an International Court in a Community of Liberal States

If the Community, as Moravcsik argues, remains primarily an intergovernmental regime, then lawyers must reverse the presumed 'constitutionalization' of the Treaty and once again conceptualize the ECJ as an international court (Moravcsik, 1991). I suggest seeing it as an international court in a community of liberal states, states with well-functioning autonomous legal systems.[6] Within this framework, the Community becomes not an anomaly but a paradigm for the potential reach and effectiveness of international law at least among some states. This reconceptualization requires international lawyers, whether located in law schools or political science departments, to pierce the veil of sovereignty and differentiate between types of states based on their domestic political systems. Theorists such as Doyle (1983, 1986), Maoz (1989, Maoz and Abdolali, 1989), Russett (1990, 1993), and many others have argued, following Kant, that liberal democracies do not go to war with one another. I have argued elsewhere that the underlying factors contributing to the distinctive nature of political–military relations among liberal states also give rise to distinctive legal relations (Burley, 1993).

In particular, legal relations among liberal states are distinguished by the possibility of at least a quasi-independent transnational judicial dialogue. Judges in these countries apply one another's law – domestic law – subject to formulæ for interest-balancing that are themselves premised on the twin precepts of mutual respect and reciprocity. Both of these concepts, often muddled together under fuzzy labels such as 'comity', themselves assume the

[6] Following Doyle, I define 'liberal states' as states with some form of representative government, constitutional protections of individual rights, and some form of market economy based on private property rights.

existence of a repeat game that depends on underlying economic, political and social conditions favourable to long-term individual and group interaction across borders.[7] Paradoxically, this underlying convergence in institutions and fundamental political and economic values renders courts of such states more willing to adjudicate disputes involving other liberal states than non-liberal states, and thus more willing to entertain the possibility of rejecting or overrriding each other's law. States in the liberal zone can thus be said to possess permeable sovereignty, subject to multiple intrusions by not only transnational actors, but also the regulatory and judicial organs of fellow states.

The EC affords the chance to examine the impact of a 'vertical' judicial network on legal relations among liberal states. Again we witness at least a quasi-independent dialogue among judges, but instead of a transnational dialogue it is a supranational–national dialogue. The deliberate efforts of the judges of the ECJ to cultivate their national brethren is now well documented, and attested to by many of the judges themselves. Would or could this dialogue take place outside the framework of a treaty professing at least the goal of integration? Imagine, for instance, an international environmental treaty in which states established an international tribunal and declared their allegiance to broad environmental goals. Is it not equally possible here, at least in the absence of *direct* executive objection, that a similar judicial dialogue could take place? Is not the key link a common training and language, buttressed by a common commitment to the autonomy and necessity of the rule of law (however loosely conceived)?[8]

Parallels to the EC need not be so narrowly drawn. The EC experience with the 'constitutionalization' or, as I would prefer to call it, the 'domestication' of an international treaty may have broader lessons. It may be, for instance, that liberal states are more likely to make their international commitments, *where*

---

[7] Compare Judge Wilkey's description of comity in *Laker Airways* v. *Sabena Belgian World Airlines*: '"Comity" summarizes in a brief word a complex and elusive concept – the degree of deference that a domestic forum must pay to the act of a foreign government not otherwise binding on the forum. ... Comity is a necessary outgrowth of our international system of politically independent, socio-economically interdependent nation states. As surely as people, products and problems move freely among adjoining countries, so national interests cross territorial borders. But no nation can expect its laws to reach further than its jurisdiction to prescribe, adjudicate and enforce. Every nation must often rely on other countries to help it achieve its regulatory expectations. Thus comity compels national courts to act at all times to increase the international legal ties that advance the rule of law within and among nations. 731 F.2d 909,921 (1984).

[8] Interestingly, Bieber has recently sought to generalize the EC legal experience in a similar fashion as an example of the 'externalisation' of a legal order: 'the ability of a legal order to attract, subsequently to become part of and ultimately to supersede surrounding legal orders' (Bieber, 1992, p. 6). He describes the preconditions for this phenomenon as follows:'a certain economic and legal environment is necessary to generate such an effect: A minimum of economic homogeneity, comparable constitutional rules on interventions in the economy and – paradoxically – a minimum awareness of the public for the parallel existence of differing legal orders'. I would suggest that these preconditions are far more likely to obtain in liberal states.

*those commitments are limited to other liberal states,* domestically enforceable through a variety of measures, above all a greater willingness to undertake national implementing legislation or administrative orders. Treaties and executive agreements with other liberal states may be more likely to be declared self-executing, thereby requiring no additional domestic enforcement for their enforcement by domestic courts. A wealth of research is being conducted into the phenomenon of compliance with international commitments, and many of these researchers are beginning to look at variance in *domestic* political structures and institutions as a source of explanation. If they identify significant differences attributable to domestic variation, the next frontier of debate will be whether the credit for taking advantage of those differences lies with the nature of the international institution or the domestic political system. For instance, are the designers of a particular treaty likely to enhance its effectiveness by allowing the prospect of domestic ratification debates to influence the negotiating process, or do treaties concluded by states with constitutional provisions for domestic ratification display different compliance or effectiveness rates?

Nor need this reconceptualization of the EC as an international legal paradigm be limited to courts. The phenomenon of mutual recognition, as Nicolaidis has demonstrated, may be occurring worldwide among states above a minimum threshold of common political and economic values (Nicolaidis, 1993). This phenomenon extends to areas as diverse as forum selection in which, beginning in the 1970s, US courts were willing to enforce the contractual selection of foreign fora even where the result under foreign law or procedure enforceable by the foreign court would be less favourable to US plaintiffs. Mutual recognition principles also appear in international banking, merger agreements, and even extradition treaties. It can be described as the instantiation of a conviction of 'legitimate difference', extending far beyond Article 100 of the Treaty of Rome.[9]

To pursue this research, EC lawyers and political scientists alike must imbibe a mixture of liberal political theory and international relations research. The lawyers among them must shed 300 plus years of conditioning to respect the monolith of sovereignty. The political scientists must re-examine law not in terms of concrete rules, but of judicial relations, modes of reasoning, and the convergence of underlying values and institutions. The result may challenge the institutionalists as well as the realists, portending a description of the contours and dynamics of non-institutional legal integration. Nevertheless, it offers an important new dimension of international legal studies.

---

[9] Compare Ehlermann's discussion of the importance of decentralized enforcement of Community law through the Article 177 procedure rather than the mechanisms of Articles 169 and 170. Ehlermann emphasizes the overriding significance of the interpenetration of Community and national law in domestic civil society (Ehlermann, 1987).

## Conclusion

Political scientists are rediscovering, or in many cases discovering, the importance of law in many contexts. The EC is no exception. I would argue that Community legal studies offers the richest imaginable lode for comparativists in both law and political science, as well as for both legal and international relations theorists.

In the last ten years the *Journal of Common Market Studies* has published only four articles on law, and only three full-length articles. These have been exemplary, but nevertheless few. I have sought to suggest three potential directions of scholarship that I hope and expect will yield a considerably richer harvest in the coming decade.

## References

Bickel, A.M. (1986) *The Least Dangerous Branch: The Supreme Court at the Bar of Politics* (New Haven: Yale University Press).

Bieber, R. (1992) 'The European Economic Area: Taming European Elephants in the Alps, or On the Externalisation of Legal Order'. Mimeo.

Burley, A.-M. (1992) 'Law among Liberal States: Liberal Internationalism and the Act of State Doctrine'. *Columbia Law Review*, Vol. 92, No. 8, pp. 1909–96.

Burley, A.-M. (1993) 'Democracy and Judicial Review in the European Community'. *University of Chicago Legal Forum*, Vol. 1992, pp. 81–91.

Burley, A.-M. and Mattli, W. (1993) 'Europe Before the Court: A Political Theory of Legal Integration'. *International Organization*, Vol. 47, No. 1, pp. 41–76.

Cappelletti, M., Seccombe, A. and Weiler, J. (eds.) (1985–) *Integration through Law: Europe and the American Federal Experience* (Berlin: de Gruyter).

Doyle, M. W. (1983) 'Kant, Liberal Legacies, and Foreign Affairs'. *Philosophy and Public Affairs,* Vol. 12, No. 3, pp. 205–35.

Doyle, M.W. (1986) 'Liberalism and World Politics'. *American Political Science Review,* Vol. 80, No. 4, pp. 1151–69.

Ehlermann, C.-D. (1987) 'Ein Plädoyer für die dezentralle Kontrolle der Anwendung des Gemeinschaftsrecht durch die Mitgliedstaaten'. In Capotorti *et al.* (eds.) *Du Droit international au droit de l'intégration: Liber Amicorum Pierre Pescatore* (Baden-Baden: Nomos), pp. 205–26.

Garrett, G. (1992) 'International Co-operation and Institutional Choice: The European Community's Internal Market'. *International Organization*, Vol. 46, No.2, pp. 533–60.

Garrett, G. and Weingast, B.R. (1991) 'Ideas, Interests and Institutions: European Community's Internal Market'. Mimeo, Stanford University.

Hart, H.M. and Sacks, A.M. (1957) The Legal Process: Basic Problems in the Making and Application of Law. Mimeo, Cambridge, Mass.

Hockett, J.D. (1992) 'Justices Frankfurter and Black: Social Theory and Constitutional Interpretation'. *Political Science Quarterly*, Vol. 107, No. 3, pp. 479–99.
Maoz, Z. (1989) 'Joining the Club of Nations: Political Development and International Conflict, 1816–1976'. *International Studies Quarterly*, Vol. 33, No. 2, pp. 199–231.
Maoz, Z. and Abdolali, N. (1989) 'Regime Types and International Conflict, 1816–1976'. *Journal of Conflict Resolution*, Vol. 33, No. 1, pp. 3–36.
Moravcsik, A. (1991) 'Negotiating the Single European Act: National Interests and Conventional Statecraft in the European Community'. *International Organization*, Vol. 45, pp. 19–56.
Nicolaidis, K. (1993) 'Mutual Recognition among Nations: Europe 1992, the Uruguay Round, and Trade in Services'. Doctoral dissertation for the Departments of Government and Economics, Harvard University.
Russett, B. (1990) 'Politics and Alternative Security: Towards a More Democratic, Therefore More Peaceful, World'. In Weston, B.H. (ed.), *Alternative Security: Living Without Nuclear Deterrence* (Boulder, Col.: Westview) pp. 107–36.
Russett, B. (1993) *Grasping the Democratic Peace: Principles for a Post-Cold War World* (forthcoming).
Shapiro, M. (1993) 'The Giving Reasons Requirement'. *University of Chicago Legal Forum*, Vol. 1992, pp. 179–220.
Stone, A. (1993) 'Judging Socialist Reform: The Politics of Coordinate Construction in France and Germany'. *Comparative Political Studies* (forthcoming).
Wechsler, H. (1959) 'Toward Neutral Principles of Constitutional Law'. *Harvard Law Review*, Vol. 73, No. 1, pp. 1–35.
Weiler, J.H.H. (1986) 'Eurocracy and Distrust: Some Questions Concerning the Role of the European Court of Justice in the Protection of Fundamental Human Rights Within the Legal Order of the European Communities'. *Washington Law Review*, Vol. 61, No. 3, pp. 1103–42.

# Index

290

INDEX